Seasonal European Dishes

ELISABETH LUARD

GRUB STREET • LONDON

ACKNOWLEDGEMENTS

I am greatly indebted to many people for assistance with this book, both those mentioned in the text and those who have helped me in my research. This last includes the courteous staff of the London Library (my private university); and particularly the Librarian at the time of writing, Douglas Matthews. Practical assistance with recipe testing came from Priscilla White, Chrissie MacDonald and Venetia Parkes: patient fryers of fritters, uncomplaining stuffers of chickens. And to my good friend and much-valued editor and publisher Anne Dolamore of Grub Street for returning this book to print.

This new edition is dedicated to the memory of my beloved daughter Francesca, who dearly loved a party.

This paperback edition published in 2013
by Grub Street
4 Rainham Close
London SW11 6SS
Email: food@grubstreet.co.uk
www.grubstreet.co.uk

Text copyright © Elisabeth Luard 1990, 2013
Copyright this edition © Grub Street 2013
Cover design by Sarah Driver
Formatting by Sarah Driver
General index by Douglas Matthews
Recipe index by Amy Davies Dolamore

This book was previously published under the title European Festival Food

The right of Elisabeth Luard to be identified as author of this work has been asserted in accordance with sections 77 and 78 of the Copyright Designs and Patents Act 1988.

A CIP record for this book is available from the British Library

ISBN 978-1908117-43-4

Author's note
Quantities are given in both imperial and metric measurements. Please use only one or other throughout a recipe. Metric equivalents occasionally differ between recipes, particularly in baking: for example, 4oz may in one case be given as 100g and in another 125g. This occurs in order to keep proportions of ingredients correct, and when using a recipe you should follow the amounts as given.

CONTENTS

Introduction

This book began with the games of children, the last refuge of ancient custom.

For those of us who grew up in post-war Europe, it seemed that the thread of understanding which linked us to the rhythms of the past was abruptly, violently severed. The war altered for ever the pattern of Europe's daily life – including the way we chose to celebrate our holidays. The old celebrations of the changing year, and the necessary tributes to the powers who controlled it, came to an end. They were no longer relevant to the new, urbanized, seasonless pattern of our lives. Such festivities as we retain have increasingly become municipal events. Our feasts, once orgies of eating and merrymaking to compensate for times of hardship, are nowadays altogether more decorous and orderly affairs.

The changes are entirely suitable for the responsible law-abiding citizens we have become in our historical maturity. Children, however, are less easily diverted from their natural rhythms. They delight in ritual and ceremony. But they also – natural disciples of the outlaw gods of Greece and the topsy-turvy mirror world of the Celts – love nonsense and disorder. Deprived of the old festivals, children demand new ones.

As my own young ones grew, they clamoured for special feasts to mark rites of passage – and I found myself with only a faint understanding of what form such celebrations should take. The little I *did* know seemed woefully inadequate, a mere twig floating on an ocean of possibilities. How were we, a new post-war urban family, to organize a christening feast? What, and above all why, were the rituals proper for Christmas, Easter, May Day, Hallowe'en? It may be true, as Jung suggested, that ancestral memory forms part of the collective unconscious – but my individual unconscious was of little assistance when under pressure from four small children to produce an appropriate feast at the drop of the conjurer's hat. Memory needed more than a little jog: mine had to re-learn the whole vocabulary.

At first we invented our own traditions. No sooner was the ritual performed than it was enshrined in custom. Birthdays acquired a seasonal slant: with six of us to mark the passage of years, we averaged a feast-day every two months. A high concentration of winter birthdays meant that chocolate cake, bonfires and toasting-forks outnumbered the picnics and strawberries of summer.

Later, when we lived for many years deep in rural Spain, we acquired a taste for these rhythms and needed to mark the seasonal feasts: the stripping of the cork-trees which surrounded our house, the gathering of the chestnut harvest, the annual pig-killing. So we shared the dishes which our neighbours thought proper for the occasion. As our lives were peripatetic, we soon began to celebrate the major church festivals according to the practice of whoever we found ourselves among. Neighbours – caught up in the general festive spirit – were happy to advise us deplorably ignorant visitors on the proper conduct of, say, the fasting supper of the Provençal Christmas Eve, and, naturally, on the disposition and significance of the thirteen desserts which followed the midnight Mass and *pastorale*. In Andalucian Spain, we were swept up bodily in the glorious open-air picnics of the Whitsun pilgrimages. Later we were made welcome guests for the cracking of red eggs and the roast lamb which concludes the candlelit vigil of a Greek island Easter.

Long though it is, the shortcomings of this book are many. I have not attempted to delineate *all* the customs and ceremonies, the feasts and the festivals, which enlivened the passing seasons in our grandparents' time, and of their grandparents before them. No doubt I have failed to mention your own favourite festival, not included your own special feast-day dish – omissions which, in the spirit of the celebration, you will have to forgive. If you remember them, they must still be alive and real – and will no doubt remain so.

Nor have I included the Jewish festivals, except to acknowledge the massive and obvious debt that the rituals of Christianity owe to the great temples of Jerusalem and Antioch. To have attempted that would indeed have made the book completely unmanageable.

As for the geographic and cultural scope of the book, there are no easy divisions to be drawn. Europe's frontiers have drifted back and forth throughout her history. As far as possible, particularly with the major festivals, I have tried to work within the limits, give or take wide margins, of four spheres of culture: the old area of influence of the Ottoman Turks in the East; the ancient Celtic strongholds in the West; in the South those provinces which came most strongly under the rule of the Romans, with acknowledgement to the Moors who followed them; and in the North the predominantly Germanic culture which embraces, although it by no means engulfs, Scandinavia. Nonetheless, every country, village and family is a law unto itself. There are no rules in this fluid anarchic tradition which governs our festivals. All edges are blurred: it is indeed a wise child who knows its own father.

Our horizons are not limited by the old restraints of time and distance, and the need to sow corn, pasture cattle, trawl seas, or gather harvest. Such matters are no longer our daily bread. That is earned in other ways, and we have new playthings in our toy-cupboard, more manageable monsters to fill our dreams. Celluloid ghouls have replaced the man-wolf who once patrolled the Mediterranean forests. Small-screen romance has routed the dancing fauns of May. The seasons are reduced to the inconvenience of rain on city pavements: the thunder-god who rode the northern storms now shares his skies with transoceanic jets.

It is only at our festival feasts that we lift the lid of the trunk in the attic just a crack, and warm our hands at the ancestral fires. The banquet we spread is naturally of the best – nothing less will do. The guests, as always, are far less predictable. It is wise to lay a place for a stranger at the table – who knows what ancient sprites might be offended at the lack of a formal invitation? Our ancestors would never have overlooked so elementary a precaution.

Elisabeth Luard

December

CHRISTMAS AND NEW YEAR: WINTER FESTIVALS OF RENEWAL

Our Christmas and New Year celebrations mark a festival of renewal which has survived for at least 4,000 years. When we welcome the anniversary of the birth of the Christ Child with evergreens, blazing logs and an exchange of gifts, we lay offerings on the tombstones of our most ancient and dangerous gods.

In Mesopotamia, 2,000 years before the Christian era, the New Year was celebrated with a twelve-day festival. Plays, fires and present-giving marked the yearly victory of Marduk, god of spring and new birth, over the forces of winter darkness. Bonfires were lit to strengthen the sun. Evergreens decorated dwellings, a reminder to the barren twigs and unborn seeds that they must soon sprout and grow. Farmers went out into the empty winter fields, banging drums and shouting to frighten away malevolent spirits. The Romans, those powerful arbiters of custom, replaced the winter solstice celebrations with the Saturnalia, the winter festival of Saturn the god of agriculture, who was in his turn overthrown by great Jupiter – war-god and ruler of the skies.

In the lineaments of the Roman Saturnalia can be traced the outlines of our modern Christmas and New Year festivals; friends visited each other, taking with them good luck presents of fruits, cakes, candles, clay dolls, grains of frankincense, and gold and silver ornaments. Masters feasted with their slaves, who were allowed free licence and could wear the pointed hat of the freeman. A Mock King of the Revels was appointed – of which our Christmas-cracker paper hats and crowns are a reminder. In the streets the common people danced in animal skins, their faces blackened. December 25th in the old Julian calendar, introduced by Julius Caesar to replace the Egyptian and Chinese moon-phase calendar, marked the turning point of the year, when the sun was at its lowest and weakest.

In Persia, the triumph of Mithras – custodian of daylight and lord of the shining heavens – was celebrated with thanksgiving fires as the sun started its climb back from the winter solstice. The rites of Mithraism share much with Christianity – particularly after the Persian god added wisdom and truth to his portfolio of attributes. Mithraism gave Christianity a good run for its money; by the second century AD it was the more popular religion – particularly among the Roman army, who exported their habits and beliefs throughout Imperial Rome's extensive colonies.

Meanwhile, the northern barbarians of Europe were keeping their own similar festival of Yule, its practice adapted to local requirements. In the cold winter, logs were burned in honour of Odin and Thor; people drank mead (fermented honey water) and huddled round the bonfires, listening to the story-tellers retelling the old legends. Mistletoe and evergreens were cut and sacrifices were made to encourage new life.

We still burn the Yule log – although now, in our centrally-heated houses, it is often replaced with a log-shaped, decorated cake. In Britain, the flaming Christmas pudding does double duty as a symbol of fire and feasting. The true Yule log should burn for twelve days, and the stump must be kept for lighting the next year's log.

John Lawson, travelling in Greece in 1900, found paganism and Christianity in uneasy truce. 'Precautions had to be taken against the Centaurs or Callicatzari, who are active for the twelve days between Christmas and Epiphany. These creatures are malevolent, swift-footed beast-men with black faces, usually hairy, cloven-hoofed and half-goat or wolf or ass, half-man. They have large heads and priapic sexual organs.'

Christians had to mark a cross in black on the house door on Christmas Eve, on the jars and vessels which contained food, and on unbaptized infants. Precautions included lighting a fire and keeping it burning all through the twelve days, to prevent the wild men coming down the chimney. Lawson noted that one huge log was set on end up the chimney and allowed to go on burning for the whole period. Ground thistle, hyssop and asparagus were suspended at the door or by the chimney as magical charms against the marauders.

Patrick Leigh Fermor found things not much changed in the isolated Greek villages of the Mani peninsula in the 1950s:

A banished mythology was left to skulk and roam in the mountains, eventually, it was hoped, to die of neglect. But from a mixture of ancient awe and perhaps, Christian charity, the country people befriended them, and they are with us still. Lesser gods, rag tag and bobtail of the sea and woods, nymphs, nereids, dryads, oreads, gorons, tritons, satyrs, centaurs – *ta paganá*, outsiders. At Christmas, they try to break in from the outside and steal the roast pork and pancakes which is the Greek Christmas fare.

They are, Leigh Fermor observes, not seen as dangerous or destructive, but as trying to join in the festivities of the season.

In many places they are humorously tolerated and placated with left offerings. The invariable time for this yearly outburst is the twelve days between Christmas and Epiphany. This span includes the great winter feasts of the Dionysia (the most licentious) and the Kronia, and after the Roman Conquest, the imported Latin fasti of the Brumalia and the Kalendae.

The pagan celebrations were marked by orgies and human sacrifice. The concluding festival, the New Year feast, was transmuted into the Greek Kalends – some of whose customs can be traced in our modern Christmas festivities. The Roman emperor Trajan's colonization of Dacia left *calinda* as the Romanian word for Christmas carol. As Christianity gained ascendancy, the four Graeco-Roman feasts merged into twelve days of underground pagan *kermesse* – celebrations which, in the early years, re-surfaced regularly to trouble the early Fathers. St Paul's correspondent Bishop Timothy met his death attempting to suppress one such pagan outbreak.

The struggles of the early Church are echoed in the modern Greek Orthodox Church's deep distrust of 'folklore' and associated superstition – and in the Orthodox emphasis on Easter as the pure festival of renewal and rebirth, with Christmas taking third place in the calendar of festivals, behind the Feast of the Assumption. St John Chrysostom preached against the Kalendae in the fifth century. Basamon was still trying to suppress the celebration of the Kronia and Kalendae in the twelfth century, when drunken masqueraders even appeared in the nave of his church.

'It was the pagan, more than the indecent aspect – improper disguise and transvestism – which was the chief target of ecclesiastical anathema; men in women's clothes, women in men's, and mad drunkards dressed and horned as devils, their faces darkened or masqued, their bodies clad in goat-skin and simulating quadrupeds.' These tricks, Patrick Leigh Fermor points out, were different in no detail from the mummers who career through the streets of Greek towns and villages today, both at the identical magic period of the twelve days and during the Carnival that precedes Lent. That they also, within living memory, rampaged through the slumbering fields and orchards of northern Europe is testimony to their hold on the imaginations of men.

These pagan excesses still surface in the modern Carnival/*Kermesse* – now outlawed to the dark days of February, clenched between the twin fists of Epiphany, last of the Christmas feasts, and Lent, sombre pathway to Easter.

In Britain our Celtic ancestors left a garland of mistletoe, sacred to both the Druids and the Norsemen, to stake their claim on the modern celebrations. Until the arrival of the turkey from the New World, the traditional meal was the roast boar's head – the chosen sacrifice due to Frey, Norse goddess of fertility. The gleaming tusker, dressed with rosemary for the returning summer, with an apple in its mouth to symbolize the rebirth of the sun, was gilded and greeted with trumpets.

Christmas took a long time to settle into its slot on December 25th. By the third century AD there were various candidate dates for Christ's birthday. January 6th, the date of his baptism, was favoured, as it was thought he would have been baptized on the anniversary of his birth. In some eastern parts of Europe, January 6th is still celebrated as Christmas Day. December 25th was gradually settled on to coincide with the winter solstice, the Yule and the Saturnalia – with a nod also to the Jewish Feast of Lights, held on December 20th or 21st, and itself keyed into the winter solstice. The sixth-century chronologist Dionysius Exiguus was the first to try to calculate the exact date of Christ's birth – and he made an error of at least four years.

The several feasts of Christmas remained movable and regional throughout Europe until the twentieth century, when modern mass communications and centralization have succeeded in making conformists of us all. In central Europe the dates were still more or less in transition until the Second World War. In Bavaria and Austria the twelve days of Christmas ran from Christmas Day to Epiphany; in Silesia they were the twelve days preceding Christmas; in Mecklenburg the twelve days started on New Year's Day.

The hooligan demi-gods of Greece still cast long shadows, too. All over central and eastern Europe, Christmas and New Year remain a time for magic, witchcraft, and devil-animals. In Tyrol, in the 1950s, the *Perchtenmasken*, masked men dressed as devils, were still leaping around in the fields to make them fertile. In Britain up to the Second World War, people still went into the orchards around Christmas time and fired shots into the branches to scare away malevolent spirits. The poet Sacheverell Sitwell recalled, as war-clouds darkened the skies of Europe, similar scenes encountered on his pre-war travels. 'At Budaors, a village near Budapest, they celebrate the winter solstice with mimes and processions, the actors being known as *regos* in Hungary, *turony* in Slovakia, and *turka* in Roumania, feasts in honour of the victory of the sun god, and games and pantomimes of carnival, with shouting to drive away evil spirits, loud and discordant drumming, a relic of the ancient Shamanism.'

Károly Viski, reporting from Hungary in 1932, confirms that these minstrel-actors were respected professionals in 170 villages. Their part in the winter festival remained central long after the arrival of Christianity. Viski quotes a fifteenth-century Transylvanian writer: 'Immediately after the celebrations on the birthday of our Lord Jesus Christ, follows the great feast of the devil on Minstrel Monday, after that comes Carnival … minstrelsy never seeming to come to an end. Hungarian minstrelsy belongs to that group of customs which celebrated the winter solstice; that is the memory of the sun-god.'

The minstrels, singing of the magic stag of St Stephan or telling the riddle of the enchanted bull, can trace a direct line to the Shamans, the priests of the religion of the ancient Siberian tribes of northern Asia, who shared many of their beliefs with the Indians of North America. The Shaman foretold the future and combined the offices of doctor and magician, being capable of curing illness with incantations and songs.

The minstrels' traditional instruments include a 'singing drum' – an earthenware pot covered with a bladder pierced with a vibrating stick. Relics of the ancient cult make guest-appearances all over Europe. The singing drums are to be found on sale today in the Christmas markets of Andalusia, keeping company with wood-and-parchment gypsy tambourines.

Although both the Protestant and Roman Catholic Churches of Europe nominally rank Easter as the most important of the Church festivals, in practice their older and wiser congregations have long since dictated that Christmas comes first. The Orthodox Church, on the other hand, celebrates Easter as the major family festival of the Christian year – and makes comparatively little of Christmas. In non-conformist lands where the Church is at her most stern, particularly Scotland and the strongholds of the Lutheran Saxons, Christmas was until recently preserved as a holy day – secular feasting and merrymaking being considered inappropriate on such a day. Hogmanay, the festival of the New Year, remains the major winter celebration in Scotland, and it is this festivity which has inherited the ancient pagan trappings.

The Catholics of the romantic Mediterranean – and up into Hungary – have built up a fine tradition of religious celebrations for the Christmas period. Festivities include the traditional fasting supper of Christmas Eve, which reaches its apogee in Provence with sophisticated crib-scenes set up in the churches, and the performance of nativity plays on Christmas Eve. The cribs – known as Bethlehems – were inspired by the descriptions of early pilgrims returning from the Holy Land, who had seen the remnants of the manger in the famous rock cave at Bethlehem. In the seventh century Pope Theodosimus ordered that all the remaining Holy Land relics be brought to Rome, and this confirmed the custom of building little local 'Bethlehems' – rocky caves peopled with carved wooden kings, shepherds and animals paying homage to the Child and his family.

Later on real people began to replace the dolls, and gradually festive plays developed round the simple re-enactment of the story. As the secular imagination got to work, the plays began to wander off the subject. By the thirteenth century Pope Innocent III decided that they were profane enough to warrant banishment of all live performances from the churches. His contemporary, St Francis of Assisi, responded by taking the Bethlehem out into the forest of Greccio, where tame live animals were his cast. St Francis's two proselytizing orders, the Franciscans and the Poor Clares, made this 'mystery' popular wherever they established themselves. No doubt the sylvan celebrants of the Saturnalia would have been entertained by the apparent completion of their circle.

Our modern secular Christmas has grown into a voracious hybrid, capable of consuming such fearful gods as the hoary wolf-skin-cloaked Old Man Winter – and disgorging him as a chubby-cheeked round-bellied old gentleman in a red dressing-gown and cotton-wool bib. The Scandinavian *tomte*, saintly old Bishop Nicholas, the subterranean scarlet-eyed *kallikantzaros* of the Greeks, Attis's sacred fir-tree, the frantic orgies of the Romans, all have fed his iron digestion. It would not be surprising if the tender Babe in the manger was next on his menu.

ADVENT

Advent is the four weeks which lead up to Christmas. The First Sunday in Advent – the Sunday closest to November 30th – is the beginning of the Church's year, and marks the start of the Christmas festivities. In Sweden families go to church to sing carols and people decorate their homes and streets. In Germany the Advent wreath is hung in the window, and its four red candles are lit.

All over Europe a scattering of small ceremonies left over from the old pagan midwinter festivals prod sleeping Mother Earth into an awareness of the responsibilities. In Germany, on December 4th, St Barbara's Feast, cherry twigs are traditionally taken indoors and put in water so that they sprout in the warmth of the chimney-piece. Once a gentle nudge to Ceres's elbow, the new buds now form part of the Christmas celebration. On the same day in Provence, a handful of seed-corn must be scattered on a piece of wet flannel and set to germinate by the fire in time to decorate the table for the Christmas Eve fasting supper (see p 51). Further up the Rhône valley, in the high villages of the Baronnies and Vaison-la-Romaine, the sprouting grain is usually lentils – they have lovely little frizzy leaves. The buds may vary, but the sentiment is the same.

Italy and Catholic Europe have their own Advent ceremonies, keeping rather closer to the old Roman Saturnalia than the northern Protestants. Mrs Hugh Fraser, Edwardian diplomat's wife, remembered a Christmas spent in Rome as a young girl in the 1880s. The festival she describes visually, at least, recalls the feast of Saturn, Roman god of agriculture, which in pre-Christian Rome was celebrated from December 17th to the 19th: 'The year began for us with the first Sunday in Advent, when hundreds of Pifferari, the bagpipe players from the mountains of Romagna and the kingdom of Naples, entered the city in little companies to play their wild, haunting music before the many street shrines, where, in those days of faith, the lamps were kept burning and the flowers fresh all year round.'

Christmas fairs are still held during Advent all over northern Europe – particularly throughout the densely populated heartland of northern France, Germany and the Low Countries. When the population of Europe was still largely agricultural and dependent on the seasons, this was a fine time of year for a fair. People had put up the winter preserves, filled their larder from the pig-killing, and were ready to think about next year. Seasonal workers had their harvest-money to spend.

In northern Europe the spice salesman had pride of place at the markets of Advent. He often had an allotted corner – as I found a few years ago in the Romanian town of Sibiu – in a special 'foreigners' market', keeping exotic company with the coffee merchant, the fez-hatted Turkish carpet salesman, and the ribbon and lace pedlar (some towns were famous for their beautiful ribbons – Galician girls saved up to buy the beautiful woven satins of Lyons). Spices have always had a special appeal for those trapped in the cold northern winter – without them the wine cannot properly be mulled, or the Christmas biscuits and cakes spiced.

In Britain, the St Ives Pig Fair, or Fair Mo, fell on the Saturday before Advent Sunday. As the pilchard-fishing season generally ended in November, there was plenty of money available and the fair was the great event of the year. In pre-war days, the main street of St Ives was crowded with stalls, *stannens*, many of them selling little gingerbread figures – including pastry pigs with currant eyes sold by the pig-pie man – in the same tradition as the north European spicebread-men (see p15). Tom, Tom the piper's son stole a pastry piglet, not a real porker, before he ran away. Young men could spend their hard-earned cash on packets of fairings – traditionally gingerbread, later mutated to sugared almonds and macaroons – for their sweethearts.

ADVENT MARKET FAIRINGS
St Ives Pig-Fairings (England)

Pig-fairings are delicious made with the currant-spiked sweet pastry used for Cornish *hevva* cake, the traditional quick snack the fishermen took to sea to fortify them for the work of hauling in the huge autumn shoals of migrating pilchards – the *hevvas* – which were common between the Lizard and Land's End until the turn of the century. Hevva cake – mixed with home-made clotted cream and swiftly baked as soon as the cry of 'Hevva! hevva!' went up from the cliff – is marked with a criss-cross pattern, like a fishing net, so that it can easily be broken by a man with his hands fully occupied.

Quantity: Makes a dozen market piglets.
Time: Start 1–2 hours ahead. Takes 20–25 minutes, with 30 minutes cooking time.
Equipment: A sieve and a large mixing bowl. A rolling pin and board. Piglet biscuit-cutter (optional). Baking trays and a cooling rack.

1lb/500g plain flour	10oz/300g currants
grated rind of 1 lemon	1 teaspoon powdered mixed spice
½ teaspoon powdered nutmeg	3oz/75g caster sugar

Either (method 1): 4oz/125g lard and 4oz/125g butter (well chilled) and 2 large eggs (lightly mixed)	Or *(method 2, traditional):* 10oz/300g clotted cream (well chilled)

Sift the flour into the mixing bowl. Lightly fork in the currants, lemon rind, spices and sugar. (Save enough currants for the piglets' eyes.)

Either (method 1): using either your fingertips or a couple of knives, rub or chop in the lard and butter (or freeze it and grate it in) – not too thoroughly, as you are aiming for a rough-puff mix, not a shortcrust. Bind together with the beaten eggs. You may need a little water.

Or (method 2): work in enough chilled clotted cream to give a soft firm dough – lovely stuff, rich and golden yellow.

Leave the pastry, wrapped in a clean cloth or clingfilm, in a cool place to rest for 1–2 hours.

Heat the oven to 350°F/180°C/Gas 4.

Roll the pastry out to a thickness of ½in/1cm. Divide into 12 rectangles and clip with a sharp knife into the rough shape of a short-legged, curly-tailed piglet – or any other festive shape which takes your fancy. Use a biscuit-cutter if you prefer. Transfer to the lightly buttered baking trays, and finish each piglet with a raisin for an eye.

Bake for 30 minutes, until deliciously brown and well risen. Cool on the rack.

The piglets will store well in an airtight tin. Next time, make the same dough into a batch of *hevva* cakes to take fishing.

MARKET FAIRINGS
(England)

These crisp ginger biscuits are made with butter and honey. The dough can be sliced into rounds, or rolled out like pastry and cut out into any shape you please. Gingerbread hearts, perhaps, to give to those you love; or gingerbread men and women to tuck into the stockings of good boys and girls; or stars of Bethlehem to dunk into the mulled wine on a cold evening in Advent.

Quantity: Makes 2 dozen biscuits.
Time: Best to start 1–2 hours ahead. Takes 20–25 minutes, with 10–15 minutes cooking time.
Equipment: A sieve and a mixing bowl. A small saucepan. Fancy biscuit-cutters, board and rolling pin *(optional)*. Baking trays and a cooling rack.

8oz/250g self-raising flour
½ teaspoon salt
1 teaspoon mixed spice
4oz/125g cold butter

1 teaspoon bicarbonate of soda
1 teaspoon ground ginger
4oz/125g soft brown sugar
icing sugar for dusting *(optional)*

Sift the flour with the bicarbonate of soda, salt and spices. Mix in the sugar.

Rub in the butter with the tips of your fingers until the mixture looks like fine breadcrumbs. Warm the honey to finger-temperature, stir it into the mixture, working in enough to make a firm paste.

Heat the oven to 425°F/220°C/Gas 7.

Either cut the dough in 4 pieces, roll each into a fat sausage, and cut into ¼in/0.5cm slices. Or leave to cool and set for 1–2 hours, then roll out the paste to a thickness of ¼in/0.5cm with a rolling pin, on a board dusted with plenty of icing sugar, and cut the dough into the desired shape with biscuit-cutters. Transfer the biscuits to the baking trays.

Bake for 10–15 minutes, until well browned. Transfer to the rack to cool and crisp.

These biscuits store beautifully in an airtight tin.

ALMOND MACAROONS
(England)

The Cornishmen were (and still are) sailors and traders. The Phoenicians braved the Pillars of Hercules for the sake of Cornish tin, and may well have brought almonds and saffron along with the spices they offered as trade goods. This Cornish taste for the exotic, shared by all sea-going people from the Vikings to the Greeks, was later fed by links with Spain – sometimes voluntary in the course of business, sometimes involuntary in war.

Quantity: Makes about 24 macaroons.
Time: 15 minutes, with 10–15 minutes cooking time.
Equipment: A mixing bowl. 2 baking trays and a cooling rack.

8oz/250g caster sugar
3–4 drops almond essence
2–4 sheets rice paper (or filo pastry)

4oz/125g ground almonds
2 egg whites
flaked almonds

In the bowl, mix the sugar, ground almonds and essence, and egg whites (there's no need to beat the whites first).

Oil the 2 baking trays and line with rice paper.

Heat the oven to 350°F/180°C/Gas 4.

Using a teaspoon and a wet finger, form small balls with ½ teaspoon of the mixture. Space the balls out on the rice paper and top each ball with a flaked almond.

Bake the macaroons for 10–15 minutes, until lightly browned. Cool on the rack and tear off any excess rice paper.

FESTIVAL OF ST NICHOLAS: DECEMBER 5TH-6TH

The eve of December 6th, the festival of St Nicholas, is the traditional present-giving day over much of northern Europe. The legend of St Nicholas can be traced back to the fourth century Bishop Nicholas of Myra in Asia Minor, imprisoned by Diocletian during a purge of the Christians.

St Nicholas began his career as the patron saint of fishermen – a position he still holds in his Orthodox homeland, where model ships are considered more to his taste than Christmas trees or reindeer. As the patron saint of sailors he rides the storms and rescues mariners in distress. Greek and Russian seamen always kept a little statue of St Nicholas in the ship's forecastle and prayed to him when danger threatened. Dutch and Portuguese boats carried his image as a figurehead. Reindeer-herding Lapp fishermen in the far north of Scandinavia adopted him. The Bishop also looks after the welfare of parish clerks, scholars and pawnbrokers. By the fourteenth century, with a little help from the sixth-century Bishop Nicholas of Pinora, St Nicholas had children in his care as well. This completed the Bishop's metamorphosis into Sünnerklas or Santa Claus – the saintly old gentleman who, preferring his generosity unrecognized, slips gifts to his young favourites under cover of darkness.

Bishop Nicholas keeps motley company on his travels. The fearsome Knight Rupprecht (sometimes called Krampus or Hans Muff) accompanies him in many parts of central and northern Europe. The knight's origin is obscure: a wild creature of the snowy wastes, he wears animal skins and eats up naughty little children. His master has, as he lashes his reindeer through those stormy northern skies, perhaps inherited the mantle of mighty Odin, Norse god of war and wisdom.

In northern and eastern France, children stuff their *sabots* and stockings with hay and grain to feed the saint's donkey, the fodder being replaced with sweets, biscuits and nuts, and a sugar-powdered gingerbread Saint, hatted rather than mitred, mounted on his donkey. Over in the Vosges and into the mountains of Switzerland, the Bishop keeps company with a wild man, Le père Fouettard, when he knocks on the door to deliver the children's biscuits, gingerbreads and sweets.

Holland was something of an innovator. The Dutch Bishop Nicholas makes his entrance from Spain accompanied by Black Peter, his dark-skinned Moorish servant – a tradition which dates back to the sixteenth century, when Holland was under Spanish rule. Resplendent in the costume of a sixteenth-century Spanish don – plumed hat and all – Zwarte Piet drops little presents down the chimney into good children's stockings and shoes. He also carries a birch rod to beat delinquents – and sometimes stuffs the really naughty children into his sack and carries them off back to Spain. His master the Bishop, magnificent in scarlet cape and gilded mitre, leaning on a golden crook, also makes his entrance from southerly, rather than polar, climes.

Dutch families hide presents all over the house in the run-up to St Nicholas's Eve. Gift-wrappings are intended to camouflage rather than embellish, and the presents are chosen for humour and personal significance rather than expense. Each present is accompanied by a Sinte Klaus verse – a poem poking fun at the foibles of the recipient. Marzipan, a more friendly Moorish import than Zwarte Piet, is the great treat. From six weeks before the celebration, Dutch pastry shops blaze with beautiful marzipan fruits and delicious spiced cakes and biscuits in the form of moulded animals and human figures. Good children get a *banketletter*, a pastry initial filled with almond paste, or a tall chocolate initial.

In the seventeenth century Sinte Klaus and Black Peter emigrated to the USA with the Dutch who settled New Amsterdam. There the old gentleman was annually led through the streets on a white horse. He was re-exported back to Europe in more or less his modern incarnation as the polar-based Santa-cum-Father-Christmas no more than a century and a half ago – an English writer in 1827 described the American tradition as 'unknown to us in England'.

Father Christmas's empire is expanding rapidly at the expense of his rivals, gaining ground annually both from old Bishop Nicholas's festival and from the Three Kings or Wise Men, whose January 6th festival is celebrated in southern Europe with a similar exchange of gifts.

ST NICHOLAS SPICED SHORTBREADS
Speculaas (Holland)

At this time of year in Dutch shops and markets there are special moulds for shaping these deliciously spicy shortbreads. There are a variety of theories about the name – my favourite is that it is from *spek*, titbit, and *klaas*, the diminutive of Nicholas. The biscuits are traditional festival treats in neighbouring Germany as well. The recipe also makes delicious everyday biscuits – popular in Holland for dunking in breakfast coffee, and as an addition to a lucky schoolchild's packed lunch. *Speculaas* moulds themselves are made of wood – traditionally beech, pear or walnut – shallow and relief-carved on the same principle as those used for Scottish shortbread. They are usually 6–12 ins/15–30cm long and feature the Bishop himself, his donkey, or his servant Black Peter. Smaller ones might be evergreen leaves and Christmas wreaths or little figures of children. The shapes can of course be moulded freehand or with a biscuit-cutter, like gingerbread men.

Quantity: Gives 2–6 moulded figures, or 3 dozen ordinary biscuits.
Time: Start 20 minutes ahead. Takes 20–25 minutes, with 15–20 minutes cooking time.
Equipment: A sieve and a mixing board. The proper wooden figure moulds would be lovely – otherwise a biscuit-cutter or a sharp knife will have to do. A baking tray and a cooling rack.

1lb/500g self-raising flour	8oz/250g soft brown sugar
7oz/200g softened butter	1 teaspoon crushed cardamom seeds
½ teaspoon powdered cloves	1 teaspoon powdered cinnamon
4oz/100g ground almonds or hazelnuts	2 eggs, lightly whisked together

Sieve the flour in a pile on to the mixing board and make a deep well in the middle.

Into this hollow tip the sugar, softened butter, spices, ground nuts and whisked eggs. Mix them together with your fingers, then draw in the flour from the outer ring, quickly working in as much as necessary to give a soft dough – you may need less or more flour depending on the size of the eggs and the water-content of the butter.

Cover the dough with a cloth or clingfilm, and leave to rest in a cool place for 20 minutes.

Heat the oven to 400°F/200°C/Gas 6.

Flour your carved wooden moulds well if making figures – knock out excess flour. Divide the dough into the appropriate pieces, flatten into the right shape with the tips of your fingers, and press firmly into the moulds. Cut off extra dough with a sharp knife. Tip out the figures on to the buttered baking tray. If they do not come out easily, work a little extra flour into the dough or flour the moulds more thoroughly.

If you have no moulds, cut out a paper pattern to use as a template. Pat the dough out into the rough shape required and put it on the buttered baking tray. Trim with a sharp knife round the template, and outline the main features of the dough-man with your knife. It will not be perfect, but it will taste delicious.

If you would like to make non-festive *speculaas*, then before you put the dough aside for 20 minutes, roll it into a long thin bolster. Slice the bolster with a sharp knife into discs ½in/1cm thick, and transfer them to the buttered baking tray. They can be rolled out and cut with a biscuit-cutter if you prefer.

Bake the biscuits, moulded or plain, in the hot oven for 15–20 minutes depending on the thickness (particularly thick ones should be cooked for longer, at 375°F/190°C/Gas 5), until pale gold and crisp. Transfer carefully to the cooling rack.

Speculaas store well in an airtight tin.

SPICED HONEYBREAD
Lebkuchen (Germany)

St Nicholas figures are the traditional gift from godparents to their godchildren on St Nicholas's day in northern France and Germany. Such honeybread and *pain d'épices* recipes are among our most ancient festival treats. Their very name comes from the Roman *libum* – a flat cake. In the Christian era the monasteries, which always had their own beehives for honey, specialized in these richly spiced celebration breads. In modern, more secular, times, various towns – particularly Dijon and Nürnberg – have become famous for their manufacture. They can be found on sale in European markets all year round. The gingerbread mixture can be pressed into the moulds used for *speculaas*, if you have them (see p. 15).

Quantity: Makes 2 large figures, or 4 dozen iced fingers.
Time: Start a day ahead. Takes 25–30 minutes, with 20–30 minutes cooking time.
Equipment: A sieve and a bowl. A small pan and a whisk. A pastry board and a rolling pin. 2 baking trays and a cooling rack.

1lb/500g self-raising flour	6oz/150g soft brown sugar
4oz/100g honey	1 teaspoon powdered cinnamon
4oz/100g ground almonds	4–6oz/100–175g crystallized mixed peel
2 eggs	

To finish

2 tablespoons kirsch or any type of brandy	8oz/250g icing sugar

Sieve the flour into the bowl.

Melt the sugar and the honey together over a gentle heat. Off the fire, stir in the cinnamon, flour and ground nuts, and the crystallized peel, roughly chopped.

Lightly whisk the eggs and beat them into the cooling honey and flour mixture. Beat until you have a smooth soft paste. Cover and leave to rest in the refrigerator overnight.

Next day, using the board and rolling pin, both well dusted with icing sugar, roll the paste out into a large rectangle ¼in/0.5cm thick. Cut it in half to give you two large flat biscuits.

Heat the oven to 325°F/170°C/Gas 3.

Transfer the two sheets of dough to the buttered baking trays. Bake for 20–30 minutes, until the biscuit is crisp and well browned. Lift carefully on to the rack to cool.

Sieve the icing sugar to get rid of its lumps, and mix to a smooth coating icing with the kirsch or brandy and a tablespoon of water.

When the biscuits are cool, ice them both smoothly and leave the icing to set for a few hours before you paint on the mitred figure of Bishop Nicholas, with or without his donkey. It's the thought that counts – but if this makes too heavy a demand on your artistic skill, the iced biscuits can be cut into fingers 6in/15cm long and 2in/5cm wide. Your favourite children will find the small biscuits just as delicious, and they will be perfectly within the tradition of St Nicholas.

INITIAL-PASTRY
Banketletter (Holland)

The initials are made with a rough-puff pastry – half-way between shortcrust and puff, but still deliciously buttery and much simpler to make than a puff pastry. It's a lovely idea for children's tea-parties, as well as being the traditional St Nicholas gift for good little Dutch children.

Quantity: Makes about 8 initials 4in/10cm high.
Time: Start 1 hour ahead. Takes 30–40 minutes, with 8 minutes cooking time.
Equipment: A sieve and mixing bowl. 2 sharp knives. A rolling pin and board. Baking trays and a cooling rack.

The pastry

8oz/250g flour	½ teaspoon salt
8oz/250g very cold butter	4 tablespoons iced water

To finish

1 egg white	4 tablespoons chopped almonds
4 tablespoons sugar	

Sift the flour and the salt into the cold mixing bowl.

Using 2 sharp knives, cut the butter roughly into the flour. Sprinkle in 3 tablespoons of the iced water and work into a dough with one of the knives. Add extra water until all the flour is taken up into a soft pliable dough. Cover and put aside in a cool place for 30 minutes.

Roll the pastry out into a large rectangle on the well-floured board. Fold it into three as if it was a letter. Put it aside in a cool place to rest for 30 minutes. Repeat three times.

Roll the pastry out to a thickness of about ½in/1cm.

Heat the oven to 475°F/240°C/Gas 9.

Cut out the initial letters (they can be as large or as small as you please) appropriate to the recipient or the occasion. Paint each letter with egg white, and sprinkle with almonds and sugar.

Rinse the baking trays with cold water and transfer the letters to them.

Bake the pastry in the very hot oven for 8 minutes, until puffed and pale gold. Turn the oven down to 350°F/180°C/Gas 4 and finish cooking for another 5–10 minutes, until the pastry is set and crisp. Open the oven door and let the house fill with the fragrance of hot butter and almonds.

Put the letters to cool on the rack. Then it's each to his own.

SANT CLAUS BREADMEN
Klausemänner (Germany)

Good German children hope to find a *Klausemann* perched on top of their sweets and treats on the morning of St Nicholas's Day. Breadmen are nicest made with an enriched dough, such as this lemon-scented milk bread – delicious to dip into a cup of hot chocolate or coffee at breakfast.

Quantity: Makes 4 *Klausemänner* or 1 small loaf.
Time: Start 2–3 hours ahead.
Equipment: A sieve, a large bowl. A baking tray and a cooling rack.

1lb/500g plain flour
scant ¼ pint/150ml warm milk
3 eggs
½ teaspoon salt (it makes sweet things taste sweeter)

1oz/25g fresh yeast (or a ½oz/12g packet of dried)
3oz/75g sugar
3oz/75g melted butter
grated rind of 1 lemon

To finish
2 tablespoons milk

1 tablespoon raisins or currants

Sieve the flour into the warm bowl and make a well in the middle. Mix the yeast with the warm milk and a teaspoon of sugar in a cup, and wait until it liquifies. (If using dried yeast, follow the packet instructions.) Pour the frothy liquid into the well in the middle of the flour. Sprinkle a little flour over it and leave it to bubble up on a warm place for 10 minutes.

Break in the eggs and pour in the butter, then add the salt and lemon rind. Work all together with your hand, drawing in the flour from the sides. Knead it well until you have a soft elastic dough – you may need more flour or liquid. Cover the doughball, still in its mixing bowl, with a damp cloth. Put it in a turned-off, still warm oven with a roasting tin of boiling water on the base – or use whatever is your preferred method for making bread dough rise.

Leave it until it has doubled in size – 1–1½ hours is usually enough in a warm damp atmosphere.

Bash the dough down and knead it for 1–2 minutes. Divide the dough into 4 pieces. Form each into a doughman – a boy for a boy and a girl for a girl. Transfer the figures to the well-buttered baking tray. Finish with a lick of milk, and use raisins or currants for eyes, and for the buttons.

Leave to prove again for about 10–15 minutes, until nicely risen and spongy.

Meanwhile heat the oven to 400°F/200°C/Gas 6. Bake the doughmen for about 30 minutes, until light and golden.

Transfer to the rack to cool – and the *Klausemänner* are all ready for a snowy morning.

ST LUCIA'S DAY: DECEMBER 13TH

The feast of St Lucia of Syracuse is a northern celebration and marks the twelve days which precede Christmas, as Epiphany marks the twelve days which follow. The festival is celebrated above all in Scandinavia and Hungary.

In Hungary, the twelve days before Christmas are called 'St Lucia's calendar'. They precede the feast by the same number of days as Christmas in the Gregorian calendar precedes the Christmas of the ancient (Julian) calendar. Throughout eastern Europe, the twelve days before or after Christmas (it varies from region to region) are the time of werewolves and magic. In the old days country people would dress up, and put on masks and dance in the fields, to frighten away the demons who harm the crops. On St Lucia's night itself, it was well known that witches could be seen face to face.

The Hungarian writer Károly Viski reported in 1932 that most of the customs and superstitions of the winter solstice were crowded together on St Lucia's Day. Precautions had to be taken against harm. Girls were not to sew, housewives could not spend money. In the evening the mistress of the house had to frighten the hens with a stick – driving them off their nests with a broom held in her left hand. Alternatively, she might steal a little wheat from the mill and feed the hens through a sieve. And when the kotyolok, the village's white witch, came to visit, the household had to welcome her with dried pears. Then the hens would lay eggs and all would be well for the rest of the year.

The origins of the Swedish festival can be traced back to the men-only feasts which were held on what was the longest night of the year in the medieval calendar. Eighteenth-century records are the first to describe young girls dressed in white and wearing crowns of lighted candles, serving the feast. Now a young girl is chosen in all Swedish communities. A kind of snowy May queen, she is dressed in a white gown, crowned with candles, and has a train of similarly clad attendants singing Lucia carols. It is her duty to bring to the table special curly saffron buns, ginger biscuits and a bowl of glögg – spiced mulled wine.

LUCIA'S SAFFRON BUNS
Luciasaffransbröd (Sweden)

These saffron-scented golden buns, rich with butter, currants and almonds and curled like ringlets, are traditionally served by the chosen Lucia and her pretty attendants – with morning coffee, or with mulled wine (see p. 21).

Quantity: Makes 2 dozen buns.
Time: Start 3 hours ahead. 40–45 minutes.
Equipment: A mixing bowl. A pastry board. Baking trays and a cooling rack.

10–12 filaments of saffron
½ teaspoon salt
1 pint/600ml warm milk
8oz/250g butter, melted
3oz/75g almonds, roughly chopped

2lb/1kg strong white flour
1oz/25g fresh yeast (or a ½oz/12g packet of dried)
1 egg
8oz/250g sugar
6oz/175g currants

To finish
1 egg, lightly beaten
2–3 tablespoons slivered almonds

2–3 tablespoons sugar

Put the saffron into a warm oven for a few moments to become dry and crisp. Crumble it into a cup and pour in a splash of boiling water. Leave it to infuse – it can be left to steep for 2 days if you have time.

Sift the flour and the salt into the warmed bowl, and make a well in the middle. Dissolve the fresh yeast in a cupful of warm milk and pour it in to the well. Sprinkle with a little flour and leave it in a warm place for 10–15 minutes while the yeast gets working on the flour. (If using dried yeast, follow the packet instructions.).

Beat the egg lightly with the rest of the milk. Pour the milk and egg, the saffron with its liquid, the melted butter and the sugar into the flour. Work it all together with your hand until you have a soft pliable dough. Work in the chopped almonds and the currants and knead thoroughly. Put the dough to rise in a warm damp place (a turned-off oven with a tray of boiling water in the base is my own favourite) for a couple of hours, until it has doubled in size.

Turn the dough out on to the floured board and knock it down to distribute the air bubbles. Cut it into 24 pieces. Roll out each piece into a long thin sausage and use your imagination to braid it into curls and ringlets. Transfer the buns to the oiled baking trays, cover with a clean cloth and set them to rise again for 20–30 minutes.

Meanwhile heat the oven to 425°F/220°C/Gas 7.

Finish the buns with a lick of egg, a sprinkle of sugar and a few slivers of almond.

Bake them in the hot oven for 12–15 minutes, until well risen and golden brown.

Serve them fresh and warm – if possible at the hands of the chosen Lucia and to the sound of carols. If not, a lit white candle will have to do instead.

LUCIA'S GINGER SNAPS
Luciapepparkaka (Sweden)

This delicately spiced cream-rich mixture gives a fine-textured crisp biscuit. The dough must be allowed its overnight rest to develop the body for rolling and cutting – it looks soft and sticky when first mixed. The *pepparkaka* accompany the saffron buns (see previous recipe) – an essential ingredient of the Lucia Day merrymaking.

Quantity: Makes about 3 dozen biscuits.
Time: Start the day before. 30–40 minutes.
Equipment: A whisk and small bowl. A small saucepan. A mixing bowl. A rolling pin and a pastry board. Shaped biscuit-cutters (*optional*). Baking trays and a cooling rack.

¼ pint/150ml treacle
8oz/225g brown sugar
juice and grated rind of 1 lemon
icing sugar, sieved, for dusting

¼ pint/150ml double cream, whipped until stiff
1 teaspoon ground ginger
1lb/500g flour, sieved

Heat the treacle until it is runny. Mix all the ingredients together except the lemon juice, then work in enough lemon juice to form a soft dough. Put it to rest, covered, in the refrigerator – overnight if possible.

Next day, knead the dough lightly and roll it out – about as thin as a coin – dusting the board and the rolling pin generously with icing sugar.

Heat the oven to 350°F/180°C/Gas 4.

Using biscuit-cutters or a knife, cut out pretty Christmas shapes – stars, trees, hearts, gingerbread men. Grease the baking trays, rinse them with cold water, and transfer the biscuits to them.

Bake the biscuits for 12–15 minutes, until crisp and brown. Slip them carefully on to the rack to cool. They're lovely to dip into coffee or glögg (see next recipe) on a cold winter's evening, whether it's St Lucia's night or just an ordinary winter evening.

Store any leftovers in an airtight tin.

MULLED WINE
Glögg (Sweden)

This brew should keep the witches and trolls at bay – the making of it is a ritual which adds spice to any evening. Aquavit and claret are the traditional liquors for glögg – the first home-made, the second a major trade item of the Hanseatic League, the consortium of Lübeck merchants who controlled the Scandinavian salt-cod and herring trade during the Middle Ages. All Scandinavia developed, and still has, a taste for red wine with cod.

Quantity: Serves 6–10.
Time: 15–20 minutes.
Equipment: A large saucepan. A small-meshed baking rack. A ladle.

1 litre bottle aquavit (or vodka or white brandy)	1 bottle claret (or any robust red wine)
6 cardamom pods	6 cloves
2–3 curls of orange peel	4 dried figs
1 small cinnamon stick	8oz/250g lump sugar (or solid cone-sugar if you can find it)

To finish

4oz/100g blanched almonds	4oz/100g raisins

Put all the ingredients except the lump sugar and the finishing ingredients in the pan. Heat them gently, and remove the pan from the heat immediately they come to the boil.

Put the sugar on the baking rack and balance it over the pan.

Take a ladleful of the glögg and light it with a match. Pour the burning liquid over the lump sugar, and repeat until all the sugar has melted. Remove the rack and cover the pan to kill the flames. The burning sugar caramelizes and adds a lovely roasted flavour to the wine – it has the same effect as thrusting in a red-hot poker.

Serve the glögg hot, poured into glasses into which you have put a few almonds and raisins.

The glögg can be prepared ahead, strained and stored in well-corked wine bottles. Re-heat, but do not let it boil or all the alcohol will vanish in a puff of steam.

SCANDINAVIAN CHRISTMAS COLD TABLE

In Scandinavia, Christmas is the longest and most important holiday of the year. The Christmas tree was introduced from Germany during the sixteenth century, but it is only in this century that the custom of bringing a whole live fir-tree indoors and decorating it with glitter, lights and straw ornaments has become widespread. The tree is kept watered until the twentieth day after Christmas, January 13th, Knut's Day in Sweden, when it is planted out again.

On Christmas Eve, no one works – farmers may only see to their livestock – and the family have their Christmas *smörgåsbord*. Traditional dishes include ham, dip-in-the-pot soup, jellied brawn and trotters, lut-fisk (lye-soaked dried cod – the only remnant of the pre-Reformation Catholic fasting supper) – and rice porridge. If there is a large gathering, different families will bring their own specialities, a kind of bring-your-own catering which, in the old days, ensured that the feast did not completely empty any one family's storehouse.

After the meal, the *tomte*, the Christmas gnome, makes his scheduled (if proxy) appearance on the doorstep with a sack of presents. For the rest of the year he lives under the floorboards of the farmhouse and keeps a weather eye on the family.

It was midsummer harvest-time a few years ago when I visited the Erikson farm in the little mountain village of Bortnan in the south of Swedish Lapland. Sweden was for long a nation of peasant farmers – freeholders of a few fields which, if carefully husbanded, yielded a reasonable living for a family. Today it is no longer so. The cash crop must be earned in the city.

The three men and two women in the field beside the road had rolled up the sleeves of their faded shirts. All wore the tattered work-trousers of the farm labourer. There was no trace of the city in their appearance or their strong bodies; Margaret Erikson, however, the old man's daughter and the elder of the two women, was a hospital administrator in Stockholm General. As the daughter of a farmer, she was typical of the changing patterns of Swedish life. Few Scandinavians are more than a couple of generations away from the land.

The grandfather was driving a threshing device pulled by a small cream and brown pony of the Norwegian Fjord breed. I climbed the ramp to the hay-loft to look at the wooden sleigh which had been pulled into shelter. Below me the cows stirred and breathed, munching steadily.

Margaret laughed in answer to my query about the sleigh.

No. We haven't used it since the war. But you should have seen us on Christmas Eve when I was a child. My mother would dress us up in our warmest clothes and my father would come round to the front of the house with the pony harnessed into the sleigh, all lined with reindeer-skins to keep us warm. We would creep under the furs and wait for my father to climb into the front. Then the sled would slide out into the darkness and the snow and head for the church in the valley down there. You can see the spire from here. The neighbours came from the hills around – they all had sleighs with ponies then. Everyone had lanterns hanging to light the way. You could hear the harness bells, and see the lights coming into the valley from all around, the people all coming to the church. It was the most exciting thing in the world.

She stroked the pale smooth birchwood and elegant curves of the sleigh. It was large enough to accommodate the whole family with ease. Slung over the beam beside it were the reindeer-skins. On a hook nearby hung the lantern. Ready for bright Christmas faces in the snow. She went on:

When we came home there would be dip-in-the-pot – our Christmas ham with a big tureen of its own broth, and creamed potatoes to go with the ham. We had cream porridge with an almond in it for the children to find, and for the grown-ups, Christmas ale, brewed specially strong. There were always herring salads, of course, to eat first – no celebration is without its herrings.

PICKLED HERRINGS WITH SOURED CREAM AND POTATOES
Sillsallad (Sweden)

Salt-pickled herrings are the most important dishes on a Scandinavian *smörgåsbord* – and participants are expected to choose them first. On a Christmas table you would also probably find *lutfisk* – rather less easy to obtain as it is wind-dried cod, stockfish, which has been soaked in a solution of lye to give it its golden colour and oddly ancient flavour – plain-boiled, it is usually served with melted butter and puréed peas. Matjes herring is a mild Dutch cure, now the most popular and widely available prepared pickled herring. Invent your own herring salads – there should be equal proportions of herring and vegetables. Or set out separate dishes of pickled beetroots, sliced tomatoes and vinegar-dressed cucumber for guests to make up their own herring mixes.

Quantity: Serves 6.
Time: 25–30 minutes.
Equipment: A large saucepan. Small serving dishes.

2lb/1kg potatoes
1 onion, peeled and thinly sliced
6 tablespoons chopped chives
½ pint/300ml soured cream

12oz/350g pickled (matjes) herrings
dill sprigs
2–3 hard-boiled eggs

Boil the potatoes in their jackets in salted water. Drain well, dry for a moment over the heat, and serve hot in a deep bowl. Guests may peel their own.

Meanwhile cut the herrings neatly on the diagonal and arrange them on a dish. Sprinkle with onion rings and dill sprigs. Moisten with a little of the pickle liquor.

Serve with the hot potatoes, the chives in their own dish, the chopped eggs in another, and the soured cream in another. Accompany with crisp rye bread and unsalted butter. The traditional drink is aquavit (*schnapps* – make it at home by dropping a few seeds of caraway into a bottle of good vodka and leaving it to macerate for a week or so) with a beer chaser. Festival beer is specially good, and pretty strong.

CHRISTMAS HAM AND DIP-IN-THE-POT
Kryddskinka (Sweden)

A lightly salted ham and its broth are essential to the spirit of a Scandinavian Christmas. The ham is sometimes smoked as well – traditionally, it would have been hung in the chimney for a few days. The joint makes its first appearance on the Christmas Eve *smörgåsbord* buffet, and after that it is left on the side to provide easy meals throughout the holiday. A communal pot of simmering ham broth, with bread to dip into it, awaits churchgoers on their return from a snowy midnight Mass. A pig's head for brawn might be included, if the pot is large enough. Leftover broth can go into a winter pea soup for Christmas Day.

Quantity: Serves around 6 for 3 meals.
Time: Start the day before. Takes about 20 minutes, with 4–5 hours cooking time.
Equipment: A very large pot. A roasting tin.

1 whole salt-cured ham (uncooked, rind left on	2 onions
– a whole ham on the bone weighs	2 carrots
12–20lb/6–10kg, off the bone 7–12lb/3.5–6kg	celery and leek tops
½ teaspoon whole peppercorns	1–2 bay leaves
water	1 pint/600ml light beer

To finish

1 egg white	1 tablespoon mustard powder
3 tablespoons brown sugar	4–5 heaped tablespoons home-made breadcrumbs

Soak the ham overnight in cold water to get rid of excess salt.

Wipe the joint. Wash and quarter the onions, leaving the skin on to add colour to the broth. Rinse and roughly chop the other vegetables.

Lay a bed of the vegetables and aromatics in the bottom of the large pot and put in the ham. Pour in enough cold water and beer to submerge the meat completely.

Bring all to a rolling boil. Lid the pot, turn down the heat and simmer steadily, adding boiling water when necessary to keep the ham submerged. Cook the ham until tender – for 4–5 hours, calculating 20 minutes per lb. Leave the ham to cool overnight in its own broth.

Next day, drain the ham (strain and save the broth for the dip-in-the-pot), pat it dry and trim off the skin. Transfer the joint to the roasting tin.

Score the fat in a diamond pattern. Mix the egg white with the mustard and sugar, and paint the joint all over with the mixture. Finish with a coating of breadcrumbs. Bake in a hot oven, 450°F/230°C/Gas 8, for 15–20 minutes to crisp and brown the topping.

Serve with prunes, soaked and simmered in a little of the stock, pea purée and apple sauce, as the centrepiece of the Christmas buffet. Accompany with a tureen of steaming ham broth for dipping.

CREAM-SIMMERED DILLED POTATOES
Stuvad potatis (Sweden)

Dairy products, including cream and milk, both soured and fresh, are very important in the Scandinavian diet. In the old days both were available throughout the winter even in the most isolated northerly farms, as the cattle were overwintered indoors – snug in huge airy barns, fed on stored hay from the summer meadows. The inclusion of onion is traditional in the south although not in the north – but they add a delicious flavour.

Quantity: Serves 4.
Time: 30 minutes.
Equipment: A roomy lidded saucepan.

1½lb/750g old potatoes
2oz/50g butter
¾ pint/450ml milk
3 tablespoons finely chopped dill, chives,
    leeks, parsley (one or a mixture)

1 mild onion
¼ pint/150ml double cream
1 teaspoon salt

Peel the potatoes and cube them small. Skin and chop the onion. Melt the butter in the saucepan and add the onion and potatoes. Fry for 4–5 minutes, until the vegetables soften a little. Pour in the cream and milk and bring to the boil. Add the salt and turn down to simmer for 15–20 minutes, until the potatoes are done. Stir in the chopped herbs. Serve the potatoes in their own creamy juices, as an accompaniment to the ham.

ALMOND CREAMED RICE
Risgrynsgröt (Sweden)

The Christmas porridge, found throughout Scandinavia and sometimes served before the meat to blunt winter-sharpened appetites, sometimes after, has an almond hidden in it to bring whoever finds it good luck all year. If you have plenty of children around, a few extra almonds will encourage them to eat it all up.

Quantity: Serves 6–8.
Time: About 1 hour.
Equipment: A large heavy-bottomed saucepan.

8oz/250g round rice
1oz/25g butter
1 pint/600ml milk
1 tablespoon ground almonds

½ pint/300ml water
½ teaspoon salt
1 pint/600ml cream
1 curl lemon peel

To finish
1–6 blanched almond(s)
brown sugar

1 teaspoon powdered cinnamon

Pick over the rice. Bring the water to the boil in the pan and stir in the rice. Bring back to the boil and add the butter and the salt. Simmer for 10–15 minutes, uncovered, until the water has all disappeared. Pour in the milk and cream, stir in the ground almonds, tuck in the lemon peel, and cook slowly, stirring regularly, for 30 minutes until the rice is quite soft.

Stir in the blanched almonds and pour the mixture into a pretty, deep dish. Sprinkle with cinnamon and brown sugar. Hand more brown sugar and cream separately. It's lovely, too, with a sharp raspberry sauce (the Scandinavians conserve their precious harvest of late summer berries as jams, sauces and cordials).

CHRISTMAS PLUM STARS
Joulutähti (Finland)

Finland has its Christmas ham too, although it is more likely to be roasted than pot-boiled. The Finns have a tradition of oven-cooking dating back to the days of room-sized baking ovens built into the wall behind the stove – which, as they cooled, were used as saunas. Christmas in urban Finland is a very jolly affair, with tomtes in their scarlet suits handing out ginger biscuits, pine-log fires at the street corners, the pavements lit with candles stuck into buckets of frozen water (no need for any but natural refrigeration). Christmas baking in Finland is a serious undertaking, with ginger cakes (see p.41) and spiced biscuits (see p. 20), conserved fruit tarts and plaits of rich sweet bread as an essential ingredient of the winter festival.

Quantity: Makes a dozen stars.
Time: Start the day before. Then allow 2 hours intermittent attention.
Equipment: A small saucepan. A large bowl and a sieve. A pastry board and rolling pin. A baking tray and a cooling rack.

The filling
6oz/175g dried prunes	¾ pint/450ml water
3oz/75g sugar	1 stick cinnamon
3–4 cloves	

The puff pastry (you can use 1lb/500g of bought pastry if you prefer)
9oz/275g flour	½ teaspoon salt
7oz/200g unsalted butter	approx. 2 tablespoons water

Put the prunes to soak in the water overnight. Next day, simmer them with the sugar and the spices until they are soft and the cooking liquid is reduced to a thick syrup. Discard the spices, stone the prunes and chop the flesh finely. Moisten with syrup and leave to cool.

Meanwhile, make the pastry. See that the butter is firm without being hard.

Take the large bowl and sieve in the flour with the salt. Cut in 3oz/75g of the butter with a sharp knife until you have a mixture like fine breadcrumbs. Mix in enough water to make a paste which does not stick to the fingers. Knead lightly. Set the dough aside for 20 minutes, with the rest of the butter beside it so that pastry and butter both reach the same temperature.

Roll out the pastry to a thickness of about ¼in/0.5cm. With your fingers place on it small pieces of butter the size of hazelnuts, using a third of the butter left over. Then fold the pastry into three, like a napkin, and again in the other direction. Set aside for 20 minutes.

Go through the last process twice more, until the butter is finished. Set the pastry aside for 20 minutes after each process. Then leave it another 20 minutes before using it. These intervals allow the pastry to lose some of its elasticity.

Roll the pastry out on the well-floured board to a thickness of ¼in/0.5cm. Cut it into two ½in/1cm squares. Make two cuts in from each corner to form the points of a star. Dampen the side flaps. Put a teaspoon of prune filling in the middle of each star and fold in the sides, leaving the points flat on the board. Pinch the flaps together to enclose the prune filling. Transfer carefully to the baking tray.

Bake the stars in a hot oven (425°F/220°C/Gas 7) for 15–20 minutes, until the pastry is crisp and golden.

Transfer them to the rack to cool. Reheat them gently to serve warm on Christmas Eve.

CHRISTMAS BUTTER-BREAD PLAIT
Joululeipä (Finland)

Spicy butter-enriched breads, particularly this plaited ring, are baked to mark all festivals in Finland – including weddings, birthdays and name days (the feast of the saint for whom you are named). Such breads are usually served at the conclusion of a meal with a sweet porridge or 'fruit soup' (see plum porridge, p.28, and *rødgrød*, p. 162). These fruit fools are delicious with biscuits or a piece of plain cake on non-feast days, and the perfect companion to this cardamom-scented Christmas bread.

Quantity: Makes an 8–10in/20–25cm ring.
Time: Start 3 hours ahead. 40–45 minutes.
Equipment: A mixing bowl. A pastry board and rolling pin. A baking tray and a cooling rack.

1¼lb/600g strong white flour	1 teaspoon ground cardamom
½ teaspoon salt	1oz/25g fresh yeast (or ½oz/12g dried)
½ pint/300ml warm milk	2 egg yolks
4oz/100g butter, melted	4oz/100g sugar

To finish

1 egg, lightly beaten	2 tablespoons sugar
2 tablespoons slivered almonds	

Sift the flour, cardamom and salt into the warmed bowl, and make a well in the middle. Dissolve the yeast in a cupful of the warm milk with a little sugar and pour it into the well. Sprinkle with a little of the flour and leave it in a warm place for 15–20 minutes while the yeast gets working on the flour. (If you are using dried yeast, follow the instructions on the packet.)

Beat the egg yolks lightly with the rest of the milk. Pour the milk and egg, melted butter and sugar into the flour. Work all together with your hand until you have a soft pliable dough. Put the dough to rise in a warm damp place (in a bowl covered with clingfilm) for a couple of hours, until it has doubled in size.

Turn the dough out on to the floured board and knock it down to distribute the air bubbles. Cut it into 3 pieces. Roll out each piece into a long sausage about 1in/2.5cm thick. Plait the sausages and join them, with a dampened finger, into a ring. Transfer to the buttered baking tray, cover with a clean cloth and set the bread to rise again for 20–30 minutes.

Meanwhile heat the oven to 400°F/200°C/Gas 6.

Finish the bread ring with a glaze of egg, a sprinkle of sugar and the flaked almonds.

Bake the ring in the hot oven for 25–30 minutes, until well risen and golden brown. Turn down the oven a little after the first 15 minutes – this reproduces the natural cooling process of an oven which has been pre-heated with raked-out fire.

CINNAMON-SPICED PLUM PORRIDGE
Rusina-soppa (Finland)`

Sweet porridge/soups are served in Finland after the meat, accompanied by a little basket of sweet breads – although elsewhere they often make their appearance as a first course. The soup is either a thickened flavoured milk – rather custard-like – or a thickened *compote* of fruit, fresh or conserved, including apples, prunes, dried apricots and raisins, and some lovely berries – of which Finland has an enviably large natural store. The thickening agent varies, but 2oz/50g of flour thickens 2 pints/1 litre of liquid to the correct consistency – try ground rice, cornflour, wheat flour, potato flour, semolina, barley or oatmeal (least favourite in Finland – too much of it about).

Quantity: Serves 4.
Time: Start the day before. Takes 20 minutes.
Equipment: A medium saucepan.

8oz/250g prunes
2 pints/1.2 litres water
1 short stick cinnamon
1 tablespoon cornflour

2oz/50g semolina
4oz/100g sugar
juice and rind of 1 lemon

To finish
1 teaspoon powdered cinnamon
whipped cream

1 tablespoon flaked toasted almonds

Put the prunes to soak in the water overnight. The next day, when they are well plumped up, take out the stones.

Bring the prunes to the boil in their soaking water with the sugar and the stick of cinnamon, then lower the heat and simmer for 10 minutes, until they are half-cooked. Stir in the semolina gradually, so that it does not form lumps, and tuck in the lemon rind. Simmer for 20–30 minutes, until the prunes are puréed and the semolina is soft. Remove the cinnamon stick and lemon rind. Stir in the lemon juice mixed with the cornflour and reboil to thicken.

Remove the mixture from the heat, and either heat it with a wooden spoon for 10 minutes, until you have incorporated enough air for the mixture to be pale and light, or put the whole lot into a food processor and give it a good beat for 1 minute.

Pour into a pretty glass bowl and leave to cool. Finish with a sprinkling of powdered cinnamon and some flaked toasted almonds. Serve with whipped cream and slices of Christmas plait (see p. 27).

This *compote* is also lovely when made with dried apricots – you will need only 6oz/175g if they are already halved and de-stoned.

CHRISTMAS WREATH CAKE
Kransekake (Norway)

This pyramid of crisp almond-macaroon rings, built up rather like the French wedding *croquembouche*, is the favourite Norwegian celebration cake, an essential at weddings and confirmations as well as

Christmas. The rings, once baked, keep beautifully in an airtight tin, ready to be finished and decorated as you please. Children love it – not nearly so heavy as our own traditional fruit cake.

Quantity: Makes an 18-ring tower.
Time: Allow about 1½ hours, as it is a bit fiddly.
Equipment: 2 bowls. A whisk. 3–4 large shallow cake tins and a cooling rack.

1lb/500g whole almonds (or ground almonds)
3 tablespoons flour
butter for greasing

1lb/500g caster sugar
3 egg whites

The cake is nicest made with a mixture of skinned and unskinned whole almonds, ground up not too finely in the coffee or nut grinder. But it can be made with ready-ground almonds – which gives a smoother paler macaroon.

Mix the ground nuts with the sugar and flour. Whisk the egg whites until aerated but still soft. Work them into the nut mixture and knead until you have a soft but firm dough – this can be done in an electric mixer.

Roll the dough into ropes as thick as your finger. Cut them into 18 lengths, starting with the smallest at 5½in/14cm long. The next should be just under 1in/2cm longer, and so on. Splice the ropes together as rings, smoothing down the join.

Butter the cake tins thoroughly and dust with flour.

Preheat the oven to 400°F/200°C/Gas 6.

Arrange the rings in the cake trays, leaving plenty of room between for them to expand – one inside the other, the first tray should have rings 1, 5, 11, 17 – and so on.

Bake for 8–10 minutes until crisp and golden. Transfer to the rack to cool.

Finish the cake now, or store the rings in an airtight tin with a piece of fresh bread to maintain the meringue's proper chewiness. Or freeze it.

Assemble the rings into a handsome pyramid, using a little caramelized sugar to stick the layers together. Decorate exuberantly with holly, crackers, miniature Santas and reindeer, candles, icing-sugar snow – whatever pleases you.

Eat the wreath cake by lifting the top rings off and tackling the bottom rings first, so that the pyramid remains intact.

It's delicious served with whipped cream flavoured with rum and grated orange rind.

TREACLE BISCUITS
Sirupsnipper (Sweden)

Make these to hang on the Christmas tree – you can even bake loops of strong thread into the shapes. They can be stored and decorated later with icing-sugar piping – a lovely job for children on Christmas Eve.

Quantity: Makes about 3 dozen biscuits.
Time: Start the day before. About 40 minutes.
Equipment: A small saucepan and a mixing bowl. A rolling pin and board. Biscuit-cutters. Baking trays and a cooling rack. String and icing-piper *(optional)*.

6 tablespoons dark treacle	4oz/125g butter
1 large egg	8oz/250g sugar
13oz/400g flour	¼ teaspoon finely ground pepper
½ teaspoon powdered cloves	1 teaspoon powdered ginger
1 teaspoon powdered cinnamon	2 teaspoons baking powder
grated rind and juice of 1 lemon	icing sugar for dusting
blanched almonds for decoration *(optional)*	

Heat the treacle until it is runny, then beat in the butter. Beat the egg lightly with the sugar. Mix all the ingredients together except the last three, then work in enough lemon juice to form a soft dough. Put the dough to rest, covered, in the refrigerator – overnight if possible. Some of these mixtures are left to mature for a week or two before they are rolled out.

Next day, knead the dough lightly, and roll it out thinly, dusting the board and the rolling pin generously with icing sugar.

Heat the oven to 350°F/180°C/Gas 4.

Using biscuit-cutters or your skill with a knife, cut out pretty Christmas shapes – stars, trees, hearts, gingerbread men. Finish, where appropriate, with a blanched almond and a loop of button thread. Transfer the biscuits to the well-buttered baking trays. Bake for 5–6 minutes, until crisp and brown. Slip the biscuits on to the rack to cool. Store in an airtight tin.

The same dough can be baked as flat sheets to make into a gingerbread house – two straight-sided and two topped with a triangle for the walls, and a pair for the roof, with the leftovers to shape into a chimney. Stick it together with melted sugar caramel. Draw on the windows, door and roof tiles with finely-piped icing, and finish with Scandinavian-style curls and hearts.

BUTTER RINGS
Smörkranser (Sweden)

Deliciously rich and very simple to make, these are lovely to dip into as a special Christmas treat, for elevenses or tea-time (Scandinavians much prefer coffee-time).

Quantity: Makes about 3 dozen.
Time: 25–30 minutes.
Equipment: A mixing bowl. A rolling pin and board. Baking trays and a cooling rack.

10oz/300g butter	6oz/175g sugar
14oz/425g flour	2 tablespoons brandy (or vodka)

Cream the butter with the sugar. Work in the flour and enough liquor to give a smooth soft dough. Let it rest covered in the fridge for an hour or two. Turn it out on to the well-floured pastry board and roll out to the thickness of a pound coin. Cut into thin strips about 4in/10cm long. Twist two strips together and join them into a ring with a dampened finger.

Heat the oven to 350°F/180°C/Gas 4.

Arrange the rings on the well-buttered baking trays, and bake for about 15 minutes until golden. Transfer to the rack to cool. Store in an airtight tin.

CHRISTMAS POOR MEN
Fattigmann (Sweden)

There are many versions of these rich fried biscuits found throughout Scandinavia; made with the best in the larder, their shape is as important as the mixture. Each family has its own tried and true version, and its favourite spicing. Frying predates oven-baking, so this is a venerable tradition.

Quantity: Makes about 3 dozen.
Time: Start an hour ahead.
Equipment: A mixing bowl. A rolling pin and board. A pastry wheel, baking trays and a cooling rack *(optional).*

6oz/150g flour
3 egg yolks
½ teaspoon ground cardamom
grated rind of ½ a lemon

2oz/50g butter
2oz/50g caster sugar
1 tablespoon brandy or vodka
deep fat (traditional) or oil (healthy modern) for
    frying

Work all the ingredients (except the frying oil) together until you have a soft firm dough. You may need more or less brandy. Leave to cool in the refrigerator.

Roll out the dough as thin as a pound coin. Using a crinkle-edged pastry wheel or a sharp knife, cut out ribbons ¾in/1.5cm wide and 3in/7.5cm long, either rectangular, or cut on a gentle diagonal. Cut a slit in the centre parallel to the long side, and pull one end through the gash, to give a characteristic slick twist in the middle.

Fry the biscuits in deep fat and drain on absorbent paper. Store, if necessary, in an airtight tin. They keep wonderfully well. The mixture can be baked on trays in a medium oven 375°F/190°C/Gas 5 for 10–15 minutes, until crisp and golden, and cooled on a rack.

CHRISTMAS IN GERMANY

In Germany, Christmas Eve – *Weihnachten* – is the night for magic, as well as for present-giving and for eating the traditional fasting meal of baked carp. On Christmas Eve, mountains burst open to reveal hidden treasure, long-drowned church towers toll their ghostly bells, trees burst into blossom and fruit, and the pure in heart can understand the language of animals.

This witching hour stretches into the twelve days between Christmas and Epiphany. On Christmas Eve and New Year's Eve, German country-dwellers used to fire shots over the fields and meadows, into shrubs and trees – a tradition echoed in the orchards of England, when it was considered appropriate to bang drums and fire guns into the apple-tree branches. Thirty years ago Richard Thonger reported a sleepless Twelfth Night at Brunerne on the Lake of Lucerne, when gangs of boys carried flaming torches into the countryside, blowing horns, ringing bells and cracking whips to scare away the two female spirits of the wood, Studeli and Stratteli, who might otherwise blight the fruit crop.

Gyula Illys reported similar habits in pre-war Hungary: 'On Christmas Eve the whiplashers ushered in the feast with a positive barrage of crackling fire, and from noon onwards the *puszta* re-echoed to the noise like a battlefield.' In Silesia, tradition dictates the burning of pine-logs all night long between Christmas and the New Year so that the pungent smoke will drive away evil spirits.

A tree decorated with paper roses, little biscuits and apples was reported from Strasbourg in 1604 – the first recorded reference to a modern Christmas tree. A few years later the custom was still unusual enough for Liselotte von der Pfalz, writing home to her daughter from northern France, to describe little box-trees decorated with lit candles. Prussian officers took the custom back to Germany as far as Danzig, and Ludwig I's wife Thérèse brought them to Bavaria. Queen Victoria and Prince Albert introduced the tree to Britain – including the habit of stacking presents round its base, although they did not also import the German custom of giving out the presents on Christmas Eve rather than Christmas Day.

Christmas present-giving dates from the Protestant 1500s, when the Infant Jesus would send a *Christbürde*, Christ's burden, to good children – a sackful of presents, to be laid out on the table for the *Bescherung*, the giving. Traditionally the bag contains five presents – something delicious to eat, something to spend, something to play with, something to learn with (maybe a pencil case or a pen) and something new to wear.

Hans Karl Adam, in *German Cookery* (Wine and Food Society, 1967), remembers his own pre-war Silesian childhood:

> Christmas was the great moment of the year at table. This is the season for baking *Pfefferkuchen*, honey-spiced cakes; and *Stollen*, rich fruit breads of which the most famous are those of Dresden. On Christmas Eve, everyone who could possibly contrive it ate carp and followed it with poppy-seed dumplings. On the first Holy Day they would eat a noodle soup, followed by a roast goose, crisp on the outside and garnished with red cabbage and *Klösse*; on the second Holy Day, roast hare larded with bacon fat and served with cream sauce and *Sauerkraute*. On New Year's Eve, too, there would be carp, but cooked au bleu because of the scales which (if you kept them) meant money for a whole year. And on New Year's Day there used to be another goose. On January 2nd, whatever might be left over was warmed up for the last time, and then everyday life resumed its usual rhythm.
>
> Nobody grumbled. What was there to grumble about?

CHRISTMAS EVE

SPICED CARP
Polnische Karpfen (Germany)

This fasting meal is most common in the eastern parts of Germany and all over Austria. The large-scaled, succulent mirror carp, originally bred in monastery moats as a live larder for fasting monks, is the fish most widely available in eastern Europe – huge specimens are stored live in big tanks in the inland markets of eastern Germany, Austria, Hungary and throughout the Balkans. This is how Hans Karl Adam remembers his Christmas Eve carp.

Quantity: Serves 6.
Time: 1 hour intermittent attention.
Equipment: A large fish-kettle.

2½lb/1.25kg whole mirror carp, cleaned and scaled (save a few scales for your purse, and you will be rich all year)

The cooking liquor

2 pints/1.2 litres water

1 leek, washed and roughly chopped

½ head celeriac (or celery)

2 lemon slices

1 teaspoon salt

2 carrots, scrubbed and chopped

2 onions

1 small bunch parsley

1 onion stuck with 2 cloves and a bay leaf

The sauce

2 pints/1.2 litres brown ale

2oz/50g peeled blanched almonds

5oz/150g spiced cake (see *Pfefferkuchen*, p. 41)

2oz/50g raisins, soaked in a little of the ale

To finish

1–2 tablespoons chopped parsley

1 tablespoon toasted flaked almonds

lemon slices

Wipe the carp.

Put all the ingredients for the cooking liquor into the fish-kettle and bring to the boil. Cover, turn down the heat, and simmer gently for 10 minutes.

Slip in the fish, and pour in the beer. Bring to the boil and allow it one big belch. Cover, turn down the heat, and simmer for another 10 minutes, until the fin can easily be pulled out.

Transfer the fish to a large warm dish and keep it warm while you finish the sauce.

Strain the cooking liquor and return it to the pan. Boil it rapidly until you have 2 pints/1.2 litres of liquid. Stir in the crumbled cake, roughly chopped almonds and soaked raisins. Reboil, and simmer for a few minutes to thicken.

Spoon the sauce over and round the fish. Finish with chopped parsley, an extra scattering of toasted flaked almonds and a few slices of lemon.

Serve the spiced carp with plain boiled potatoes and good German beer.

The finishing beer-sauce can be used to reheat some slices of boiling sausage or frankfurters – a lovely medieval mixture for one of the non-feasting of the twelve days.

SILESIAN POPPY-SEED STOLLEN
Schlesischer Mohnstollen (Germany)

These sweet breads are sometimes boiled as dumplings. Over the border in Austria, and further across in Hungary, where the Ottoman Turks influenced the kitchen, the same stuffing is wrapped in Turkish filo pastry and becomes a strudel. I have eaten it in Yugoslavia wrapped as here in bread dough but spread merely with poppy seeds and a little egg and butter. This is a sophisticated version based on a deliciously rich custard, and it is given by Silesian-born Hans Karl Adam in his *German Cookery*.

Quantity: Serves 6.

Time: About 2½ hours intermittent attention.

Equipment: A sieve and mixing bowl. A rolling pin and board. 2 shallow baking tins and a cooling rack.

The dough

1lb/500g plain flour
8 fl oz/200ml finger-warm milk
3oz/75g sugar

½ teaspoon salt
1oz/25g yeast
5oz/150g butter

The poppy-seed filling

5oz/150g poppy seeds
¼ pint/150ml milk
3oz/75g softened butter
6 tablespoons mixed candied peel
3 tablespoons chopped almonds

4 egg yolks
4oz/100g sugar
3 tablespoons sultanas, soaked in 4 dessertspoons
   brandy

The icing

10oz/300g sieved icing sugar
4 tablespoons brandy

4 tablespoons hot milk

To finish

poppy seeds

Sieve three-quarters of the flour with the salt into the warmed bowl.

Pour a little warm milk over the yeast in a cup, sprinkle in a teaspoon of sugar, and leave for a moment or two to liquidize. Make a hollow in the flour and pour in the yeast mix. Sprinkle with some of the flour and leave for 10–15 minutes to start the sponge working. Pour in the rest of the milk and work in the flour, drawing it in gradually from the sides, until you have a soft smooth dough. When it no longer sticks to your hands or the bowl, cover it with clingfilm and put it in a warm place to rise until doubled in bulk – about 1 hour in a warm turned-off oven with a tray of boiling water in the base.

Mix all the filling ingredients together and heat them gently, stirring all the time, until you have a thick rich custard. Do not let it boil or the eggs will curdle. Leave the custard to cool while you finish the bread dough.

Sieve the remaining flour on to the pastry board. Knead the dough for a moment or two to distribute the oxygen bubbles. Melt the butter and work it and the remaining sugar into the dough, drawing in the extra flour to absorb the extra liquid.

Divide the dough in half. Pat it or roll it into rounds as big as a dinner plate. Put it back to rise for 20 minutes or so. Spread the filling on half of each round, and roll it up into a loose bolster.

Bake at 400°F/200°C/Gas 6 for 45–50 minutes, until nicely risen and firm to the finger. Transfer to the rack to cool.

Mix the icing ingredients together, and ice the bread-cakes when they are cool. Finish with a sprinkling of poppy seeds.

NOODLE SOUP
Spätzlesuppe (Germany)

This soup is served before the roast goose on Christmas Day. The base is a clear strong broth – made with a boiling fowl or a piece of shin beef which, having given all its richness to the soup, could then be passed on, in a peasant farming household, to the over-wintering mother pig – her yearlings having long gone for wurst and bacon.

Quantity: Serves 8.
Time: Start 3–4 hours ahead. About 20 minutes full attention.
Equipment: A large, lidded saucepan. A mixing bowl. A grater.

The broth
6 pints/3.5 litres water
1 boiling fowl or a hunk of shin beef
top of a celery head
1 leek, washed and roughly chunked
salt and black peppercorns

2lb/1kg beef bones, browned in a hot oven
2–3 large carrots, scrubbed
2 large onions, peeled and quartered
2 cloves

The noodles (8oz/250g dried noodles can substitute)
1lb/500g white flour
4 whole eggs

1 teaspoon salt
4 tablespoons water

To finish
2 heaped tablespoons chopped parsley

Simmer all the broth ingredients together in the loosely-lidded saucepan for 3–4 hours, until you have 4 pints/2.5 litres of good strong liquid. Skim off the grease, strain, and bring back to the boil just before you are ready to serve.

Meanwhile make the noodle dough. Sieve the flour and salt into a mixing bowl. Make a hollow in the middle and break in the eggs. Work the eggs into the flour, drawing it in gradually from the sides, and adding as much water as you need to make a firm dough.

When the broth has reboiled, flour the grater and grate the noodle dough straight into the boiling broth. This is the easy way. The Swabians, noodle experts of Germany, do highly technical things with boards and knives and scrapers.

Reboil the broth, stir in the parsley, and serve the soup piping hot. Lovely on a snowy Christmas Day.

ROAST GOOSE WITH APPLES, RED CABBAGE AND POTATO DUMPLINGS
Gänsebraten mit Äpfeln, Rotkohl and Kartoffelklösse (Germany)

This is the traditional Christmas Day meal in Germany. The goose remains an obdurately seasonal bird – modern hormones and husbandry have not altered its determination to breed within its natural cycle.

This brings the current year's goose to the table no earlier than Michaelmas, and at its succulent maturity for the winter solstice.

Quantity: A young plump bird will weigh 9–12lb/3–4kg and serve about 8–10 people. The bones weigh heavy but the meat is rich.

Time: Allow 4 hours intermittent attention.

Equipment: A large roasting pan. 2 saucepans (one with a lid). A grater, mixing bowl and draining spoon.

The bird

1 goose, neck and head left on, all giblets
   supplied
2 cloves
salt and pepper

4 cooking apples
4 medium onions
1 stem of wormwood or a spring of sage

The red cabbage

1 small red cabbage
   (1½–2lb/750g–1kg in weight)
8 fl oz/200ml wine vinegar
pepper
2–3 cloves
1 large cooking apple, peeled, cored and sliced
3–4 tablespoons redcurrant jelly
   (or strawberry or blackcurrant jam)

1½ pints/900ml stock (poaching liquor from
   the goose-neck would be appropriate)
½ teaspoon salt
3 tablespoons brown sugar
1 large onion, skinned and chopped
1 tablespoon goose dripping

The potato dumplings

2lb/1kg potatoes, boiled in their skins
   and peeled – they should be firm
1 teaspoon grated nutmeg
black pepper

3 eggs, forked together
1 tablespoon cornflour
1 teaspoon salt

Trim off the neck as required for the stuffed goose-neck recipe on p.37. Wipe and trim off excess fat from the interior cavity. Tie two pieces of the fat over the bird's breast.

Heat the oven to 350°F/180°C/Gas 4.

Peel, quarter and core the apples. Peel and chop the onion. Stuff the goose with the apple, onion and cloves, with the wormwood or sage in the neck end. Sew up the cavity. Sprinkle with salt and pepper, and put the bird breast-down on a rack in the oven, over a dripping tray. Pour a mug of boiling water over the bird and into the tray.

After 30 minutes, turn the bird breast up. Prick the skin (not through to the flesh), particularly round the throat and the base of the wings, to let the fat run. The goose will need 3½–4 hours roasting in all, depending on the size of the bird. Pour out the goose fat regularly every 30 minutes or so, basting the bird when you do so.

(Save the fat – it's lovely for sautéing. Goose fat is snowy white and very pure. The Romans held it in higher esteem than butter, and our great-grandmothers made face creams and embrocations with it.)

Meanwhile, shred the red cabbage and bring it to the boil with the stock, vinegar, salt, pepper, sugar and cloves. Brown the onion and the apple slices in a little goose fat before adding them to the cabbage. Lid the pan and turn the heat down to simmer for an hour or so, until the cabbage is tender – keep an eye on it and add extra water if it looks like drying out. If too much liquid, uncover and boil fiercely to evaporate. Taste and adjust the seasoning. Finally add the redcurrant jelly – it will keep warm for as long as you please.

Prepare the dumplings. Grate the potatoes into a bowl, and mix them to a firm dough with the eggs, cornflour and seasonings – adding extra cornflour if necessary. Make the dough into about 30 balls about the size of a pigeon's egg – it may be easier to roll the dough into a sausage about 2in/5cm in diameter, and then chop off short lengths. Leave till the goose is nearly cooked.

Sprinkle cold water (from the ends of your fingers) over the bird 10–15 minutes before the end of the cooking – this will crisp the skin. When you judge your goose cooked, thrust a skewer into the base of the thigh – if the juice runs pink it is not yet done, if it runs clear, it is ready.

Scoop out the apple-onion stuffing. Mash it well and stir it into the pan juices (skim off the excess fat first) to thicken them. Leave the goose to rest in the turned-off oven for 20 minutes for the meat to firm up.

While the goose is resting, finish the dumplings. Bring a large saucepan of salted water to the boil. Drop in the dumplings. Bring the water back to the boil, take it off the heat, and leave for 20 minutes, until the dumplings float to the surface. Remove each carefully with a draining spoon and transfer it to a warm dish with an upturned saucer inside it, so that the water can drain down and leave the dumplings dry. You could fry the potato balls in little patties in the goose dripping, if you prefer – these are called *Patzek*, and children love them.

Make sure each person gets a slice of breast and a slice of leg, and a good helping of apple gravy, red cabbage and potato dumplings.

STUFFED GOOSE-NECK
(Germany)

This dish used to be popular in Britain, where it was known as goose pudding. The stuffed neck can be roasted with the goose if you prefer – but it will be crisp and not so juicy.

Quantity: Serves 3–4 as a dish on its own (8–10 if it accompanies the goose).
Time: 15–20 minutes. 40 minutes cooking.
Equipment: A mixing bowl. A mincer or food processor. A large saucepan.

the goose's neck and liver	3 slices bread
1 small onion	8oz/250g pork belly
2–3 slices streaky bacon	2 eggs
1 tablespoon chopped parsley	1 teaspoon dried marjoram
2oz/50g blanched almonds	2oz/50g shelled pistachios (optional)
½ teaspoon salt	pepper

Cut the goose-neck as close to the head as possible, and the base close to the breast. Loosen the skin from the neck and peel it carefully off the bone. Turn the skin inside out and trim off the windpipe and other bits and bobs. Turn the skin the right way round again and sew up one end.

Soak the bread in a little water, then squeeze it dry.

Chop the onion and brown it in a little goose dripping. Strip the meat from the neckbone and mince it roughly with the pork, the goose liver and the bacon. Mix the bread, onion, eggs, herbs, nuts and seasonings.

Fill up the neck with the mixture. Sew up the open end.

Prick the stuffed neck all over (it should be like a fine plump sausage), and poach it in enough water to keep it submerged for 40 minutes – the poaching water can be used for the red cabbage. Leave it under a weight overnight. Slice it and eat it cold with pickles. Or sauté it in goose fat and serve it with the goose if you have extra mouths to feed.

SUNDAY AFTER CHRISTMAS

ROAST HARE WITH CREAM SAUCE AND SAUERKRAUT
Hasenrücken in Sahne mit Sauerkraut (Germany)

German forests and well-watered meadows were always rich in game – particularly in Silesia, where rivers and mountains provided good fodder and cover. Industry and population pressure have reduced the wild land – but roast hare remains the traditional meal for the Sunday after Christmas. The practice of eating feathered game before Christmas, fur afterwards, remains an old country custom.

Quantity: Serves 4.
Time: Start 4 hours ahead, or the day before. 2 hours intermittent attention.
Equipment: A mixing bowl. A small and a large heavy saucepan. A roasting tin. A sieve or food processor.

1 saddle of hare weighing about 2lb/1kg
  (if the hare is small, leave the back legs on)

4–5 rashers fat bacon or thin strips pork fat

The marinade

2 glasses red wine
1–2 sprigs thyme
1 bay leaf
5–6 crushed juniper berries
1 stick celery, rinsed and chopped
6–8 crushed peppercorns

2 cloves garlic, peeled and sliced
rind of 1 lemon, matchsticked (the juice goes in
  the gravy)
1 large carrot, scrubbed and sliced fine
2 medium onions, skinned and chopped

The sauerkraut

2lb/1kg sauerkraut (salted cabbage)
2 medium onions, peeled and sliced
3oz/75g dripping or good lard
3–4 cloves
1 glass white wine
1 tablespoon cornflour, slaked in a little water

1 bacon rasher, chopped
2 apples, peeled, cored and sliced
4–6 crushed juniper berries
1 bay leaf
sugar and salt

To finish the hare

2 tablespoons brandy

¼ pint/150ml double cream

juice of 1 lemon

salt and pepper

With a sharp knife, remove the outer membrane from the saddle (and the back legs if you have included them — tie them neatly to the body, chicken-fashion). The removal of this tough pale blue membrane is important, or the hare will never be tender.

Mix all the marinade ingredients together, pour them over the joint, and leave it for 4 hours or overnight.

If you are using raw sauerkraut, attend to it first, so that it is ready at the same time as the meat. (If the sauerkraut is ready-prepared, follow the instructions on the container, adding the extra onions, apples and flavourings.) Using a couple of forks, tear the sauerkraut into its shreds so that it doesn't end up lumpy. Taste it: if it's too sour, rinse it — but don't wash out all the piquant flavour.

Sauté the bacon, onions and apples briefly in the dripping or lard in the large heavy saucepan. Add the sauerkraut and the flavourings, including a little sugar and salt. Pour in the wine and enough hot water to submerge everything. Bring to the boil, cover the pan and leave to simmer gently until tender. It will take between 30 and 50 minutes — the older the cabbage, the longer it will take to cook. Do not let it become so soft that it loses its texture.

Tie the bacon or pork fat round the joint, and place it in the roasting tin. Roast the hare for 15 minutes in a hot oven, 450°F/230°C/Gas 8. Turn the meat after 10 minutes.

Meanwhile bring the marinade to the boil, then turn down the heat and simmer while the meat has its preliminary roasting.

Pour the marinade over the hare, turn the oven down to 400°F/200°C/Gas 6 and cook for another 20–25 minutes, basting regularly — the meat should still be pink in the middle. Total cooking time is 35–40 minutes. If you prefer the meat cooked right through, return it to the turned-off oven for 10 minutes.

Warm the brandy and pour it over the joint. Flame it with a match. Keep the meat warm while you finish the sauce and the sauerkraut.

Check the sauerkraut's seasoning, and add extra salt and sugar if necessary. Stir in the cornflour and boil it up to thicken the juices.

Strain the stewing juices from the meat into the small saucepan, pushing down hard to extract all the lovely flavours — for a thicker sauce, liquidize everything in the food processor. Reheat and stir in the lemon juice, then the cream. Taste and add salt and pepper.

Carve the hare, still wrapped in its bacon, in long slices down the fillets. Pour a little of the cream sauce over the hare fillets, and the rest separately.

Serve the hare on a beautiful big dish, flanked by a fragrant heap of sauerkraut and plain-boiled buttered noodles (see p. 55) or rice, and a good red wine.

CHRISTMAS BAKING AND DRINKING

CHRISTMAS FRUIT BREAD
Christstollen (Germany)

These traditional Christmas breads are a speciality of Dresden – from where they are exported around the world. *Stollen* are not at all difficult to make at home. Being a rich moist fruit bread (compare them to the English rich fruit cake), they improve with keeping – some families keep the last piece to be eaten at Easter.

Quantity: Makes 4 *Stollen*.
Time: About 3 hours intermittent attention.
Equipment: A mixing bowl. A small saucepan. A pastry board. A baking tray and a cooling rack.

2lb/1kg flour
3oz/75g fresh yeast or 1½oz/40g dried (rather more than usual – this is a heavy mixture to lift)
5oz/150g finely chopped mixed candied peel
4oz/100g blanched almonds

approx. ¾ pint/450ml warm milk
4oz/100g sugar
1lb/500g raisins
4oz/100g currants
grated rind of 2 lemons
6 tablespoons dark rum

To finish
1 knob of butter to glaze

vanilla-flavoured icing sugar for dusting

Sieve two-thirds of the flour into the warm bowl.

Pour a little warm milk over the fresh yeast in a cup, sprinkle in a teaspoon of sugar, and leave it for a moment or two to liquidize. (If using dried, follow the packet instructions.) Make a hollow in the flour and pour in the yeast mix. Sprinkle with some of the flour and leave for 10–15 minutes to start the sponge working. Pour in the rest of the milk and work in the flour, drawing it in gradually from the sides, until you have a soft smooth dough. When it no longer sticks to your hands or the bowl, cover it with clingfilm and put it in a warm place to rise until doubled in bulk – about 1 hour should be fine, as you have a high proportion of yeast to flour.

Meanwhile, put the dried fruit, peel, lemon rind and nuts to soak in the rum.

Sieve the remaining flour on to the pastry board. Knead the dough for a moment or two to distribute the oxygen bubbles. Work in the soaked fruit and nuts and the rest of the sugar, drawing in the extra flour to keep the dough firm but soft. Don't overwork it, or the dough will turn grey.

Divide the dough into 4 pieces. Quickly knead each piece into a ball and then flatten it into an oval. Make a dent in each oval with a rolling pin lengthways, more to one side than the other. Fold the wide side over the other. Repeat with the other pieces and transfer the *Stollen* to the buttered baking tray. Cover and leave in a warm place for 20 minutes to prove.

Bake in a hot oven, 450°F/230°C/Gas 8, for 40–45 minutes. If you want to make larger *Stollen*, divide the dough in half and bake at the same temperature for 60 minutes. The oven has to be good and hot, or the *Stollen* will be speckly because of all the butter.

Take the *Stollen* out of the oven when they are well risen and firm to the finger. Transfer to the rack to cool. Paint them while still warm with melted butter and dust very generously with icing sugar. You can, if you would like to make them look really sumptuous, ice them with a thin coat of plain white icing or a sugar glaze (1 tablespoon sugar melted in 1 tablespoon water), and finish with a sprinkle of candied peel and flaked almonds.

GINGER SPICE CAKE
Pfefferkuchen (Germany)

Spices are special for northerners starved of sunny flavours – a wide range of these 'pepper' cakes and biscuits are to be found as celebration food throughout northern Europe. In the Middle Ages, northern Europe's merchant sailors, usually bankrolled by the Hanseatic League, the all-powerful consortium of merchants based at Lübeck, ensured their countrymen's access to such eastern spices. All ginger cakes improve with the keeping. Remember that spices vary in their strength, so add more if you think the mixture needs it.

Quantity: Makes a 1½lb/750g cake.
Time: 20 minutes. 55 minutes baking time.
Equipment: A sieve and mixing bowl. A cake ring-mould.

4oz/125g butter	8oz/250g honey
3 eggs (size 2)	1 teaspoon powdered cinnamon
1 teaspoon powdered ginger	½ teaspoon powdered cloves
4oz/125g white flour	3oz/100g rye flour
1 teaspoon baking powder	¼ pint/150ml soured cream
butter and breadcrumbs for the cake ring	

Melt the butter and the honey together and leave to cool. Beat in the eggs and spices. Sieve the white flour and the baking powder into the rye flour, and fold it lightly into the honey-butter with a metal spoon, adding the soured cream alternately to keep the mixture soft and light.

Heat the oven to 325°F/170°C/Gas 3.

Generously butter a cake ring-mould and sprinkle it with breadcrumbs. Drop in the mixture, spreading it evenly round. Bake for 15 minutes, then drop the oven temperature to 250°F/130°C/Gas 1 to finish the cooking – about another 40 minutes. When the cake is well risen and firm to the finger, take it out, let it rest for a few minutes, and then unmould on to a rack.

Store in an airtight tin until needed. Delicious with Christmas mulled wine (see below).

Leftovers can be made into a *pfefferkuchen* sauce for Christmas carp or a sauce in which to reheat boiling sausages (see p. 32).

SILESIAN PUNCH
Schneeschipperpunsch (Germany)

This mulled wine cup, spiced with cinnamon and cloves, is sure to keep the witches at bay on a cold winter night. Lovely to serve to guests on Christmas Eve, particularly with a slice of rich Christmas *Stollen* (see p. 40) to dunk into it.

Quantity: Serves 8–10.
Time: 10–15 minutes.
Equipment: A saucepan or kettle, and a ladle.

6oz/175g sugar	½ pint/300ml water
twist of orange rind	twist of lemon rind
1–2 short sticks cinnamon	4 cloves
1 bottle white wine (a flowery German Moselle, perhaps)	1 bottle red wine
	3 wine glasses brandy

Put the sugar, water, orange and lemon rind and spices in a saucepan and heat, stirring until the sugar dissolves. Simmer for 5 minutes to develop the scents.

Tip in the white and red wine and the brandy. Heat gently until bubbles start to rise. Remove from the heat and serve with a ladle, avoiding all the bits and pieces.

AN ENGLISH CHRISTMAS

All families have their own Christmas tradition. My family's is a traditional English celebration, evolved as a working compromise between the habits of two families. My four children will no doubt make similar adjustments in their own households – and a new and individual celebration will be born. Living in rural isolation in a cork-oak forest in southern Spain, as we all did for many years when the children were growing up, we had to work particularly hard for our rituals.

Our Christmas timetable, as with all such traditions, adjusted to suit circumstance. In our neighbourhood in Spain there was no nativity play, something everyone had enjoyed at English primary school. Instead, neighbouring Spanish households had a *Belen*, a model Bethlehem scene which featured a cork-bark stable, the Holy Family and all the usual participants, but to which new figures of local interest – fisherwoman, boot-maker, egg-seller, baker, chickpea-roaster, gypsy dancer – were added every year. We acquired our own household crib, and added a live version – the nativity play. This became an annual one-day event – the limits of a small child's concentration – and it occupied most of the day before Christmas Eve. Neighbouring children were co-opted. Everyone was suspicious at first, in case our northern Protestant beliefs gave the lie to Roman Catholic orthodoxy. The morning was given over to choosing and dressing the parts. The performance took place, after lunch (chips and ice-cream) and a couple of chaotic rehearsals, at dusk. Everyone used the language in which they were most comfortable – an earnest of Pentecost to come. Herod was reckoned the plum part, with the Innkeeper playing second comic lead. In fact, the play evolved along just those lines which gave the Pope a headache back in the twelfth century.

On Christmas Eve we brought in evergreens, holly and mistletoe if we could get it, and decorated the Christmas tree. Tradition dictates that the prickly leaves and scarlet berries of the holly should not be brought indoors until they are needed to protect the household against the witching time. (Mistletoe, the druids' sacred white fire which burns between heaven and earth, was also revered by the Norsemen – in Sweden it is known as *donnerbesen*, thunder-broom, effective against Thor's thunder and lightning.) We followed midnight Mass on Christmas Eve with the ritual hanging-up of stockings outside each door.

On Christmas Day in my family the feast is in the evening, and the midday meal is light and more or less do-it-yourself, followed by the distribution of the presents round the Christmas tree. Although the

Christmas tree – but not the timing of the distribution of the presents – was popularized in Britain in Victorian times by the German Prince Albert, the roots of the tradition go far deeper, back to the most ancient symbol of all, the flowering maypole. A more recent prototype can be found in the mystery plays of the Middle Ages which grew out of the simple nativity plays. These Mysteries included a Garden of Eden play which was performed inside a ring of candles set round a fir-tree hung with apples. When the plays were banned, the tree stayed. The candles were moved on to the branches, and the tree was hung with wafers to represent the Body of Christ – replaced these days in northern Europe with gingerbread stars and figures (see p. 20). In Britain the tree elbowed out the traditional kissing bough – a half-circle of willow frame, like a Roman emperor's laurel wreath, woven with evergreens, decorated with candles above and red apples dangling below, each with a twig of mistletoe beneath. The candles were relit every evening from Christmas Eve till Twelfth Night.

Dinner was, and remains, the main celebration of my family's festival. This represents a win for my traditions – cook's prerogative – since the male side of the family always had their Christmas meal at lunch. Nothing came easy in the mid-sixties in rural Andalusia. There were no supermarkets with prepared and packaged goods. Nevertheless, most of the exotic ingredients dictated by the English Christmas pudding were available in this land of Moorish spicing – but in a form which would have been more familiar to the Crusaders who first imported them to Britain. Extraordinary festivals call for out-of-the-ordinary ingredients, and we northerners traditionally use hard-to-get southern spices in our celebration dishes. Southerners prefer such northern specialities as Atlantic-caught salt cod, *bacalao*, to mark the Christmas festival.

We made our pudding in early November to give it time to mature for Christmas – and the work of preparation was too time-consuming to be anything but a family business. There were raisins to be pipped, scalded almonds to be popped from their rough woody skins; the peel of oranges and lemons to pare off and candy. The pearly grains of raw suet had to be separated from their fine membranes with floury hands. The old gypsy spice-seller in the market-town of Algeciras weighed out the spices into little twists of brown sugar-paper with much curiosity about the *pudim inglés* for which they were destined. After the hard work, everyone felt they had taken an active enough part in the whole business for a wish to be granted when the pudding was finally ready to be stirred. As with many celebration foods, including the Irish Hallowe'en champ, the Scandinavian Christmas porridge and the French *galette des rois*, the pudding had to contain at least one lucky token. We put in the lot.

For the main course, after a brief flirtation with goose, we settled on a turkey fattened by the local baker. Turkeys were first imported into Spain from the New World by Spanish Jesuits in the wake of Columbus's discoveries, so it seemed a sensible compromise. The baker's flock of handsome bronze-feathered scarlet-wattled creatures were much closer to their American ancestors than the heavy-breasted monsters we now buy oven-ready. Semi-wild, muscularly efficient fliers when his wife forgot to clip their wings, the birds would greet us noisily and aggressively when we went to fetch the bread every day. The turkeys gleaned in the surrounding cork-oak forest with the village's herd of red-bristled sharp-snouted pigs – themselves destined to be stars of other Christmas tables. In spite of a late fattening on autumn's acorns, and the baker's excellent crusts, the birds were relatively small – no more than would feed a family of six. But their meat was firm and juicy, with a gamey flavour rather like fresh pheasant.

The rest – preparing the stuffings, the sauces and the vegetables – took up much of Christmas Day itself. Everyone helped, smallest to eldest, male or female, and the preparation of the meal remains an important part of our Christmas ritual.

Celebrations are credible only if they are the reverse of daily habit: excess is best appreciated after fast.

All over Britain, local habits reflect regional preoccupations. In Bodmin, the home of Cornish Methodist temperance, Christina Hole reported in 1975 that four gentlemen in full evening dress were accustomed to carry a wassail bowl 'full with apples and good spice' round to every door, collecting alms for the town's poor in return for a ladleful of the brew. In Scotland, the feast of Hogmanay which follows the traditionally strict observance of the Christmas festival itself is celebrated with an enthusiasm that the south, surfeited by its Christmas feasting, cannot even approach.

Southern Celtic Britain has its own traditions, many of them rooted in a rural way of life now vanished. In Devon and Somerset, the ashen faggot, a large bundle of green ash sticks cut from the double hedges grown for the purpose, was burned in the hearth instead of the Yule log. The Christmas faggot was made exceptionally thick in the middle and tightly bound with bands of ash or hazel. The young who were thinking of courting would choose a band, and if it was the first to break in the fire, then they would be the first to marry. Most feast-days have these opportunities for a little ritual courting built into the celebration – sometimes transmuted from more serious intent. The kiss under the mistletoe sprang from the pre-Christian ritual which dictated that enemies meeting under it were obliged to exchange the kiss of peace.

THE EVE OF CHRISTMAS EVE

TOM BAWCOCK'S EVE SEVEN-FISH PIE
(England)

On a visit some years ago to the fiercely independent Cornish port of Mousehole in Cornwall, I was told the story of this version of starry-gazey pie by the wife of a local fish-seller.

> I don't know how far back the story goes – hundreds of years, I expect. We never forget a good story in Mousehole. It was after a long time of storms and the boats had not been able to fish for weeks. The whole village was hungry, and it was already Tom Bawcock's Eve – the day before Christmas Eve. So the men put to sea in spite of the weather. They caught seven kinds of fish, and that was all the fish that went in the pie. The pilchard-heads would be left sticking out of the pastry so that the rich oil can drain back in and not be lost.

Such careful housekeeping is not so necessary in these easier times, but the pie remains delicious. Some households still make the clotted cream which sauces it.

Quantity: Serves 6.
Time: 40 minutes preparation.
Equipment: A mixing bowl. A rolling pin and board. A pie dish or tin.

The pastry

12oz/350g flour
3oz/75g cold lard
4–5 tablespoons cold water

1 teaspoon salt
3oz/75g cold butter

The filling

1lb/500g mixed fish fillets – choose from traditional pilchards (don't bother to skin them), mackerel, cod, bass, pollack, herring, eel, sole, skate, plaice, and include a few mussels, winkles, scallops or oysters

2 medium potatoes
salt and pepper
1 heaped tablespoon chopped parsley

To finish

¼ pint/150ml soured thick cream (or add 1 teaspoon lemon juice to fresh cream – there's nothing better for a simple sauce than thick yellow Cornish scalded cream left to stand and sour a little)

Make the pastry first. Sieve the flour and salt into the cold bowl. Chop in the lard and butter, first with a knife, then with the tips of your fingers. Leave the mixture quite rough – not fine breadcrumbs. Work in enough cold water to give a soft but not sticky dough. Leave it to rest, loosely covered, in a cool place for 30 minutes, while you prepare the filling.

Pick over the fish and chop it roughly. Peel the potatoes and sliver into rough matchsticks.

Divide the dough in half. Roll out both pieces on a lightly floured board, and use one round to line a shallow pie dish or baking tin.

Lay half the potato on the pie-base. Season with salt and pepper, and sprinkle with parsley. Lay in all the fish, with more seasoning and parsley. Finish with the rest of the potatoes. Damp the edges of the pastry and put on the lid. Trim and press the edges together in a pretty pattern with a fork. Cut a little hole in the top for the steam to escape, and decorate with the trimmings cut into fish-head shapes. Glaze with a brushful of cream.

Bake in a hot oven, 450°F/230°C/Gas 8, for the first 20 minutes. Then turn down the heat to 400°F/200°C/Gas 6, and continue to cook for 45–60 minutes.

Serve the pie hot, cut into wedges, with the cream handed separately for each person to lift the crust and add a dollop. Accompany with a glass of ginger wine and drink old Tom Bawcock's health.

CHRISTMAS EVE

MINCE PIES
(England)

These spiced pies come from an older tradition than plum pudding. Recipes for mince pies were already recorded by the end of the sixteenth century, although the ingredients were much more varied and less sweet than now, including chicken, lamb or mutton tongues, eggs, spices and dried fruit, all chopped finely, spiked with vinegar, and baked in little pastry coffins. Originally the pies were not particularly Christmas fare, but they became so when the Crusaders brought back spices from the east.

Before the Reformation, the mince pie was oblong to represent a manger, with a little figure of the baby Jesus on top. The baby was removed and saved when the pie was eaten. The Puritans under Cromwell put a stop to all such Papist nonsense. But by the end of the seventeenth century the mince pie had bounced back. It still contained meat, but now it was round, had shed its Holy Infant, and had added orange and lemon peel, eggs, raisins and sugar. Today there's a reminder of meat still in the suet –

although even that is now slipping away.

Quantity: These quantities make 3lb/1.5kg mincemeat. The recipe is for 18 mince pies, although this is enough mincemeat for 3–4 dozen.
Time: Make the filling at least the day before – best a few months ahead. 40–45 minutes preparation and baking.
Equipment: A mixing bowl. A saucepan or jam jars. A sieve, rolling pin and board. Patty tins and a cooling rack.

The mincemeat

8oz/250g prunes, stoned and chopped	8oz/250g apricots, stoned and chopped
8oz/250g raisins, picked over and pipped	8oz/250g currants, picked over
8oz/250g dark brown sugar	1 pint/600ml cold tea
2 cooking apples, peeled, cored and finely chopped	juice and grated rind of 1 lemon
	8oz/250g shredded suet
4oz/100g blanched chopped almonds	½ teaspoon powdered cloves
½ teaspoon grated nutmeg	1 teaspoon powdered cinnamon
1 large glass brandy	

The rough puff pastry

12oz/400g cold flour	½ teaspoon salt
9oz/300g cold butter	¼ pint/150ml cold milk
caster sugar for dredging	

Put the dried fruit and sugar to soak overnight in the tea. The next day, if you are going to use the mince-meat straight away, bring the soaked fruit to the boil in the saucepan and simmer for 10 minutes (add extra tea if the fruit is dry).

Mix in the remaining ingredients. Pot the mincemeat up in sterilized jars and store in a cool larder if you have the time, to mature it.

Make the pastry. Sieve the flour with the salt, and roughly rub in one third of the butter with the tips of your fingers. Mix into a smooth dough with the milk.

Roll the dough out on the lightly floured board into a long narrow strip. Divide the remaining butter into 3 equal portions. Chop one portion into small pieces, dot these over the pastry, and dredge lightly with flour. Fold evenly in three, turning the pastry round so that the folded edges lie right and left when rolling. Press the edges lightly with the rolling pin to prevent air escaping, and roll out as before. Repeat the process with the other portions of butter. Leave it to rest for 10 minutes in a cool place.

Pre-heat the oven to 425°F/220°C/Gas 7.

Roll the pastry out to about ¼in/0.5cm thickness, and cut covers for the pies. Roll the pieces out thinner, cut out rounds, and line patty-tins with the pastry. Put a teaspoon of mincemeat in each, damp the edges of the pastry, lid the pies and glaze them with a brushful of milk. Dredge with caster sugar. Bake in the hot oven for 20–25 minutes, until the pastry is crisp and golden. Transfer to the cooling rack. Serve the pies hot, with brandy butter (see p. 51) to melt into the filling.

Eat one mince pie on each of the twelve days of Christmas to make sure of twelve months of happiness in the coming year.

LAMB'S WOOL WASSAIL
(England)

The wassail – the word comes from the Saxon *was haile*, meaning 'Your health' – is traditionally served from an applewood bowl on Christmas Eve. Jesus College, Oxford, has a 10-gallon wassail bowl with a ½-pint ladle – enough to get the whole High Table merry as crickets.

Quantity: Serves 4.
Time: 20 minutes.
Equipment: A large saucepan or kettle. A ladle. A baking tray or toasting fork. A bowl and whisk.

2 pints/1.2 litres mild ale
4 small hard apples (or 8 crab apples)
¼ pint/150ml cream
4 tablespoons sugar

1 cinnamon stick, 1 small piece ginger, 6 cloves
  (tied in a scrap of cloth)
2 egg yolks
grated nutmeg

Put the ale to infuse with the spices at the side of the fire, or on a very low heat on the cooker.

Meanwhile, prick the apples and put them to roast – either in a hot oven on a baking tray at 450°F/230°C/Gas 8 for 20 minutes until they soften, or on a toasting fork in front of an open fire.

Lightly beat the cream with the egg yolks and sugar until everything is well blended.

Turn up the heat under the ale. Remove from the heat when it is almost boiling. Take out the bag of spices and whisk in the cream and egg. Float the apples on the surface, finish with a dusting of nutmeg, and serve hot – don't reboil it, or the egg will curdle.

Accompany with a batch of freshly made spicy biscuits (see the Scandinavian St Lucia recipes, p. 47). They should keep forever – everyone knows that anything baked on Christmas Eve will never go mouldy.

CHRISTMAS DAY

ROAST TURKEY WITH ALL THE TRIMMINGS
(England)

The turkey was first documented in an English larder – that of Archbishop Cranmer, reviser of the book of Common Prayer and himself destined to be roasted at the stake – in 1541. Chief among its predecessors on the festive table of the great houses of England (and as far back as the Saxon halls) was the pagan garlanded and gilded boar's head. The supporting cast included venison, swan, bustard, peacocks rewrapped after roasting in their spread-tailed finery, pork, beef, goose and, particularly in Yorkshire, a huge pie stuffed with a great variety of game and tame birds.

Sixty years ago, north-countrywoman Dorothy Hartley confessed she had no enthusiasm for the turkey, even though the best were reared in Norfolk. 'Northern farmers have chicken for Easter, duck and green peas for Whitsun, and a fine meaty goose for Christmas.' The housewives of Germany and eastern Europe still choose a goose for the festive bird (see p. 35), but the turkey has reigned over the English Christmas table since the seventeenth century.

Quantity: A 10–12lb/5–6kg turkey serves 8–10.

Time: 4 hours.

Equipment: 2 skewers. A small frying pan. A large and a smaller roasting tin. 2–3 large saucepans and a colander. A small ovenproof dish, a steamer (*optional*). 2 small saucepans. A liquidizer.

The bird

1 turkey with giblets

salt and pepper

3–4 thin slices cold butter

8 rashers fat streaky bacon or pork fat

Lemon and almond stuffing

1lb/500g bread, crumbled and soaked

1 egg, lightly mixed

4oz/100g flaked almonds

1 tablespoon thyme

salt and pepper

1 onion, peeled, chopped and softened
   in a little butter

grated rind of 1 lemon

1 heaped tablespoon chopped parsley

Pork and chestnut stuffing

1lb/500g minced pork or sausagemeat

1 teaspoon crumbled sage

salt and freshly milled pepper

1 small glass white wine

8oz/250g dried chestnuts, soaked overnight, or
   1lb/500g fresh chestnuts, roasted in a hot oven
   for 10 minutes and skinned

The vegetables

2 medium swedes, peeled and chopped

butter and milk to finish

salt and pepper

extra dripping or lard

8oz/250g cranberries

2lb/1kg sprouts

2 carrots, peeled and chopped

1 egg

4lb/2kg old potatoes, peeled, quartered and
   parboiled

1 tablespoon sugar

nutmeg

The bread sauce

12oz/350g white day-old loaf, chunked

1 pint/600ml milk

½ teaspoon powdered cloves

½ onion, sliced

1 tablespoon butter

salt and freshly milled black pepper

The gravy

1 tablespoon flour

1 pint/600ml stock, made with the turkey giblets

1 glass white wine

salt and pepper

Optional extras

redcurrant jelly

bacon rolls and little chipolatas roasted for the last
   30 minutes with the turkey

Wipe the bird inside and out. Lift the skin of the breast and slide thin slices of cold butter in between the flesh and the skin. Season the bird inside and out with salt and pepper. Trim the rind off the bacon.

Mix all the ingredients for the lemon and almond stuffing and use the mixture to stuff the neck end of the bird.

Mix all the ingredients for the pork and chestnut stuffing and put it in the cavity of the bird.

Skewer up both openings. Tie the bacon over the breast and legs of the turkey.

Start the bird breast down in a hot oven, 425°F/220°C/Gas 7, for 20 minutes. Then turn the oven down to 375°F/190°C/Gas 5. Roast it for 3½–4 hours, allowing a total of 20 minutes to the lb, weighed before stuffing. Turn the bird breast up after 2 hours.

About 1 hour before the turkey is scheduled to be taken from the oven, pour off any dripping into a second roasting pan. Add extra dripping or lard, heat it in the oven, and turn the parboiled potatoes in the hot fat. Put them to roast for 40–60 minutes.

Meanwhile, peel and chunk the swedes and the carrots. Put them to boil in plenty of salted water until soft – 25–30 minutes. Mash them thoroughly and beat in 3–4 tablespoons milk, a large knob of butter, the egg and the seasoning. Transfer the mixture to a buttered ovenproof dish and put it to bake in the oven for 20 minutes or so to brown the top – it rises a bit, like a soufflé, but is very good-natured and won't mind being kept warm.

Baste the bird and the potatoes regularly – watch the oven temperature, as it drops swiftly when the oven is full.

Meanwhile make the bread sauce. Put all the ingredients in the liquidizer and process thoroughly. Bring the mixture gently to the boil in a small pan, then turn down the heat and simmer until thick. Beat in an extra knob of butter. Taste and adjust the seasoning.

Put the cranberries to simmer until soft with the sugar in a splash of water.

Remove the bacon from the turkey breast for the last 20–30 minutes of the cooking. Check if the bird is done by pushing a skewer through the second joint of the leg and the thick white-meat cushion above the wing. When the juices no longer run pink, the turkey is ready.

Transfer the bird to a warm serving dish and let it rest, covered, for 20 minutes to firm the meat for carving, while you finish the trimmings.

Steam the brussels sprouts or boil them in plenty of salted water. Drain them and toss them in butter. Season with salt and pepper and a sprinkle of nutmeg.

To make the gravy, scatter the flour into the roasting tin and let it fry for a moment over the heat. Pour in the stock and wine and bubble it all up, scraping in all the dark delicious bits stuck to the pan. Add the drainings from the serving dish. Taste, and add salt and pepper and a little gravy browning (burnt sugar and water) if you like dark gravy.

Serve everything on hot plates, with the sauces, vegetables and gravy handed separately. A successful Christmas dinner is a triumph of careful timing, so settle down and enjoy it – the Lord of Misrule dictates that there's no need to clear away till tomorrow.

CHRISTMAS PUDDING
(England)

The ancestor of our modern pudding was plum porridge, a substantial soup of meat broth, wine and fruit juices, raisins and spices, thickened with breadcrumbs. This was served as the first course of Christmas dinner, and was eaten with a spoon (see the German carp recipe on p. 32, which produces a similar blend of sweet-salt flavours). By the mid seventeenth century the soup had solidified into the familiar rich dark steamed pudding.

Here's my own family recipe.

Quantity: Makes two 6lb/3kg puddings.
Time: Start the day before. 25–30 minutes to prepare. 7 hours boiling + 2 for reheating.
Equipment: A large mixing bowl. 2 large pudding basins. A large saucepan. Tokens: a ring for a wedding, a thimble for the old maid, a button for the bachelor, a miniature horse-shoe for good luck, money for fortune.

1½lb/750g finely shredded suet
1lb/500g raisins
1lb/500g mixed candied peel
1lb/500g stoned, finely chopped dried apricots
12oz/350g blanched almonds, roughly chopped
½ teaspoon powdered cloves
1 teaspoon powdered cinnamon
1 large wineglass brandy
juice and grated rind of 1 lemon and 1 orange

2lb/1kg brown breadcrumbs
1lb/500g currants
1lb/500g stoned, finely chopped prunes
1lb/500g dried figs, finely chopped
1lb/500g dark brown sugar
1 teaspoon powdered nutmeg
2 pints/1.2 litres dark beer
8 eggs (size 2)

Mix all the dry ingredients in the large bowl. Add the beer, the brandy, and the eggs beaten to a froth with the lemon and orange juice. Mix thoroughly with a wooden spoon. You may need more beer if the mixture is not wet enough to drop from the spoon easily.

Call the household in to stir the pudding and make a wish.

Leave the mixture in its bowl to stand for at least 12 hours in a cool place. Butter the pudding basins and divide the mixture between them, pressing the pudding well down. Cover with buttered greaseproof paper, pleated in the middle to allow for expansion. Tie a clean cloth over all, stringing round and knotting on top to make a handle. (Baking foil will do, but it is not so easy to lift in and out of the boiling water.)

Set the pudding, the bottom resting on a heatproof dish or metal ring, in a large pan of boiling water to reach half-way up the side of the bowl. Bring back to the boil, turn down to a fast simmer, lid the pan and leave it to cook steadily for 7 hours – topping up regularly with boiling water. This can be done in a moderate oven, 350°F/180°C/Gas 4 – a rather less nerve-racking process, as the bowl is not apt to clatter around like a demented morris dancer if the water gets too hot.

When the pudding is ready, firm to the finger and well shrunk from the sides, lift the bowl carefully out of the water and let the pudding cool. Remove the old coverings, cover with clean paper and cloths, and store in a cool larder.

You can of course eat the pudding straight away, when it will be lighter and paler. The longer you store it the darker, richer (and heavier) it becomes.

To reheat the pudding on Christmas Day, reboil it for 2 hours, tip it out of the basin on to a warm plate and carefully bury the tokens as best you can in the sides. (If you bury them when you make the pudding, they can come up with some peculiar chemical reactions after a month or two.)

Top the pudding with a sprig of holly, pour a small glass of warm brandy over it all, set it aflame, and bring it to table.

Hand separately a jug of pouring cream, a lightly egg-thickened custard laced with brandy, or brandy butter (see below).

Now for the leftovers – or the second pudding. It is delicious sliced and fried in butter, but there are other good ways of serving it.

Lancashire makes a kind of Eccles cake with the crumbs. Pack as much as you have into a pastry case. Lay a pastry lid over the top, turn it over, and roll it lightly. Then cut slashes in the top, gild with egg and milk and sprinkle with sugar. Bake at 375°F/190°C/Gas 5 for 30–40 minutes until the pastry is crisp and golden. Serve it hot for tea.

The dairy farmers of Devon like their leftover pudding cooked in a rich custard. Cut the leftovers into wedges and put them in a pie-dish, criss-cross fashion like open brickwork. Make an egg custard mixture – ½ pint/300ml cream whisked with 3 eggs – and pour it over, so that it fills all the gaps. Bake in a slow oven, 300°F/150°C/Gas 2, for 40 minutes.

BRANDY BUTTER
(England)

The Americans call this fridge-firmed sweet butter 'hard sauce' and can take responsibility for its popularity as a replacement in England for the more traditional custard. As a paid-up member of the school-prunes-and-custard generation, I much prefer brandy butter with my pudding.

Quantity: Serves 6 – people eat masses of it.
Time: 15 minutes.
Equipment: A bowl and a wooden spoon, or an electric mixer.

12oz/350g unsalted butter	8oz/250g caster or icing sugar
juice and grated zest of 1 orange	wine glass of brandy (or rum or whisky)

Soften the butter to a cream, then beat in the sugar with the orange juice and grated zest. Keep beating it until it is really pale, light and fluffy, as for a cake – easiest with an electric mixer.

Beat in as much brandy as the mixture will take without curdling. Pile it into a bowl and refrigerate until it is solid.

CHRISTMAS ORANGE JELLY
(England)

In Yorkshire, where many of our best native dishes originate, an orange jelly was the traditional Christmas treat back as far as Tudor times. The fresh fruit flavour is delicious after roast turkey, as an alternative to the heavy pudding. In this recipe, contributed to Florence White's English Folk Cookery Association in the 1920s, with a note that Christmas wouldn't be Christmas without an orange jelly, the juice is not heated so the flavour is really fresh.

Quantity: Serves 6.
Time: Start the day before.
Equipment: A grater. A small and large bowl.

8 juicy oranges	2 lemons
1 glass (¼ pint/150ml) medium sherry or Marsala	1oz/25g leaf gelatine
6 level tablespoons sugar	½ pint/300ml boiling water

Wash, dry and pare the rind off 4 oranges and 1 lemon. Soak the rind in the sherry or Marsala for 1 hour.

Put the gelatine and sugar into a bowl, pour in the boiling water, and stir until all is dissolved.

Strain in the orange-flavoured liquor, discarding the rind. Squeeze the juice from all the oranges and the lemons and stir it in without straining. Pour the liquid into a pretty, old-fashioned mould (rinse it with cold water first) and leave it to cool and set overnight.

If you prefer, you can pour the jelly mixture into halved and scooped-out oranges. Serve with the scooped-out segments of orange and you will be in royal company: Charles I liked his orange jelly served this way as a refresher before he tackled a more serious pudding.

SOUTHERN CHRISTMAS

Christmas is celebrated throughout Roman Catholic Europe in high romantic style, with nativity scenes in the churches, midnight mass, and a nativity play performed by the local schoolchildren. The most important traditional meal is the fasting supper of Christmas Eve – from the simple rural Portuguese *bacal-hanu* supper, to the extravaganza of a full Provençal *gros souper* followed by the ritual thirteen desserts.

Regional nativity plays share more than divides them. Sometimes performed in the church, sometimes outside, they are usually a simple re-enactment of the Bethlehem story, with Herod as the villain and the shepherds to provide a little comic relief. Károly Viski described a typical 'Bethlehem play' performed in the open air in a Calvinist village in the 1920s:

Seven boys, aged fourteen to sixteen, make up the cast; King Herod, Joseph, the runner (the envoy), two angels, two shepherds. The terrible king is dressed as a Hussar – red trousers, blue dolman, fur cap, hussar shako, curved sword, boots with big spurs. The angels are dressed in white petticoats and blouses borrowed from their mothers, worn over their ordinary clothes. Two shepherds complete the group – their shaggy fur coats touching the ground, big sticks in their hands, sheepskin caps on their heads.

By the fourteenth century these Bethlehems, live offspring of the model Bethlehem scenes so popular inside the churches, were being performed in the markets and streets of the towns – in much the same way as the Easter Passion plays and processions. Sometimes they were performed by girls only, led by an older woman, or marionettes were mixed up with live actors. In some villages, freed from the constraints of the church, the plays developed into comic-shepherd plays with little or no religious content. Anyone who has ever been involved with the organisation of a modern children's nativity play can easily see how this would happen.

In Portugal, Rodney Gallop found many of the old traditions still in full flower in the 1930s.

In Portugal, Christmas is essentially a family festival at which as many relatives as possible are re-united. The bonfires and *galheiros* of June are replaced by the *cepo de Natal*, the Yule log (of oak wherever possible), which blazes in the churchyard or, more usually, indoors on the *fogueira da consoada*

(Yule fire), while the family eat the consoada, or Christmas banquet, in the small hours of Christmas Day. The ashes and charred remains of the fire are burned later in the year when there are thunderstorms. Where their smoke goes, no thunderbolt will fall. The *alminhas* – souls of the dead – are welcomed at the feast. Crumbs are scattered for them on the hearth, or the table is left spread after the consoada, in order that they may share in its plenty.

Italians celebrate Christmas Eve with a non-meat fasting supper – fish, vegetables, cheese – followed by attendance at midnight Mass. The major feasting is saved for the secular New Year's Eve, and the sweet breads and special confectionery such as *panettoni* and almond *torrone* are the specialities of Twelfth Night, when the *Befana*, the witch, slips down the chimney with presents for good children.

But it is the fasting supper of Provence, the *gros souper*, which has survived in all its glory until the present day. It has not changed much since the Provençal poet Frédéric Mistral recorded the *gros souper* as celebrated at Saint-Rémy around the turn of the century – a ritual whose roots go well back into the pre-Christian era:

> Ah the blessed table, truly blessed surrounded, as it is, by the whole family, at peace and content. The lamp hanging from the ceiling, which, during the rest of the year, lights us with its pale glow, this particular evening has been replaced with three candles. And if the end of the wick should by chance turn towards one of the diners, that is a sign of some disaster to come.
>
> On the white cloth are placed, in appropriate order, the sacramental dishes. The snails, which each diner winkles from the shell with a brand-new pin, the fried salt-cod, the muge [gurnard] stuffed with olives, chard, cardoons, *céléri à la poivrade*, followed by a host of delicious sweetmeats, such as the *gâteau à l'huile*, grapes, nougat, quinces, and above all, the Christmas bread – not to be broached until one quarter has been given to the first poor man who passes by.
>
> At each end of the table, in a little dish, sprouts a tuft of wheat which on St Barbara's feast was planted and watered so that it would germinate.

My own favourite Christmas ritual is somewhat gentler – that celebrated further up the Rhône valley, in the scattered villages of the Baronnies which cling to the slopes of Mount Ventoux. The Christmas Eve table, as with all such festivals in France, remains a fiercely regional affair. Many years ago my own family celebration was directed by Mademoiselle Paulette of the little hill-village of Villedieu, just down the road from the Roman town of Vaison-la-Romaine. In Vaison itself, midnight Mass is accompanied by the *galoubé* and the *tambourin*, the instruments of Provence. Olives and truffles and wine are the local specialities – with mountain herbs, beautiful salt hams and sausages, salt cod, the year's new pressing of olive oil, and local seasonal fruit – *reinette* apples and William pears – on sale in all the Christmas markets. It is traditional, explained Paulette, to use, if not your own home-grown ingredients to celebrate the Christmas festival, then at least those which are as local as possible. This has safeguarded regional differences.

Paulette, now retired from her work as an accountant, lives in Villedieu in the house in which she was born – at that time it belonged to her grandfather the village baker: 'The bakers cannot make a good living any more – people do not eat so much bread – and the bakers have to make cakes and other things to make ends meet. Up here the *pompe à l'huile*, traditional down by Marseilles, is replaced by the *fougasse*. My grandfather made it with good butter, and offered it to his customers as a Christmas gift.' Paulette now has time to sing in the church choir, providing an accompaniment to the Christmas nativity play performed at midnight on Christmas Eve by the local schoolchildren. The *pastorale* is quite short, and the children, these days, mime to their own recorded voices. 'Otherwise,' says Paulette, 'it goes on all night.' In addition to the Holy Family and the usual characters, there is a miller, a *catéchisme*, a schoolchild, and a blind man – played by a small boy wearing his own pebble glasses. The four-footed worshippers are represented by a stuffed sheep, replacing the live one of the old days, who accompanies the shepherds on their way to Bethlehem. The Three Kings do not appear – their moment comes on January 6th.

Some habits, such as the *tréfoir* or Yule log – brought in and put on the fire on Christmas Eve and put back in the fire every night to be burnt a little more until Twelfth Night – are shared with the northern celebrants.

Mademoiselle Paulette's Christmas Eve celebration starts after sundown, at about seven o'clock. The central dish of her family's *gros souper* is the *soupe aux lasagnes*, with a variety of vegetable dishes – particularly cardoons and chard – with snails and a salt-cod dish to support it. A substantial soup is the traditional evening meal in rural France – hence *souper*: supper.

Soup is never served at lunch time. To finish we would have a home-made cheese — many people in Villedieu had a goat for milk and cheese. If they were *tommes fraîches* they were little round white fresh cheeses, or, if they have been matured on drying trays – the *cannisses* – they were *picodons*, and we would sometimes pickle them in our own new olive oil. Everyone had a lime-tree for their *tilleul*, and most people had access to a truffle-bearing oak for an *omelette aux truffes*.

After midnight mass the family return home for a glass of mulled wine and the traditional thirteen desserts, symbolizing Christ and his twelve disciples. The correct composition of the thirteen desserts is a thorny subject. It is most traditional to choose home-grown treats rather than imported luxuries – and the shopping list varies from place to place. In the uplands of Haute Provence, Paulette stipulates muscat grapes, picked right at the end of harvest, and hung to conserve them till Christmas in the cool of the rafters. Speckled yellow pears, the stalks dipped in scarlet sealing wax, and the fragrant yellow *reinette* apples are *de rigueur*.

We dried our own apricots, made quince paste, and we always had *les mendiants*, the four begging orders of friars: almonds for the Dominicans, figs for the Franciscans, hazelnuts for the Carmelites, dried currants for the Augustines. We made the dark nougat at home with hazelnuts and honey, and it was so hard you needed a hammer to break it. But we always bought the white nougat, which is a factory-made speciality of Montélimar.

Paulette includes tangerines rather than oranges – but both can be disputed and replaced with prunes on regional grounds.

It may be that those down by the sea had more access to these things – citrus fruit and dates from Africa. In addition we had the *panade*, a tart filled with apple purée. Sometimes the *panade* might be a savoury – made with spinach or pumpkin. Everyone would take their own tarts to my grandfather the baker, to be popped into the oven after the bread had been baked. Sometimes the roast would go in too, after the baking was done – you know, not everyone had ovens. The pace of life was slower and things were appreciated more. People celebrated in the family – and there was plenty of family.

For the midday meal on Christmas Day, the *dîner de Noël*, we had game — perhaps a thrush or wild boar pâté — then roast lamb or poultry. Usually we had lamb, as it's very good round here. For New Year there was not a party or anything. Just on New Year's Day, the younger people would visit the older and wish them a happy New Year. And the children would receive a glass of orange syrup and maybe a bit of cake or a piece of chocolate.

CHRISTMAS EVE IN PROVENCE

SOUP WITH RIBBON NOODLES
Soups aux lasagnes (France)

This light and delicious winter-vegetable soup is the traditional Christmas Eve *souper maigre* in the rural uplands, round Vaison-la-Romaine. The *lasagne* paste was, when time was of no real consequence in the winter, always made at home — using the housewife's own beautiful rich-yolked eggs. The vegetables, too, were, and still are, likely to be home-grown and stored for the winter. The olive oil which enriches the soup is that delicious peppery, fruity juice of the first-picked olives of the new season. Milling goes on all through Christmas until mid January.

Quantity: Serves 6.
Time: Start 30 minutes ahead if making your own pasta. 20–25 minutes.
Equipment: A large soup-pot. A rolling pin and board if making your own pasta.

6oz/175g dried lasagne (look for the ones like very broad tagliatelle with frilled edges) or 12oz/350g fresh noodle dough (make your own with 8 oz/250g flour and a pinch of salt kneaded to a soft dough with 2 large whole eggs)
bay leaf, parsley, thyme
3 pints/2 litres water
5–6 stalks chard, washed and cut into short lengths

3–4 stalks celery, washed and cut into short lengths
3–4 large mature carrots, scraped and roughly chopped
3–4 young turnips, peeled and roughly chopped
1 clove garlic, crushed
salt and pepper
¼ cabbage cut into strips
3–4 leeks, trimmed, well-washed and cut into thin rings

To finish
3–4 tablespoons olive oil, or a garlicky *aioli* or mayonnaise

Prepare the noodle dough if you are making your own — easily done with an electric mixer. It should rest for 30 minutes before you roll it thin and cut it into bite-sized squares ready for poaching in the soup. (If using dried sheets, break them up.)

Put the root vegetables and aromatics into the cold water (no preliminary frying is necessary) and bring to the boil with a teaspoon of salt. Simmer until the vegetables are nearly done — about 10–12 minutes. Stir in the dried *lasagne* (if using fresh, add it last) and bring it all back to the boil. Add the green vegetables in the order given, bringing everything back to the boil in between additions. Taste and add salt and pepper.

Finish with a swirl of olive oil, or a generous spoonful of *aioli*.

GRATIN OF CARDOON
Carde au gratin (France)

Spinach, chard or celery can replace cardoons in this recipe. *Cynara cardunculus*, a close relative of the globe artichoke, is a popular winter vegetable all round the Mediterranean, where it is blanched like celery. Don't forget to trim off all the leaves and take out the leafy yellow bits on the heart – the leaves are terribly bitter and cardoons should never be bitter. If you can afford, or find, a truffle to include, it will make the dish all the more delicious. Most Provençal *paysan* households have access to a truffle oak or two, and will save a find for Christmas – either gathered fresh, or sterilized for storage in a jar with a sprinkling of salt. The truffles go into everything – omelettes, scrambled eggs, to stud a Christmas dinner capon or turkey, or as here, to add a flavour of the best fillet steak to the Christmas fasting supper.

Quantity: Serves 4–6.
Time: 50–60 minutes.
Equipment: A roomy, lidded saucepan. A colander. A gratin dish.

1 head of cardoon, trimmed of all leaves and chopped into short bite-sized lengths (use the tender inside stalks only) or 1–2 heads celery
1 black truffle, brushed and cut into slivers (*optional*)
salt and pepper

juice of ½ a lemon
4 tablespoons olive oil
2 tablespoons whole black olives, squashed with a rolling pin
2 tablespoons flour
½ pint/300ml white wine
3 tablespoons grated cheese

Cook the cardoon pieces in boiling salted water in the saucepan for 10–15 minutes, until tender. Drain and toss with the lemon juice.

Heat the oil in the pan and turn the cardoon pieces in it to dry them off a little. Add the olives and the optional slivered truffle. Heat again. Sprinkle in the flour and stir it in. Splash in the wine and bubble it all up. Simmer for 10–15 minutes to cook the flour and evaporate the alcohol. Taste and add salt and pepper.

Spread the cardoons in their sauce in the gratin dish, finish with a generous sprinkling of grated cheese, and slip it under a hot grill to gild and bubble up.

SALT COD IN PROVENÇAL SAUCE
Morue en raito (France)

A well-prepared middle cut of salt cod, carefully soaked, is as sweet and fresh-flavoured as fresh cod. Choose pure white fish with no trace of pink down the spine – in Provence at Christmas there are special stalls selling ready-made salt-cod purée (*brandade de morue*) and ready-soaked fish. Marseille-born Josephine Besson, now Cannes's most famous cook, gives this recipe for her own family's fasting supper.

As you enjoy it, do not be too distracted to remember, on the stroke of midnight, that the tiny Baby Jesus must be popped into his miniature manger in the household's *crèche*.

Quantity: Serves 4.
Time: Start 24 hours ahead. 30 minutes.
Equipment: A bowl. A shallow saucepan.

1lb/500g salt cod (or 1½lb/750g smoked haddock, which will need no soaking)
1 large onion, peeled and chopped
1lb/500g tomatoes, scalded, skinned and chopped

1–2 tablespoons flour
4 tablespoons olive oil
2 cloves garlic, peeled and chopped
1 tablespoon capers
1 tablespoon gherkins, chopped pepper

Put the salt cod to soak in plenty of clean water for 24 hours, changing the water 3–4 times. Keep it in a cool place – cover it if it is in the refrigerator, otherwise everything will smell of fish.

Cut the fish into bite-sized pieces and flour it lightly.

Heat the olive oil and fry the fish on each side until golden. Remove the pieces, and replace them with the onion and garlic. Fry gently until they soften and take colour. Stir in the chopped tomatoes. Allow it all to bubble up and cook down into a thick sauce. Slip back the fish pieces, with the capers and chopped gherkins. Season with pepper. Simmer gently, without allowing the sauce to boil, for 10–15 minutes.

Serve with a big bowl of plain boiled potatoes.

SNAILS WITH SPINACH AND WHITE WINE
Escargouillade aux épinards (France)

I used to pick the small *petit gris* snails used in this dish when I lived in the Languedoc. I knew exactly where to find the delicately striped molluscs when, as dawn broke, they would climb to the top spikes of a particular thicket of broom. The timing was crucial: as the sun rose into the sky, they would slide quickly back down into the dewy grass below.

Wild snail stocks have been so depleted in France that the creatures cannot now be picked from the hedgerows for sale in the markets – although those collecting for their own table continue to do so. When I was in Provence last year there were thousands of *petits gris* aestivating in the summer grass. All land snails are edible, including the British garden snail – many of which are direct descendants of the Roman farmed snail.

As for the need to starve them, this is done to get rid of what the snails have ingested and retained in their intestines – whether pesticides, lead paint or simply odd bits of vegetation the French call *mauvaises herbes*, which can upset the human digestive system. When picking from the wild, starve the snails for a week or so until they have emptied their cloaca of any alien nibbles (they can be fed with thyme, fennel, or vine leaves if you feel so inclined).

When you are ready to prepare them, leave them overnight in a well-lidded bucket with a handful of coarse salt. The following day, wash them patiently in running water until there are no more gluey bubbles and the water runs clear. Put them in a large saucepan with a *bouquet garni* and cover with clean warm water – the temperature of summer rain. The snails will soon pop their heads out, which makes them much easier to eat. When they do so, bring the water to the boil fast. Throw in a small glass of vinegar to cut the froth. Simmer them for 40–60 minutes (the larger the snail, the longer the cooking) and drain them. Then they are ready for their sauce.

The dish can be made without snails and just with spinach, celery or chard. Or you can make it with lambs' hearts, simmered for 1 hour and cubed, instead of the snails.

Quantity: Serves 4–6.
Time: 40 minutes after the initial preparation of the snails.
Equipment: A lidded saucepan. A roomy casserole.

1lb/500g ready-prepared snails in their shells	1lb/500g spinach
3–4 tablespoons olive oil	2–3 cloves garlic, peeled and chopped
6–8 anchovies in oil (1 small can)	1 tablespoon flour
1–2 glasses dry white wine	salt and pepper

Pick over the snails and reject any empty shells – or any where the snail has not come to the mouth of its shell.

Pick over and rinse the spinach. Put it to cook in a lidded saucepan in the water which clings to its leaves. Drain it as soon as it collapses. Press out the water and chop the spinach roughly.

Warm the oil in the casserole and toss in the garlic, turning it in the hot oil until it is soft. Add the anchovies and mash them in briefly. Stir in the spinach and keep turning it over the heat until the oil is all absorbed. Sprinkle in the flour and turn it well in. Pour in the wine and let it all bubble up to evaporate the alcohol. Stir in the snails, shells and all, season (not too much salt), and turn them in the sauce until everything is piping hot.

Serve with plenty of bread, and provide each person with a pin (or, if you are in Provence, an acacia thorn) to pick the snails out of their lairs.

TRUFFLE OMELETTE
Omelette aux truffes (France)

Should you be so fortunate as to find yourself in truffle country for the *gros souper*, look for a man with a dog and a patch of truffle oaks and persuade him to dig you your very own supply. The magnificent flavour is far too ephemeral to survive more than a couple of days from its cradling earth, so what's the point of buying it any other way? Leave the truffle overnight with eggs in a covered bowl so as not to waste any of that heavenly breath.

Quantity: Serves 2.
Time: 5 minutes only, so warm the plates first.
Equipment: A bowl, fork and omelette pan.

5 perfectly fresh eggs from free-spirited barnyard hens	salt and pepper
first-pressing olive oil	2oz/50g butter, or 2 tablespoons
	1 whole truffle, brushed lightly, showered free of sand, and matchsticked

The difference between scrambled eggs (a delightful alternative vehicle for the truffle) and omelettes is in the mixing. For the omelette, the forking has to be light – a mere few flicks of the wrist, so that the yolk and white are swirled together. For scrambled eggs, it is a thorough mix. Season the eggs with salt and pepper.

Heat the pan first, and throw in the butter or oil. As it heats (the butter will froth), toss in the match-sticked truffle. An instant later, pour in the eggs. Let the base set over a high heat. Turn over the set egg to let the liquid run underneath. While the egg is still very soft and frothy, turn one third into the middle. Flip the omelette over itself on to the warm plate.

Serve immediately.

You will never taste anything so perfect if you live to be a hundred.

THE THIRTEEN DESSERTS
Les treize desserts (France)

In the uphills of Provence, round Vaison-la-Romaine, the thirteen desserts, prettily arranged on their dishes round the fougasse – the rich sweet bread which symbolizes Christ – are grapes, apples, pears, dried apricots and figs, quince paste, hazelnuts, walnuts, dried currants, black and white nougat, and tangerines.

On the littoral Calena, as Christmas is called round the sea-ports of Provence, it is the olive-oil bread, the pompe, which takes the place of the fougasse in the central position, and the apricots and pears are often replaced by almonds and dates. Passions run high as to which are the traditional ingredients. Josephine Besson, of La Mère Besson in Cannes, explains the presence of the dates:

> Do you know why the date has the two sides of its stone in the form of a double letter O? It is because the Virgin Mary, on her way to Bethlehem, paused in the shade of a date tree, and, glancing heavenwards, she exclaimed 'Oo, what lovely fruit!' so the date-stone, ever since, has born the double mark of her delight.

CHRISTMAS BREAD
Fougasse (France)

Nowadays this pretty lacy Christmas bread from the uplands of Provence can be bought all year round all over the region. Salted versions, to be eaten with the main course, are made with a few anchovies worked in, or with crisp bits of salty pork scratchings. Sweet ones are flavoured with orange rind. The lowland version, the pompe (the recipe is given in my book European Peasant Cookery), is scented with orange-flower water, a simple home-made infusion used as a holy benediction. Olive oil is the usual enriching ingredient for dough – but village bakers would, in pre-war days, make it with the more luxurious (in this country of the olive) butter as a gift for favoured customers at Christmas.

Quantity: Makes a loaf for 6.
Time: Start 3 hours ahead. 25–30 minutes.
Equipment: A sieve and mixing bowl. A rolling pin and board. A baking sheet and cooling rack.

1lb/500g plain flour
4oz/125g sugar
grated rind and juice of 1 orange

1oz/25g fresh yeast (½oz/12g dried)
2 eggs
3oz/75g butter, melted to a cream but not oiled

Sieve the flour into a warm bowl.

Pour a little warm water over the fresh yeast in a cup, sprinkle in a teaspoon of sugar, and leave it for a moment or two to liquidize. Make a hollow in the flour and pour in the yeast mix. Sprinkle with flour and leave for 10–15 minutes to start the sponge working. (If using dried yeast, follow the packet directions.) bBeat the eggs and make up to ½ pint/300ml with orange juice. Pour into the well in the middle. Work in the flour, drawing it in gradually from the sides, until you have a soft smooth dough. When it no longer sticks to your hands or the bowl, cover it with clingfilm and put it in a warm place for about 1–2 hours to rise, until doubled in bulk.

Knead the dough on a well-floured board, knocking it down to distribute the oxygen bubbles. Work the creamed butter and the rest of the sugar into the dough. You may need extra flour.

Roll the dough out into a large oval – it should be about as long as from your fingertips to your elbow.

Transfer to an oiled baking tray. Slash the dough in the rough shape of a hand, with a long slash at the heel of the thumb, and two lines of slashes following the curve of the dough in the rough positions of knuckles. Pull the dough sideways to fan out the slashes.

Cover loosely with clingfilm, and leave in a warm place for 20–30 minutes to rise again.

Heat the oven to 425°F/220°C/Gas 7.

Bake the bread for 20–30 minutes, until well puffed and brown. Transfer to a baking rack to cool.

PUMPKIN AND APPLE TART
Panade (France)

All the bakeries of upland Provence have this delicious tart on sale at Christmas. The bought tarts are filled with a sweetened apple purée, but at home they are often made with pumpkin, either sweet and mixed with apple or a savoury version on its own, or with spinach. In this version pumpkin adds its sunny colour and delicate flavour to the apple.

Quantity: Serves 6.
Time: Start 30 minutes ahead.
Equipment: A medium saucepan with a lid. A sieve and mixing bowl. A rolling pin and board. An 8-in/20cm tart tin.

The filling
2 cooking apples, peeled, cored and roughly
  chopped
grated peel and juice of 1 orange
4oz/100g sugar
pine-kernels or slivered almonds

6oz/175g ripe pumpkin, peeled, de-seeded and
  roughly chopped
2oz/50g butter
2 tablespoons lightly roasted

The pastry
6oz/175g flour

½ teaspoon salt

1oz/25g icing sugar

1 egg yolk

4oz/100g butter, chopped into dice

1–2 tablespoons cold water

Put the apple and pumpkin pieces in a saucepan with the orange juice. Bring to the boil, lid, and turn down to simmer until quite soft.

Meanwhile, make the pastry. Make sure all the ingredients are cold. Sieve the flour with the salt into a bowl and sprinkle in the icing sugar. Using the tips of your fingers, rub the butter into the flour roughly – it does not need to be too finely mixed.

Fork the egg yolk lightly with a tablespoon of water and mix it into the flour and butter until you have a soft dough ball. You may need the extra water – the amount always depends on the size of the egg yolk and the wateriness of the butter.

Leave the dough to rest under cover in a cool larder or the fridge for 30 minutes, while you finish the filling.

Mash the apple and pumpkin together over the heat until any excess liquid is evaporated and you are left with a thick purée. Beat in the butter and sugar. Put the purée aside to cool.

Reserve a third of the pastry and roll out the rest to line the tart tin. Fill with the fruit purée.

Heat the oven to 350°C/180°C/Gas 4.

Roll out the reserved third of pastry and cut it into strips. Finish the tart with a neat latticework of pastry. Sprinkle the units into the spaces between the lattice.

Bake for 30–40 minutes, until the pastry is crisp and golden.

Serve with a sweet white wine – perhaps a fragrant, flowery Beaumes de Venise from the high shoulders which link the jagged grey precipices of the Dentelles de Montmirail.

HONEY AND HAZELNUT NOUGAT
Nougat noir artisanat (France)

Home-made nougat is delicious – but notoriously as hard as a paving stone. Take a hammer to it. Almonds can be used instead of hazelnuts. Honey is a speciality of Provence, where a great many different kinds are available. Lavender, thyme, rosemary (grown commercially for perfume and herbs), spring meadows, orange, acacia and lime trees, even pine forests, all have their season when the bees are busy collecting. The honey is flavoured according to the flower from which the nectar is gathered – which is, in its turn, dictated by the blossoming season and the positioning of the hives. Those who have their own swarms will often move the hives from place to place to take maximum advantage of the different blooming times and places – a welcome service to those whose crops need pollination.

Quantity: makes 2lb/1kg.
Time: 20–25 minutes.
Equipment: A heavy-bottomed saucepan. A sugar thermometer. A baking tray.

1lb/500g honey

2 sheets rice paper

1lb/500g lightly toasted hazelnuts

Put the honey and the hazelnuts in the saucepan. Bring gently to the boil. Simmer delicately, stirring regularly, until the nuts begin to froth and the sugar thermometer records hard crack.

Meanwhile, line the baking tray with a sheet of rice paper.

Pour the honey and nut mixture on to the rice paper. Top with the remaining sheet. Leave to cool.

FEAST OF ST STEPHEN AND BOXING DAY: DECEMBER 26TH

St Stephen, one of the seven deacons of the early Church, earned himself the distinction of first place in the Christian calendar when he was stoned to death in Jerusalem just after the Ascension. The saint somewhat mysteriously became the patron saint of the horse – possibly because of a Swedish St Stephen who loved horses. His enthusiasm is reflected in the tradition of a Boxing Day foxhunting meet in Britain, and in the race-meetings which are held all over northern Europe on the day after Christmas.

Lady Diana Cooper, young daughter of the house at Belvoir Castle in Rutland at the turn of the last century, leant over the balcony to watch the gathering of the Boxing Day meet:

> The ladies wore top hats or billycocks with very black veils drawn taut across their cold noses, and fringes and buns. The men were in pink, with glossy white 'leathers', swigging down cherry brandy from their saddles to keep out the cold. Hounds making a faint music of excitement were dexterously and mercilessly whipped into a pack. Then they would be off, with a flinty clatter of hooves and suppressed oaths and the language horses are thought to understand, through the bare woods to the open Vale, the second horsemen following demurely. They would hack home cold, weary and fulfilled in the twilight, generally caked in mud and smelling of horse, and fall upon the tea and boiled eggs, and discuss the runs and falls and scandals until the gong rang for dressing-time, getting louder and louder as it approached down the unending passages.

In Britain, the day after Christmas was the day when servants emptied their tip-boxes and tradesmen received their annual sweetener – a generosity rooted in the tradition that this was the day the local priest emptied the church alms box and distributed its contents to the poor of his parish.

Gifts of food were usual in rural areas. The farmer's wife baked pies for the farm-workers, and the parish priest treated his parishioners to bread and cheese and ale.

BOXING DAY TATIE POT
(England)

The rolling fells and wooded slopes of the northern Lake District provide the best of sport for the keen foxhunters of Cumbria, birthplace of John Peel himself. This black-pudding enriched lamb stew is the hunt's traditional meal – washed down with a nip of sloe gin, or a swig of brandy.

The local Herdwick mutton, pastured on the heathery moors, was the preferred meat, although lamb has now taken its place in the stewing pot. With the long cooking, the black pudding melts in to give a deliciously dark gravy. It is a good simple meal after all the roast meat of Christmas.

Quantity: Serves 4 hungry huntsmen.
Time: Start the day before. 30 minutes.

Equipment: A deep baking tin.

3½lb/1.75kg neck of lamb on the bone, chopped
3–4 carrots, scraped and roughly sliced
1½ pints/900ml boiling water
salt and pepper
2lb/1kg potatoes, peeled and thinly sliced

1–2 onions, skinned and thinly sliced
1 large swede or turnip, peeled and chopped into
    bite-sized pieces
1lb/500g black pudding (in skin or in the piece),
    sliced

Put the lamb, onions, carrots and swede or turnip into the baking tin with enough boiling water to cover. Season with salt and pepper.

Bring everything back to the boil. Cover with foil. Cook in a very low oven, 250°F/130°C/Gas 1, for 4–5 hours, until the meat is so soft it is falling off the bone.

Ladle out the juice and leave it to get cold, overnight perhaps, so that you can lift off the hat of fat.

Take out the bones and cut the meat into bite-sized chunks. Arrange the meat and vegetables back in the baking tin. Cover with slices of black pudding. Boil up the juices, taste and adjust the seasoning, and pour the boiling liquid over the meat so that it covers it. Lay overlapping discs of potato over the top. Dot with lamb fat. Season, cover with foil, and return the dish to a hot oven, 375°F/190°C/Gas 5, to bake for 50–60 minutes.

Remove the foil after 30–40 minutes, when the potatoes are soft, to crisp and gild them at the edges. Serve with pickled red cabbage (below).

PICKLED RED CABBAGE
(England)

A sharp-flavoured, rosy pickle which cuts the richness of the meat, this is the perfect – and traditional – companion for the tatie pot above.

Quantity: Makes 3lb/.kg.
Time: Start a month ahead. 20 minutes.
Equipment: A shallow dish. A small saucepan. 3 pickle jars.

2lb/1kg red cabbage
2–3 slices raw beetroot (for extra colour)
1–2 pints/600ml–1.2 litres cider vinegar

1 tablespoon salt
2–3 slices raw onion (for extra flavour)
1 teaspoon pickling spice

Slice the cabbage into fine ribbons, spread it in a shallow dish, and salt it thoroughly. Leave it overnight. Next day, drain it and pack it into jars. Top each with a slice of beetroot and a slice of onion.

Boil up the vinegar with the spices and simmer for 15 minutes. Strain over the cabbage and seal the pots down.

Ready in a month – although you can eat it after a week.

CUMBERLAND RUM NICKY
(England)

Every household in Cumberland has its own family recipe for the Nicky – much like a large mince pie, it still had beef marrow in it until recent times.

Quantity: Serves 4–6.
Time: Start the day before. 1½ hours intermittent attention.
Equipment: A small bowl. A sieve and mixing bowl. A rolling pin and board. An 8–10in/20–25cm diameter shallow tart tin.

The filling
8oz/250g dates, chopped
1 tablespoon crystallized stem ginger, chopped small
1 large Bramley apple, peeled, cored and chopped small

8oz/250g raisins and currants, mixed
1 glass dark rum (Lamb's Navy – this is seafarer's country, looking to Jamaica)
2oz/50g butter, softened
2oz/50g soft brown sugar

The pastry
8oz/250g flour
3oz/75g butter
4–5 tablespoons cold water

½ teaspoon salt
3oz/75g lard

To finish
1 tablespoon milk

1 tablespoon unrefined granulated sugar

Put the dates, raisins and currants and ginger to soak overnight in the rum in a covered bowl.

Next day, make the pastry first.

Make sure all the ingredients are cold. Sieve the flour with the salt into a bowl. Using the tips of your fingers, rub the fat into the flour until you have a mixture like fine breadcrumbs. Work in enough cold water to give a soft dough.

Leave the dough to rest under cover in a cool larder or the refrigerator for 30 minutes.

Mix the rest of the filling ingredients with the soaked fruit and brandy.

Heat the oven to 400°F/200°C/Gas 6.

Cut the dough in two. Roll out into rounds on a floured board, and use one round to line the tart tin. Spread in the filling. Damp the edges of the pastry and lay on the second round. Press the edges together lightly with a fork. Cut a little hole in the top of the pie, brush it with milk and sprinkle with the granulated sugar.

Bake for about 45 minutes, until the pastry is crisp and brown.

Transfer carefully to a wire rack to cool. Lovely hot or cold – in Cumbria it is sometimes served with a dollop of rum butter (see facing).

RUM BUTTER
(England)

Nutmeg is a favourite spice in Cumberland, where traditional recipes rely on spices rather than herbs in the cooking pot. The trading ports of Silloth, Whitehaven and Maryport supplied the surrounding countryside not only with the spices the housewives loved, but also with West Indian rum and sugar.

Quantity: Serves 4–6.
Time: Start 1–2 hours ahead. 5 minutes.
Equipment: A bowl and a wooden spoon.

4oz/125g butter
¼ whole nutmeg, grated (plenty)

8oz/250g soft brown sugar (dark or light)
2–3 tablespoons rum

Cream the butter with the sugar and nutmeg till well blended. Not too much beating – the sauce should remain gritty. Beat in the rum.

Let the sauce harden in the refrigerator for an hour or two. Serve it cool with a hot Rum Nicky (see previous recipe).

January

New Year's Eve everywhere is the night to listen and watch for signals of joy or sorrow in the coming year. 'First-footing' in Scotland is one of the many rituals which ensure future good fortune, and requires that the first person to enter a house on the first day of the year should be a dark stranger. Some regions prefer a fair-haired visitor – a prejudice which may have something to do with the characteristics of expected marauders. The stranger should enter carrying a piece of peat or coal, which he puts on the fire. He is then rewarded with a bannock or a slice of cake and a dram of whisky. In some areas, the stranger brings in a sprig of mistletoe as well, and places his own bread and salt on the table. In Germany there is a similar tradition which requires that the first person met must be a young boy.

In rural Sweden on New Year's Day, it was customary for the farmer to go out into the fields and listen to the sounds of the long Arctic night: if he caught the soft breezy whisper of a scythe cutting grass, there would be a good harvest in the summer; if he heard the stormy clashing of swords, he must batten down against a bad year, with wars and troubles to compound the loss.

In Germany a young lover's fortune might be told with the help of the *Bleigiessen* – pouring molten lead into a bowl of cold water and reading from the shapes. In the Alps, the old folk stay at home and drink punch, and forecast the weather for the coming year with an 'onion calendar', made by cutting an onion into twelve slices – one for each month. When laid in order and sprinkled with salt the one which weeps the most juice will be the rainiest month.

In the south of England, similar preoccupations held until the turn of the last century, when in Herefordshire's cider-apple orchards the year's end was celebrated with the Burning of the Bush – a ball of hawthorn twigs (blackthorn over the border in Worcestershire) which, together with the mistletoe, hung in the farmhouse kitchen from one New Year's Day to the next. At dawn on January 1st the ball was taken down, carried to the first sown wheatfield and burnt on a large fire of dry straw. The Bush was then carried flaming all through the fields, to a rhythmic chant of 'Aud Ci-der'. This ritual completed, all the participants would settle down to a feast of cider and plum cake back at the farmhouse.

Over in rural southern France, Mary Eyre, spirited Victorian hiker and author of *A Lady's Walks in the South of France*, recorded a similar ritual in the Bearne in the 1860s:

On the last day of December, every family in that part awaits with anxiety the coming of the fairies, for whom a feast is prepared in the most private recess in the house. They come, say the mountaineers, in the middle of the night, to visit those who love them. Happiness, under the guise of a beautiful child, whose wavy silken hair is crowned with roses, is carried in their right hand; and Misfortune, under the form of a child in a torn robe, with tear-stained cheeks, and wearing a crown of black thorns, is in their left. Numerous flocks to pasture on the neighbouring mountains, and abundant harvests are the recompense they bestow on the inhabitants of the dwelling where they are received with true love and rustic display. The fairies know and grant the most secret wishes of the young girls, if they have attended properly to the fresh milk, the curds, and the fine white bread prepared for them.

Further north, at Hervé in the Pays de Liège, a well-garnished *choucroute* of salt-soured cabbage, pork and sausages is eaten on the first day of the year – a belly-rounding feast to ensure a well-padded wallet all the year long. In France, as in Britain, it has recently become the custom for family parties to go out to a restaurant for the New Year's Eve dinner, where everyone, young and old, tucks into a *grande bouffe*, starting with oysters. This new habit seems compatible with the more ancient tradition of visiting relatives on New Year's Day to wish them good health. The young would visit the older members, who would welcome them with rich sweet wine and cakes, and home-made fruit syrups and biscuits for the children.

With the rise of Protestantism in northern Europe, the Christmas feasting which had once marked the pagan midwinter celebrations and survived the transition into the Christian festival almost disappeared under the thumb of Puritanism. The midwinter riot became a decorous Christian celebration, with most of the day spent in church – and no opportunity to misbehave. This paved the way for a return to popularity of the old New Year celebrations – which had never been attached to a Christian ritual, and so were no business of the church.

The traditions of the New Year concern themselves with future prosperity. The plentiful food and liquor act as a message to the gods, old or new – a reminder that divine help is required, even demanded, to ensure a full store-cupboard and a grateful populace in the coming year.

SCOTTISH HOGMANAY SUPPER

The stern non-conformists of Scotland have let their hair down at the New Year since the Reformation. Today the Scots' festival of Hogmanay, with its attendant ritual of first-footing, is celebrated with an enthusiasm unmatched anywhere in Europe.

Hogmanay – also known as Cake Day since Scottish children expected the gift of an oatmeal bannock – has its name from the Old French *aguillanneuf* or New Year gift, which becomes *hoguinané* in the Norman dialect.

Good rich food made with the best ingredients, and plenty of it, distinguishes festival food from everyday food in Scotland. Spices were an important trade item in the days when the puffers called at the islands, with their cargo of flour and other essentials for the isolated inhabitants of the Hebrides, where I used to live for much of the year. A *ceiledh* (a 'cayley', or party, in its English rendition), with a bit of dancing the old reels and some singing of the old songs, follows the supper – then it might be time for a slice of cloutie dumpling and a dram of whisky. Bagpipes and accordions welcome the New Year – usually with a sentimental and spirited rendering of 'Should auld acquaintance be forgot'.

THICK VEGETABLE BROTH WITH BARLEY
(Scotland)

This fine broth is made with the milky juices used in the gigot recipe which follows. It can be made with plain water or with milk and water on non-feast-days, when it is a good hearty winter soup – a meal in itself if accompanied by a round of home-baked scones and a bit of cheese.

Quantity: Serves 6.
Time: Start the day before.
Equipment: A large soup pot.

3 oz/75g barley
½ large swede, peeled and chunked
2 large carrots, scraped and chunked
3 leeks, with their green, washed and chopped
1 small cabbage or a handful of turnip tops, trimmed and finely sliced

2 pints/1.2 litres lamb stock made with milk (make the quantity up with water if you don't have enough)
1lb/500g potatoes, peeled and chunked
1 heaped tablespoon chopped parsley

Soak the barley overnight in enough water to cover.

Put all the ingredients except the potatoes, cabbage and parsley into the soup pot. Bring to the boil, lid, and turn down to simmer for 30 minutes. Add the potatoes. Bring back to the boil, turn down the heat, and cook for a further 15 minutes. Add the cabbage or greens. Bring back to the boil and cook for another 5–10 minutes.

Stir in the parsley just before serving the hot broth. You could always add a stir of cream to make it really rich.

MILK-SIMMERED GIGOT OF LAMB WITH CAPER SAUCE
(Scotland)

At Hogmanay the hardy mountain-pastured lambs which have been on the market since September are still not yet at their first birthday, after which they will be classified as hogget – mutton. Judge Lord Henry Cockburn enjoyed a fine gigot (leg) of hogget at Braemar in 1853 (*Memorials of His Time*, Edinburgh, 1856):

> I think it my duty to record the unmatched merits of a leg of mutton which we had to-day at dinner. It was a leg which told how it had strayed among mountains from its lambhood to its death. It spoke of winter straths and summer heights, of tender heather, Alpine airs, cold springs, and that short sweet grass which corries alone can cherish. These were the mettle of its pasture. It left its savour on the palate, like the savour of a good deed on the heart.

Boiling and braising were the traditional cooking methods in all but the wealthiest households, as roasting takes too much precious fuel. A well-grown leg or shoulder of lamb is doubly delicious when oven-simmered in milk with some of the liquid used to make the caper sauce – a rich but economical party dish for the many guests expected at the *ceiledh*. Use the rest of the cooking liquor in the vegetable broth which precedes the meat.

Quantity: Serves 8–10.
Time: Start about 4½ hours ahead. 30 minutes.
Equipment: A saucepan. A large heavy stew-pot or oven-proof casserole. A draining spoon and a whisk.

1 leg of well-grown lamb (about 5lb/2.5kg)
3–4 large carrots, scraped and chunked
1 small head celery, well washed and thickly
  sliced
1 bay leaf
about 2½ pints/1.5 litres milk

3–4 onions, peeled and chopped
1 large swedish turnip (neep), peeled and chunked
3–4 leeks, rinsed and roughly chopped
salt and pepper
a handful of parsley, roughly chopped

To finish the sauce
either the trimmed fat from the gigot, or
  2oz/50g butter
4 tablespoons capers

2oz/50g flour
2oz/50g flour
salt and pepper

Wipe over the meat. Trim off and reserve any excess fat. Season the meat all over. Wipe the stewing-pot or casserole round with a bit of the trimmed fat. Put all the vegetables in the bottom of the pot to make a bed for the meat. Season the vegetables and lay in the gigot. Tuck the herbs round it.

Bring the milk to the boil and pour it over the meat. Bring everything gently back to the boil and remove from the heat immediately. Lid the pot, transfer it to a low oven, 300°F/150°C/Gas 2, and leave to cook very gently for 3–4 hours – turn the oven down if the milk starts to boil. You can simmer the dish on top of the stove if you prefer, but make sure you use a pan with a very heavy base.

When the meat is really tender, pour off the milk and leave the gigot to settle while you make the sauce. You will need 1½ pints/900ml of the liquid.

Render down the reserved fat from the leg in a saucepan, until you have about 2 tablespoons of liquid. Remove the solids with a draining spoon and discard (instead of rendered fat, you could use butter). Turn the flour in the hot fat until the mixture is sandy. Gradually pour in the hot lamb milk, whisking steadily. Stir in the capers, season, and cook the mixture over a low heat for 5–8 minutes, until the sauce is thick and shiny.

Serve the gigot sliced on to a bed of its cooking vegetables, with the caper sauce handed separately. Accompany the dish with large baked potatoes, scrubbed, pricked, lightly salted and popped in the oven for the last 1½-2 hours of the gigot's cooking time. There's nothing better than a Hebridean potato dug from the rich peaty loam of the tattie patch, unless it be a well-flavoured leg of lamb from the hill.

CLOUTIE DUMPLING
(Scotland)

Chrissie MacDonald, my neighbour on the island of Mull in the Inner Hebrides, makes this rich boiled fruit cake for special occasions – perfect to offer the first-footer on the first day of the year. Her own family likes its dumpling cold, served sliced like a baked fruit cake. Nevertheless she concedes that some, particularly round Glasgow, like theirs hot and served with cream or custard. I lean towards the Glaswegians. City and town dwellers can buy a black bun, the baker's treat, instead. This is either a richly fruity bread enclosed in a casing of plain dough; or a rich fruit cake baked in a pastry casing. Both these recipes are oven-baked, which in the old days put them beyond the reach of all but the big house and the town bakeries.

Quantity: Serves at least 8 (there's no fun in a small dumpling).
Time: Start 4–5 hours ahead. 25–30 minutes.
Equipment: A mixing bowl. A large boiling saucepan. An 18in/45cm square of clean white cloth – maybe from an old sheet. A baking tray. A small saucepan and a whisk.

The dumpling

1lb/500g self-raising flour
4oz/100g soft brown sugar
5oz/150g vegetable fat or butter
1 tablespoon black treacle
8oz/250g sultanas
1 grated mature carrot
¼ pint/150ml milk

6oz/175g soft fresh brown breadcrumbs
1 teaspoon mixed spice, plus a little extra powdered cinnamon
8oz/250g currants
2 grated apples (cored but not peeled)
1 egg

Sieve the flour and mix it with the breadcrumbs, brown sugar and spices. Melt the vegetable fat or butter gently with the treacle. Stir in the breadcrumb mixture, the currants and the sultanas. Mix all well together with the grated apple and carrot – using your hands. Add the egg beaten up in the milk. Add more milk if necessary to give a soft mixture which drops easily from the spoon.

Bring a saucepan of water to the boil and put in the cloth. When it comes back to the boil, take out the scalded cloth (Chrissie remembers her mother could put her hands straight into the boiling water). Sprinkle the cloth with flour and put in the dumpling mixture, patting it into a rough-shaped ball.

Draw up the edges of the cloth over the mixture, and tie it up firmly with string, leaving enough room for the pudding to expand. Slip an upturned saucer into the base of the cooking pot and lower the dumpling back into the boiling water, so that its base rests on the upturned saucer. Keep the water topped up with boiling water so that the pudding is submerged throughout its cooking time. Bring the water back to the boil. Boil steadily but gently for 4 hours. It can be longer but it shouldn't be less.

Remove the dumpling – be brave and use your hands, or hook a wooden spoon through the tied top. Dip the dumpling straight in and out of cold water, and unwrap it on to a serving plate. The skin will initially be white from the flour. Put the dumpling on its plate in a very low oven, 250°F/130°C/Gas 1, to dry off for 20 minutes and develop its characteristic fine dark glossy skin.

The dumpling cuts wonderfully rich and dark. Leftover slices are delicious fried in butter – lovely with cream.

LENTIL POTTAGE
Lenticchie in umido (Italy)

Seeds are customarily offered as hostage to future prosperity – as with wedding rice and confetti. In many regions of Italy lentils, smallest and therefore most numerous of pulse vegetables, are eaten at midnight on New Year's Eve or on New Year's Day in order to bring wealth in the coming year. Here is Milan-born Anna del Conte's favourite recipe for the celebration's appropriately thick lentil soup-stew. A happy and prosperous New Year cannot fail to follow.

Quantity: Serves 4.
Time: About 1 hour.
Equipment: A heavy saucepan.

1 tablespoon olive oil
1 small onion, very finely chopped
12oz/350g brown lentils (they need no
  previous soaking)

2oz/50g pancetta
4–5 sage leaves or ¼ teaspoon dried sage
salt and freshly-ground black pepper

Put the oil and the *pancetta* in the saucepan and heat for a couple of minutes. Add the onion and the sage and sauté for 5 minutes.

Add the lentils, and as soon as they are well coated with fat, pour over about 1½ pints/900ml of boiling water. Lid the pan and simmer for about 1 hour or until the lentils are soft but still whole, and nearly all the liquid has been absorbed. Add salt and pepper to taste.

The dish is even more delicious if you serve it with poached boiling sausage, *zampone*. Use the poaching liquid to cook the lentils.

ROAST SUCKING-PIG
(Hungary)

This is the traditional New Year feast in the rural farming districts of eastern Europe. Every independent peasant family kept at least one pig, fed through the winter on the wastage from the household, and put out to glean in the orchard after the harvest and in the forest in the autumn. The pig is the best sign of a settled, rather than nomadic, population – an important distinction in central Europe, where the nomadic herdsmen of the Russian steppes finally settled down. Unlike cattle, sheep or even reindeer, there is no way to herd a swine, as anybody who has ever tried to reason with a recalcitrant sow will confirm. The pig, too, shares the haphazard breeding cycle of its masters – kid and lamb would not have been available at this time of year.

Quantity: Serves 6.
Time: About 2½ hours intermittent attention.

Equipment: A spit is best, a large roasting tin will do.

3lb/1.5kg sucking-pig   1 large cube of fat bacon
½ pint/300ml beer

Wipe the piglet well, singe off any stray hairs, salt the belly cavity but do not salt the outside, and score the skin in a diamond pattern with a very sharp knife.

Roast the piglet on the barbecue. Or spit-roast it. If you are using the oven, preheat it to 400°F/200°C/Gas 6 and put the piglet straight on to the rack above a baking tray containing an inch of boiling water. Experts recommend tucking a champagne bottle inside the belly cavity to keep it prettily in shape.

The piglet will take 2–2½ hours to roast crisp and delicious. Baste the skin throughout the cooking with the bacon chunk spitted on a toasting fork, dipped in beer.

Serve the sucking-pig with a mountain of braised sauerkraut spiked with cumin – or fresh finely-shredded cabbage cooked in drippings and its own juices, if it has been a mild winter.

EVE AND FEAST OF THE EPIPHANY: JANUARY 5TH–6TH

Twelfth Night is the eve of the day the Three Kings, Gaspar, Melchior and Balthazar, alias the Three Wise Men, arrived in Bethlehem to lay their gifts at the feet of the Holy Infant.

The Three Kings sprang to stardom in northern Europe when their relics were brought to Cologne from Milan during the twelfth century. The miracle plays which followed their installation made popular heroes of the three: dark-skinned Gaspar had all the jokes, and eventually turned into Kasperle – the German Punch. The Reformation ousted the three from their favoured position in the church, and transferred their characters to the Punch-and-Judy shows which remain popular children's entertainment all through German-influenced Europe. I saw a fine version in Ghent last year. The sage Gaspar would no doubt have been a little surprised by his truncheon-wielding, tricorned *alter ego*.

Italy has stood by a rather older tradition. Diplomat's wife Mrs Hugh Fraser remembered the Epiphany Witch of her Roman childhood in her memoirs in 1911.

> On Twelfth Night came the Befana, the great Epiphany Fair in Piazza Navona. With wildly beating hearts we used to depart, accompanied by a trusty body-guard of servants. By that time the air was full of the wildest din, tin trumpets, penny whistles, and strident rattles all in full blast, so that speech was useless and we could only hold tight to guiding hands and let ourselves be led around the Piazza, stopping at every booth on the way to spend our money on the bright tin toys and strange sweets which were the speciality of the season. We had hardly heard of Santa Claus, but the 'Befana', the kind witch who walks on the housetops and brings toys to good children and rods to naughty ones, was a very real personage to us.

January 6th remains the day of gifts round most of the Mediterranean – even though Father Christmas is fast gaining ground as the chief present-giver from his rivals the Three Kings, old Bishop Nicholas, and the Italian Befana. At the moment some lucky Mediterranean children enjoy a double festival of gifts as the transition is made to what seems inevitably a uniform celebration on December 25th.

France celebrates Epiphany with a rich cake in which a bean is buried, the *galette des rois* – the recipient of the bean being chosen King of the Feast. The origin of the custom has been claimed by the monks of Besançon who, in the eleventh century, chose their abbot by means of a small coin buried in a loaf of bread. There is little doubt that the ritual has pre-Christian roots in the Roman Saturnalia's method of choosing a Lord of Misrule. After the Revolution, the *galette* was considered un-civic-minded. The lucky token became a miniature phrygian cap and the festive cake was rebaptized *gâteau de l'égalité*. In recent times the bean has been transformed into pretty little china favours – boats, cars, trains, or lucky cats.

In the English Midlands, a few of the old pagan crop-blessing ceremonies remained attached to Twelfth Night – the day which, in the old calendar, was celebrated as Christmas Day and still is, in some parts of eastern Europe. Gloucestershire farm-workers were given caraway cakes soaked in cider by their employers – echoing the original *galette* of northern France, which was almost certainly a cider-drenched cake. At Glastonbury, the thorn tree which grew from Joseph of Aramathea's staff was expected to bloom at midnight on Twelfth Night. After an hour the blossoms would fall, to be gathered and treasured for luck – an event witnessed among a large crowd by a Mrs Leather (as reported by the ethnologist Christina Hole) in 1908.

It was a local custom to light twelve bonfires – and then, with a fine sense of theatre, a thirteenth one for Judas Iscariot, which would be stamped out immediately. In Herefordshire and Worcestershire, where cattle were important members of the household, the wassail bowl and a large ring of plum cake was carried out to the cattle byre. The cake was hung on the horns of the best ox, and if he tossed it forwards, the omens were good and the bailiff claimed it. If he tossed it backwards, it belonged to the mistress of the house, and the omens were not so good. Afterwards there was a Twelfth Night supper in the farmhouse for the farm-workers, of which the centrepiece was a magnificent cake containing a bean and sometimes a pea as well – the same tradition as that which is still found in France today. The bean marked the King of the Bean or Epiphany King, and the girl who found the pea was the Queen.

The bean ceremony disappeared in England during the eighteenth century, but the cake remained popular for another fifty years. In the run-up to Epiphany, all the pastry cooks' windows in London and the market towns would fill up with cakes – large and small, rich dark cakes, full of fruit, heavily iced, and lavishly decorated with stars, flowers, crowns, and little figures, of the Three Kings. But by the middle of the nineteenth century the newer festival of Christmas had claimed both the fun and the cakes.

Over in Sweden, Knut's Day used to be celebrated on January 6th, but the feast was moved to December 13th after a seventeenth-century reform of the calendar. Many Swedes still end their Christmas festivities on this day – dismantling the decorations, throwing out the tree, and going back to work. When the tree is stripped, the household has a little party when the children can eat up the edible ornaments which decorated it – ginger biscuits and sweets. Knut's Day used to be a time for masquerade, with men and boys dressing up as 'Old Knut' and playing tricks on the neighbours – a custom particularly energetically observed in Uppland, just north of Stockholm, an area settled by Walloons whose tradition this was.

France still keeps relics of this Twelfth Night visiting. On the Eve of Epiphany in the countryside of Normandy, boys and girls go from door to door in their neighbourhood with a collecting basket, serenading the neighbours with the songs of the season, in return for which they receive little presents, sweets and a few coins.

Orthodox Europe celebrates the *Ta Fota*, the lights, with a service for the blessing of the seas and rivers – Mediterranean Europe, particularly the sailors of Greece, cradle of Orthodoxy, naturally considered the sea the most important element, providing as it did both highway and sustenance. Throughout Greece the priests lead processions to the water's edge to bless the quays and ships – a ceremony which is followed by enthusiastic celebrations in each harbour's *tavernas*.

All good things have to come to an end – and Epiphany is the last of the great feasts of Christmas. Winters were long and hard in the old days. Those dependent on the growing season, as was everyone until recent times, could only wait in patience and hope for the spring. The midwinter festivals renewed men's spirits and confirmed their faith in nature – quite apart from the efficacy of the feasting as an elbow-jog for the gods. The celebrations made more bearable the inevitable deprivations as the larder and store-cupboard emptied. The rich cakes of the Provençal Twelfth Night bring the Christmas festivities to a rousing conclusion.

THE EPIPHANY CAKES OF FRANCE

There are a great many versions of this cake-with-a-bean to be found throughout France and those neighbouring countries which share French gastronomic traditions. The most ancient recipes are the yeast-raised breads such as the *couronne de Provence*. Perhaps the most delicious are the almond-stuffed, butter-rich *galettes* of the sophisticated pastry-cooks of Paris.

Here is a seventeeth-century account of the *galette*-distributing ritual (which varies little from region to region) as performed in Marseilles:

After grace has been said and everyone is seated, the cake in which a bean has been hidden in order that he who receives it may be recognized as lord of the Feast, is placed before the head of the household by who ever has been deputized for this duty. Usually it is a young child – if not, the youngest present is selected.

The cake is served in a pretty dish or on a snow-white linen napkin, already neatly divided into pieces, so that there shall be no cheating.

The bearer of the cake asks the head of the household, with great solemnity, to whom each piece of the cake should be given. The head of the household replies that one piece should be given to God, and the rest distributed to those present, in their natural order of seniority.

ALMOND SHORTBREAD
Galette aux amandes (France)

A simple shortbread biscuit, this is a rural housewives' *galette* – the easiest and most quickly prepared of the Epiphany cakes. It remains a popular recipe in northern France, where, as throughout the whole of northern Europe, there is an ancient tradition of pastry-making based on the butter and wheat of the fertile heartland. Only the best goes into festival food.

Quantity: Serves 6–8.
Time: 1 hour intermittent attention.
Equipment: A sieve and a mixing bowl. A baking tray and a cooling rack. A golden trinket, a silver coin, or a butter bean.

8oz/250g flour	4oz/100g ground almonds
6oz/175g softened butter	4 egg yolks
4oz/100g caster sugar	1–2 tablespoons warm water

Sieve the flour into the bowl and mix in the ground almonds and the sugar.

Beat the yolks lightly together and work them, with the softened butter, into the flour mixture with the tips of your fingers. Work in enough water to give a soft, malleable dough ball. Stick the trinket, coin or bean in the middle.

Preheat the oven to 450°F/230°C/Gas 8.

Rinse the baking tray with cold water and flatten the dough ball straight on to the sheet, working it out with a floured fist until you have a *galette* about 12in/30cm across. Make sure the hidden secret cannot be seen. Mark the top with royal arabesques and curlicues of an Eastern nature.

Put the *galette* in the hot oven to bake light brown and crisp. 20 minutes should be enough, but keep an eye on it — ovens are so variable.

When the *galette* is firm and crisp, transfer it to the rack to cool.

Break the *galette* into as many pieces as there are guests present. Whoever gets the lucky morsel is monarch of the festivities, and can choose a consort.

THREE KINGS ALMOND PASTRY
Galette des rois Parisienne (France)

This is the version of the Epiphany *galette* most generally found on sale in French *pâtisseries*. In Paris it was the traditional gift of the baker to his regular customers.

Quantity: Serves 6.
Time: Intermittent attention for 1½ hours.
Equipment: A mixing bowl and a sieve. A pastry board and rolling pin. A baking tray and cooling rack. A lucky token or a dried bean.

The pastry

9oz/275g flour	½ teaspoon salt
7oz/200g unsalted butter	approx. ¼ pint/150ml water

The filling

4oz/100g ground almonds	4 drops almond essence (this is made from bitter
1 tablespoon kirsch or brandy	almonds)
2 egg yolks	3oz/75g sugar
4oz/100g softened unsalted butter	

Make sure everything, including the utensils, are cool. See that the butter is firm without being hard.

Take a large bowl and sieve in the flour with the salt. Cut in 3oz/75g of the butter with a sharp knife until you have a mixture like fine breadcrumbs. Mix in enough water to make a paste which when worked a little does not stick to the fingers. Knead lightly. Set the dough aside for 20 minutes, with the rest of the butter beside it so that pastry and butter reach the same temperature.

Roll out the pastry to a thickness of about ¼in/0.5cm. Dot it with a third of the remaining butter, cut into small pieces the size of hazelnuts. Then fold the pastry into three, like a napkin, and again into three in the opposite direction. Set aside for 20 minutes.

Go through the last process twice more, adding the same amount of butter each time. Set the pastry aside for 20 minutes after each process. Then leave another 20 minutes before using it.

Divide the pastry in half. Roll it out into a pair of rounds about 10in/25cm in diameter and let it rest for the last time while you make the filling.

Heat the oven to 375°F/190°C/Gas 5.

Mix the ground almonds with the sugar and the butter, cut into little pieces. Add the almond essence, liquor and egg yolks and work together until you have a smooth paste.

Rinse the baking tray through cold water. Transfer one round of pastry to the tray, and spread the almond paste over the pastry, leaving a border round the edge. Bury the lucky token or bean in the almond paste. Dampen the pastry edge and cover with the second round of pastry. Press both edges together with a fork. With a sharp knife, mark the top with a lattice pattern without cutting right through to the filling. Paint the top with a little beaten egg.

Bake the *galette* in the oven for 30 minutes or so, until pastry is crisp, dry and well browned. Transfer to the rack to cool.

Accompany the *galette* with a glass of kirsch or sweet wine, and see who is the Lord of the Feast.

THE CROWN OF PROVENCE
La couronne de Provence (France)

This is sometimes made with butter to make it particularly special. I rather prefer it with Provençal olive oil – the flavour is subtle and delicate and complements the citrus flavours perfectly.

Quantity: Makes a crown to be shared among 6–8.
Time: Start 3–4 hours ahead.
Equipment: A sieve. A mixing bowl. A clean cloth. A baking tray and cooling rack. Lucky tokens.

12oz/350g flour	1 teaspoon salt
1oz/25g fresh yeast (½oz/12g dried)	1 tablespoon milk
1 whole egg	4oz/100g sugar
2 tablespoons olive oil	zest and juice of 1 orange and 1 lemon
2 tablespoons chopped crystallized fruit	2oz/50g slivered almonds

Make sure everything is at room temperature – nice and warm.

Sieve the flour into the warm bowl with the salt. Put the fresh yeast to dissolve in the milk, with a pinch of sugar to get it all going. Pour the yeast mixture into a well in the flour and sprinkle the surface with a little flour. Leave for 10 minutes or so for the yeast to start working. (If using dried yeast, follow the packet directions.)

Meanwhile fork the eggs lightly together with the sugar and the orange and lemon zest and make up to ¼ pint/150ml with orange and lemon juice. Add the oil and pour the mixture into the well in the flour with the yeast.

Knead all together thoroughly, pulling and pushing with the ball of your hand, until the dough is smooth and elastic. Add extra flour or warm water if necessary. Form the dough into a smooth cushion, ends tucked neatly underneath. Put the dough back into the bowl, cover loosely with a damp cloth or clingfilm, and put it in a warm place to rise for 1–2 hours, until doubled in bulk. This is a rich dough, so it takes longer than usual to rise.

Knock the dough down and knuckle it well to distribute the air. Work in the fruit and nuts quickly. Bury the tokens in the middle. Form the dough into a round flat cushion about 1in/2cm thick, and dig a hole in the middle with floured fingers. Pull the hole out until you have a round crown of dough – it needs coaxing as it bounces back.

Transfer the crown to the buttered baking sheet. Cover it as before and put it back into your chosen warm place to rise once more. This should take about 30 minutes – the dough is ready when it has doubled in thickness and bounces back when you press a fingertip into its surface.

Preheat the oven to 375°F/190°C/Gas 5.

Nick the crown round its rim with kitchen scissors (dipped in cold water to stop the dough sticking to the blades). Brush the top with egg yolk and sprinkle with roughly crushed lump sugar to give the crown a pretty sparkle.

Bake for 35–40 minutes, turning the oven a little lower after the first 15 minutes, and keeping a careful eye on it to see it doesn't burn. Tap the base: if it sounds hollow, the bread is ready.

Remove from the oven and transfer to the rack to cool.

Serve with glasses of fruit syrup for the children, and sweet wine for the grown-ups.

ST VINCENT'S DAY: JANUARY 22ND

January 22nd 1863: January is come and well-nigh gone too, and winter is nearly over. Today is the Feast of St Vincent, the patron Saint of Bagnères, and the people are all in holiday costume, feasting and dancing. You cannot imagine what a pretty sight it was. Fancy a regular drop scene for a theatre. A green meadow by the road side, in the middle of which three *ménétriers*, or fiddlers, were seated in chairs placed upon a deal table, fiddling away merrily to two or three hundred peasant lads and lasses, all decked out in their holiday suits . . . The Pyrenese are passionately fond of dancing, and, although the priests reprobate it, take advantage of every holiday to pursue their favourite amusement. (From Mary Eyre's *A Lady's Walks in The South of France*)

Miss Eyre's rural idyll was one of the many small local festivals which enrich the lives of the country-dwellers of the Mediterranean – exceptional only because it is so early in the year, while the weather is still wet and cold (see p. 226 for the midsummer pilgrimages). Such celebrations are always held in the open air, and often take the form of a walk to the local shrine – whether saint or Virgin – after which a simple portable meal is enjoyed. This is usually matured cheese (made from ewe's milk in this shepherding area), home-cured salt ham, good fresh bread from the local baker, wine or cider, and may be a slice of onion or a rub of garlic for bite. The festive element is provided by the setting, the music and dancing, and the sweetmeats and cakes special to the occasion – across southern France, these are likely to include a variation on the Provençal enriched sweet bread (see fougasse, p. 59) – here known as a *pastis*. But there will be others, such as this beautiful *croustade*, which reflect regional strengths.

PYRENEAN PRUNE PIE
Estirat or *croustade aux pruneaux* (French Basque)

This delicious flaky double-crust tart – crisp, buttery, and combining the techniques of noodle-making, puff pastry and filo – is sometimes made with apples.

The autumn's crop of plums, plentiful in the orchards tucked into the fertile narrow valleys of the Pyrenees, the range which divides France from Spain, are dried in the crisp frosty air of the early winter. Hams and prunes are best cured in the cold dry breezes of the mountains – those who live down on the wet plain will send their produce up to their hill-dwelling cousins for wind-curing.

Quantity: Serves 6.
Time: Start the day before. 2 hours intermittent attention.
Equipment: A sieve and mixing bowl. A rolling pin and board. An 8–10in/20–25cm round baking tin and a cooling rack.

2lb/1kg prunes
1 glass Armagnac or brandy
1lb/500g plain flour
2 eggs, lightly forked together
10oz/300g butter, creamed
4oz/100g sugar

½ pint/300ml orange-flower water, or the juice and
 grated rind of 1 orange
½ teaspoon salt
approx. ¼ pint/150ml water
2oz/50g goose fat or lard, melted

Put the prunes to soak overnight in the orange and Armagnac.

Next day, make the pastry. Sieve the flour and salt into the mixing bowl. Make a well in the middle and pour in the eggs. Work the flour into the eggs with your hands, pulling it in gradually from the edges, adding the water as you go, until you have a soft smooth dough – exactly as for home-made pasta. Cover the ball of dough and put it aside to rest for 10 minutes to develop the gluten.

Stone the prunes (crack a few stones and extract the kernels) and chop them roughly with enough juice to moisten them.

Roll out the dough to ¼in/0.5cm thick. Spread all the softened butter over it, leaving a finger's width of a rim. Fold the dough over itself in three and roll it out again – you will need to flour it well. Leave it to rest again for 10 minutes. Repeat the operation three times. Finally roll it out as thin as possible – paper-thin shows real skill. Leave it to dry for 1 hour.

Heat the oven to 450°F/230°C/Gas 8.

Brush the sheet of pastry with drops of melted goose fat or lard – easy to do with a paint-brush. Use a quarter of the pastry to line the tart tin – you should manage 3–4 layers laid gently on top of each other. Spread in the prune filling and sprinkle on half the sugar. Damp the edges of the pie, and top with more layers of pastry and the rest of the sugar. Trim and neaten the edges, glaze the top with a little egg-yolk or milk, and scatter with the trimmed leaves of pastry.

Bake for 30 minutes, until the pastry is crisp and well browned.

Sprinkle the pie with a little extra Armagnac as it comes out of the oven.

BURNS' NIGHT: JANUARY 25TH

January 25th is the night on which all good Scotsmen celebrate the anniversary of the birth, in 1759, of their national poet, the great Robert Burns. It is an occasion to be marked with piping, poetry, haggis and malt whisky – a good rumbustious *ceiledh* as befits the roistering, womanizing customsman.

The Burns' Night dinner should be well punctuated by readings – or even recitals by the more dedicated – of the great man's better-known works (this is not a night for subtleties). 'The Cotter's Saturday Night', followed by 'Holy Willy's Prayer', concluding with a spirited rendering of 'To a Mouse' and 'Tam O'Shanter', would fit the bill.

The haggis, essential fodder for the celebrants, must be greeted with its Ode, accompanied by the appropriate gestures:

> Fair fa' your honest sonsie face,
> Great chieftain o' the pudding race!
> Aboon them a ye take your place,
> Painch, tripe, or thairm:
> Weel are ye worthy o a grace
> As lang's my airm.

And so on and so forth, with the magestic haggis (a great deal larger than any of our modern offerings) daggered open in the third verse, to gush forth their entrails bright, warm-reekin', rich. The whole eight stanzas can be found in any popular anthology.

HAGGIS
(Scotland)

A ready-made haggis is already fully cooked. It's just a matter of reheating it. This, as the English soldiers discovered when outflanked by the fast-moving Scots, makes it perfect convenience food for eating on the run.

Quantity: Serves 4.
Time: Allow 30 minutes.
Equipment: A large pan with a lid. A draining spoon.

a haggis weighing 1½–2lb/750g–1kg   water

Bring plenty of water to the boil in the large pan. When it is boiling properly, take the lid off and put in the haggis. Bring the water back to the boil again, but allow only a single belch, then turn the heat down to simmer. Give it 25–30 minutes at least – the water can be kept at a gentle simmer for an hour if necessary.

Be warned: if you bring the haggis to the boil from cold and leave it boiling, it will burst.

Alternatively, heat the haggis in a tightly-covered casserole in a low oven – 30 minutes will be fine.

Serve the haggis as piping hot as the piper who accompanies it to table, with mashed potatoes and mashed 'neeps' – swedes.

You may if you please now pour a dram of whisky over your reekin' spoonful. If you prefer, as I do, to take your haggis in its natural state and your whisky likewise, it is time to drink to the health of HM Customs and Excise who were far-sighted enough to give employment to Scotland's favourite prodigal poet. If poor old Rabbie had had a penny of the duty payable on every bottle drunk in his honour since then, he would never have died with a pair of begging letters dropping from the tip of his pen.

PAN HAGGIS
(Scotland)

If you're prepared to forgo the Poet's trenching of the gushing entrails, a simple pan haggis doesn't take long to prepare and is almost as 'warm-reekin'.

Quantity: Serves 4.
Time: Start 2 hours ahead.
Equipment: A large lidded pan.

1lb/500g pig's or lamb's liver
1 pint/600ml water
salt and pepper
1 teaspoon dried thyme

3 medium onions, skinned and quartered
4oz/125g pinhead oatmeal
6 oz/175g grated butcher's suet

Simmer the liver and onions in the water for 30–40 minutes.

Meanwhile toast the oatmeal in a heavy pan or in the oven until nicely browned. When the meat is well cooked, remove it with a draining spoon. Reserve the stock.

Grate the liver and onions (in a processor if you prefer), and stir in the toasted oatmeal, suet, thyme, salt and plenty of freshly ground black pepper. Moisten with sufficient stock to give a softish consistency. Lid tightly and cook gently on the top of the stove. Check the pan and stir frequently, adding more liquid as necessary, for 1–1½ hours.

If you prefer, the pan haggis can be cooked in a heavy lidded casserole in a low oven – these habits of using top-heat and boiling evolved in a kitchen where scarce fuel ensured there was no baking oven.

CHRISTENING FEASTS

The Christian Church requires that babies be baptized – brought to church, blessed with water and given their chosen saint's name – and vouched for by godparents as soon as possible after their birth. In much of Catholic Europe, the given-name is often that of the saint on whose day the child was born. This includes the various dates consecrated to the Virgin Mary, so there are plenty of Immaculate Conceptions and Assumptions in Spain and Italy. It is customary to celebrate your saint's day as your own anniversary, even if your real birthday does not coincide.

Kâroly Viski detailed pre-war rural births in Roman Catholic Hungary:

In some places the baptism feast is on the day on which the christening took place, in others it is three or four days, occasionally even three of four weeks later, that is, once the worst days are over and the mother can also be up and take part in the entertaining. At a strict baptism only the women may take part, but often the men of the household are also allowed in. In some places there is a christening dinner, in others a supper. Amongst the Matyos, even in the poorest house, there are at least five or six courses. The menu: beef soup, boiled meat, cabbage with pork, chicken soup with noodles, a milk pudding with butter or honey, or sprinkled with sugar; 'paprika' chicken; fried sweets and naturally, wine.

At the end of supper the child is put on the table for a little while in beautifully clean swaddles, and then everyone gives something for the babe.

In Germany, christenings also involved considerable expense for the godfather and godmother – they were reckoned glory for the Lord and hard on your pocket. In Silesia at the christening lunch the pastor would sit at the head of the long table – men on one side and women on the other. It was the schoolmaster's duty to ladle out the soup, and the proud father's to refill the glasses. Outside the house, a beer-barrel announced free drinks for all comers – an expensive round in these days of motorized transport.

In France, the celebration remains a family affair. Childless herself, Mademoiselle Paulette of Villedieu in upper Provence remembered, in 1988, the christening parties given for her nephews and nieces before the war.

We had the meal at midday, after the service. The food was always the best available, mostly prepared in advance. We had big plates of home-cured pure-pork sausages cut in slices, served with sweet unsalted butter, cornichons and bread, salt-dried ham, chicken – never soup, no one has soup at lunchtime. And salads of course – whatever could be found in season, wild-gathered as well as from the vegetable patch; chicory, frisée, dandelion, the big hairy leaves of les mourres, and big dishes of fried aubergines with tomatoes, cooked slowly with olive oil and herbs in my grandfather's bakery.

The housewives of Britain were kept busiest before the birth, before they themselves retired to handle the equally specialized demands of labour, making rich fruit cakes for the Merry Meal. These goodies, including a 'groaning-cake' and a huge cartwheel of 'groaning-cheese' were left out on the table for the father and any other interested, but not directly involved, visitors. Meanwhile the mother and midwives concentrated on the serious stuff in the birth-chamber.

The cheese and cake would be divided into portions – called 'whangs-o'-luck' in some districts – usually by the father, sometimes by the attending doctor. If the cake-cutter cut himself in the process dire misfortune would fall on the baby within the year. Unmarried girls might tuck their portion under their pillow so that they would dream of a future husband. In Oxfordshire, the cake was cut in from the middle to leave a lucky ring of cake for the baby to be passed through on its christening day.

The 'groaning' victuals echo an allied ritual, recorded in her pre-war English Folklore by Christina Hole, who found traces, in mid-twentieth-century Herefordshire, of that primitive activity known as the 'couvade' – in which the father-to-be is thought to suffer some of the symptoms of pregnancy and may well retire to bed for the actual birth. Ethnologist G.L. Gomme mentions a further refinement in Yorkshire, where the relatives of a mother who refused to finger the father of an illegitimate baby would search the village until they found a man ill in bed. The invalid was then reckoned the missing parent by virtue of his simulated accouchement. Today's view of the joint responsibility and involvement of both parents in the processes of pregnancy and giving birth may perhaps be an echo of a far older preoccupation.

GROANING-CAKE
(England)

A slice of this delicious fruit cake, and a piece of cheese, should be offered for luck to the first person of the opposite sex encountered on the way back from the christening. Hamilton Jenkin had a report of being made such a gift in St Ives in 1932. Make the cake at least 2 weeks ahead and store it in a tin to mature. Serve it with a slice of mature cheese – Cheddar, Lancashire or Cheshire. The same mixture makes a fine Christmas cake.

Quantity: Yields a 4lb/2kg loaf.
Time: Start 2 weeks ahead. 20–25 minutes. Allow 2½ hours oven time.
Equipment: A sieve and mixing bowl. A large round cake tin and a cooling rack.

11oz/325g self-raising flour	11oz/325g butter
10oz/300g soft brown sugar	6 eggs
1lb/500g currants, sultanas and raisins	4oz/100g glacé cherries
4oz/100g mixed peel	1 glass sweet sherry
1 teaspoon mixed spice	½ teaspoon grated nutmeg
4oz/100g ground almonds	

Sieve the flour. Cream the butter and sugar together with a wooden spoon until light and fluffy. Beat in the eggs one by one, adding a tablespoon of the flour if the mixture goes grainy. Fold in the flour and all the rest of the ingredients.

Heat the oven to 325°F/170°C/Gas 3.

Butter the cake tin and line it with buttered paper. Pour in the cake mixture. Bake the cake for about 2–2¼ hours, until a skewer thrust into its heart comes out clean.

CHRISTENING TIAN
Tian d'aubergines (France)

In Provence and throughout Italy, Greece and Turkey, housewives will dry the final crop of aubergines, sweet and firm from the last of the summer sun, for the winter larder. Alternatively, in areas where the olive plantations ensure a good harvest from November to February, the crop might be put up in jars with last year's olive oil, in anticipation of the winter's replenishment.

Quantity: Serves 10.
Time: Start 3–4 hours ahead. 40 minutes. 2–2½ hours cooking time.
Equipment: A frying pan. A sieve and bowl. A large shallow earthenware dish (*tian*).

3lb/1.5kg aubergines	approx. 1 pint/600ml olive oil
2–3 cloves garlic	2 onions, skinned and sliced
1lb/500g tomatoes, sliced	1 teaspoon dried thyme
1 teaspoon dried rosemary	salt and pepper
1 glass white wine	8oz/250g home-made breadcrumbs

Hull and thickly slice the aubergines. Heat the oil in the frying pan and, when it is not yet smoking, put in the garlic and onions. Let them soften and take a little colour for 6–7 minutes. Remove them to a sieve over a bowl and let them drip while you gently fry the aubergines. You will need to return the extra drippings to the pan as you fry. As the aubergine slices soften, transfer them into the sieve. Continue until all are used up. Layer the aubergines, garlic and onions and uncooked tomatoes in the *tian*, sprinkling with herbs and salt and pepper as you go, and finishing with a layer of tomatoes. Shower in the wine and trickle over any remaining oily drippings from the bowl, or use extra oil.

Heat the oven to 325°F/170°C/Gas 3.

Bake the *tian* for 2–2½ hours. After an hour, sprinkle on a hat of the breadcrumbs and an extra trickle of oil.

Serve with slices of salt ham and sausages and the most diverse green salads you can gather, dressed with olive oil, wine vinegar and spring's first tender leaves of wild garlic.

HUNGARIAN FRIEND'S BASKET

These are the traditional offerings of the godmother to the mother of her godchild. Delivered beautifully wrapped and ready-prepared, the gift offers a practical solution to two perennial problems – fortifying the mother and feeding her family. As a gift, it beats a silver spoon or a baby-shower into a cocked hat. Apart from the following two made-up dishes, the basket should contain plenty of bread, a solid storable cake made with dried fruit, and some spicy biscuits and a few sweets for the rest of the children.

BEEF AND SAFFRON BROTH
(Hungary)

A good strong beef broth is ideal for setting any new mother on the right road to recovery.

Quantity: Makes 4 pints/2 litres.
Time: Allow 6 hours at least for the simmering.
Equipment: A roasting tin. A large soup pan. A thermos for transport.

1 beef shin bone, sawn into pieces	1 oxtail, jointed
2lb/1kg shin of beef	2–3 onions, not skinned but quartered
2–3 carrots, scrubbed	2–3 sticks celery, washed
1 sprig of marjoram	1 small bunch of parsley
½ teaspoon peppercorns	3–4 strands saffron (just enough to add fragrance
1 heaped teaspooon salt	and colour)

Roast the shin bone in a hot oven until it is brown and shiny – this preliminary toasting improves the flavour and colour of the broth out of all recognition.

Put the roasted bones and all the rest of the ingredients in the soup pot, with 6 pints/3.5 litres of water to cover.

Bring to the boil, skim, and turn down to simmer. Leave overnight, loosely lidded, if you have a very gentle and good-natured hot-plate. Or leave it simmering (no bubbles should break the surface) in the oven or on the top of the cooker for at least 6 hours.

Strain and pour into the thermos – there should be about 4 pints/2.5 litres. Put a packet of egg-noodles in the basket as well – they cook quickly in the broth and will give added strength where it is needed.

MUSHROOM PAPRIKA CHICKEN
(Hungary)

Probably more suitable for fortifying the fortunate father and his friends, this is a deliciously rich dish, with plenty of paprika to keep the winter cold at bay.

Quantity: Serves 4–6.
Time: 2 hours intermittent attention.
Equipment: A roomy lidded casserole.

1 chicken
2 day-old white bread rolls
4oz/100g chopped mushrooms (Hungarians
   have a wide year-round repertoire of
   wild-gathered fungi)
2 tablespoons chopped parsley
1 tablespoon paprika

salt and pepper
8 fl oz/200ml milk
2oz/50g lard
4oz/100g minced pork or bacon
2 eggs
2 onions, peeled and chopped
8 fl oz/200ml water

To finish
8 fl oz/200ml soured cream (or cream with a squeeze of lemon)

Wipe the chicken and loosen the skin of the breast and second joints. Salt it inside and out.

Crumble the bread and put it to soak in the milk for 10 minutes. Fry the mushrooms for a few minutes in a little of the lard. Work the mushrooms, minced meat, eggs and parsley together with the soaked bread until you have a soft stuffing. Season it – not too much salt if you have included bacon. Stuff the mixture under the chicken's loosened skin anywhere you can.

Melt the rest of the lard in the casserole and turn the chicken in the hot fat until it is lightly browned all over. Remove the bird and put in the chopped onions. Let them fry for a moment to take colour. Stir in the paprika and pour in the water. When it boils, return the chicken to the pot. Lid and simmer over a low heat, shaking the pot every now and again and turning the chicken, until the bird is quite tender.

Remove the chicken and joint it. Stir the cream into the pan juices and heat gently. Return the chicken joints to the sauce in the casserole. Pack it all up neatly in the basket.

CHRISTENING CHINE
(England)

In Lincolnshire the chine – the long fillet which runs on either side of the backbone – was the proper joint to celebrate a christening. In the 1920s, a correspondent of Florence White's English Folk Cookery Association supplied the anatomical direction for the joint: 'The christening or fore-chine was cut down each side of the backbone of a pig and it was so called because one was generally saved for a christening.'

Quantity: Serves 12–16.
Time: Start a day ahead. 30 minutes to prepare. 2 hours to cook.

Equipment: A large saucepan. String and a boiling bag.

a neck chine of bacon (about 12lb/6kg), boned
1 lettuce, shredded
½ pint/300ml roughly chopped chives or
   leek tops

4 pints/2.5 litres parsley, roughly chopped (lots)
a dozen blackcurrant and raspberry leaves
2 tablespoons roughly chopped marjoram
1 teaspoon ground mace

Soak the bacon overnight if your butcher thinks it necessary. Lay the joint skin side down on a board and cut deep slits ½in/1cm apart in the meat, taking care not to cut through the skin.

Stuff the cuts with the herbs and mace, thoroughly mixed together – a food processor does the job beautifully.

Tie the joint up neatly, wrap it in a boiling bag, and submerge it in a large panful of cold water. Bring it to the boil, turn down the heat, and simmer for 2 hours from the time the water boils.

Let the joint cool in the water.

February

Candlemas is the festival which marks, in Catholic countries, the Presentation in the Temple of the infant Christ by the Virgin Mary. In post-Reformation Britain, the feast left behind one or two baby-related customs – this is the day to rock an empty cradle in the hope of a child. The feast takes its name from the white candles which light the procession into church.

As usual, the roots of the celebration go deeper than the two millennia of Christianity. The glittering candles also mirror, and coincide with, the lighting of the Carnival fires – a victory of profane over sacred in which the Church has long agreed to concede the battle in order to win the war of Lent.

In France there are regional specialities which mark the day – various *beignets* and *galettes* and *crêpes* whose traditions are also shared with the celebrants of Carnival. The *mariottes* or *marionettes* of Montbard and the Côte d'Or are the most obviously pagan in origin. These are little cut-out puff-pastry figures of girls and boys, strongly reminiscent of the old fertility figurines. At Montbard they have their own legend: the washerwomen were at their labours in the town's fountain on a misty February 2nd when the spray from the stream wreathed up and revealed a company of water-fairies, crowned with spring blossoms, who danced in the mist like graceful *marionettes*.

The ladies went home and ever afterwards commemorated the delightful experience by baking biscuits in the shape of the fairies, decorated with five beans to indicate the crown, the eyes, the nose and the mouth. The pastries would then be taken to the fountain, where the heads were broken off and thrown in the water. If the fairies were pleased with the offering, the young people might expect to marry in the following year. This ritual was celebrated until 1939 – when most such customs vanished, leaving behind only the girl and boy figurines.

In Marseilles the *Candelouso* is celebrated with special little boat-shaped breads, called *navettes* or *naveto de Sant-Vitou* for St Victor, patron saint of the ancient port. Marseilles is naturally most concerned with ships, and the festival of the Purification evokes the legendary escape from the Holy Land and subsequent landing near Marseilles of the two Marys – the mother of James, and the Magdalene – who brought Christianity to Provence.

The *navettes* are distributed from, among other places, the church of Notre Dame de la Chandeleur/Feu-nouveau, shrine of the immortal Black Virgin, whose legend reaches back to Isis the seafarer, and whose image was said to have been carved by St Luke from a fennel root. To add a little extra spice, the Greeks who founded Marseilles always carried live coals high on the prows of their ships, enclosed in hollowed-out roots of the self-same giant fennel.

CANDLEMAS BOATS
Navettes de la Purification (France)

They came in all sizes. Little tiny ones the size of a toggle on a doll's bonnet; most of them narrow as a drumstick, marked with a pale line down the middle; others, mostly from the bakery, of impressively large dimensions worthy of those grand gentlemen, the lawyers and the rich merchants. All, made with snow-white flour and well-gilded by the oven, were perfumed with orange water. And there were too, in the rich *quartiers*, in the *pâtisseries*, enormous boats, as long as a child's canoe, gaily decorated with ribbons. (Renée Jouveau, *La Cuisine Provençale de Tradition Populaire*, Nîmes, 1976).

Quantity: Makes 12 little breads or 1 enormous one – whatever you please.
Time: Start 2–3 hours ahead. 1 hour intermittent attention.
Equipment: A sieve and a bowl. A baking tray and cooling rack.

12oz/350g flour
4oz/125g sugar
4oz/125g butter

1 teaspoon salt
1oz/25g fresh yeast (½oz/12g dried)
approx. ¼ pint/150ml orange-flower water (infuse a handful of orange-flowers [or zest] in boiling syrup for 10 minutes)

Sieve the flour and salt into the bowl, add the sugar, and rub in the yeast and the butter cut into little pieces. Work in enough orange-flower water to make a soft dough.

Knead all together thoroughly, pulling and pushing with the ball of your hand, until the dough is smooth and elastic.

Put the dough back into the bowl, cover loosely with a damp cloth or clingfilm, and put it in a warm place to rise for 1 hour.

Knock the dough down and knuckle it well to distribute the air.

Cut the dough into as many pieces as you mean to make *navettes*. Form each piece of dough into a long thin pointy sausage.

Put the *navettes* on the buttered baking tray and slash each one down the middle so that the dough parts in rising. Cover as before and put back into your chosen warm place to rise once more. This should take about 30 minutes – the dough is ready when it has doubled in thickness and bounces back when you press a fingertip into its surface.

Preheat the oven to 425°F/220°C/Gas 7.

Bake the *navettes* for 20 minutes, keeping a careful eye on them to see that they don't burn.

Remove and transfer to the rack to cool. Serve the Candlemas breads by candlelight, of course.

The lawyers of Marseilles have their annual banquet on this day, and after the *grand bouffe* they enjoy the first early strawberries from Beaudinard with their *navettes*.

ST VALENTINE'S DAY: FEBRUARY 14TH

The Roman martyr St Valentine is probably a composite of several saintly gentlemen — Valentine being as common a name in classical Rome as Smith or Jones in modern Britain. The leading contender, Bishop Valentine, was thrown into prison by the Emperor Claudius for aiding and abetting the outlawed Christians. So powerful was the good bishop's oratory that he managed to convert and baptize his jailor, Asterius. In recompense for this inconvenience, the Emperor, not unnaturally, had Valentine flogged and beheaded, as a warning to other such troublesome priests, on the Flaminian Way on February 14th, AD 269. It is this bloodthirsty, if everyday, event that we commemorate with hearts and flowers.

The anniversary does of course have little to do with the well-earned martyrdom of Bishop Valentine. The early Church merely substituted the name of a saint for a pagan festival — finding a simple renaming easier than trying to rewrite the calendar with one sweep of the pen. The re-baptized celebration was the Lupercalia, the festival of Juno and Pan, which began around the middle of February. One of the attendant ceremonies was the placing of the names of unmarried girls in a box, from which they were drawn by would-be partners at random — a custom clearly reflected in the unsigned Valentine cards of today. Throughout Europe the most popular form of this lottery became the placing of girls' names in one box and boys' names in another — future pairings being indicated as drawn.

The St Valentine's Day customs were taken up with enthusiasm in England. That prudent man of letters, Samuel Pepys, recorded the events of his own conjugal St Valentine's Day in his diary on February 14th, 1667:

> This morning came up to my wife's bedside (I being dressed myself) little Will Mercer to be her Valentine, and brought her name written upon blue paper in gold letters, done by himself, very pretty and we were both well pleased with it. But I am also this year my wife's Valentine, and it will cost me £5. But that I must have laid out if we had not been Valentines.

By the end of the Victorian era, these love-missives had changed character somewhat. George Long, writing in 1930, remembers the vulgar fun to be had in the stationers' shops of his youth, when the windows were:

> Full of gross caricatures of the most offensively personal character, known as Valentines. These criminal libels consisted of a most insulting portrait of some individual together with a quatrain of feeble verse calling attention to some physical or moral characteristic of the person, so worded as to be likely to lead to murder if he found out who sent it.

To each his own. The romantic Hungarians, in common with much of Europe, celebrate St Valentine's Day with honey-cake hearts pressed in centuries-old moulds. In Hungary, these are a speciality of the bakeries of the beautiful medieval town of Sarospatak. Such fairing-hearts were sold at church-ales — village festivals held on chosen Sundays in northern and eastern Europe, equivalent to the *romerías* and *ferias* of the south — for the young men to present to their sweethearts.

SAROSPATAK GINGERBREAD HEARTS
Gyömbérikalacs szív (Hungary)

Most of Europe has a repertoire of these moulded *pains d'épices* for feast-days. The basic dough, although it has to be prepared in advance, is beautifully easy to handle and mould – the precious imported spices make it festival food. To accompany this token of your affection – much more interesting than a Valentine card – offer your sweetheart a glass of the fragrant dark golden wine of Tokaj, rich and sweet as new honey. You would not have to go far to fetch it – Hungary's most famous vineyards are only just over the hills from Sarospatak.

Quantity: Makes 6 large hearts or 2–3 dozen small ones.
Time: Start a day ahead.
Equipment: A sieve and a mixing bowl. A rolling pin and board. 2–3 baking trays and a cooling rack.

14oz/425g flour	½ teaspoon salt
1 teaspoon baking powder	4oz/100g ground almonds
5oz/125g ground almonds	5oz/125g honey
5oz/125g molasses	3oz/75g brown sugar
5oz/125g butter, creamed	1 egg
juice and grated rind of 1 orange	1 teaspoon powdered cinnamon
½ teaspoon grated nutmeg	½ teaspoon powdered cloves

To finish
6oz/175g sieved icing sugar, mixed to a stiff paste with an egg white

Mix all the biscuit ingredients together to a smooth soft dough. Wrap it in clingfilm and leave it to rest overnight – you'll find it much easier to work in the morning.

Roll the pastry out with a rolling pin on a board to a thickness of ¼in/1cm, dusting everything well with icing sugar to stop it sticking.

Heat the oven to 450°F/230°C/Gas 8.

Cut out hearts as small or as large as your fancy dictates. Lay them out on the baking tray. Bake them in the hot oven for 10–12 minutes, until well browned. Transfer them to the rack to cool.

Use all your skill with the icing sugar to pipe Hungarian gypsy patterns on the hearts – flowers and curls and baroque featherings and furbelows.

CARNIVAL AND PRE-LENT: EARLY FEBRUARY

Prince Carnival, changeling offspring of the Roman Saturnalia and the Greek Kronia, is celebrated with varying degrees of enthusiasm throughout Europe. An uneasy truce holds until the Christian fast of Lent beats the masked monarch into reluctant retreat. Even so, the Christian rituals of Shrove Tuesday and Ash Wednesday are not easily unravelled from the pagan excesses which precede them.

Carnival is dependent for its dates on the peripatetic festival of Easter. Traditionally the period begins on the Saturday night three weeks before the beginning of Lent, and runs up to Ash Wednesday, which in the Western (Julian) calendar falls between February 9th and March 15th. The Orthodox Catholic Church sticks to the old calendar, which puts the start of the Orthodox fast some two weeks later.

Such movable feasts do not suit the convenience of the municipal officials who run today's popular events. The authorities have mostly managed to settle on a fixed date – the first week in February seems preferred – to welcome the forces of disruption. But the enforcers of law and order have not completely won the battle – after all, the wily princeling has not yet lost his 2,000-year war with mother Church herself. He, as befits his unruly nature, is liable to pop up any time from mid-November to Ash Wednesday, masked and wild-eyed, beribboned and insulting, strumming his discords, from a darkened archway in old Seville, round a sharp street-corner in Arles or Utrecht. He is most at home among the young, in the university towns, where he is the chief instigator of those rites of passage most appropriate to the rising sap of his worshippers.

The most obvious features of the ancient festivals are maintained in our modern carnivals. Disguise was (and remains) the essence of Carnival – men dressed as women, girls as soldiers, both sexes costumed as animals. Secure in their anonymity, the celebrants could give themselves up to the wildest of orgies. In Orthodox Greece today, the celebration of *aprokriess* is viewed by the Church with considerable disapproval – particularly in impoverished rural areas where the old gods still warm a seat at the hearth. The early Church's struggle against pagan authority was too long and hard to allow the least accommodation of such dangerous enemies. She surrendered too many hostages in her time. At Ephesus the Dionysiac orgies which predated Carnival included human sacrifice – Bishop Timothy, St Paul's correspondent, was in all probability a victim.

Anthropologist John Lawson had first-hand experience of the remnants of these customs in Greece in 1910:

Although the savage orgies of old time have dwindled into harmless mummery, their most constant feature, the wearing of strange disguises, remains unchanged; and the occasion too is still a winter-festival—either some part of the Twelve Days, or the carnival preceding Lent. I myself saw such a custom enacted in Scyros. The young men of the town array themselves in huge capes made of goat-skin, reaching to the hips or lower, and provided with holes for the arms. . . Thus in various grades of goat-like attire, the young men and boys traverse the town, stopping here and there to leap and dance, or anon at some friendly door to imbibe spirituous encouragement to further efforts.

In northern Europe, *Fastnacht* or *Fasching* or *Karneval* is celebrated with particular enthusiasm throughout Germany and her neighbours. People wear fancy dress, dance in the streets and hold the authorities to ridicule. In Basle the festival lasts for three days and nights, during which everyone dresses up in fraternity livery, dictated by the brotherhoods each year: ducks, fairies, chocolate bars or whatever. Prince and Princess Carnival parade through the streets accompanied by a troupe of girls dressed as Hussars – a custom which the United States has to thank for its drum majorettes.

In Alpine villages tradition stayed, until recent times, close to the spirit of the original Dionysiac orgy. In pre-war days, the men of the village would don heavy wooden carved masks and grotesque costumes of towering straw and feathers which added six feet to their height, and dance to the discordant music of swinging cowbells. The old wooden masks have now mostly been retired into folk museums, joining the Tarascon and the rest of the shaggy-haired dream creatures who patrol the borders of our conscious minds.

In southern Europe, it is Portugal and Italy which continue to celebrate Carnival with uninhibited pleasure. Rodney Gallop, travelling among the seafarers of Portugal in the 1930s, puts forward an interesting theory to explain it.

> There is a theory that [Carnival] was originally connected with the opening of navigation each spring, and the name derived from *carrus navalis* [the ship of the goddess of navigation: Isis in the Mediterranean, Nehalennia in Northern Europe]. The carnival period was a time when normal restraints did not apply – whole populations gave themselves up to mirth and jollity and darker passions which would not be allowed them in the more staid and sober course of ordinary life.

The Danish ethnologist Henning Henningsen, writing in 1949, corroborates the water connection. He describes the *dystoløb* held on Carnival or Shrove Monday all over Denmark. These boat-tournaments or jousts in which the participants have to knock each other into the water were still common in his day, although they were not held every year in each place.

> During the winter the sailing-ships had to lie up, as the sea was frozen over. This left plenty of time at their disposal for preparing festivals. Carnival marks the close of a 'fat' time and the beginning of lean times. It also means the end of idleness and the beginning of regular work: the ice having melted, sailing and fishing can begin again.

In Holland around Carnival time there are ice-skating races across the frozen canals and lakes – whole towns and villages turn out to watch, with feasting and drinking afterwards. The most famous is raced through eleven towns of Friesland.

In Portugal Rodney Gallop observed a Carnival theatre which reminded him of similar theatricals in his own country.

> It was our good fortune to chance on a Carnival mumming play in the village of Cadriceira near Torres Vedras on Carnival Sunday . . . On reaching an open space near the church, they stopped and arranged a rough curtain to screen an imaginary stage from the assembling village audience. The mummers retreated behind it, and then, each in this turn, made their entry through the 'curtain'. The first wore a battered top hat and frayed frock coat, and carried a black bag. Singing unaccompanied, he announced that he was a doctor. Two more characters now entered, a peasant and his wife (played skilfully by a man in a kerchief, veil and petticoat). Offered a chair, she sat down with heartrending groans to be examined by the doctor. A sudden surmise leapt into my mind. Would the subject of this Portuguese mumming-play be the traditional theme of such performances from Roumania to the Yorkshire dales? It was. A moment later, with a deft gesture, the doctor slipped his hand under the chair and whipped out a celluloid doll.

As for Citizen Carnival in Italy, Mrs Hugh Fraser enjoyed his revels in Rome at the turn of the last century.

> A few weeks after epiphany the excitement of the Carnival illuminated life for ten days. To be dressed in a real domino and stand on a balcony in the Corso, flinging bushels of confetti and hundreds of posies at all and sundry, was something to dream of for the rest of the year. Every window in the street was hung with tapestries and garlands; the bands were playing in every

square; the towering cars, wreathed with flowers and filled with men and women in dazzling costumes, passed up and down in endless procession; the crowd below surged and screamed and danced a thousand antics, till the great moment struck when a company of mounted dragoons came pounding along to clear the way. Breathless silence followed their passage. Then far away, from the Piazza del Popolo, sounded a muffled thundering of hoofs and a roar of voices, ever nearer and more and more deafening, till the 'Barberi', the riderless race-horses, wild with fear at the yells of the populace and the clattering of tinsel hung all over their bodies, swept into sight, flew past, and were lost to view as the crowd broke and closed in behind them – and the day was over!

Tracing Carnival's demise in France, Mary Eyre quotes Rivares's *Chansons et airs populaires de Béarn*:

For a curious custom nearly obsolete at Pau, but still existing in full force in Béarn and Gasconey [sic]. This is the trial and condemnation of the Carnival (a stuffed figure, like our Guy Fawkes), on Ash Wednesday:

'His advent has been celebrated by songs and cries of joy; but, woeful example of the fluctuations of popular favour, he is now exposed to the hatred of the same persons who exalted him to the skies a few days ago. He is a fallen monarch, and his reign is ended. At a fixed hour, which has been loudly announced beforehand, a crowd of masks throng in a theatre prepared the previous day. The judges take their seats, the advocates are at their posts. The unhappy Carnival arrives on a cart drawn by an ass, and surrounded by gendarmes, and most grotesquely dressed. He is lifted into his place; the accusation is made; the witnesses against him examined; he is defended by his lawyers, but in vain. He is condemned to an ignominious death. He is conducted to the bridge, when the president of the court executes the sentence he has himself pronounced, by setting fire to the accused's clothes, and precipitating him thus flaming into the river.'

Pre-war Catholic Hungary, reported Károly Viski, had a riotous time in Carnival.

The entertainments at the end of Carnival last from its last Sunday to Ash-Wednesday. The last day of the Carnival, Shrove Tuesday, is the time of the freest entertainments and most generous feast. Compared to it Christmas is nothing. In some places they carry out jail birds on Carnival's tail. Two lads are wound round from top to toe with straw ropes, on the head of one they put a plumed hat, on the head of the other they tie a scarf; their faces are blackened with soot, they have to hold a hatchet or an axe, both are chained and they are paraded from house to house, collecting food. From this they arrange a grand dinner.

In the English Midlands, Christina Hole recorded a pre-war repertoire of superstitions associated with the making of the traditional Shrove Tuesday pancakes. An unmarried girl would give the first pancake to the cockerel: however many hens came to share it with him would be the amount of years before she was wed. At Olney in Buckinghamshire, housewives summoned by the pancake Bell race to the church, tossing pancakes as they run. The first to arrive receives a prayer book from the vicar and a kiss from the verger – a nice compromise between sacred and profane.

In Britain, too, Shrove Tuesday is celebrated as the 'last day of Shraft' – the end of the short festival season which includes Egg Saturday with its egg-rolling ceremonies, Quinquagesima Sunday and Collop (bacon) Monday. 'Shrove' derives from the pre-Reformation practice of going to be shriven on that day in preparation for the severe fast of Lent, present in Carnival, some say, in the name, *carne vale* – Latin for 'farewell to meat'. The three days which precede Lent were marked in England until modern times by all kinds of rowdy entertainments: cock-fighting, wrestling, dancing, pancake-feasts, thrashing the fat hen, throwing the cock, greasing the pig, guessing names for sweethearts – a feature of all celebrations, the subject being of such paramount interest to humanity.

Carnival food, in common with Shrove Tuesday's specialities, is primitive and simple, made with ingredients which are customarily begged, borrowed or stolen from more staid and sober citizenry. Recipes must be quickly and easily prepared – fritters, pancakes and omelettes feature prominently in country districts where children and young people, unskilled in kitchen matters, are the most important celebrants.

My own children took part in just such a Shrove Tuesday/Carnival ritual in the Languedoc in the late 1970s. The four of them, along with all the children of the small rural community whose life we shared, repaired in secret to an isolated barn, with the eggs they had sequestered from their families, and cooked up a gigantic flat round omelette in a huge iron pan. After the omelette had been torn up and eaten, the event developed into an unruly party with much ragging and hooliganism – during which, I learned several years later, my son (then fourteen), uncharacteristically pinned the village bully to the floor and boxed his ears for cheeking his three young sisters. None of them knew in what ancient ceremony they had assisted – but all admitted to a feeling that the day was somehow disreputable and should not be openly discussed.

In urban areas it is often street food which is the most typical – the grilled sausages, kebabs and pork fillets of the Mediterranean, the Carnival doughnuts of Germany and the airy fritters and *beignets* of France.

CARNIVAL

PORK KEBABS
Hirinó souvlakia (Greece)

The Greeks traditionally feast on pork for the first and second week of the three-week Carnival. This is the time to slaughter the household pig, fattened throughout the previous summer and cosseted through the winter until this moment. Kebabs are popular fast food wherever the Moors and Turks settled – additional flavourings make the difference from one country to another. Spain likes complicated Moorish spicing. In Greece the flavours are simple, dependent on fine raw vegetables, with olive oil as the main seasoning.

Quantity: 12–15 kebabs.
Time: Start several hours, or a day, ahead. 20 minutes.
Equipment: 12–15 skewers.

1lb/500g lean pork, in bite-sized cubes	2 green peppers, hulled and de-seeded
2 onions, skinned	2 firm tomatoes
3–4 tablespoons olive oil	several bay leaves
1 tablespoon dried oregano	salt and pepper

To finish

bread	lemon quarters

Check over the meat and trim if necessary. Cut all the vegetables into pieces the same size as the lamb cubes. Thread the meat and vegetables alternately, with a bay leaf piece on each, on the skewers. Paint with oil and dust with oregano and freshly milled pepper.

Grill the kebabs over a very high heat, turning them frequently. Lower the heat at the end of the cooking time to let them cook through. Sprinkle with salt.

Serve hot on their skewers, with plenty of thick-chunked bread and a lemon quarter each.

BRAISED SPICED LAMB
Arnaki kampamás (Greece)

This subtle hot-spiced lamb is braised so long and gently it needs no knife (it can be made with chicken too). In Carnival it accompanies the macaroni cheese on p.99. It traditionally has neither onion nor garlic – witches and fairies, welcomed at the Carnival hearth, hate them. The tomato and chilli, New World ingredients, are considered aphrodisiac – much needed in Carnival time.

Quantity: Serves 5–6.
Time: Start 2–3 hours ahead. 20–25 minutes.
Equipment: A frying pan and/or a heavy roasting tin – the Greeks have ones with handles especially for these gently braised dishes.

2lb/1kg lamb, chunked but with bone left in (shoulder is excellent)	1 small lemon, diced (flesh, pith and skin)
	salt and pepper
1 tablespoon seasoned flour	2 tablespoons olive oil
1lb/500g tomatoes	1 large glass white wine
2 tablespoons tomato paste	1 stick cinnamon
3–4 cloves	1 small red chilli, de-seeded and chopped

Work the lamb chunks thoroughly with the lemon and seasonings of salt and pepper. Leave to marinate for 10–15 minutes. Toss the meat in the seasoned flour. Heat the oil gently in a frying pan, or in the Greek roasting pan. Turn the meat in the hot oil till it browns deliciously. Add the tomatoes and heat till bubbling.

Splash in the wine mixed with the tomato paste. Add the spices and the chilli, and enough water to come up to the top of the meat. Cover loosely with foil and put in a low oven, 300°F/150°C/Gas 2, to cook very gently for 2–3 hours, until the meat is falling off the bone. Uncover for the last 30 minutes to brown the meat and evaporate the juices down to a small quantity of lovely sticky rich sauce – just enough to robe the meat.

Serve with the Lent macaroni cheese on p.99.

GRILLED SPICED HAMBURGERS
Churrasco (Portugal)

This is a re-import from Brazil, Portugal's erstwhile colony and now the Mecca of all serious Carnival-addicts. *Churrasco* is the name given to all grilled meats. These little spiced hamburgers are cheap and tender – Portuguese (and Brazilian) meat is on the tough side.

Quantity: 6 small hamburgers.
Time: Start a few hours ahead. 20 minutes.
Equipment: A mixing bowl. A griddle or heavy frying pan.

1lb/500g minced pork or beef
1 egg, lightly beaten
1 tablespoon finely chopped onion
1 tablespoon paprika
salt and pepper

2–3 tablespoons fresh breadcrumbs
2 garlic cloves, peeled and chopped
1 tablespoon chopped parsley
1 teaspoon cayenne pepper
olive oil for greasing the griddle

To finish
bread

lemon quarters (*optional*)

Work all the ingredients (except the oil) together with your hands until you have a smooth slightly sticky mass. Divide the mixture into 6 balls, and flatten them into thin discs.

Heat the griddle (or a heavy iron frying pan or skillet). Slick it with oil. When it is smoking, smack on the hamburgers. Cook them quickly, turning once.

Serve hot on rounds of bread or in buns. Accompany with lemon quarters – the favourite instant sauce right round the Mediterranean.

SPICED GRILLED CHICKEN
Frango grelado (Portugal)

Portuguese chickens in rural households do sterling duty as egg-layers and only make it into the pot when they are stringy old ladies. This makes a bit of spiced grilled chicken doubly festive because so rarely enjoyed.

Quantity: Serves 6, with plenty of bread.
Time: Start a few hours or a day ahead. 30 minutes.
Equipment: A bowl. A barbecue, grill or heavy iron pan.

1 whole chicken, jointed into 16 pieces
1 teaspoon cayenne
1–2 garlic cloves, crushed with 1 tablespoon
   rough salt

2 tablespoons paprika
1 teaspoon crushed bay leaves
2–3 tablespoons olive oil
oil for greasing the griddle

To finish
bread

lemon quarters (optional)

Check over the chicken – the 16 pieces should include the back. Mix the paprika, cayenne, bay leaves, garlic and salt with the oil. Rub the chicken pieces thoroughly with this mixture. Put them into the bowl, cover, and leave in the refrigerator overnight at least.

When you are ready to cook, heat the barbecue, grill or heavy iron pan until really hot. Smack on the chicken pieces. Grill them for 5–6 minutes, turning once. Then lower the heat and cook them until the juices no longer run pink when you prod down to the bone.

Serve with bread and lemon quarters.

CARNIVAL DOUGHNUTS
Berliners (Germany)

Shape dictates the naming of these fried doughballs – Berlin likes them round and stuffed with jam. They're quite easy to make – particularly if you have a batch of bread on the go. Children love them.

Quantity: Makes a dozen or so.
Time: Start 2–3 hours ahead.
Equipment: A large mixing bowl. Baking trays. A deep frying pan and a draining spoon.

1lb/500g flour	1 teaspoon salt
3oz/75g sugar	2oz/50g butter
1oz/25g fresh yeast (½oz/12g dried)	grated rind of 1 lemon
¼ pint/150ml warm milk	3 eggs
jam	fat or oil for deep frying

To finish
caster sugar for dusting

Sieve the flour into a basin with the salt. Stir in the sugar, and rub in the butter, yeast and lemon rind with the tips of your fingers. Work in enough warm milk, whisked with the eggs, to make a soft dough.

Knead all together thoroughly, pulling and pushing with the ball of your hand, until the dough is smooth and elastic. Form the dough into a smooth cushion, ends tucked neatly underneath. Put the dough back into the bowl, cover loosely with a damp cloth or clingfilm, and put it in a warm place to rise for 1 hour.

Knock the dough down and knuckle it well to distribute the air. Roll it into a fat sausage, and cut it into 12–15 lengths. Knead each piece into a ball, flatten it and drop a teaspoon of jam in the middle. Close the dough up over the jam. Turn so that the join is underneath, and set out the doughnuts, well spaced out, on the flour-dusted baking trays.

Cover as before, and put the doughnuts back into your chosen warm place to rise once more. This should take about 30 minutes – the dough is ready when it has doubled in thickness and bounces back when you press a fingertip into its surface. A friend of mine leaves them uncovered on the side of her Aga – she says she loves to watch them rise like little sponges.

Heat the frying fat or oil. When it will fry a cube of bread a beautiful golden brown in a few seconds, drop in the doughnuts – not too many at a time or the oil temperature will drop. Fry them, flicking them over with a draining spoon. When they are golden and firm and cooked right through (4–5 minutes), remove and drain on absorbent paper.

Continue until all are ready. Roll the doughnuts in caster sugar – if you eat them straight away you'll burn your tongue on the jam.

ACACIA-BLOSSOM FRITTERS
Beignets de fleurs d'acacia (France)

These delicious little Provençal Carnival frivolities can be made with any edible blossoms. The acacia is an overgrown member of the pea family – *leguminosae*; its clustering violet blooms blaze in the ravines of upper Provence and the Baronnies, providing early nectar for the bees. Pea or bean-blossom, nasturtiums, marrow or pumpkin flowers, rose-petals, elderflowers, all take kindly to frittering. The recipe comes from my favourite *traiteur* in Vaison-la-Romaine.

Quantity: 30 fritters.
Time: 1 hour intermittent attention.
Equipment: A mixing bowl, a small bowl and a whisk. A deep-fryer and a draining spoon.

30 sprays of acacia blossoms	8 oz/250g flour
½ teaspoon salt	1 tablespoon sugar
2 tablespoons olive oil	3 tablespoons brandy
3 eggs, separated	2½ pints/1.5 litres light beer
oil for frying (olive oil is best)	

To finish:
icing sugar

It is better if the blossoms do not need to be washed – if it cannot be avoided, do it gently.

Sieve the flour with the salt, make a well in the middle, and mix in the sugar, the olive oil, and the brandy mixed with the egg yolks, and work in enough beer to give you a thick batter which will coat the back of a wooden spoon. You may need some extra water. Put the batter aside for 1–2 hours for the flour to swell.

Heat the oil until it is hazed with a faint blue smoke.

Whisk the egg whites until stiff and fold them into the batter just before you are ready to fry.

Dip the sprays of blossom in the batter and drop them in the hot oil – not too many at a time. Turn them once, and when they are well puffed up, remove them with a draining spoon and put them on paper to drain.

Sprinkle the fritters with icing sugar, and serve them as soon as possible. Accompany with a glass of fragrant *tilleul* (lime-blossom tea) sweetened with a spoonful of acacia blossom honey – very sybaritic.

NORMANDY APPLE FRITTERS WITH CALVADOS
Beignets normands aux pommes (France)

There are many variations on the beignet theme throughout France. Differences reflect the strengths of the local larder – from the yeast-raised *bottereaux* of Nantes to the vanilla-scented *cruchpeta* of the Basques, the cream-rich *foutimassons* of Poitou to the rum-spiked *bugnes* of the ancient Roman city of Arles – once capital of the Empire's western provinces, including Britain.

Quantity: Makes about 30 fritters.

Time: 1 hour intermittent attention.
Equipment: A mixing bowl and whisk. A deep-fryer and draining spoon.

4oz/100g flour
3oz/75g icing sugar
¼ pint/150ml milk
4–5 apples

½ teaspoon salt
¼ pint/150ml cider
2 tablespoons Calvados
frying lard (typical of the area) or oil

To finish
caster sugar

Sieve the flour, salt and sugar into the mixing bowl. Gradually beat in the cider and milk (alternately), and the Calvados, until you have quite a thick batter which will coat the back of a wooden spoon. Leave aside to rest for 20 minutes or so.

Heat the fat or oil in the deep-fryer.

Peel and core the apples neatly and cut them into rings. When the frying fat is hot enough to fry a cube of bread immediately, dip each ring into the batter and drop it in – not too many at a time.

Turn once. Remove and drain when beautifully puffed up and golden. Serve hot, sprinkled with caster sugar. Accompany with a short glass of Calvados and a long draught of cider.

CENTURION'S EARS
Oreillettes (France)

These deep-fried pastry medallions are named for the unfortunate centurion who had his ear sliced off by the Apostle Peter – only to have it restored as good as new by his Master. This is the version made in Toulouse.

Quantity: Makes about 20 ear-sized biscuits.
Time: Start 2–3 hours ahead. 40 minutes.
Equipment: A mixing bowl. A rolling pin and board. A deep-fryer.

8oz/250g flour
3 eggs
3 tablespoons sugar
oil for frying

½ teaspoon salt
1 tablespoon Cointreau
4oz/100g softened butter

To finish
icing sugar

Sieve the flour with the salt and work in the eggs, Cointreau, sugar and butter until you have a smooth soft dough. Cover and leave it aside for 2–3 hours to rest.

Roll the dough out on a well-floured board. Cut out into rounds.

Heat the oil. When it is lightly hazed with blue, slide in the pastry ears, a few at a time. Turn them once. When they are light and well gilded, remove them with a draining spoon and transfer them to absorbent paper. Dust them with icing sugar.

Serve them warm, with a glass of Cointreau, and perhaps a sip of chilled Blanquette from nearby Limoux – my favourite sparkling wine.

CHEESE SUNDAY: LAST SUNDAY BEFORE LENT

MACARONI CHEESE
Makaronáda (Greece)

In Greece, cheese is eaten on the last Sunday before Lent – after that, there are no more dairy products until the cheese-pies of Easter Sunday. This is the traditional dish for Cheese Sunday. Greeks call all types of round pasta *makarónia*, including spaghetti, harking back to the old days when tube pasta was the only shape made, with the exception of that even more ancient preparation, the rice-like grated dough *rizaki* or *manéstra* used for soups and porridges. *Makarónia* can be bought in sizes from 1 to 10, number 1 being the fattest. On non-fast days pre-boiled macaroni is often layered with meat sauce and cheese *béchamel* and slow-baked in the oven like a *moussaka*. This meat-less version – known as 'orphaned', since it has no succulent companion – is served with a thick rich braised stew on non-fast days (see *Arnaki kampamás*, p. 94).

Quantity: Serves 4 as a main dish.
Time: About 1 hour.
Equipment: A small and a large saucepan. A wide earthenware gratin dish.

The sauce
2oz/50g butter
1 pint/600ml milk
½ teaspoon grated nutmeg

2 tablespoons flour
salt and pepper

The pasta
1lb/500g fat macaroni
4 eggs
6oz/150g grated cheese
salt and pepper

4oz/125g butter (Greek concentrated butter gives the right flavour)
2 tablespoons fresh breadcrumbs

Make the *béchamel* sauce first. Melt the butter in the small saucepan. Sprinkle in the flour and let it foam up without taking colour. Whisk in the milk gradually over the heat, stirring vigorously so that the sauce is not lumpy. Add salt, pepper and nutmeg. Simmer for 5–7 minutes until the sauce is thick and smooth. Take it off the heat and let it cool.

Cook the macaroni in plenty of boiling salted water until it is quite soft (none of the Italian *al dente* in Greece). Drain and toss with half the butter.

Beat the eggs and half the cheese into the cooled *béchamel*. Stir half the sauce into the macaroni and spread in the gratin dish. Layer the rest of the *béchamel* sauce on top. Sprinkle with the remaining cheese, the breadcrumbs and the rest of the butter.

Cook in the oven at 350°F/180°C/Gas 4, for 30–35 minutes until brown, crisp-hatted and bubbling.

SHROVE OR COLLOP MONDAY: LAST MONDAY BEFORE LENT

BACON AND EGGS
(England)

This is the day for eating bacon and eggs together – and there is no better bacon than a thick collop cut from a well-cured side of a typical old-fashioned English pig. Perhaps from the stocky Berkshire, descendant of the medieval half-wild porker; or from a long-sided Tamworth, the cottager's pig: or from the handsome Gloucester Old Spot, fattened on windfall apples in the orchards of cider country.

Quantity: Serves 4.
Time: 10–15 minutes.
Equipment: A cup. A frying pan.

8 eggs
1–2 tablespoons butter

8 lean thick-cut bacon rashers

Crack 2 eggs into a cup. Warm the frying pan. Put 2 rashers of bacon to fry in a little butter. When they are nicely browned, slip in the eggs. Fry the eggs, spooning the butter over the top to set the white and leave the yolk runny. Continue until all are used up. Serve with home-made bread.

SHROVE MONDAY PEA SOUP
(England)

In eastern Cornwall, Shrove Monday was known as Paisen Monday, as it was traditional to eat pea soup.

Quantity: Serves 4 as a main dish.
Time: About 1 hour.
Equipment: A large saucepan. A sieve and/or a liquidizer.

1lb/500g dried marrowfat peas soaked overnight
    in cold water
1 carrot
1 small parsnip
1 pint/600ml meat or vegetable stock

salt and freshly milled pepper
1 onion
3 sticks celery
1oz/25g butter or lard
½ pint/300ml milk

Drain the soaked peas, cover with fresh water and add ½ teaspoon salt. Cook the peas until mushy – about 30 minutes will see them tender. Push them through a sieve, or process to a purée in the liquidizer.

    Meanwhile prepare the vegetables. Cut them into small pieces and fry for a few minutes in the butter or lard. Add the mushy peas and the stock. Stir well and season with salt and pepper. Bring to the boil. Stir in the milk. Taste and adjust the seasoning.

    Serve with crusty brown bread.

SHROVE TUESDAY COCKEREL SOUP
(England)

All over Britain, Shrove Tuesday was the day for cock-fighting as well as pancake-making – clearing out the barnyard just in time for the eggless fast of Lent. The tough-sinewed casualties of the fights went into a chicken broth stewed up into variations on the Scots cock-a-leekie.

Quantity: Serves 6.
Time: Start 3 hours ahead. 10 minutes.
Equipment: A large soup-pot.

1 large boiling fowl	4lb/2kg leeks
3–4 sprigs parsley, roughly chopped	3–4 stalks celery, rinsed and chopped
2 bay leaves	6–8 peppercorns
about 5 pints/3 litres water	2–3 potatoes, peeled and sliced
1lb/500g spring greens, washed and shredded	salt

Wipe the fowl inside and out, and truss it neatly. Cut the leeks into thick rings, keeping the dark green end of the leaves separate, and rinse them well. Reserve the best half – the middle green – of the chopped leeks, and put the rest, including the dark green tops, in the soup-pot with the fowl. Add the parsley, celery, bay leaves and peppercorns and salt. Pour in enough water to submerge the bird. The aim is to end up with about 3 pints/1.5 litres of broth.

Bring to the boil, skim, turn down the heat, lid tightly and leave to simmer very gently – just so that a few bubbles occasionally pit the surface – for about 2–3 hours, until the broth is good and strong and has reduced by a third. (The lower the cooking heat, the clearer the broth.)

Add the potato slices and the rest of the leeks. Bring the broth back to the boil and simmer for 10–15 minutes to cook the potatoes. Add the spring greens after 5 minutes.

Season with salt and serve the broth, chicken and vegetables in deep soup-plates – the chicken should not even need a knife to cut it by now.

PANCAKES WITH SUGAR AND LEMON
(England)

Pancakes were – for those who like rational explanations – designed to use up the good things in the larder before Lent. Others find more subtle symbolism in the circular shape of the omelettes and pancakes which mark the end of Carnival, including the idea that the sunny discs are an ancient sacrifice to the returning sun. Shackle eggs was the popular Shrove Tuesday game in the West Country. Each child had to carry an uncooked egg to school. Each egg was marked with the owner's name and put with all the others in a sieve. The sieve was then shaken until all but one of the eggs cracked. The owner of the last egg was the winner and was crowned with a special cap – the eggs were then used to make pancakes. Show your mettle as a pancake-flipper, and lead a merry wake for the passing of Carnival. Tomorrow is fasting and we shall all be sober.

Quantity: Makes about 20.
Time: Start 1-2 hours ahead. 25-30 minutes.
Equipment: A bowl. A small pancake pan.

8oz/250g flour
4oz/100g sugar
½ pint/300ml milk

½ teaspoon salt
4 eggs
butter for frying

To finish
sugar

lemon quarters

Sieve the flour with the salt and stir in the sugar. Make a well in the middle and work in the eggs and enough milk to give you a batter like single cream. Leave it to develop for an hour or two.

Heat the pan. Roll a small knob of butter round it. When it foams, pour in enough pancake batter to coat the base of the pan. Let the batter set over the heat – when the top surface is dry, flick the pancake over. (You'll get better at it with practice.)

Continue until all the batter is used up.

Serve the pancakes hot, with sugar and lemon quarters.

MARDI GRAS OMELETTE
(France)

This recipe is for children only: gather all the kids of the neighbourhood and beg, borrow or steal the eggs and a bit of bacon to fry them in. Then find a secret place to make the largest omelette ever dreamed of. It doesn't matter if it's clumsily done – that's part of the treat. Then get out into the fields and play hooligan games. That's it folks: enough is enough.

Quantity: Serves 10.
Time: 20 minutes.
Equipment: A roomy mixing bowl. The largest frying pan you can find.

6oz/175g fat bacon
1 tablespoon salt

24 eggs
1 tablespoon pepper

Heat the frying pan. Dice the bacon and, when the pan is hot, put it to fry gently until all its fat has run and the bacon is just crisp little pieces of crackling which will add texture to the omelette.

Crack the eggs into the bowl, add the salt and pepper and mix them roughly with a fork. Pour the eggs into the hot fat.

Lift up the omelette as it sets to let the mixture run underneath. Make sure everyone has enough bread, and distribute the omelette. No forks or plates or niceties should be necessary: King Carnival is not yet buried.

ALMOND SOUP
(Finland)

This sweet almond soup is traditionally served with cream buns on Shrove Tuesday throughout Finland – a celebration meal to welcome the turning year. At this time the days are lengthening from their midwinter night, the ice is breaking up on the rivers and lakes, and all living creatures, human, animal or vegetable, can feel the oblique rays of the returning sun.

Quantity: Serves 4.
Time: 10 minutes.
Equipment: A saucepan.

2 pints/1.2 litres rich milk
1 teaspoon cornflour, slaked in 1 tablespoon milk
6 tablespoons ground almonds
3oz/75g sugar
a curl of lemon peel

Put all the ingredients in the saucepan and bring to the boil. Simmer for 10 minutes. Remove the lemon peel. Serve hot, with sweet buns stuffed with whipped cream and toasted almonds.

ASH WEDNESDAY: FIRST DAY OF LENT

ASH WEDNESDAY BEAN SOUP WITH PISTOU
Soupe d'haricots au pistou (France)

The French were always adept at slipping round the demands of the Lenten fast – resorting to such underhand tricks as dipping a leg of lamb in the well so that it might qualify, by virtue of its swim, as fish. Dishes such as this Ash Wednesday bean soup, and the Grand Aioli – also the Ash Wednesday fasting dish (a full recipe for which can be found in my book, *European Peasant Cookery*) – hardly seem to represent a gastronomic deprivation.

Quantity: Serves 4.
Time: Start a day ahead. 1½ hours intermittent attention.
Equipment: A soup-pot. A liquidizer or a pestle and mortar.

The soup
6oz/175g white beans, soaked overnight
2 small turnips, peeled and chunked
a *bouquet garni* – bay leaf, parsley, thyme
2 pints/1.2 litres water
¼ cabbage, shredded
salt and pepper

2 large carrots, scraped and chunked
2–3 sticks celery (the unblanched is nicest in soup), washed and chopped
1 large potato, peeled and cubed
2 leeks, washed and cut into fine rings

The *pistou*

4 cloves garlic (one each), peeled and roughly chopped

¼ pint/150ml olive oil

½ pint/300ml basil leaves, stripped from their stems

1 slice stale bread

salt

Drain the soaked beans and rinse them. Put them in the soup-pot with the carrots, turnips, celery and *bouquet garni*. Add the water, but no salt yet. Bring to the boil, turn down to simmer, cover, and leave to cook gently for 1½ hours, until the beans are soft. After an hour, add the potato.

Meanwhile, make the *pistou*. Put all the ingredients in the liquidizer, or pound up the first three ingredients in the mortar, and add the oil gradually.

Just before you are ready to serve the soup, take out the *bouquet garni* and stir in the cabbage and the leeks. Taste and add salt and pepper. Bring it all back to the boil, and serve.

Let everyone stir in their own *pistou*. Heaven is a Lenten bean soup. Plenty more tomorrow and tomorrow.

LOFOTEN COD FESTIVAL –
TORSKENS DAG: END OF FEBRUARY

Torskens Dag, the Day of the Cod, is a modern festival celebrating the most ancient of harvests. On an appropriate day at the end of February, the citizens of the Lofoten islands' capital, Svolvaer, throw a dinner to mark the return of the cod shoals, plump with roe and ready to spawn in the warm waters of the Gulf Stream which bathe the Arctic archipelago.

Lying inside the Arctic Circle off the cost of Norway, the Lofotens in winter are magnificent. By February the Arctic night is already shortening. As the sun sets the great Lofoten 'wall' is irradiated with ice-cream colours: palest apricot, blackberry, strawberry and deep raspberry. The sea is a deep Arctic indigo, punctuated occasionally with a raft of brilliant-feathered king eider, or the lacquer-black flashes of killer whales as they crop the shoals. Clouds of gulls and an occasional sea eagle scavenge in the wake of the fishing boats, plucking the heavy silver fish from the nets as they are winched aboard the little vessels.

The first-caught fish, its curds creamy and firm, is eaten fresh, prepared according to custom – simply and perfectly, as befits the best of ingredients. The bulk of the annual catch is salted as *bacalao/morue* for export to Catholic Europe where, once fasting food, it is now a much esteemed luxury in dishes such as *brandade de morue*. Some customers, including the Norwegians themselves, and also the Italians and West Africans, prefer the more venerable stockfish or wind-dried cod. For this the fish, gutted but left whole and unsalted, is simply hung up to dry on huge outdoor racks, to pickle in the natural salt carried on the sea-breeze. The fish cannot be hung on the racks until the temperature rises above its winter sub-zero – if it freezes it spoils.

Stockfish is, with skins and furs, Norway's oldest trading commodity. The hard planks of protein doubled up as both ship's stores and trading items for the Vikings' long voyages. The cod harvest remains an important economic factor in Norway – not surprisingly when every household in northern Norway was, until 100 years ago, dependent on the fishing industry for money to purchase all trade items.

Norway's population of land-owning farmers was traditionally versatile: they fished, farmed, traded and went to sea as the seasons dictated. Their bankers – fishing being a notoriously unpredictable undertaking – throughout medieval times were the Lübeck-based merchants of the Hanseatic League. The Hansas moved into Bergen, the clearing house for the northern fishermen, in the thirteenth century, probably to fill the vacuum left by the Great Plague. Their fine wooden-walled warehouse-cum-dwellings are preserved on the Bergen waterfront today. The League replaced itself in the fifteenth century with the Monopolies – still dominated by the descendents of the Hansa merchants, who were now permitted to take out citizenship. Bergen remains an important centre for banking, and the town still recognizes Hansa blood in its leading citizens.

The Hansa merchants, with 500 miles of Arctic waters between them and their suppliers, did well enough out of trade as long as they had stamina and patience. The arrangement was to mutual advantage. There were years of 'black sea' when the shoals simply did not appear at all – and at such times the merchant bankers were obliged to advance enough for the purchase of next year's fishing equipment, however bad the season. In a good year, the fishermen received wheat flour, red wine and fabrics in exchange for their stockfish and barrels of cod liver oil. Their annual arrival was well heralded. Since the visitors used the cod oil to waterproof their sealskin outerwear, the sensitive inhabitants of Bergen swore they could smell the fishing fleet on its way home when it was still 100 miles away.

The seventeenth century saw the introduction of klipfish – salt cod or *bacalao* – but the natives never really took to it. Salt cod is to this day an export-only item. Stockfish remains popular not only in Norway but also with the Italians and West Africans. 'We do not cook it nearly as well as the foreigners,' a salting-factory owner and wholesaler told me. 'The Italians make the most wonderful stews with the stockfish, using tomatoes and peppers.' His face lit up at the thought. 'I make a selling trip there every year, and I try a different recipe each time.' Much of the work of salting and drying the catch is now carried out in factories on the Svolvaer waterfront, although there are other centres, such as Henigsvaer, just down the coast, which specializes in *lutefiske*, similar to stockfish but finished in a lay cure.

In spite of industrialization, one lone fisherman can still net, gut and hang his catch out to dry all in the same day, and even find a local market for his wares – affording an unusual independence to this hardy race of solitary men and women.

The menu for *Torskens Dag* is built around *Skrei mølje* – a one-pot soup-stew which takes full advantage of the different textures and flavours available from the one fish. Here from the skipper of the M/K *Skarheim Senior*, my host for the day on an icy but magnificent fishing trip in his Arctic grounds, is the recipe for the dish – as prepared on the flat-topped iron stove which heats the crew's communal cabin. On special occasions cod is served, not with Norway's everyday aquavit with a beer chaser, but with red wine – a preference which dates back to the Hansas' time, when wine was used to ballast the ships on their return trip from the Mediterranean. The land-based dinner itself was, when I attended it in 1987, punctuated by specially written or selected songs about the cod, speeches about the state of the fishing grounds, and a fund of lyrical cod stories from a visiting television cook.

I give both the modern and a simple version of the old recipe – through there is nothing to beat the traditional one-pot boat stew, particularly since you can skip the speeches and get straight on with the singing.

COD SUPPER
Skrei mølje (Modern Norway)

Really fresh fish doesn't smell or taste 'fishy', and when cooked it has a delicate creamy curd between the flakes. A cod straight from the net has a bright eye, a faint, slightly metallic scent, and a firm feel to the inquiring finger. Such delights are hard for most of us to come by – we do not share the good fortune of the inhabitants of the Hanseatic town of Bergen, who still buy their cod live from tanks on the harbour. Make this supper when you can persuade a cod fisherman to supply you with fish an hour or two away from its watery bed.

Quantity: Serves 10–12: well, it's a festival, after all.
Time: 1 hour.
Equipment: Greaseproof paper. A large soup-pot. A draining spoon. A small saucepan.

The soup and fish

a 6–8lb/3–4kg whole spring cod, skrei, with
   its own liver and both wings of roe
2–3 onions, skinned and quartered
7 pints/4 litres water

4–5 sticks of celery
3–4 carrots, washed and chunked
2 bay leaves
plenty of salt

The sauce

8oz/250g cod liver for sauce
2 tablespoons vinegar

1 pint/600ml water

To finish the soup

3–4 carrots, scraped and matchsticked
1 pint/600ml soured cream
juice of 2 lemons
salt and pepper

2–3 leeks, washed and slivered
1 pint/600ml fresh cream
4oz/100g pickled pearl onions

First wipe the cod's roe and wrap it in a double envelope of greaseproof paper. Bring a pan of salted water to the boil and lay in the packet of roe. Bring it back to the boil and then turn down the heat immediately. Simmer until the roe is firm – a medium-sized roe takes about 25 minutes. Leave the roe in the water to cool.

Fillet and skin the cod. Put the bones, head and tail into a soup-pot with the water and bring to the boil. Skim. Add the rest of the soup ingredients. Boil for 20 minutes – not longer, or the soup will taste bitter.

Meanwhile make the cod-liver sauce. Clean the liver in a bowlful of water – pulling it apart with the fingers and removing the membranes as you find them. Bring one third of the water to the boil with a tablespoon of vinegar, and throw in the liver. Bring it all back to the boil, and add another third of cold water and the rest of the vinegar. Bring back to the boil and add the third cup of water. When it reboils, the sauce is ready. Add salt to taste. It has a lovely rich buttery flavour like beef-marrow.

Now turn back to the soup and fish. Strain the broth, return it to the pan and reheat to boiling. Add the fillets of fish and poach them for 3–4 minutes – just long enough for them to turn opaque. Take them out and transfer them to a warm deep dish. Ladle over enough broth to submerge the fish fillets and the cod's roe, and keep it all warm. This allows the roe to reheat, and the cod to finish cooking while you serve the soup.

Finish the soup. Add the matchsticked strips of carrot and leek and bring all back to the boil. Off the heat, stir in the sour and the fresh cream, the pickled onions and the lemon juice. Taste and correct the seasoning.

Serve the soup first, accompanied by Norwegian flatbrød – very thin crispbread.

Serve the poached cod with the roe and some plain-boiled potatoes, with the rich liver sauce handed separately.

Accompany the fish with a glass of red wine – Beaujolais, as imported from Bergen, courtesy of the Hansas' descendants.

Offer brandy, coffee and Danish cookies to follow – the Danes were the occupying power in the area for a long time, and the cook who prepared this dinner was Danish. Conquerors, as well as bankers, sometimes have their virtues.

COD SUPPER (2)
Skrei mølje (Traditional Norway)

The wooden fishing smacks which still make up the Lofotens' inshore fleet have changed their habits little over the centuries. Many still salt and dry their catch in the old way, although the skippers now have sophisticated radar-trackers and modern machinery to manage their nets. Below decks the crew's cabin is heated with a simple wood-burning stove on which the fishermen brew their coffee and simmer their fresh-caught supper of spring skrei cod, much as they did when the Hanseatic merchants were trading wheat and wine for salt-stiff planks of stockfish and barrels of cod-liver oil. They topped off the pot with the cod's own liver, cleaned and torn into pieces in the fingers, never cut with a knife, providing a rich sauce with the consistency and flavour of beef-marrow (see preceding recipe). Egg-and-butter sauce is the substitute the fishermen's wives recommend.

Quantity: Serves 4.
Time: About 40 minutes.
Equipment: A heavy oven-proof casserole.

4 cod steaks (4oz/100g each)	1 fresh cod's roe (both 'wings')
salt and pepper	1½lb/750g potatoes
1 tablespoon vinegar	6oz/175g butter
2 hard-boiled eggs	

Wipe over the cod steaks and roe and salt them lightly.

Peel the potatoes, slice them thickly and put half in the base of the casserole. Lay the roe on top. Finish with the rest of the potatoes. Pour in enough water, salted so that it tastes like seawater, to come to within a finger's width of the top. Add the vinegar. Bring to the boil, lid tightly and simmer for 30 minutes, either on the top heat or in a medium oven at 350°F/180°C/Gas 4, until the potatoes are soft and the roes are firm.

Melt the butter in a small pan and stir in the chopped hard-boiled eggs.

Five minutes before the end of cooking, lay the fish steaks on top of the potatoes. Lid the casserole.

The fish steaks will take no longer than 5 minutes to cook through.

Serve the helpings scooped through the layers. Hand the butter sauce separately.

Norwegians like their *Skrei mølje* with a glass of red wine, the trade item the Hansas exchanged for salt cod. Beer with a chaser of aquavit would substitute in years when the catch was small. The proper toast is *skol*.

March

LENT: FORTY DAYS' FAST – FEBRUARY/MARCH/APRIL

The fasting period of Lent is a period of abstinence acknowledging Christ's forty days in the wilderness. It lasts from Ash Wednesday to Easter Sunday. In medieval times, Wednesdays, Fridays and Saturdays as well as Lent were declared meatless, partly as a penance and partly as a kind of crowd-control – meat-eating was held to inflame the passions and heat the blood. When the early Church fathers imposed the Lenten fast during the third and fourth centuries AD, the discipline was by no means unfamiliar to their congregation.

'The modern Greek celebration of Lent, Holy Week and Easter is, so to speak, the Christian counterpart of the old mysteries, and seems to own much to them,' observed classicist and anthropologist John Lawson in 1910.

It so happens that Easter falls in the same period of the year as did the great Eleusian festival – the period when the re-awakening of the earth from its winter sleep suggests to man his own re-awakening from the sleep of death; and it is probable that the Church turned this to good account by making her own festival a substitute for the festival of Demeter after the pagan pattern; for it would seem that the Church, when once her early struggles had secured her a firm position, exchanged hostility for conciliation, and sought to absorb rather than to oust paganism.

As a period of abstinence was required of the mystae of Demeter, so during Lent and still more strictly during Holy Week the Greek peasants keep a fast which certainly predisposes them to hysterical emotion during the services; and *en revenance*, just as the initiated are said to have indulged themselves too freely when the mysteries were over, so the modern peasants, when the announcement of the Resurrection has been made, disperse in haste to feast upon their Easter lamb.

Pope Gregory the Great, architect, *circa* 600 AD, of the eventual split between the Patriarchs of Constantinople and the Bishop of Rome, adhered to the inherited asceticism of eastern religion and decreed Lent a total fast until sundown, with no meat or dairy products to be taken during the forty days. This interdict included eggs from creatures either feathered or scaled. Naturally the barnyard hens had no such obligations, and continued to lay. Their product had to be stored – hard-boiling was the easiest method – ready to celebrate the Resurrection.

Observance was more or less strict according to the historical period and the demands of the established Church. Lenten abstinence can range from a single voluntary privation, such as a favourite food or drink, to a complete day-long fast, with bread and water taken only after sundown. This enforced lean period, strictly observed, according to regional habit, throughout the Middle Ages, provided a natural balance. It offered the whole population the sanction of Church and establishment for an annual physical and spiritual spring-clean – and a chance to recover from the rowdy excesses of the winter festivals.

The western Church, both Roman Catholic and non-conformist, cut her Lenten clothes to suit her cloth. In the main, she contented herself with simply abstaining from meat – both fur and feather – during Lent and on the Friday fasts. Fish, cheese and milk were usually permitted on these days, but eggs were not. Northerners – Scandinavians in particular – were permitted fish eggs and cod-liver oil, since there was no other cooking oil available. The mainstay of the diet, particularly among inland populations, was grain dishes, dairy products and storable winter vegetables – with salted fish as the chief source of protein.

The Church timetable was perfectly tuned to the natural cycle of the seasons. For this her congregations have to thank the early Church's practicality in stepping into the shoes of the old pagan seasonal festivals. It was no accident that the post-Carnival Lenten fast coincided with a time of reduced agricultural activity and the rapid emptying of winter's larder. The Lenten timetable also accommodated the fishermen. Late February to early March sees the storms of the Atlantic abate, and the ports of northern Europe freed from the ice which confines the fishing boats through the winter. This timing allowed those with access to the sea to enjoy the first catches of the year with the Church's blessing. The strictures of Lent also ensured that the Atlantic fishermen's conserved wind-dried wares, particularly stockfish and salt cod, found eager customers in the markets of the devout Catholic south. This valuable bulk trade, bankrolled during the Middle Ages by the Lübeck-based merchants of the Hanseatic League, led to a vigorous two-way exchange of both goods and ideas.

In the Low Countries – Holland and Belgium – the Lenten period coincided with the spring herring shoals. Pig-butchers and *charcutiers*, the mainstay of the well-fed burghers' laden sideboard, took to selling herring during Lent to make up for lost business. In the Middle Ages, people feasted on the new herring: for rich and poor alike, herring – smoked, salt or fresh – was the great bastion against famine.

Henry Wolff, in the Black Forest *circa* 1890, took note of the celebrations of Spark Sunday:

> For the celebration of the advent of spring, the first Sunday in Lent, Spark Sunday, is set apart, and the peculiar custom observed is popularly termed *Scheiben-schlagen*. It is of distinctly pagan origin, bearing some resemblance to the heathen Gaelic Beltan or Belstien which used to be practised in Scotland and Ireland. It consists in throwing burning discs of beech wood – which represent the sun up in the air at night, accompanied by particular words and speeches designed to benefit a sweetheart. for such wishes the lady rewards her swain next morning with a present of cakes – likewise formed in the shape of discs – which are baked while he is throwing his fiery missile. In some villages in the place of discs girls bake *bretzeln*, plain cakes twisted in the shape of a double O. But these are really wholly out of place. They are distinctly Christian, and represent the ropes with which our Saviour's hands were tied before the crucifixion.

Journal-keeper William Brockedon, mountaineering the Swiss Alps around 1830, found familiar sanctuary among the snowy peaks. He reported as excellent the fasting supper he shared with the Augustine monks of the St Bernard pass – and had occasion to admire the monks' best friends – decked out with a miniature barrel of that which, under the circumstances, must have been manna from heaven: festival food indeed.

At supper we were placed at the head of the table; it was a day of fasting; the soup, though *maigre*, was excellent – the fish, pieces of salt cod, dressed with cream and currants, delicious omelettes, cheese and fruit, completed our repast. The *vin ordinaire* was good, and an extra bottle was served to us of some delicious Italian wine.

The Eastern Orthodox Church, for whom the festival of Easter outranks that of Christmas, stipulates a rigorous Lenten fast – still adhered to in the remoter highlands and islands where the people are poor and faith remains strong. All animal products are forbidden throughout the forty days, requiring total abstinence from meat, cheese, milk, butter, poultry, and eggs. Also proscribed was all seafood judged to contain blood – hard rules for a nation of seafarers – although crustaceans and cephalopods, including shrimp, crab, lobster, octopus, squid and cuttlefish, were permitted. The mainstay of the eastern housewife is a well-stocked larder of pulses – chickpeas, beans, lentils, dried broad beans. These basics could be combined, in the temperate Mediterranean, with an almost uninterrupted supply of winter-crop vegetables – cabbage, potato, cauliflower, turnip, beet, carrot, leek, stored onions and garlic. These fine ingredients, cooked over the slow fires of winter, with a seasoning of juicy lemons and the thick peppery green olive oil of the annual winter pressing, not only conformed to dietary stipulations but remain a delight to the palate and a welcome relief to the digestion.

As for the rest of Christendom, Orthodox pre-Revolution Russians ate only vegetables, fruit, bread and honey during Lent. The Romanians ate only Indian corn and beans. Bulgarians ate only black food for mourning – black bread, black olives, black beans in olive oil and prunes. The full fast was often limited to the first and last weeks only.

Lent falls in the fallow time before the sap of spring begins to rise, and it remains the ideal time for abstinence. Such a period of deprivation and semi-hibernation (no drunken excesses or riotous behaviour) refreshes both body and soul – an enforced lull naturally designed to reconcile all living things with the demands of the changing season. The medieval housewife, who observed the forty-day fast in the normal cycle of the year, baked no cakes or biscuits during the period (with the exception of Britain's Mothering Sunday cake, which was in any event saved for Easter); avoided sugar, honey, and sweetmeats; served no alcohol; used butter, oil and other enrichments only sparingly in her recipes. Instead she served simple seasonal dishes, mostly based on vegetables but admitting of regional variations: fresh soups made with plain water and winter legumes enlivened, in more temperate climes, with the first green leaves; in the north, unleavened breads and porridge were supplemented by the first fresh fish of the spring.

The disciplines of Lent offered an annual challenge to the cook, which led to many fine inventions, including the herring dishes of the Low Countries.

GREEN HERRINGS
Groene herring (Holland)

The Dutch like their plump spring-run herring *au naturel* – the backbone slipped out, the sparkling viridian-flanked fish held by the tail and swallowed right down in one gulp, like a sand-eel disappearing into a heron's throat. There is a modern ceremony which requires the first crate of new herring to be delivered with considerable ceremony to the monarch – after which everyone else can rush down to the port for their own supplies.

The burghers maintain that Amsterdam itself is built not on the windy promontories which flank the dyke-bound pastures, but on a foundation of 1,000 years of herring bones. The Dutch prefer to buy their favourite street-food from herring kiosks parked at the interstices of the elegant semi-circle of canals which dictate the contours of their ancient port. For the rest of the year, the carts sell various lightly-salted and pickled herrings.

The salting of herring has to be carefully monitored. The fish must lie in salt for at least eight days if the herring is to be kept. The slightly salted or sweet herrings which are the ones most widely marketed are fish that have been salted for 24–48 hours. Rollmops are filleted herrings which have been salted and then pickled in vinegar with onion.

The Dutch and the Belgians like their pickled herrings with bread and butter, with a chaser of thick-cut crisp-fried chips. Conveniently to hand from a neighbouring kiosk, the chips come with a choice of tomato sauce, chopped onion, or a delicious yellow dollop of perfect mayonnaise. If you ask for the *spetziale* you get all three – but that, although conforming to the letter, might not be true to the spirit of the fast.

Quantity: Serves 1.
Time: 5 minutes.
Equipment: A sharp filleting knife.

2 raw herrings   chopped raw onion

Scale the herrings vigorously – there should be only a fine veil of silver-green skin left on. Press the fish down its flanks to loosen the backbone. Neatly half-sever the head from the back, leaving it attached to the backbone. Then pull the head towards you, bringing out the guts, backbone, rib-cage and all. Finish the process with a sharp filleting knife. Sever the backbone just above the tail – otherwise you won't have a handle to catch hold of the fish.

You should now have double fillets of fish, held together by the tail: perfect for a Lent-bent Dutchman.

Serve with chopped raw onion and a pint of the best beer – in Holland it was likely to be a foaming mug of *Oranjeboom*.

GRILLED BLOATERS
Lammekenzoete (Holland)

A fifteenth-century Dutchman, William Beukels, lays claim to the invention of kippering – although the principle of using smoke to increase the shelf-life of salted meat and fish has been understood, in primitive form, since pre-history.

The perfecting of the primitive process was important economically and practically, as it permitted the conservation of the spring bounty delivered into the fishermen's nets when the herrings shoaled from the North Sea.

Bloaters are whole fish, salted for a few hours only, threaded through the gills on to sticks, left to drain, and then put near the fireplace in which a beech fire has been lit – the hot air dries the herrings and gets rid of excess oil. It is all the smoke generated which gives the fish its flavour. In Britain bloaters are traditionally a speciality of Yarmouth, much appreciated throughout East Anglia.

Kippering, on the other hand, is a cold-smoking process. The fish is hung some distance from the fire and smoked at about 25°C. The largest red herrings are called *gendarmes* – the story goes that a fish-seller, not much enamoured of the law, saw a likeness to the old tricorn hat worn by the *gendarmerie*, and cried his wares accordingly. He was immediately summonsed for insulting the majesty of the law. The other merchants all followed suit in sympathy – and that was the end of it: *gendarmes* they remain.

Quantity: Serves 1.
Time: 10 minutes.
Equipment: A grill or a frying pan.

1–2 bloaters per person
freshly milled pepper

butter

Cut off the bloaters' heads and tails. Slit them down the back and grill or fry in a dry pan over a high heat until the skin is crisp and the fish heated right through.

Serve piping hot with a knob of butter and a turn of the peppermill. Accompany with a baked potato and a helping of celeriac, boiled and mashed with milk, butter and seasonings.

SMOKED RED HERRING
Boestring (Belgium)

Red herrings, a speciality of Ireland as well as of Belgium, are well-salted bloaters. The Belgians like to eat them raw – although they can be grilled like bloaters or kippers. The modest little mustard sauce makes all the difference, as it somehow cuts the saltiness of the fish – if you include chopped dill, it is the same sauce as that served for the Scandinavian dilled salmon, *gravlax*.

Quantity: The sauce serves 4.
Time: 5–10 minutes to set out.
Equipment: A small bowl and a fork.

1 smoked herring or bloater per person
cored diced apples (with the skin left on)
peeled, diced cooked beetroot

cold diced boiled potatoes
gherkins
chopped hard-boiled eggs

The sauce
1 tablespoon mild mustard
6 tablespoons oil
salt and pepper

1 tablespoon vinegar
½ teaspoon sugar

Cut off the heads and tails of the fish and open them down the back.

Set out all the ingredients on separate dishes, so that each person can make up his own salad.

Make the sauce when you are ready to eat. Mix the mustard and sugar with the vinegar and then work in the oil with a fork until you have a thick, almost mayonnaise-like, *rémoulade* sauce. Season. It's wonderful what a mustard emulsion will do – but it will not last. If it separates, try working in a splash of boiling water, or start again with another dab of mustard.

FOUR-GRAIN CARAWAY BREAD
La Loée (France)

The ever practical French had a repertoire of plain rough breads designed to get the vital organs working again after the fritters and meat of Carnival. This one was a speciality of Abbeville in Picardy. Itinerant pedlars used to announce their oven-hot Lent-bread to the housewives with cries of 'Loée – la loée caaoude!'

Quantity: makes 2 x 2lb/1kg and a 1lb/500g loaf.
Time: Allow 4 hours intermittent attention.
Equipment: A mixing bowl. 3 loaf tins and a cooling rack.

2lb/1kg stone-ground wholewheat flour
4oz/100g barley flour
8oz/250g medium oatmeal
1½ pints/900ml warm water

4oz/100g rye flour
1 teaspoon salt
1 tablespoon caraway seeds
3oz/75g fresh yeast (1½oz/40g dry)

Sift the flours and salt into the bowl. Mix in the oatmeal and caraway seeds. Mix the fresh yeast with ½ pint/300ml of the warm water and a pinch of sugar, wait until it liquifies, and pour it into a well in the flour. Sprinkle with flour and leave in a warm corner for 10–15 minutes, so that the yeast can begin to work. (If using dried yeast, follow the packet directions.)

Knead everything together, adding enough of the water to give you a soft, slightly sticky dough. Work it well, pulling and pushing with the ball of your hand, until the dough is smooth and elastic.

Put the dough back into the bowl, cover loosely with a damp cloth or clingfilm, and put it in a warm place to rise for at least 2 hours – it needs longer than a plain wheat dough.

Knock the dough down and knuckle it well to distribute the air.

Divide it into 3 pieces, work each piece into a smooth fat sausage and press them into the greased baking tins. Cover and put back to rise once more. This should take about 1 hour – the dough is ready when it has doubled in thickness, and bounces back when you press a fingertip into its surface.

Preheat the oven to 350°F/180°C/Gas 4. Bake it for 60–80 minutes – it is ready when the bread is well shrunk from the sides of the tin and sounds hollow when you tap it. Tip it out of the tin and pop it back into the oven for 5–10 minutes to brown the sides and base.

Transfer to the rack to cool.

CABBAGE AND PAPRIKA SOUP
(Hungary)

Variations on this basic fasting soup, often using the salty liquor from the sauerkraut barrel, provided the usual pre-war Lenten fasting supper in Hungary. As with all simple recipes, it depends on the excellence of its ingredients and the skill of the cook. On other days the meal might have been a *kisze* (fruit soup), or a slice or two of oat bread, similar to the French four-grain recipe above, eaten with milk, honey and stewed plums.

Quantity: Serves 4.
Time: 1 hour intermittent attention.

Equipment: A soup-pot.

2 tablespoons vegetable oil (pumpkin oil is home-milled throughout eastern Europe)
1 heaped tablespoon paprika
1–2 tablespoons dried mushrooms or wild-gathered winter fungi, soaked in warm water for 1–2 hours (*optional*)
½ small cabbage, shredded

2–3 cloves garlic, skinned and chopped
1–2 onions, skinned and chopped
2 pints/1.2 litres water
8oz/250g celeriac, peeled and cubed
1 fine large potato, peeled and cubed
salt and pepper

To finish

2 tablespoons lemon juice or wine vinegar
3–4 generous tablespoons parsley

1 teaspoon cayenne pepper (or a fresh green chilli, de-seeded and chopped)

Heat the oil in the soup-pot and toss in the garlic and onions. Let them fry gently for 4–5 minutes. Sprinkle in the paprika and toss it with the oil. Immediately pour in the water – paprika burns quickly – and add the optional mushrooms, the celeriac and the potato.

Bring to a rolling boil, turn down the heat, add salt and pepper and simmer for 30 minutes. Five minutes before the end, add the cabbage. Finish with the lemon juice or vinegar, and a sprinkle of cayenne and parsley.

Serve with the four-grain bread

APPLE POTTAGE
(Croatia)

Thick soups made with the remaining stored apples or dried fruit from the previous autumn were popular Lent dishes in pre-war eastern Europe. A satisfying fruit soup – lemon, quince, plum, prune, whatever is seasonal – is served at the beginning of the meal, although in Lent the soup might be the only dish offered, maybe with a slice of corn bread to fill the belly. This cinnamon-scented version (the spice-loving Turks occupied most of eastern Europe for six centuries) makes a delicious dessert. In non-Lent times it is delicious with a topping of thick yogurt (at least I haven't suggested whipped cream, honey and a sprinkle of chopped toasted nuts).

Quantity: Serves 4.
Time: 30 minutes.
Equipment: A soup pan and a potato masher.

The pottage

6 cooking apples, peeled and sliced
1 pint/600ml dry white wine
3 cloves

grated zest and juice of 1 small lemon
1 short cinnamon stick
2 tablespoons sugar

To finish

1 tablespoon cornflour slaked in 1 tablespoon
white wine

2 tablespoons brown sugar

1 tablespoon butter

1 teaspoon powdered cinnamon

4 tablespoons fresh breadcrumbs (or small cubes of
bread) fried in butter

Put all the pottage ingredients in the soup pan and bring to the boil. Turn down the heat, lid the pan, and leave to simmer for 20 minutes, until the apples are quite soft.

Remove the cinnamon stick and fish out the cloves if they are easy to find. Mash the apples into the juices. Stir in the slaked cornflour and return the pan to the heat. Bubble it up. Beat in the butter.

Serve in bowls, sprinkled with cinnamon and brown sugar and a tablespoon of fried breadcrumbs. Who said fasting food was a hardship?

ORANGE AND RAISIN CORNBREAD
Bobóta (Greece)

Greek rural households all have their own recipe for Lenten cornbread. Maize is a staple grain all over eastern Europe. The cobs are harvested late and fully mature, then dried and stored in tall. thin. cage-like wooden storehouses which punctuate the landscape from Macedonia to Transylvania. The Greeks, like the Turks, have a ferociously sweet tooth, and at times other than Lent this crumbly golden cake would be drenched with sugar syrup or honey. It makes a lovely breakfast (particularly accompanied with non-Lenten crisp bacon).

Quantity: Makes 1 large loaf, or 12–15 individual buns.
Time: 1 hour intermittent attention.
Equipment: A sieve and a mixing bowl. A small saucepan. A baking tin.

12oz/350g cornmeal

3 teaspoons baking powder

¼ pint/150ml olive oil (use sesame oil in
Holy Week)

2–3 tablespoons sugar or honey

6oz/175g plain flour

1 teaspoon salt

juice and grated rind of 4 oranges

8oz/250g currants, plumped in 1 small glass brandy

1 glass warm water

Sift the cornmeal, flour, baking powder and salt into a mixing bowl. Heat the olive oil in a small pan, and stir it, hot, into the flour. Mix it in with your fingers. Add the orange juice and grated rind, the currants and brandy, the sugar or honey, and enough warm water to make a thick batter.

Heat the oven to 375°F/190°C/Gas 5.

Oil the baking tin and pour in the mixture.

Bake the cake for about 50 minutes, until it is a deep chestnut colour and feels firm to the finger. If you would prefer small individual buns – American-style corn muffins – allow them 20 minutes in a slightly hotter oven.

Serve warm, with or without warm syrup or melted honey poured over.

TIMBALE OF SPINACH AND MUSHROOMS
Sformato di spinaci e funghi (Italy)

Rural Italian housewives do not traditionally use a great deal of meat in their everyday meals. The Lenten fast offers an opportunity for ingenuity with vegetable dishes, in which Italian cooks in any event demonstrate a mastery all year round. The richer households and those who lived by the sea would replace meat with fresh fish, but the ordinary *contadina* relied on her own store-cupboard – including dried *porcini* and bottled or sun-dried tomatoes – and supplemented it in the early spring with the first wild gathered leaves and fungi. Nettles (the top four leaves only), young dandelion and morel mushrooms are all there to be gathered at this time of year – I give substitutes, but use the real thing if you can. Later in the year, make the *sformato* with aubergines, fennel, green beans – any combination which takes your fancy. It's a lovely dish and very pretty.

Quantity: Serves 6–8.
Time: 1 hour preparation. 55 minutes cooking time.
Equipment: A saucepan. 2 small bowls. A frying pan. A ring mould.

1lb/500g spinach (fresh or frozen)
1½oz/40g flour
1 pint/600ml milk
4 eggs, forked together
2oz/50g grated parmesan

8oz/250g mushrooms (or 2oz/50g dried *porcini*, soaked for 20 minutes in hot water)
salt and pepper
1 teaspoon grated nutmeg
1 tablespoon fresh breadcrumbs

To finish
Fresh tomato sauce – skinned tomatoes simmered till thick with a spoonful of olive oil, a little chopped garlic and a seasoning of nutmeg and cinnamon

Cook the spinach briefly in the water which clings to its leaves after washing or freezing. Squeeze it dry, chop, and reserve it in a bowl.

Slice the mushrooms and sauté them in 1oz/25g of the butter. Reserve them in another small bowl.

Melt the rest of the butter in a small pan and stir in the flour. Let it fry for a moment, until it looks sandy. Beat in the milk over the heat, using a wire whisk to avoid lumps. Add salt and pepper and mix half the sauce into the spinach and the rest into the mushrooms.

Stir half the egg into the spinach mixture and spice it with grated nutmeg. Stir the remaining egg and the grated parmesan into the mushroom mixture.

Heat the oven to 375°F/190°C/Gas 5.

Butter the ring mould and sprinkle it with breadcrumbs. Spoon one of the mixtures into one side, and the rest into the other. Set the mould in a baking tray and pour in enough boiling water to come two-thirds of the way up the side.

Bake for 50–55 minutes, until the egg has set firm.

Remove from the oven and leave to settle and shrink for 5 minutes. Be brave and unmould the timbale on to a warm plate: put the plate on the top and turn the whole thing over at once.

Pour tomato sauce into the hole in the middle, and the rest round the side: very pretty, and it tastes divine. Lent is no real hardship in Italy.

SALT COD WITH CREAM AND CURRANTS
Morue à la crème (Switzerland)

The market stalls of central and southern Europe still offer, from Christmas to the end of Lent, a surprisingly wide range of dried cod and stockfish. There are various cuts of *morue*, from the fatty belly to expensive middle cuts to bits of tail-end for croquettes. It comes from pre-soaked to plank-hard. Ready-made *brandade* is always popular – enthusiastically recommended as being made with the best cut of the *morue*, the purest of mashed potato and, naturally, the richest and fruitiest olive oil.

Quantity: Serves 4.
Time: Start 24 hours ahead. 30 minutes.
Equipment: A bowl. A saucepan. A frying pan.

1lb/500g salt cod (or 1½lb/750g smoked
  haddock, which will need no soaking)
4oz/100g currants, pre-plumped in a glass of
  white wine

1oz/25g seasoned flour
2oz/50g butter
½ pint/300ml single cream
salt and pepper

Put the salt cod to soak in plenty of clean water for 24 hours, changing the water 3–4 times. Keep it in a cool place – covered if it is in the fridge, or everything will smell of fish.

Cut the fish into bite-sized pieces and flour it lightly.

Heat the butter and fry the fish on each side until golden. Remove the pieces, and replace them with the soaked currants and their liquor. Allow it all to bubble up and cook down into a syrup. Pour in the cream. Simmer gently, without allowing the sauce to boil, for 10–15 minutes. Season.

Serve with noodles, or floury potatoes, plain-boiled in their skins.

BAKED BUTTER BEANS
Gigantes plaki (Greece)

The Greeks love their pulse vegetables and cook them beautifully – but simply. I have included a little olive oil in this dish – even devout Greeks would permit a little of their favourite ingredient as long as it was not during Holy Week.

Quantity: Serves 4.
Time: Start the day before.
Equipment: A large saucepan.

8oz/250g dried butter beans, soaked overnight
  in plenty of water
1 large carrot, scraped and sliced
3–4 ripe tomatoes (or a 14oz/400g tin)
1 bay leaf

1 large onion, skinned and chopped
2 cloves garlic, skinned and chopped
2–3 sticks celery (the green, unblanched type has
  the best flavour)
salt and cayenne pepper

To finish

¼ pint/150ml olive oil (use sesame oil in
  Holy Week)
lemon quarters (optional)

1 heaped tablespoon chopped parsley
juice of ½ a lemon

Drain the beans and cover with fresh water to a depth of 2 fingers. Bring to the boil, turn down the heat and simmer, covered, for 1½-2 hours until soft. If necessary, add boiling water during the cooking time. After 1 hour, add the vegetables and aromatics. Season with salt and cayenne.

Stir in the olive oil and the parsley just before serving, and squeeze in the juice of ½ a lemon.

Serve with lemon quarters, if you like, and a dish of capers, or pickled caper shoots, separately. (The Cypriots in particular love to cut the heaviness of bean dishes with these vinegar-sharpened pickles.)

The beans need no sauce except the pan juices and rough salt.

BROAD BEANS WITH ONION AND DILL
Koukia yachni (Greece)

Broad beans were the original European bean, both for eating fresh and for drying for winter storage. They were not supplemented by the haricots (including runner beans) until the New World vegetables returned in Christopher Columbus's luggage. This fine simple dish can be made with dried or fresh vegetables. By the end of Lent in Greece, the new beans will have swelled in the pod. Feathery fronds of anis-flavoured dill weed (very good for the digestion) grow wild all round the Mediterranean.

Quantity: Serves 4 as a main dish.
Time: Start a day before if using dried beans. 1 hour intermittent attention.
Equipment: A large saucepan with a lid.

2lb/1kg shelled broad beans (or 1lb/500g dried,
  soaked overnight in water)
4–5 fat spring onions, rinsed and chopped
salt and pepper

¼ pint/150ml best Greek olive oil (use sesame oil
  during Holy Week)
4 tablespoons chopped fresh dill
1 pint/600ml water

To finish

1 tablespoon chopped dill

quartered lemons

Pick over the broad beans. If they are dried, nick out the little black 'key'. If they are young and tender, include some of the young pods – they have a lovely asparagus-like flavour.

Heat the oil gently in the saucepan, add the onions and fry them for a moment. Add the beans, dill and seasoning. Pour in the water and bring it all to the boil, then lid the pan and simmer for about 30 minutes (longer if you are using dried beans).

When the beans are quite soft, remove the lid and allow to boil down over a fierce heat until the liquid is almost reduced back to oil.

Sprinkle with the chopped dill and serve with quartered lemons – and thick strained yogurt at any other time of year but Lent.

CABBAGE LEAVES STUFFED WITH PUMPKIN
Capouns farci au citrouille (France)

Mi-*Carême*, the mid-Lent break, is traditionally celebrated in Provence on the Thursday of the third week of Lent. Pumpkins, *polichinelles* and lanterns figure prominently in the celebrations, which echo, if faintly, the jollities of Carnival – with a courtesy knee bent to the Church.

Quantity: Serves 4.
Time: 30 minutes to prepare. 1 hour's cooking.
Equipment: A small sauté pan. A mixing bowl. A baking dish and foil to cover.

12 large cabbage leaves	10oz/300g cooked pumpkin purée
4 tablespoons cooked rice or fresh breadcrumbs	1 egg, lightly beaten
2 tablespoons strong grated cheese	1 onion, chopped and sautéed in olive oil
1 clove garlic, chopped and sautéed in olive oil	2 tablespoons chopped parsley
1 teaspoon chopped marjoram	1 tablespoon chopped lovage or celery tops
salt and pepper	

To finish

1lb/500g tomatoes, scalded, skinned and chopped	1 glass white wine
1 glass water	4 tablespoons olive oil

Scald the cabbage leaves with boiling water, drain, and lay them out flat.

Mix the pumpkin purée, rice or breadcrumbs, egg, cheese, vegetables, herbs and seasoning into a soft stuffing. Put a tablespoon of the filling on each cabbage leaf, tuck in the sides and roll up into a small fat bolster. Secure with toothpicks if the leaves are a bit bouncy.

Arrange the stuffed leaves in an oiled gratin dish. Tuck the chopped tomatoes round. Pour in enough wine and water to come two-thirds of the way up the cabbage. Trickle on the oil.

Cover with foil and put in a hot oven, 425°F/220°C/Gas 7 for 10–15 minutes to heat everything through. Then turn the heat right down and cook for 1 hour at least in a low oven, until the cabbage leaves are tender and the tomatoes have melted into a delicious rich sauce.

This recipe can be prepared a day ahead, as it reheats beautifully.

MOTHERING OR REFRESHMENT SUNDAY: END OF MARCH/EARLY APRIL

The fourth Sunday in Lent is Mothering Sunday in England – a celebration triggered by the day's appointed psalm, 'Rejoice ye with Jerusalem, and be ye glad with her', combined with the day's epistle, which speaks of Jerusalem as the 'mother of us all'.

Until the First World War changed the social arrangements of Britain's aristocracy, Mothering Sunday was the day when servants were allowed to go home to their mothers both spiritual and physical: mother church and mother parent. During the last century the festival applied to a sizeable proportion of the population: in 1820, before the beginning of Victoria's reign, over half the wage earning population was employed in domestic service, including a large number of unmarried girls. These young women were allowed to bake a rich cake to be carried home and stored away in the family larder, ready for the Easter festival three Sundays ahead. Just enough time for the cake to mature – all fruit cakes improve with keeping.

Naturally, full advantage had to be taken of such an infrequent perk, and the cake was made of the very best ingredients in the mistress's larder. Into it went the finest white flour, well sifted and dried in the oven first, raisins-of-the-sun, Jordan almonds, crystallized fruit, sweet butter and fresh eggs, and expensive spices from the locked cupboard where the precious supplies were kept. Some households made a point of including figs, symbols of fecundity quite proper to motherhood – all those little seeds. If the employer was affluent and the housekeeper open handed, there would be a layer of delicious almond paste baked in the middle of the cake and another one on top. Such generosity reflected well on the mistress of the house. A rich cake, perfectly baked, would reassure anxious mothers that their daughters were being well cared for and properly instructed.

In countries where Carnival is kept, the fourth Sunday in Lent is known as Refreshment Sunday. It was a feast for both body and soul, when the sins of Carnival might be confessed and absolved and the rest of the day spent in the company of the family, enjoying an alfresco picnic – an affirmation of Christian institutions in reparation for pagan misdemeanours.

In the hills above Nice in the old days, pre-war and beyond, reported local resident Léopold Massiera (*Fêtes en Provence*, 1982), an open-air mass was held, following which, in a state of grace, families picnicked together on the grass – a homage to the Sermon on the Mount and the subsequent feeding of the five thousand.

One cooked noodles in the *taiaran* [an earthenware casserole] and reheated rabbit civet brought from home. And the whole afternoon was given over to a kind of children's fair where one could buy pumpkin souvenirs, hollowed and carved to make a kind of music, and gourd (*cougourdons*) seeds to be planted on Holy Saturday, sold by country people down from the hills for the day, their wares spread out for sale on clean clothes on the ground. In addition there were friandises, soft marzipans perfumed with orange-flower water, or hard bonbons flavoured with liquorice, and jujube syrup and lemonade sold in bottles stoppered with coloured marbles.

SIMNEL CAKE
(England)

This recipe combines boiling with baking – the easiest and most ancient way of making a rich cake. There is virtually no beating and absolutely no machinery required.

Quantity: Makes a 6lb/3kg cake.
Time: About 20 minutes active. Approx. 3 hours oven time.
Equipment: A large saucepan. A mixing bowl. A deep 9in/22cm cake tin.

8oz/250g butter
1½lb/750g mixed dried fruit
4oz/100g glacé cherries, cut in half
grated rind and juice of 1 orange and 1 lemon
2 teaspoons mixed spice

8oz/250g black treacle
4oz/100g dried figs, chopped to raisin-size
4oz/100g whole blanched almonds
12oz/350g self-raising flour
4 eggs

The marzipan layer
8oz/250g ground almonds
1 egg

8oz/250g icing sugar

Line the base of the cake tin with a double layer of well-buttered paper. If yours is not one of those tins with a hinged side, line the sides as well with a double thickness – raisins are terrible for sticking. Always use butter to grease a cake tin – then even if you have used margarine in the mixture, the cake will taste buttery. Dust a little ground almond round the tin since you have it to hand, for a really nutty flavour.

Put the butter, treacle, all the dried fruit, the whole almonds and the orange and lemon rind and juice into a roomy saucepan, and heat until the butter and treacle have liquidized. Simmer gently, stirring, for a few minutes, and then leave aside to cool.

Prepare the marzipan by working all the ingredients into a stiff paste. You may need a little lemon juice to make it pliable. Knead it into a ball and roll out into a disc to fit the cake tin – dust with icing sugar to stop it sticking to the rolling pin. Ready-prepared marzipan is no good for this – it is usually made without the egg which holds the mixture together in a single luscious layer as it cooks.

Sieve the flour and spice into the pan with the syrup-fruit mixture and crack in the eggs. Turn it all together thoroughly until you have a soft mixture which drops easily from the spoon. Spoon half the mixture into the lined cake tin. Lay in the disc of marzipan, and cover it with the rest of the cake mixture. Smooth the top down so that it dips a little in the middle – this encourages the cake to bake with a flat top.

Bake in a low oven at 300°F/150°C/Gas 2 for 2½–3 hours. The cake will feel firm to your finger when it is done. Another test is to listen to it – an excited hissing means it is still evaporating moisture and not yet ready.

It you can bear to store your handiwork for so long, keep it for Easter. Top it with another layer of marzipan (same quantities again) and decorate it with 12 marzipan balls to symbolize Our Lord and his 11 apostles – Judas had dropped out of the picture by Easter Sunday. Pop the cake under the grill for a moment to brown the apostles.

RABBIT CASSEROLE PROVENÇALE
Civet de lapin (France)

The sauce of a civet – a rich dark stew usually made with furred game – should be thickened and enriched with the blood saved from the animal. This is really possible only if you have killed your own. However, 2oz/50g of crumbled black pudding will do very well instead. Nevertheless, a rich stew such as this herb-scented Provençal version is fine picnic food on a crisp spring day. The stew doesn't have to be served piping hot – just leave it in its cooking-pot and transport it wrapped in an old duvet or blanket. Make sure you take plenty of bread for mopping up the sauce – unless you can manage noodles, with which the picnicking penitents of Nice used to accompany the dish.

Quantity: Serves 4.
Time: 1–1½ hours intermittent attention.
Equipment: A large heavy-bottomed pan. A small frying pan.

1 plump rabbit, neatly jointed and including the head (split), liver and kidneys
1 glass plain water or home-made stock
3 large tomatoes, scalded, skinned and chopped
4oz/100g salt fat bacon (streaky), cubed small
salt and pepper
4oz/100g mushrooms or ceps, wiped and sliced

4-5 tablespoons olive oil
1 glass white wine
2oz/50g black pudding
8 garlic cloves, in their skins
1–2 sprigs thyme (the cooks of Provence use wild serpolet)
4oz/100g black olives (ripe-pickled French, Italian or Greek)

Pick over the rabbit, removing stray fur and sharp splinters of bone. Heat the oil in the large frying pan. Sauté the rabbit joints in it until they seize and brown a little. Remove them and put them aside.

Pour in the wine and the water or stock and allow it all to bubble up. Add crumbled black pudding, the tomatoes and the whole unskinned garlic cloves, the chopped bacon and the thyme. Season with salt and pepper.

Add the rabbit joints, bring to the boil, turn down the heat, and leave to simmer gently, loosely covered, for as long as it takes for the rabbit to be so tender that it can be eaten with a fork. A young animal will be ready in 30–40 minutes – an older one may take over an hour.

When the rabbit is nearly done, fry the mushrooms in the reserved oil in the small frying pan. Add the olives and stir until they are hot. Stir the contents of the pan into the stew 5 minutes before the end of cooking.

Complete the picnic in traditional style with marzipans and macaroons (see p. 13), and refreshing fruit syrups.

April

ALL FOOLS' DAY: APRIL 1ST

The custom of playing tricks on children and the simple-minded on April 1st seems to be very ancient – those who translate such habits into Judeo-Christian terms suggest that it is a reminder of the dove who left Noah's Ark 'finding no rest for the sole of her foot'.

However, April 1st is the date on which the sun emerges from the zodiacal sign of the fishes, which may explain the various references to fish in rhymes which mark the day – Sweden's 'April, April, you silly fish, I can fool you as I wish'; and the French term for an April Fool – *Poisson d'Avril*.

Only Spain in all Europe lacks an All Fools' Day. The rest of Europe enjoys its fun and games on April 1st. The most usual trick is to send someone on a fruitless errand – particularly children. In Scotland the favourite task was a letter to be delivered. The recipient opened it and told the bearer it should have been for someone else – and so on for as long as the joke held. When the bearer finally read it, he found the couplet: 'The first and second of April, Hound the gowk [cuckoo] another mile.' In France children were dispatched to fetch a dozen cocks' eggs. In England they were sent for a pound of elbow grease, a leather hammer or a quart of pigeon's milk. In Brittany they are sent to fetch a litre of sweet vinegar.

GREEN BAKED CARP
(Yugoslavia)

We are still in Lent, and fish is standard Lenten fare all over Europe. The favourite in central and eastern Europe is mirror carp, a strain perfected by the medieval monks. The carp can be bought live from huge tanks in the market, and are a startling sight to those prospective purchasers unused to purchasing their fish on the fin. Enormous fish-eyes, magnified by the glass walls, stare out gloomily as they wait to be netted and weighed. I first made their acquaintance in Belgrade.

Quantity: Serves 4.
Time: 1 hour.
Equipment: A long narrow baking dish.

a whole carp, weighing about 3lb/1.5kg before scaling and cleaning, or a grey mullet

2 cloves garlic or a handful of fresh wild garlic leaves
1 large bunch sorrel or watercress

1 large bunch green celery leaves
juice of 1 lemon
¼ pint/150ml oil

1 small bunch flat-leaved parsley
salt

Wipe the carp inside and out. Chop all the aromatics up together and mix them with the lemon juice and a teaspoon of salt. Stuff the herbs into the cavity of the fish.

Heat the oil in the baking dish and lay in the carp. Bake for 20 minutes at 350°F/180°C/Gas 4. Pour a glass of boiling water over the fish and continue to cook it for another 25 minutes.

Serve with plain boiled new potatoes, and sauce it with its own juices into which you have stirred the herbs from the stuffing.

WESTERN EASTER: BETWEEN MARCH 22ND AND APRIL 25TH

The western Church, Roman Catholic and non-conformist alike, celebrates the feast of the Resurrection according to the Julian calendar, on the first Sunday after the full moon which follows the vernal equinox. The first Christians, following the rituals laid down by the Jewish faith they shared with their founder, observed Passover – Pesach, 'He passed over', the commemoration of the deliverance of the Israelites from Egypt. The Christian feast gradually replaced the Jewish festival, but remained lunar derived. The etymological lineage is obvious in the Latin derived names for Easter – *Pâques* in France, *Paach* in Holland, *Pasqua* in Italy, *Pascua* in Spain, and *Pascoa* in Portugal.

In northern Europe, where the festival is known as variants on the word Easter, the etymology is different, a distinction also subtly echoed in the attendant rituals. Northern egg ceremonies – egg hunting, egg rolling or pace egging – were known to the eighth-century scholar monk the Venerable Bede, who linked them to Eostre, the Norse goddess of spring and of the dawn, whose month of April was called Eosturmonath by the Anglo-Saxons, and whose sacred animal, the hare, was believed to hide eggs, symbols of rebirth, in gardens and outhouses for children to find.

Most of Germany still adheres to the Easter hare as the layer of Easter eggs – and Easter egg bread (see p. 137) is baked in the form of a hare, with a whole egg tucked under its tail. There is a rival menagerie in different districts: in Upper Bavaria the cock is held responsible, Franconian Thuringia blames the stork, and the fox features around Hannover. To add to the general exuberance of the German Easter, the bakeries are full of special unleavened and butter-enriched Easter breads, including the Pomeranian *Osterwolf* – baked in the shape of a wolf with four paws and open mouth, and Vienna's enormous *Osterkuchen*.

Eggs, forbidden food during the strict Lenten fast, play a central part in the Easter rituals all over Europe – in part because eggs have been a talisman of rebirth long before Christianity appropriated the symbolism, but not least because the fast ensured that there were plenty of eggs available. In medieval times, in Britain and Ireland as well as all over the Continent, eggs were offered as Easter tithes to landlords, both secular and spiritual. In rural France, some parishes still make gifts of baskets of eggs to their priest on Easter Day.

In rural Hungary, the simple plain coloured eggs of the rest of Europe become works of art. The women folk artists of Kalocsa, Nograd and Matyo-land are particularly admired for their skills – these days they even travel to the big cities to paint murals on the walls of modern flats. This same skill in decorating domestic articles and interiors with the special designs peculiar to their district or village or family is used to embellish Easter eggs. The distinguishing stylized flower-motifs also appear in the richly embroidered clothes that many people still wear on high days and holidays. Those who know can distinguish, say, the roses of Palots from the roses of a neighbouring village as easily as a Scot can between clan tartans – a far less venerable tradition. The technique which produces the sophisticated designs is ancient: the patterns are drawn on the eggs with wax, and the eggs are then dipped into cold paint to take the base colour, and finished by hand.

It was not only in Hungary and eastern Europe that the eggs were beautifully decorated. Traveller Nicholas Dorcastor described the breaking of the Holy Week fast in Italy in the mid-sixteenth century:

> As soon as the eggs are blessed, everyone carries his portion home and causeth a large table to be set in the best room of the house, which they cover with their best linen, all bestrewed with flowers, and place round it a dozen dishes of meat, and the great charger of eggs in the midst . . . The Easter eggs themselves yield a very fair show, for the shells of them are all painted with divers colours and gilt . . . sometimes no less than twenty dozen in the same charger, neatly laid together in the form of a pyramid.

All visitors in the following week are invited, and must not refuse, to eat an egg – a tradition which has survived until modern times: eggs are still the centrepiece of the traditional Italian Easter meal.

The important ingredients of Easter festival food – bread, eggs, meat and the year's supply of salt (bought in April) – were traditionally taken to church to be blessed: a wise precaution in rural communities faced with the coming hazards of the farming year.

In the highlands and islands of Scotland, where, in the old days, oatcakes were the staple fare, Easter Sunday's batch was finished with an egg glaze, and then eaten with crowdie – a soft fresh cheese – mixed with butter. Belgium and the Lowlands celebrate Easter with blazing displays of brilliantly tinted marzipan fruit and animals in all the confectioners' shops. Marzipan was named from the 'pains de St Marc' made by a Venetian baker – St Mark being his city's patron saint – in time of great wheat shortages. Dutch housewives have special lamb-shaped moulds for the butter on the Easter table.

The hot cross buns of England, the equivalent of the Mediterranean's Easter egg studded breads, seem to be one of the last relics of the fine white cakes which were offered and eaten at the Greco-Roman spring festival of Diana, and the pre-Christian Saxons also prepared them in anticipation of good fortune. The buns kept their magic properties long after they were marked with Christianity's symbol. Until recent times, a few buns saved from Good Friday were believed to protect the house from fire and the granary from rats. Taken on board ship, they would avert wrecking. Folk needed all the protection they could get on Good Friday, as it was held to be an unlucky day anyway: blacksmiths would not shoe horses because of the nails on the Cross, miners felt it too dangerous to go below ground, housewives would not wash clothes for fear they would emerge from the tub spattered with blood. No one swept the floor on Good Friday – or on New Year's Day either – as it would sweep away good fortune and result in a death in the family.

Easter is nowhere immune from the old gods. In Scandinavia it was the time when the witches, encouraged by the re-awakening earth, were particularly energetic. On Holy Thursday they were thought to fly off on broomsticks to rendezvous with the devil at the mythical Blåkulla. In order to repel their attentions, everyone, particularly in the Western provinces, lights bonfires – the bigger the better – and lets off fireworks and paints their doors with crosses and stars to scare the intruders away. These 'Easter hags' are still commemorated by Swedish girls and boys who dress up as witches and tour the neighbours, unseen and unidentified, to leave a little card – the Easter letter – hoping for a treat to be left out in return. In Sweden, too, Easter has a rite-of-spring ritual: people pick birch twigs and willow branches in Lent and bring them indoors so that they bud by Palm Sunday, conveniently available as substitute palm-trees. The holy intent is somewhat belied by some households, where the father makes play on Good Friday morning to beat his children and other dependents with the budding birch twigs. The explanation often offered is that it is in sympathy with Christ's beating and his sufferings on the way to Golgotha. Now the ritual is no more than a children's game, and children's games, it seems, have always been the last refuge of pagan custom.

In Spain and Portugal the villagers got together to beat, hang or burn effigies of Judas on the anniversary of the Crucifixion – a habit translated to Liverpool via the Spanish merchant ships which brought in wine and fruit, and where Good Friday was known as Spanish Day. Jack-o-Lent was the English Judas, a stuffed man who was dragged about on Ash Wednesday – although his true ancestor was probably Old Man Winter. In addition to these ceremonies, Iberia has its magnificent Holy Week processions, of which Seville has the most dramatic. Day and night the brotherhoods of barefooted Nazareños, anonymous in mourning colours of purple and dark crimson, black and cream, midnight blue and plum, badged, cloaked and hooded like Grand Inquisitors, make their way through Seville's rambling alleyways of the poor, and the broad avenues of the rich, to the cathedral, some bearing the life-sized carved wooden Pasos, Stations of the Cross, some themselves weighed down under heavy crosses, others making the whole journey on their knees, their slow progress punctuated by the spontaneous mourning songs – keening laments – which suddenly issue from the overhanging balconies and shadowy doorways to remind the spectators of the holy women who wept at the foot of the Cross.

The Passion plays which are the live performances of the carved tableaux, much as the model Bethlehems are given flesh and blood in the nativity plays, still form part of the Easter ceremonies in towns and villages throughout Europe. All, nevertheless, are overshadowed by the once-in-ten-years re-enactment of the events of Holy Week by the entire population of the Bavarian Alpine village of Oberammergau.

Catholic Europe continues to celebrate Holy Week with those rituals which remind its congregations of the Easter calendar, as did Britain until the Reformation. The ceremony which commemorated Jesus's washing of the feet of his disciples on Holy Thursday has its echoes in the English monarch's annual distribution to the deserving poor of the Maundy Thursday money at Westminster Abbey. Although the gift of coin of the realm has now replaced the rather more humbling ablution (the last English monarch to perform the ritual was James II), a reminder of the original function remains in the white towels worn by both officials and recipients of the bounty.

The grandees of Rome demonstrated a more robust view of their responsibilities in 1900. Mrs Hugh Fraser, author and diplomat's wife, took delight in reporting the ceremony:

By Holy Thursday many thousands of pilgrims from all parts of Italy, but more especially from the South, had arrived in Rome. They were made the personal guests of the Holy Father, and were made to feel they were his especially beloved children. The vast building of the Santo Spirito was portioned out into dormitories and refectories, where food and lodging were provided for all who had brought the necessary recommendation from their parish priest. When the Ave Maria rang, they came crowding into the spacious hospice, to find a splendid supper prepared and good beds for their weary limbs. The Roman princes and princesses, in Court dress of black velvet and a long black veil, and wearing their most magnificent family jewels, came to do honour to the Pope's guests. They received the contadine and their babies, and led them to the tables loaded with good things which ran down the hall, and guided them to their places, where each found her supper separately laid out. But before enjoying this, the poor dusty feet that had travelled so far must be washed, and the princesses, following Christ's example, went round from one to another on their knees to perform this kindly act.

The capital of western Catholicism, Mrs Fraser continued, put on a fine *son-et-lumière* Easter display – but with a kick in its tail:

On Easter Sunday we climbed the long twisted stairs leading to the tower terrace, and in the soft April darkness, gazed at St Peter's outline covered from portico to pinnacle with stars of silver light. Far away across the dusky city we could trace every detail of cross and dome and column, quivering with mysterious radiance against the velvet gloom of sky. Not a sound was to be heard. We knew that the entire populace of the city and the peasants in every hamlet in the mountains were watching with us in that intense silence. Then, from Sant' Angelo, one cannon boomed out its signal, and ere its echoes died away the silver summit of the cross on the dome had flamed to molten gold, which ran in a torrent of glory down, down, from dome to roof, from roof to pillar, from pillar to colonnade, till the whole was one breathing hive of gold. We crept down to our little beds in the friendly old nursery, holding hands tightly and asking each other, 'Did he get down alive?' For the task of changing the topmost light on the towering cross, four hundred feet above the ground, was so desperately perilous that a condemned criminal was granted his pardon if he chose to undertake it; and in those days of faith confession was made and absolution received before attempting that climb for freedom.

Had the prisoner tumbled from that glittering dome high above the holiest altar in Christendom, no doubt the grinning goat-god, at home among the silent watchers on the Seven Hills, would have been the first to applaud the sacrifice.

PALM FRIDAY

The Friday before Palm Sunday is celebrated in the Catholic Church as the Feast of the Seven Sorrows of the Blessed Virgin Mary. There are three from the early life – the prophecy of Simeon, the flight into Egypt, and the three-day separation from Jesus mentioned in Luke's Gospel. The remaining four are from the Passion itself: the meeting with Christ on the way to Calvary, the Crucifixion, the removal of the body from the Cross, and the burial.

SEVEN-HERB SOUP
Siebenkräutersuppe (Germany)

In central Europe Our Lady of the Seven Sorrows is traditionally consoled with this fresh flavoured fasting soup prepared with seven bitter herbs. I give alternatives for those wild gathered leaves which may be hard to find – or, in the case of primroses, illegal to pick in those countries which have protective legislation.

Quantity: Serves 4.
Time: 15–20 minutes.
Equipment: A large saucepan.

The herbs

4oz/100g watercress, washed and finely chopped
2 leeks, well-washed and chopped into fine rings
4oz/100g clover leaves (mint can substitute)
4oz/100g primrose leaves (sorrel can substitute)
6oz/150g spinach, rinsed and finely shredded

4oz/100g parsley, washed and finely chopped
4oz/100g nettle tops (top 4 leaves only and use
gloves to pick them – but radish or turnip-tops
can substitute), washed and chopped

The soup

2 pints/1.2 litres vegetable stock or plain water
with a glass of wine
2 large potatoes, peeled and sliced
salt and pepper

1–2 sticks celery, washed and finely chopped
(the green unblanched type is best)
1 bay leaf
1 tablespoon wine vinegar

To finish (*optional*)

3–4 tablespoons soured cream

Pick over and prepare the herbs.

Bring the stock or water and wine, with the celery, potatoes and bay leaves, to the boil in the saucepan. turn down the heat as soon as it boils, and cook until the potatoes are soft – no more than 6–8 minutes if they are thinly sliced. Mash the potatoes a little into the soup. Stir in the herbs. Bring it all back to the boil, taste, and season with salt, pepper and the vinegar.

Finish, if you like and if your view of Lent permits, with soured cream. Accompany with black bread and white radishes.

PALM SUNDAY: THE SIXTH SUNDAY IN LENT

Northern Europe had trouble finding palm fronds to decorate its houses on Palm Sunday to commemorate the frond-strewn entrance of Jesus into Jerusalem.

In England the preferred palm-substitute was the catkinned willow. Palm Sunday was celebrated with figs – traditional fertility symbols long before D.H. Lawrence discovered them. Florence White reported in 1932 that the day was still known in some counties as Fig Sunday, and suggests that the connection was with the withering of the barren fig tree – the story which follows the Gospel account of Christ's entry into Jerusalem. Until the First World War, when the custom went into abrupt decline – perhaps because supplies became scarcer and more expensive – grocers sold huge quantities of dried figs for the making of the puddings and pies traditional to the day.

In Germany the problem is overcome with leafy branches of holly, willow, hazel, birch or yew – whatever comes naturally, and whatever, in pagan times, came in handy to celebrate the rites of spring. The cut wands are sometimes draped with pretzels and apples – a custom echoed in Provence, where candied fruits, little dough men, wrapped sweets and biscuit rings are hung like premature fruits on the olive and laurel branches more appropriate to the natural vegetation. The Provençaux have not so easily forgotten the significance of this ritual – a bride pregnant before her wedding day is described as having celebrated Easter before Palm Sunday.

CHICKPEA SOUP
Soupe do pois chiche (France)

This dish belongs to the Marseilles celebration of Palm Sunday, where it commemorates the miraculous arrival, during a time of terrible famine in the Middle Ages, of a ship laden with chickpeas. The soup is for grown-ups only – the children will have eaten so many sticky sweets and biscuits from the decorated twig-trees that they will not have room for anything but a few roast chickpeas – still a favourite children's snack round the Mediterranean.

Quantity: Serves 4 as a main dish.
Time: Start the day before.
Equipment: A large saucepan.

1lb/500g chickpeas, soaked overnight in cold water with 1 teaspoon baking soda (as *an aide-digestion*)
1–2 sprigs thyme and rosemary
4 tablespoons olive oil

2 onions, skinned and chopped
2 carrots, washed and chopped
2 sticks celery, washed and chopped
1–2 bay leaves
        salt and pepper

To finish
2 eggs, beaten up with 2 tablespoons grated cheese

Drain the soaked chickpeas. Bring 4 pints/2 litres of water to the boil. Add the chickpeas and the rest of the ingredients, except the salt and pepper. Bring all back to the boil. Lid tightly and leave to cook at a rolling simmer for about 2 hours. Season the soup when the peas are soft.

Pour a ladleful of the hot broth into the egg-and-cheese mixture. Off the heat, whisk the mixture into the soup. Do not reboil, or the eggs will curdle and your lovely velvety thickening will vanish.

Serve with bread, more grated cheese, and a salad of fresh spring leaves – young dandelion, lamb's lettuce, sorrel, chicory – dressed quite plainly with lemon juice, a slick of good oil, and salt.

FIG PUDDING
(England)

Florence White received this account from her correspondent P.H. Ditchfield, describing Palm Sunday customs still extant in the home counties in 1896:

> At Edlesborough, Buckinghamshire, the children procure figs, and nearly every house has a fig-pudding. For some days beforehand the shop-windows of the neighbouring town of Dunstable are full of figs, and on Palm Sunday crowds go to the top of Dunstable Downs, one of the high-

est points in the neighbourhood, and eat figs. Nor is the custom confined to Buckinghamshire; until quite lately people used to assemble on Silbury Hill on the same Sunday and eat figs, and fig-puddings were much in vogue.

Quantity: Serves 4–5.
Time: About 1 hour intermittent attention.
Equipment: A small saucepan. A bowl and sieve. A rolling pin and board. A 6–7in/12–15cm pie tin and a cooling rack.

The filling
8oz/250g dried figs

2 teaspoons cornflour

1 teaspoon mixed spice

juice and grated rind of 2 oranges

2oz/50g currants

2 tablespoons dark treacle or golden syrup

The pastry
8oz/250g flour

2oz/50g lard

3–4 tablespoons cold water

1 tablespoon brown sugar

2oz/50g butter

To finish
powdered sugar and powdered cinnamon

Tail the figs and put them in the saucepan with the orange juice and just enough water to submerge them. Simmer until they are plump and soft. Stir the cornflour, slaked in a little cold water, into the juices to thicken them. Stir in the rest of the filling ingredients, and leave it all to cool.

Make the pastry. Sieve the flour into a bowl. Stir in the sugar. Rub in the fats with the tips of your fingers and then sprinkle in enough water to give a soft smooth dough. Work quickly so that the pastry stays light. Some people freeze the fat first and then grate it in. Put it to rest for 20 minutes or so.

Heat the oven to 375°F/190°C/Gas 5.

Divide the pastry in two. Roll out one piece and use it to line the pie tin. Fill it with the now cool figs and juices. Roll out the remaining pastry and use it to lid the pie. Trim and fork the edges together to seal them. Cut a small hole in the top and decorate with pastry fig-leaves.

Bake the pie for 25–30 minutes, until the pastry is crisp and brown. Transfer to a rack to cool. Finish with a dusting of cinnamon and a sprinkle of powdered sugar – brown or white.

GREEN THURSDAY: THURSDAY OF EASTER WEEK

Throughout Europe, this is the traditional day for cleaning the house ready for Easter, green symbolizing purity and cleansing from sin, which recalls Christ's ritual washing of his disciples' feet. By the time Easter Sunday comes round, the house should be sparkling – chimneys swept, blankets aired, cupboards and larders well-scrubbed – all ready for the clear light and open doors of spring.

Don't forget to serve honey with the breakfast rolls – or the bees will not give of their best in the coming year.

HERRINGS WITH SPRING HERBS
Matjes heringe mit grün (Germany)

In Germany green things are eaten today. Serve the last of the fine fat spring herrings – northern Europe's favourite Lent dish – with the first tender leaves of spring. It is perfect for Green Thursday, accompanied by the first tiny new potatoes.

Quantity: Serves 4.
Time: 1 hour.
Equipment: A large and a small saucepan. A whisk.

fillets of 2 fresh herrings (8 fillets)
1lb/500g new potatoes, scrubbed and
  plain-boiled with plenty of salt
1 small bunch chervil
1 small bunch chives

4 hard-boiled eggs, peeled and chopped
1 large bunch young spinach leaves
1 small bunch parsley
1 small bunch sorrel
1 small bunch dill

The sauce
¼ pint/150ml soured cream
2 tablespoons chopped gherkins

2 tablespoons chopped dill

Set out the herrings on individual plates on a bed of chopped egg. Arrange the potatoes and the green herbs all around.

Combine the sauce ingredients, and hand them separately. To accompany, serve black bread with white butter, the last of the winter's pickled cucumbers, and a bowl of young radishes; all good healthy food and fresh flavours for Green Thursday.

GOOD FRIDAY

Good Friday is the blackest day in the Christian calendar – commemorating, as it does, the death of the Son of God on the Cross. Those who had not observed a strict fast during Lent usually felt themselves obliged to honour it on Good Friday. All Lenten fasting food (see pp. 109-123) is suitable sustenance for the day. The alternative is a day-long fast, broken only by water and an obligatory glass of vinegar, to commemorate the vinegar-soaked sponge offered to Jesus by the centurion.

HOT-CROSS BUNS
(England)

England bakes and eats its sweet Easter buns on Good Friday – practically everyone else in Europe waits till Easter Sunday for its sweet treat. The modern food historian Anne Wilson· dates as post-Reformation the association of hot-cross buns with Good Friday, noting that raisin and currant buns were a special Lenten food in Elizabethan times. Before then it was the custom to mark all loaves with a cross before baking as it still is in the isolated villages of the Mediterranean – in order to ward off the evil spirits who might prevent the bread rising. The Reformed Church did not approve of such popish practice, and retained the cross only for the holiest day of the year.

Quantity: Makes 2 dozen buns.
Time: Start 3 hours ahead. 1 hour intermittent attention.
Equipment: A mixing bowl and sieve. A baking tray and cooling rack.

2lb/1kg strong white flour	½ teaspoon salt
1 tablespoon mixed spice	5oz/150g butter
1oz/25g fresh yeast (½oz/12g dry)	6oz/175g soft brown sugar
¾ pint/450ml warm milk	2 eggs
2oz/50g currants	2oz/50g sultanas
2oz/50g mixed peel	

The crosses
4oz/100g marzipan or plain shortcrust pastry

To finish
4 tablespoons sugar, dissolved in 4 tablespoons boiling water

Sift the flour, salt and spice into the bowl. Rub in the butter and the yeast with the tips of your fingers.

Stir in the sugar, and knead all to a soft dough with the milk lightly mixed with the eggs. Work it well, pulling and pushing with the ball of your hand on a well floured board, until the dough is smooth and elastic.

Put the dough into the bowl, cover loosely with a damp cloth or clingfilm, and put it in a warm place to rise for 2 hours.

Knock the risen dough down on a well floured board, and knuckle it well to distribute the air. Mix in the fruit and peel (if you do this earlier in the process, the dough will be grey).

Cut off pieces of dough the size of a pigeon's egg. Flatten each nugget of dough and draw the edges up to give you a little round cushion. Put each bun, creased-side down, on the well greased baking tray, allowing plenty of space for expansion. Cover the buns and put them back to rise once more. They should take about 30 minutes to double in size again.

Preheat the oven to 425°F/220°C/Gas 7.

Top the buns with two thin strips of marzipan or pastry in the shape of a cross. If you prefer, you can mark them with a knife cut instead.

Bake the buns for 15–20 minutes, until they are well risen and as brown as berries.

Glaze the buns as they come out of the oven, with a brushful of sugar syrup. Transfer them to the baking rack to cool.

Serve hot-cross buns for a late breakfast on Good Friday – they have to be made fresh on the day or they are not what they pretend.

In medieval times, any leftover buns were kept and crumbled to be mixed with water and taken as a cure-all for stomach complaints.

EGG AND PAPRIKA SOUP
(Hungary)

In some regions of Hungary, a simple soup enriched with eggs is eaten on Good Friday. A fish soup enriched with fish eggs is the alternative. Since by now the house has been swept and scrubbed, and the Easter eggs have been decorated ready to be taken to church to be blessed, you may not want to mess up the kitchen again with more Lenten fish.

Quantity: Serves 4.
Time: 20 minutes.
Equipment: A large saucepan.

2oz/50g lard or oil
1 tablespoon paprika
4 eggs, whisked with 1 tablespoon wine vinegar
¼ pint/150ml soured cream

1 tablespoon caraway seeds
2 pints/1.2 litres water
salt and pepper

Heat the lard or oil in the saucepan and stir in the caraway seeds. When they pop, stir in the paprika and immediately pour in the water. Bring all to the boil and simmer for 5 minutes. Pour a ladleful of the hot broth into the whisked eggs. Off the heat, whisk the egg mixture into the soup. Taste and add salt and pepper. Finish with soured cream.

Serve the soup without reboiling, with hot garlic-rubbed butter-fried croûtons. You'll be surprised how good it is.

GOOD FRIDAY LIMPETS
(Isle of Man)

Limpets are called fritters on the Isle of Man, and it was customary to pick a bucketful on Good Friday and cook them for tea. Pick them off the rocks at low tide – swiftly and silently, or they clamp down and you will never prise them loose. Be careful to pick where there is no effluent – shellfish are the miner's canary of the sea, and always feel the first effects of any bad news. Limpets can be prepared in any way suitable for mussels or clams. Once they are off their rocks, wash them thoroughly in plenty of clean water and then scrape them out of their shells – with a quick twist of one large sturdy limpet shell or a sharp little knife.

Quantity: Serves 4.
Time: 30 minutes.
Equipment: A large frying pan and a draining spoon.

1 pint/600ml shelled limpets (mussels or
   clams would do)
4–5 tablespoons dried breadcrumbs
frying oil

2 tablespoons flour
1 egg beaten with 1 tablespoon milk
salt and pepper

Dry the limpets roughly, roll them lightly in flour and shake off any excess.

Heat a panful of frying oil at least 2 fingers deep, until a faint blue haze rises.

Dip the limpets in the egg and then in the breadcrumbs. Fry them quickly – not too many at a time or they will be oil sodden – turning once. Drain them on absorbent paper. Sprinkle with salt and pepper. Continue until all are used up.

Serve them hot, with a good strong cup of tea.

EASTER SUNDAY

Egg dishes are the distinguishing ingredient of Easter feasting. For the main meal most people serve roast lamb (see Greek Easter, p.154) – often accompanied by a sauce of bitter herbs, as with the English vinegar and mint. The alternative Easter feast, particularly in north-eastern Europe, is ham or pork. The Hungarians call Easter *Husvet*, festival of meat, and like to serve bacon or ham with horseradish, grated freshly in long thin strips, as the Easter treat.

Finland has an interesting if unreproducible Easter food; Mammi, a solid porridge made with malted rye flavoured with dried orange peel, baked for 3 hours in birch-bark dishes and served with sugar and cream. 'Mammi,' says Peggy Benton in her 1960 *Finnish Food*, 'is perfectly cooked when the edge of the bark is covered with a fine powder and the bottom is like a thin layer of syrup.'

Say a grace before your Easter meal. Robert Burns, occasionally required to bless the meat, offered a poetic plea for a sheep's head against a rainy day – not the same as a roast lamb on the spit, but nonetheless a tasty morsel for a hungry Scot on a lean Easter:

> O Lord, when hunger pinches sore,
> Do thou stand us in need,
> And send us from they bounteous store,
> A tup or wether head!
> Amen.

EASTER HERB OMELETTE
Omelette fines herbes (France)

This was the traditional Easter lunch when I was a child in northern France. I don't remember having roast lamb, but I do remember the huge pan, blackened outside and burnished to a near-white sheen inside, which was used to make the omelette. We children were sent out into the damp spring garden to collect the fresh herbs – under strict instructions to be careful to pick only outside leaves so as not to damage the young plants. Then we were allowed to tip the frothy eggs into the pan ourselves, and watch as the curds set almost as soon as they touched the hot butter.

Quantity: Serves 4.
Time: 15 minutes.
Equipment: A bowl. A 4 person omelette pan – failing that, the usual 1 person pan.

10 eggs

2 tablespoons chopped sorrel or watercress

1 tablespoon chopped tarragon

2oz/50g butter

2 tablespoons chopped parsley

2 tablespoons chopped chives

salt and pepper

Swirl the eggs together with a fork – they should blend rather than froth. Lightly mix in the herbs, salt and pepper.

Put a large oval plate to warm.

Heat the omelette pan. When it is hot, drop in half the butter. Swirl the butter round the pan until it froths. Pour in the eggs all at once. As soon as the bottom sets, move it over to allow the uncooked egg to run underneath. Dot the remaining butter over the surface (3–4 blobs is fine). Turn half the omelette over itself. While it is still lovely and runny, tip it out on to the warm plate so that it folds over itself to give a plump juicy bolster.

We children took the omelette to the bottom of the garden, and ate it there with our fingers.

SAVOURY STUFFED EGG BUNS
Folares do pascoa (Portugal)

The Portuguese bake a version of the sweet Easter cakes with eggs embedded in them (see Easter egg bread, facing page). this excellent savoury version is made in the northern districts. In Portugal the breads are made in the shape of a heart, or an egg, or are just round. Here I give a typical oil pastry as an easy recipe – but the buns are often made with an egg and oil enriched bread dough, such as that given for the Easter egg bread, omitting the dried fruit and nuts.

Quantity: Makes 4 buns.

Time: 2 hours intermittent attention.

Equipment: A frying pan. A bowl and a sieve. A small saucepan. A rolling pin and board. A baking tray.

The filling

2 tablespoons olive oil

1 onion, skinned and chopped

2oz/50g salt cured ham or lean bacon, diced

4oz/100g meat (pork, lamb, veal), cubed small

1 glass white wine

1 tablespoon chopped parsley

1 garlic clove, skinned and crushed

1 red pepper, de-seeded and chopped

2oz/50g diced Portuguese *linguica* or *chouriço* (or Spanish *chorizo* or salami plus 1 teaspoon paprika)

salt and pepper

The oil pastry

10oz/300g self-raising flour

4 tablespoons olive oil

¼ pint/150ml water

½ teaspoon salt

2 tablespoons white wine

To finish

1 tablespoon milk

4 new laid eggs, hard-boiled

Heat the oil in a frying pan and gently fry the garlic, onion and peppers. When the vegetables are soft, push them to one side, add the ham and the *linguica* or *chouriço* and fry that. Add the cubed meat, and sauté it until it takes a little colour. Splash in the wine and add the parsley. Bubble up, lid, and simmer until the liquid has evaporated and the meat is tender. Taste and add salt and freshly-milled pepper. Leave aside to cool while you make the pastry.

Make a well in the flour and sprinkle in the salt. Put the oil, wine and water into a small pan and heat it to blood temperature. Pour the warm liquid into the flour, and work the dry and wet ingredients together until you have a soft elastic dough. Work it some more until it is a smooth, elastic ball.

Heat the oven to 425°F/220°C/Gas 7.

Roll out the dough, not too thinly, and cut out 8 rounds, or hearts or egg-shapes, on a well-floured board with a floured rolling pin. Transfer 4 of the rounds to the oiled baking sheet, and spread the cooled filling in the middle of each, leaving a finger's width of margin all round. Wet the edges and lay the second round over the first to enclose the filling. Damp the edge, scalloping to make a rope pattern. Press a hollow into the middle, damp it with milk, and settle in the unshelled egg. Secure the egg with crosses of pastry dough made from the trimmings.

Bake the *folares* in the hot oven for 10–15 minutes to set the pastry, then turn the oven down to 375°F/190°C/Gas 5 and bake for another 20 minutes until the pastry is golden brown.

COLOURED EGGS
(England)

Until the confectioners took over, delicately tinted eggs were a favourite gift at Easter in England. Fresh from the barnyard, they were coloured with natural dyes. Spinach or anemone petals were used for green, gorse blossom for yellow, cochineal for scarlet. For a mottled yellow, the egg can be boiled wrapped in the brown skin of an onion.

PAINTED EGGS
(Hungary)

Hungarian children and young people traditionally give each other painted eggs as tokens of friendship or even engagement – Easter is a favourite time for weddings, as the new wine is just ready for drinking and the event can be celebrated in style. Sometimes the eggs are decorated with tiny horseshoes and finished with little metal loops – in the old days this was probably so that they could be hung up by the boys on the Easter trees set up on Easter night on the girls' gates. Easter marks the start of spring, and springtime is the right time for courting. A gift of an egg says all that needs to be said.

EASTER EGG BREAD
Corona de pascua (Spain)

These plaited crowns of rich sweet breads, with hard-boiled eggs nestling in the links, appear all round the Catholic Mediterranean, from Portugal to Greece. In pagan Hungary, George Lang records, the woven or braided breads signified the hair sacrifice to be placed in a fresh grave; among the people of Moldavia a special bread bracelet is baked to be placed on the arm of a still-born infant so that the baby can play with it in the next world.

In Italy an enriched bread, much like the Christmas *panettone*, is baked into a dove-shaped Easter cake – *la colomba*. The dove-cake is finished with almonds and sugar crystals. The bird seems to have local significance, rather than the role allotted to it by Noah as the universal symbol of peace. In Milan, the birthplace of the cake, the bird was a hero of the battle of Legnano in 1176.

Twenty years ago I used to buy my *corona de pascua* in my local bakery in Algeciras, southern Spain. The bread came with six snow white eggs, as it was customary to order one egg for each member of the family. Unless of course there were guests staying: everyone knew everyone else's business in those days, and such family comings and goings were a matter of great interest.

Austrian children, already stuffed with the lovely cream pastries with which the Austrians mark all special occasions, receive a *Monih* (monk) – a doughboy about a foot long with a whole egg embedded in his navel – made with a similar dough, but with softened butter instead of olive oil.

Quantity: Serves 6.
Time: Allow 4 hours intermittent attention.
Equipment: A mixing bowl. A baking tray and cooling rack.

1lb/500g flour
4oz/100g sugar
8 fl oz/100ml warm milk
8oz/250g raisins
3oz/75g peeled blanched almonds
grated rind of 1 lemon

½ teaspoon salt
1oz/25g fresh yeast (or ½oz/12g dried yeast)
4–5 tablespoons olive oil
2oz/50g crystallized peel
1 teaspoon powdered cinnamon

To finish
6 white new-laid eggs, hard-boiled

1 egg yolk, mixed with 1 tablespoon milk

Sift the flour and salt into the mixing bowl. Mix the yeast with ¼ cup of warm milk and a pinch of sugar, wait until it liquifies, and pour it into a well in the flour. Sprinkle with flour and leave in a warm corner for 10–15 minutes, so that the yeast can begin to work. (If using dried yeast, follow the packet directions.)

Add the rest of the ingredients and knead together, adding enough of the remaining milk to give you a soft, slightly sticky dough. Work it well, pulling and pushing with the ball of your hand, until the dough is smooth and elastic.

Put the dough back into the bowl, cover loosely with a damp cloth or clingfilm, and put it in a warm place to rise for 1½ hours, until the dough feels spongy and firm.

Knock the dough down and knuckle it well to distribute the air.

Divide the dough into 3 pieces and roll each into a long rope. Plait the ropes in 6 links (start in the middle – easier to taper the ends), securing at each end with a damp finger. Transfer to the greased baking tray.

Cover the bread and put it back to rise once more. This should take about 1 hour – the dough is ready when it has doubled in thickness and bounces back when you press a fingertip into its surface.

Nestle a whole unshelled egg into the V of each link – dampen the hollow first so that the egg sticks in position. Glaze the bread and eggs with the egg-and-milk.

Preheat the oven to 400°F/200°C/Gas 6.

Bake the bread for 35–40 minutes, until well risen and nicely browned.

Transfer to the rack to cool.

EASTER MONDAY

All over Europe, from the Easter parades of Britain to the all-day picnics of Greece, this is the day the whole population takes to the streets and hills to laze around and pick flowers and generally enjoy the promise of summer. Picnic food is the order of the day, from the scones and cheese piece-for-the-pocket of Scotland, to the potato omelette of Spain (see p. 187), to the deliciously light *torta pascualina* of Italy – feathery and juicy as anything the Ottoman Turks ever devised.

EASTER PIE
Torta pascualina (Italy)

This delicious vegetable and egg pie, popular at this time throughout Italy, is the Easter speciality of the province of Liguria, the coastal strip which includes Savoy and Genoa and reaches round to the French border. The people, pressed hard against the coast by the mountains behind, are sailors and fishermen by tradition, which perhaps accounts for the Arab filo pastry used in this recipe. The fine pastry is often home-made by those used to preparing their own pasta – to the skilled cooks of Liguria, any dough is plain sailing. Filo/strudel dough is now widely available in supermarkets: for this dish, 33 layers are required, one for each year of Christ's life.

Quantity: Serves 6.
Time: 1½ hours intermittent attention.
Equipment: A lidded pan. 2 bowls. A pastry brush. A 10in/25cm diameter pie tin.

33 sheets filo pastry (about 12oz/350g)
1 tablespoon butter
2–3 spring onions, finely chopped
1lb/500g ricotta (or fresh curd cheese), mashed
2 tablespoons cream
1 teaspoon grated nutmeg
6 eggs, hard-boiled and shelled

1lb/500g chard (or beet tops, or curly cabbage), rinsed and shredded finely
1 tablespoon chopped fresh marjoram
2 tablespoons grated parmesan
salt and pepper
about 6 tablespoons melted clarified butter

Take care to keep the filo pastry covered while you work – it dries out and cracks very easily.

Sauté the chard quickly in the 1 tablespoon of butter with the onions and the marjoram – cover and shake the pan over the heat for a few minutes to soften the vegetables and concentrate the flavours. Leave it to cool.

Beat the ricotta, parmesan and cream together in a bowl. Season with salt, pepper and nutmeg.

Preheat the oven to 350°F/180°C/Gas 4.

Butter the pie tin and line it with two thicknesses of filo pastry. Paint the top sheet with a slick of melted butter, lay on another two layers and paint them with butter, and so on until you have sixteen thicknesses of filo.

Spread in the chard – lightly so that you do not press the air out of the pastry layers. Cover the chard with the cheese mixture. With the back of a spoon, press out 6 hollows and lay in the eggs. Lay on 2 more sheets of filo and paint with butter as before. Continue until all is used up.

Bake for 1 hour, until beautifully light and golden brown. Let the *torta* cool and become firm. Leave it in its pie tin, tied up in a clean cloth, when you transport it to the picnic. Cut it with a sharp knife so that there is an egg in each segment.

EASTER IN LAPLAND

Frank Hedges Butler, Edwardian traveller and founder of the Royal Club, spent a turn-of-the-century Easter in Karesuando, Swedish Lapland – noting that apart from the Swedish governor and his English-speaking wife, there were no other Europeans staying there. Easter remains the time when Lapp weddings are celebrated, although these days there are likely to be rather more tourists.

It was Easter-time, March 23rd, and the great feast of the Lapps. There was no market or fair; it was simply like an English Easter, with holiday-making and religious services, confirmations, baptisms, funerals and marriages.

The Church Festival began on Good Friday and lasted until Easter Tuesday. Nominally we were five days in church. As a rule the Lapps live far in the interior and can only go to church twice a year, the first Sunday in Advent and at Easter. The church, built on the site of an old one in 1820, is a very fine wooden building, well warmed by wood stoves, and with a gallery and high steeple. The Service is Lutheran.

The Lapps were all dressed in their best clothes, and when seated in the church, the colours and different blends of blue, red, and yellow on their brown and white paesks and coloured shawls adorned with silver ornaments, was a sight not to be forgotten. The church was crowded, about one thousand Lapps attending, the men sitting on one side and the women the other. Many had to sit on the floor. Babies were there in their canoe reindeer cradles, and dogs, of a large Pomeranian breed, lay at their masters' feet or ran about the church, and in and out of the door whenever it was opened. At funerals and weddings dogs come in with the same freedom, as they are the faithful friends of the Lapp and the protectors of the reindeer.

. . . We saw four couples married at the same time, some hundred guests being present. The brides were generally dressed in red, with white shoes and red gloves, with beautiful silk scarves and tassels. The bridegrooms wore a very fine blue suit, which stood out at the sides, with white reindeer shoes and a square cap. No dress at a fancy ball can be more picturesque than a Lapp bridal dress in red.

American travel-writer Maturin Ballou in 1887 described the Lappish ceremony, and its consequences, in more detail:

When a couple of young Lapps desire to become married a priest is sometimes employed, but by common acceptation among them the bride's father is equally qualified to perform the ceremony, which is both original and simple. It consists in placing the hands of the two contracting parties in each other, and the striking of fire with a flint and steel, when the marriage is declared to be irrevocable. Up to a certain age, Lapp babies are packed constantly in dry moss, in place of other clothing during their infancy, this being renewed as occasion demands. The little creatures are very quiet in their portable cradles, consisting of a basket-frame covered with reindeer hide, into which they are closely strapped. The cases are sometimes swung hammock fashion between two posts, and sometimes hung upon a peg outside the cabins in the sunshine. Though many hours have been passed by the author among these people, he never heard a breath of complaint from the wee things.

EASTER WEDDING BANQUET
(Lapland)

Frank Hedges Butler sketched out the feast circa 1900. 'The banquet was at 9 p.m., and reindeer cream, marrowbones of the reindeer and venison were the principal dishes, with hot coffee and cakes.' The menu was not much altered until the terrible disaster of Chernobyl exposed the *Same* herds of reindeer, the nomadic northerners' equivalent of beef cattle, to enough radiation to warrant their official removal from the dinner-table.

It is not possible to reproduce such a feast accurately without access to the correct raw materials. Beef marrow (baked in the bone in a medium oven for an hour) can substitute for the reindeer and the venison marrowbones; smoked beef tongue is not quite as delicate as reindeer, but makes a passable imitation.

VANILLA AND ALMOND CREAM CAKE
Bløtkake (Norway)

Elaborate cream cakes remain the popular celebration treat all over Scandinavia. Dairy products – cream and milk both fresh and soured – have always formed an important part of the Scandinavian diet. Hay for the cattle is the one crop which can be counted on to mature in the short summer of northern Scandinavia. Serve the cream cake with coffee – I remember in Lapland the coffee was brewed in a copper kettle and poured off the top of the grounds, after a small piece of dried fish-skin had been dropped in to clear the coffee. Oddly, it works fine and doesn't taste at all fishy.

Quantity: Makes 1 large cake.
Time: Settle down for 2 hours. Most of it is washing-up.
Equipment: A mixing bowl and an egg-beater (electric is best). A 9in/22cm cake tin (removable sides if possible) and a cooling rack. A blender or whisk. A bain-marie or a small saucepan with a small basin resting in it. A bowl and clingfilm. A rolling pin and board.

The cake

3 eggs	4oz/100g caster sugar
3oz/75g plain flour	1oz/25g cornflour
1 drop vanilla essence	1 glass sherry or fruit syrup

The vanilla filling

½ pint/150ml milk

2 drops vanilla essence

2 teaspoons powdered gelatine

1 heaped tablespoon toasted slivered almonds

4 egg yolks

3 tablespoons sugar

4 tablespoons whipped cream

Topping

2 tablespoons raspberry jam (or any other good jam without too many lumps)

8oz/250g sieved icing sugar, mixed to a thick coating icing with water

8oz/250g ready-made marzipan (see simnel cake, p.121, for recipe)

2–3 tablespoons toasted slivered almonds

Preheat the oven to 350°F/180°C/Gas 4.

First make the cake. Whisk the eggs with the sugar until white and fluffy. This takes twice as long as you expect, even with an electric beater – allow 8 minutes at least. Sieve and fold in the flour, cornflour and vanilla with a metal spoon – turning the mixture well over to 'tire' it (it must be exhausted already, with all that beating).

Butter the cake tin and line it with buttered greaseproof paper. Tip in the mixture.

Bake the cake for 40–45 minutes, until well-puffed and firm to the finger. It won't increase much in size.

Let it settle and then tip it out on to a cake rack to cool. Split it ready for the filling and transfer the base to its final resting place. Soak it with sherry or fruit syrup.

Meanwhile make the filling. Whisk the milk, yolks, vanilla, sugar and gelatine together, or mix them in the blender. Heat the mixture gently over boiling water in the bain-marie or a bowl suspended over a saucepan, until it all thickens. Pour into a cold bowl, cover with clingfilm, and leave to cool. Fold in the whipped cream and the slivered almonds.

Layer the cake with the cold vanilla cream.

Spread the outside of the cake with the raspberry jam.

Dust a rolling pin and board with icing sugar and roll out the marzipan into a round wide enough to drape over the whole cake and reach down the sides.

Cover the cake with the marzipan. Trim the edges. Spread on the icing and let it set. Damp the sides (or spread them with more jam) and roll them in the toasted slivered almonds.

After that, choose your own decoration: Easter hares (no Easter eggs, let alone chicks, yet in the far north), a bride and groom. Or do something skilful with the piping bag.

EASTERN EASTER: BETWEEN APRIL AND MAY 5TH

The eastern Orthodox Catholic Church still uses the Gregorian calendar, having split in 1054 with the Rome-based Catholic Church – acknowledging the Patriarch of Constantinople as their spiritual leader leaving Pope Leo IX as Bishop of Rome. The eastern Easter usually falls in April, or sometimes in early May – about eleven days later then the western Easter. Even in countries where the state is entirely secular, Easter remains a popular folk festival. In Greece it is a far more important celebration than Christmas – it is the time when all Greeks go back to their homes to be with their families.

As with all our festivals, the traders of the big cities have been busy commercialising the celebration for centuries. A certain 'Roving Englishman', writing in *Household Words* in the 1850s, observed the noisy exuberance of an urban Orthodox Easter:

The Greek Lent is over, and it is Easter at Constantinople; all night long great guns have been firing afar off, and small arms are being discharged by excitable persons at every street corner; you might fancy the town was being stormed, instead of holding high festival, so violent is the noise and uproar. During the day the streets are crowded as a fair, and perambulated by itinerant vendors of good things, as boisterous as on a Saturday night at Wapping. Fowls, sweetmeats, rank pastry, various preparations of milk and *reakee*, seem to be the chief things which furnish a Greek merry-making at Constantinople. Little boys, with eager black eyes and tallowy complexions, are in their glory, and go yelling and whooping about, to the dismay of staider wayfarers.

Half a century later, John Lawson attended a somewhat more religious celebration on the island of Therea. For the observance of the Orthodox Easter, no one can hold a beeswax candle to the devout congregations of Greece's isolated rural communities – particularly those of the islands, which have always felt themselves more vulnerable to the gods, whether pagan or Christian.

The Lenten fast was drawing to a close when I arrived. For the first week it is strictly observed: meat, fish, eggs, milk, cheese, and even olive-oil being prohibited, so that the ordinary diet is reduced to bread and water, to which is sometimes added a soup made from dried cuttlefish or octopus; for these along with shell-fish are not reckoned to be animal food, as being bloodless. During the next four weeks some relaxation is allowed; but no one with any pretensions to piety would even then partake of fish, meat or eggs; the last-mentioned are stored up until Easter and then, being dyed red, are either eaten, or – more widely – offered to visitors.

Then comes 'the Great Week' and with it the same strict regulations come into force as during the first week of Lent. It was not hard to perceive that for most of the villagers the fast had been a real and painful abstinence. Work had almost ceased; for there was little energy left. Everywhere white, sharp-featured faces told of real hunger. Such was the condition of body and mind in which they attended the long service of Good Friday night . . . Soon after dark on Easter Eve, the same weary yet excited faces may be seen gathered in the church. But there is a change too; there is a feeling abroad of anxiety, of expectancy. To-night there is restlessness rather than silence. Some go to and fro between the church and their homes; others join discordantly in the chants and misplace the responses; anything to cheat the long hours of waiting . . . What is happening there now behind those curtains which veil the chancel from the expectant throng? Midnight strikes. The curtains are drawn back. Yes, there is the bier, borne but yesternight to the grave. It is empty. That is only the shroud upon it.

The words of the priest ring out true: 'Christ is risen! . . . A miracle, a miracle!'

Quickly from the priest's lighted candle the flame is passed. In a moment the dim building is illumined by a lighted taper in every hand. A procession forms, a joyful procession now. Everywhere are light and glad voices and the embraces of friends, crying aloud the news 'Christ is risen' and answering 'he is risen indeed.' In every home the lamb is prepared with haste, the wine flows freely. In the streets is the flash of torches, the din of fire-arms, and all the exuberance of simple joy. The fast is over; the dead has been restored to life before men's eyes; well may they rejoice even to ecstasy. For have they not left the ecstasy of sorrow? This was no tableau – it was all true, all real. In these simple folk religion has transcended reason; they have reached the heights of spiritual exaltation; they have seen and felt as minds more calm and rational can never see nor feel. As men now mourn beside the bier of Christ, so in old time may men have shared Demeter's mourning for her child Kore who, though divine, had suffered the lot of men and passed away to the House of Hades. As now men rejoice when they behold the risen Christ, so in old time may men have shared Demeter's joy when her child returned from beneath the earth, proving that there is life beyond the grave.

It was this vivid account which led me, in 1989, to attend the Easter celebrations on the holy island of Patmos, where St John wrote the Book of Revelations and where, I was assured, Easter was still celebrated in the Monastery of the Theologian with the old fervour. Patmos, tucked into the lee of the Turkish coast, is far too near the infidel for religious complacency.

Although few corners of tourist-swamped Greece could today be called remote, the Dodecanese archipelago in which Patmos is one of the smaller outposts is a twelve-hour journey by ferry from Piraeus, Athens's port. On Palm Saturday, when I joined the ship, its three decks were packed to the gunwales with Greeks returning to celebrate Easter in the collective bosom of their families. Tourists are scarce at this time of year, when the spring sunshine cannot guarantee a tan, and the Mediterranean has not yet settled to its summer aquamarine. The tourist-hordes come later, crowding into Patmos's harbour of Skala and packing out its little fishing settlements. Even then, few take the trouble to explore inland, to climb the steep hill behind Skala, bend a knee in St John's cool dimly-frescoed cave-hermitage, and continue up through the dusty olive groves to admire the craftsman-built houses of Hora. Still fewer, these days, make the pilgrimage to the 1,000-year-old Monastery of the Theologian, spreading, like a mother-hen brooding her chicks, its amber stone buttresses over Hora's clustered whitewashed terraces.

Throughout Easter week from Palm Sunday to Easter Tuesday, the monks of the monastery founded by St John Christodoulos in 1088 hold open house – throwing wide their painted chambers and shadowed sanctuaries to the congregation which sustains them. The people crowd into the monastery day and night, certain of their welcome in this most domestic of religious interiors. The population of the holy island, having paid far more than the proscribed tithe of their earthly labour in exchange for heavenly reward, feel entirely at home in God's house. Naturally, the church is open throughout all the rest of the year: it is simply that this festival of Easter is above all a community effort, with monks and laity combining in a passionate determination to see the whole terrible business of Holy Week through to a successful conclusion.

There can be nowhere in Christendom where church and congregation are so intimately entwined. Many of the monks were married before they took holy orders – only the senior clergy are expected to have been celibate. All are visited noisily and enthusiastically at Easter by mothers and fathers, sisters and brothers, wives and cousins. Children and grandchildren tumble merrily in and out of the archways and cobblestones of the monastery's maze of passages. The church's domed and painted ceilings, dim as the Cave of the Revelation, are layered with 1,000 years of incense and prayer. Every lintel, wall and vault is bathed in a sea of frescoes, filmed with a veil of smoke from the dozens of candle lamps which swing in the domed shadows. When their colours grow dim, others will be painted; a living church spring cleans, it does not restore – that is for dead museums. Time is no enemy: a grandfather clock faces the altar. The monks come and go up the snowy stairs and along the golden walls whose broad tops act as pathways between the maze of cells, communal chambers and side chapels. Everyone is busy with the domestic arrangements of bread and wine and greetings.

The first ceremony of Holy Week, the *Niptiras* – the 'basin ceremony', a re-enactment of Christ's washing of the feet of the disciples – requires the monks to come to the people. Perhaps because of this, it is the most beloved event of the year. The enactment takes place, wind and weather permitting, on a palm and flower-decorated stage in Hora's tiny main square, on the lip of a cliff which falls steeply away, past St John's cave, down to the spring dark sea. Beyond, the horizon stretches to the Holy Land – where, in Jerusalem itself, brother monks are performing the only other re-enactment of the ritual.

When I attended the ceremony, Easter fell at the end of April, and everyone hoped for a sunny day. By eleven in the morning, the scheduled time for the beginning of the ceremony, the whitewashed square and the alleyways which surround it were strewn with wild lavender, and the air was sweet with the scent of blossoms crushed underfoot by the gathering crowds. Children were hoisted on to shoulders and grandpas made comfortable on doorsteps. Everyone was neatly but soberly dressed in black, white and grey. The only colour came from the gold embroidery and ruby velvet upholstery on the stage, and a flight of migrating bee-eaters flashing aquamarine and viridian wings against the scurrying spring clouds overhead. Swallowtail butterflies, attracted by the scent of the lavender, or the damp foreheads of the spectators in the suddenly blazing sun, dipped and danced in and out of the crowd.

Suddenly the crowd was quiet. A black-robed, tall-hatted bearded brother, sheltering from the sun under a black umbrella, raised his voice in the long rhythmic cadences which underpin every Orthodox ceremony. The crowd parted to admit the procession of crimson-robed monks.

One by one the twelve disciples, played by the senior monks, took their seats on the dais. In character, each disciple nodded and greeted his fellows. Taking pleasure in the double familiarity, the crowd identified each actor and the personality he played. Finally the Master, personified by the Abbot, coped in rich deep purple encrusted with pearls and delicately faded gold embroidery, mounted his throne.

The crowd sighed gently as the Abbot/Christ turned to face his chosen twelve, Judas seated on his left hand, the empty blue sea and sky behind him. The ceremony of question and answer, the ritual bathing of the feet and kiss of brotherhood offered to eleven of his disciples, was performed with such grace and conviction that when he finally turned to Judas, his instant of hesitation at Judas's reply, followed by the completion of the ritual and the kiss – a reminder of the kiss of betrayal – was greeted with a hiss of dismay by the entire audience. It was, after 2,000 years, a performance of almost unbearable poignancy, an image as powerful today as it must have been when the Patriarchs of Byzantium first re-enacted it.

Next day the long sombre story of Good Friday unfolded in the inner recesses of the church as the monks and laymen took turns at the lectern to chant the slow rhythms of the gospel verses. The congregation crowded the chapels, genuflecting, making its double sign of the cross, kissing a favourite icon, standing a while, wandering out again – to be replaced with new faces.

The chapel walls are lined with carved wooden stalls – earmarked for the elderly or lame, mothers with babies-in-arms, or a few lonely souls, who, having no family of their own, are always welcome to spend the entire week curled in a corner, watching the comings and goings, homely as any hearthside grandma. As in all churches of pilgrimage, the altar is screened from the main body of the church, to allow pilgrims somewhere to sleep at night.

Little children crouched in the hollows behind the stalls, playing with the wax on their candles, flames glowing on excited faces, a game of tag liable to break out at any moment. Draped over a stall-end was one of the younger monks' black outer garments – the heavy ink-black wool miraculously soft, lined with a shimmer of the finest knife-pleated silk. The monastery's vestments, along with its venerable library, are its chief glory. The jewel-crusted stoles, copes and mitres designed and stitched over the last ten centuries by the women of the community, both nuns and laity, are magnificent, and the monks use them to punctuate the drama of Holy Week: now appearing in brilliant cerulean blue, now in sombre grey, now in silver-threaded amethyst.

The owner of the black robe was one of three monks detailed to call the congregation to Mass with a tattoo of mallet blows on a heavy oak beam slung up in the courtyard. A layman provides a counterpoint with a hammer on a metal bar. The sound is eerie – an echo of the hammer blows which nailed Christ to the Cross, or, later, the knuckles of the disciples rapping on the empty tomb.

There was no shortage of bodily sustenance in the church, either. It's easier to pray with something in the belly. Bread for the Host is baked each day in the village bakery – no anaemic wafers here, but great crusty wheels of prosforon 'offering bread' – a full yard in diameter, double tiered to indicate the dual nature of God, and made with the best and finest wheat flour. Only the cross-stamped central piece is distributed from the altar – the rest is laid out in wide shallow baskets to alleviate the hunger of the worshippers during the long hours of the vigils, or taken home for the Easter meals. The scent curled down the steep whitewashed streets, calling the inhabitants to Mass far more persuasively than the tolling bells. Water, too, was available in the cloister for those who were thirsty.

Everyone seemed to have brought a rosary to be blessed, to search out a cherished icon to be kissed, landing the greeting with perfect accuracy even when the images were draped in mourning-cloths. Meanwhile, outside in the courtyards, the congregation exchanged news with long lost cousins from America, or Athens, or Paris, or just the neighbouring island.

The Passion of Good Friday was drawing to its pre-ordained conclusion. The monks made the circle of church and courtyard three times, carrying the coffin on which rested an icon of the entombed Christ. The candles extinguished, the chapel shrouded in mourning cloths, the long vigil began. After dusk, long, thick double-wicked tapers, hand-dipped in dark honey-scented beeswax, were distributed free to all who kept the night-long watch. People were observing the complete fast, broken only by a glass of vinegar, so the baskets of bread were empty now. An old man handed out the tapers as new vigilants arrived. The mood was as dark as the night. At midnight the Abbot emerged to sprinkle the congregation with orange-flower water.

Here was ceremony without pomp. No distance, either spiritual or physical, separated priest from congregation. The songs of praise were sung with full-volume fervour. Christ is comforted in his agony, mourned in his tomb, willed to his Resurrection. The participants remind each other, like old men sitting round a fire of an evening, of the old story, re-living through the oral tradition a 2,000-year-old experience.

Easter Saturday sees the promise of Resurrection at the morning Mass. There was a sense of relief, not least because everyone could now have a cup of coffee. The bakery was selling round scallop-edged cheese pies scented with nutmeg, and tsoureki, plaited crowns of sweet mastic-flavoured bread with red eggs embedded in the circumference. Live kids and lambs were being carried, bleating like babies, up the hill, ready for the feast tomorrow. Through open doorways wafted the scent of the mageritsa, lamb soup, slow-simmered on the hob, ready for the breaking of the Lent fast after the Mass of Resurrection at midnight. A party of teenagers arrived back from the fields below the village with a large bundle of fennel fronds for the soup, and wild-gathered rosemary for the lamb.

Midnight, and the monastery was packed with people. Every stone step had its family group, every corner a congregation of grandfathers, every broad shoulder its precariously balanced child. A few premature fireworks crackled in the dark streets below. The moonlight was brilliant – flooding the battlements with its cold light, shimmering on the expectant faces crowding the courtyard. The young monks knocked on their wooden yoke – a triple crescendo of drumbeats announced the commencement of the service.

The altar, these past two days dark-draped and bare, was revealed as the arched doors swung wide to the congregation. The interior of the church, still dimly lit, had now been massed with brilliant columns of lilies and roses. The floor was strewn with lavender and rose-petals. From the recesses of the church the voices rose in the litany of coming salvation. Strangers smiled at each other, filling their nostrils with the fragrance of orange-blossom, rosewater and the honey scent of the as yet unlit beeswax candles.

The service continued. At a quarter to the appointed hour, the Abbot and his acolytes emerged into the courtyard. Suddenly it was midnight and the cry of 'Cristos Anesti!' (Christ is risen) swelled into a shout of triumph as the bells rang out. The crimson-robed monks lit the candles of those nearest to them and suddenly candlelight blazed and surged like a forest fire, the light racing from hand to hand up the staircases and along the balconies, illuminating faces flushed with delight. Neighbours kissed neighbours, children looked for parents, husbands searched out wives to exchange the kiss of greeting and a triumphant 'Cristos anesti!' Once again, the Lord is risen and the people can rejoice. Tomorrow, after morning Mass, the Abbot was due to distribute red eggs and his blessing to everyone, and the people could go about their business, secure in the knowledge that their spiritual advocate was once more in a position to intercede for them.

Easter Monday coincided in 1989 with May Day – a public holiday and the first day of spring, traditionally celebrated with an all-day picnic. Everyone took food out into the country or down to the beach – cheese pies, red eggs, tsoureki, fruit, leftover roast meat, tomatoes, cheese, and of course, the wine which had not been permitted in Lent – returning home at sunset with bunches of May flowers to decorate the house.

Tuesday after Easter is the day for the blessing of the icons. The service was held in the small upper square of Hora, its well-worn pavings once again strewn with lavender. The icons, both church- and family-owned, were brought out and held by young monks and small boys, a painted audience for the Abbot's service of blessing. Afterwards the people filed round the square, kissing the icons, tucking in a flower here, taking out a flower there, and finally queueing for the Abbot's benediction, given with a posy of bright spring flowers dipped in holy water scented with orange blossoms.

Then the icon-bearing procession set off round the town, everyone streaming behind, holding short services of benediction in the town's square to bless the icons from the nearby houses. The Abbot beamed with delight – a startling sight in one so old and dignified: the stern-faced dignitaries of the western Church do not accommodate such visible pleasure. One young man stepped out of the crowd to bring a blue and white embroidered stole across for the Abbot to bless. He tucked it back safely in his jacket – perhaps he was contemplating Holy orders, or was a messenger for a brother already ordained.

As we wound through the narrow streets, past the convent from which still curled the scent of the nuns' Easter baking of twist-biscuits and honey breads, we passed a sudden reminder of Sunday's feast. Glimpsed through an open gateway in a derelict courtyard was a washing-line of goat skins hanging up ready for curing – already they were stiff and dry in the morning air.

Old women leant out of windows and doorways to shake droplets from their long-spouted flasks of orange-blossom water on the passing monks and congregation. Friends stopped to chat, rubbing their hands and refreshing their faces with the sweetly perfumed water. Sometimes a waft of scented smoke curled up the street as someone lit a saucerful of incense to greet the monks' passing. The embroideresses who made their magnificent robes are named and known – this one by so-and-so, that one by the other. The interchange of even the holy instruments themselves – incense, wine, bread, icons, reliquaries – between church and congregation de-mystifies the objects but makes them somehow holier, like old friends, doubly valued for the experiences shared.

On Patmos, the monastery and the people have always suffered and prospered together – and miraculously survived the occupying waves of Turks and Christians, Arabs and Normans, Italians and Germans. The monks and their workmen arrived simultaneously 1,000 years ago, armed with the charter granted to their founding father by Emperor Alexius I of Constantinople. The Holy Christodoulos was well pleased with his rocky outpost. Here was nothing to tempt the sybaritic appetites of the pagan goat-god who had claimed so many Christian victims: 'The island is fallen to waste, covered with brambles and thorn scrub, untrodden and so arid as to be totally barren and infertile.'

The landscape has not grown much more hospitable in the last millennium – although a few lemon groves, olive trees and vegetable gardens supplement shipments from the large and more fertile islands of Samos, Kos and Crete. Small wonder the summer tourists and their dollars are so welcome in the hotels and apartment houses of Skala, in the fishermen's tavernas of Kampos and Grikos.

In modern times the monastery village of Hora, loftier and more decorous than her seaside sisters, has a respectable summer-time income catering to the rich of Athens, the new owners of the elegant mansions built by descendants of the monastery's craftsmen. Here lives an Italian princess, there a Belgian banker, and in that balconied palace a Greek politician and his mistress – but only for one month a year. The villagers of Hora render unto Caesar in the summer, but Easter is for God.

PALM SUNDAY

PALM SUNDAY FISH SOUP
(Greece)

Patmos sticks firmly to its strict Lenten fast, during which nor eggs, nor milk, nor fish nor fowl, let alone good red meat, are permitted. Palm Sunday is the exception – fish, but not eggs, are allowed back on the menu. On the Sunday before Easter, in celebration of Christ's entry into Jerusalem, the local taverna on the beach served up this delicious fish soup. Greek fish soups belong to the *pot-au-feu* school: the broth is served first, with the solid fish and vegetables appearing as the second course. The fish varies according to the fortune of the fisherman. Rascasse-type rockfish which have plenty of gluey bones are considered a good base, but this is not immutable: Greek inshore fishermen net some strange rainbow-hued creatures for the soup-pot.

Quantity: Serves 4.
Time: 30 minutes.
Equipment: A large, deep saucepan.

1½–2lb/750g–1kg whole white fish (gurnard, whiting, small haddock, pollack, ling, catfish – nothing expensive)
1 head celery (the green unblanched type has the best flavour)
2 tomatoes
2 lemons (optional)

salt and pepper
2 pints/1.2 litres water
4 tablespoons olive oil
4–5 large spring onions, or 2 mature onions
3–4 sprigs parsley
1lb/500g large new potatoes

Rinse, scale and gut the fish, leaving it whole. Salt it thoroughly and put it aside.

Put the water and oil into the saucepan with the celery (well washed and roughly chopped), the spring onions (trimmed and rinsed but with the green left on) or mature onions (peeled and chunked), the parsley, the tomatoes (roughly chunked), and the potatoes (peeled and quartered lengthways). Bring everything to the boil, and boil rapidly, uncovered, for 12–15 minutes, until the potatoes are nearly soft.

Lay the fish on top of the vegetables, lid the pan, and cook for another 8–12 minutes, until the fish is done. You will have to judge this yourself by parting the flesh down to the bone with a knife – the bone should no longer be pink.

Lift the fish and vegetables out carefully with a draining spoon and arrange them on a warm dish. Leave a few pieces of potato in the broth.

Taste the broth and add salt and pepper if necessary. Finish with a hearty squeeze of lemon, and serve. Squeeze some more lemon over the fish, and serve it flanked by lemon quarters.

No egg *avgolemono* thickening today – Lent will be over soon enough.

HOLY THURSDAY

The Thursday before Easter is sometimes called Red Thursday, because this is the day on which the red-dyed eggs are cooked. The dye used in the old days came from a special redwood – and it had to be made in a new bowl, and the dye not thrown away after it had been used. This is the day, too, to bake Easter buns and breads, the *tsoureki* which have red eggs embedded in them – in Greece the breads are flavoured with brandy and caraway seeds. (See p.137 for the Spanish version.)

RED-DYED EGGS
(Greece)

Red eggs are eaten throughout the six days of celebration which follow Easter Sunday, but they make their first appearance at the post-midnight breakfast, taken early on Easter Sunday morning after the Saturday Mass of the Resurrection, before the *mageritsa* soup is served. No eggs should be eaten before midnight on Saturday. The ceremony of egg cracking – the *tsougrisma* – is as much fun as our own cracker pulling. Each person takes his own egg and cracks it against his neighbour's – round end against round end or pointed against pointed, but never against sides – with a cry of '*Cristos anesti!*' (Christ is risen), to which the replay is '*Alithos anesti*' (truly he is risen). When there is only one egg left whole, the owner is judged the winner. No prizes are awarded, the honour is sufficient.

Papers of red dye to colour a given number of eggs can be bought from any Greek greengrocer at Easter-time.

Quantity: One egg per person.
Time: 10–15 minutes.
Equipment: A saucepan.

Allow 1 egg per person, and another 5 each for snacking over Easter

4 tablespoons vinegar to 1 pint/600ml water
red dye

To hard-boil perfectly fresh eggs, make sure they are at room temperature first. Put them in a saucepan in warm water in which the dye has been dissolved, according to the instructions on the packet, with a good splash of vinegar to act as a fixative – red food colouring or cochineal will do in default.

Bring the water to the boil. Remove the pan from the heat and lid tightly as soon as the water boils. Leave the eggs for 6 minutes. Take them out and plunge them into cold water, then give them a shine with oil. You can re-use the dye by adding more vinegar.

SPINACH PIE
Spanakopita (Greece)

This spinach pastry is baked throughout Lent and can be bought in every Greek bakery. Each family has its own favourite balance of greens and seasonings. Holy Thursday is the last chance to enjoy it before the fast of Good Friday signals that Lent is drawing to a close.

Quantity: Serves 4–6.
Time: 1 hour.
Equipment: A saucepan. A pastry brush. A baking tray.

2½lb/1.25kg spinach or mixed wild leaves – Good King Henry, fat-hen, watercress, dandelion
4–5 tablespoons sesame oil
3 eggs, lightly beaten
1 teaspoon grated nutmeg (*optional*)

6 scallions or large spring onions, minimally trimmed, rinsed and chopped
4 tablespoons chopped dill or mint
8oz/250g grated feta cheese (or 6oz/175g grated Cheddar and 2oz/50g grated parmesan)
8–10 sheets filo pastry

Keep the sheets of filo covered while you work so that they do not dry out.

Sweat the greens with the onions and herbs in 1 tablespoon of sesame oil and the water that clings to them after washing, for 5 minutes until they wilt. Sprinkle with the grated feta, or the same weight of grated Cheddar mixed with parmesan (feta is a very salty and well-flavoured cheese). Stir in the eggs and mix thoroughly. Season with salt and pepper and optional nutmeg.

Heat the oven to 350°F/180°C/Gas 4.

Layer a pastry base of 8 sheets of filo, brushing between the layers with sesame oil, in the oiled baking tray – the pastry should just reach up the sides.

Spread in the spinach mixture.

Lid the pie with another 4 sheets of filo brushed with oil. Mark with a diamond pattern and sprinkle water over the pastry, using your fingertips dipped in water. This will stop the pastry curling up.

Bake for 45–50 minutes, until the pastry is flaky and golden. The pie is at its best served just warm.

GOOD FRIDAY

Greeks who have not observed the strict Lenten fast will probably fast on Good Friday. No one works.

During Easter week the *prosforon* – a double-layered round bread stamped with a special seal – can be bought in any Greek bakery. It is customary to take it to church as a gift, to be blessed, the centre to be used for the communion – taken only once or twice a year in the Greek Orthodox Church, as a one- or two-day fast is required beforehand.

The female members of the family take sweet-scented flowers – violets, roses, stocks and lemon blossom – to the church to decorate the pall on which the effigy of the body of the dead Christ is placed after the descent from the Cross.

Food, if it is taken at all, is of the plainest: lettuce or wild greens dressed with vinegar or lemon juice; *tahinosoupa* – a universally unpopular soup made with sesame seeds and rice, seasoned with lemon juice; sesame-seed halva; or maybe a plain lentil or fava (broad) bean soup.

FASTING SOUP
Fakki (Greece)

This is Greek soul-food – a very venerable dish indeed. It should be good and thick, almost so that a spoon can stand up in it. On non-fast days it can be finished with a generous seasoning of olive oil, but it is very good without. It is the traditional fasting food during Holy Week. Vary the diet by making the soup with brown lentils or split peas and seasoning with lemon instead of vinegar.

Quantity: Serves 6.
Time: 10 minutes to prepare, 2 hours simmering – even better made the day before and reheated.
Equipment: A large soup pan.

1lb/500g yellow lentils	4 pints/2.5 litres water
1–2 onions, skinned and chopped	3 garlic cloves, skinned and chopped
2–3 stalks celery, washed and chopped (the unblanched green type has the best flavour)	a 15oz/450g tin of tomatoes
1–2 bay leaves	small handful of parsley, roughly chopped
	salt and pepper

To finish

1–2 tablespoons chopped raw onion (optional)	3–4 tablespoons chopped fresh oregano, basil and mint
2 tablespoons wine vinegar	

Pick over the lentils and put them in the soup pot with the water and the other ingredients. Bring all to the boil, lid and turn down to simmer. Leave to cook very gently for 1½-2 hours, stirring occasionally. When the soup is good and thick and puréed, it is ready. Taste and add more salt and pepper if required.

Finish with the optional chopped onion, the herbs and the vinegar. Hand more vinegar separately. Accompany with bread, and a warm salad of cooked greens – spinach, beet tops, radish tops, chard leaves, young dandelion, any edible wild greens – dressed with lemon juice, sesame oil (permitted in Lent), salt and pepper.

EASTER BISCUITS
Pascalinas (Greece)

These nutty little melt-in-the-mouth biscuits are made in advance and offered to visitors throughout the

Easter celebrations. The first time they come out might be after the funeral service on Good Friday – each family remaining true to its own tradition, taking with them a glass of red wine or a glass of white wine, or a glass of vinegar, or no drink but water.

Quantity: Makes about 4 dozen.
Time: 1 hour.
Equipment: A bowl and a sieve. Baking trays and a cooling rack.

8oz/250g butter, softened
2 egg yolks
1lb/500g self-raising flour

6oz/175g caster sugar
1 orange, grated rind and juice

To glaze
1 egg yolk, beaten with 1 tablespoon orange juice

Cream the butter with the sugar until light and fluffy. Beat in the egg yolks and the grated orange rind. Sieve the flour and fold it in, together with enough orange juice to make a stiffish dough.

Heat the oven to 375°F/190°C/Gas 5.

Break off nut-sized pieces of the dough, and roll them into ropes with well-floured hands. Join each rope together with a dab of water, in a figure of eight. Or it could be a snail shape, or a ring, or an S, or whatever you please.

Transfer the biscuits to a buttered baking sheet. Paint them with the egg yolk and orange juice mixture.

Bake for 20–25 minutes until golden. When you open the oven, the heavenly scent of oranges wafts out. Transfer the biscuits to the baking rack to crisp and cool. Store in an airtight tin.

EASTER SATURDAY

The strict fast of Good Friday can be broken with coffee after the midday service of the Little Resurrection. Then the household sets about the baking of the traditional cheese pies, making the stock for the Saturday-night lamb or kid soup, and preparing the meat for roasting on the morrow.

EASTER CHEESECAKES
Militíni Santorínis (Greece)

Milk-drinking is not permitted during Lent – leaving a surplus for cheese-making. In fact, this was the only time a poor rural household with only one cow could set aside enough of the rich milk of spring-time to make even fresh curds, such as those used in the Easter pies. The *masticha* which flavours the mixture is the resin from the masticha tree. It has an exotic flowery flavour. People chew it raw, like chewing gum, and it is used to flavour a cordial. Look for it among the spices in any Greek delicatessen.

Quantity: Makes two dozen pies.

Time: Start the day before. Next day, start 2 hours ahead. 40 minutes.
Equipment: Two bowls and a sieve. A rolling pin and board. Baking tray and a cooling rack.

The filling

2lb/1kg fresh white cheese
1 teaspoon powdered masticha or vanilla
1 tablespoon fine semolina

6 eggs
2oz/50g softened butter

The pastry

2lb/1kg flour
1oz/25g fresh yeast (or ½oz/12g dried yeast)

2 teaspoons salt
½ pint/300ml oil

To finish

1 teaspoon cinnamon

Mix all the filling ingredients together and leave overnight.

Next day, make the pastry. Sieve the flour and salt into a bowl. Crumble in the yeast and work in the oil until you have a smooth ball of dough. Cover and leave to rest in a warm place for a couple of hours to let the yeast lighten the mix.

Heat the oven to 375°F/190°C/Gas 5.

Roll out the dough on a well-floured board to a thickness of about ¼in/0.5cm – not too thin. Using a saucer as a template, cut out rounds of dough. Transfer them to an oiled baking sheet.

Put a generous tablespoon of filling in the middle of each pastry round. Pull the sides up and pinch them together so that they lap but do not enclose the filling. Finish with a quick dust of cinnamon.

Bake for 40–45 minutes, until the filling has set and the pastry is crisp and golden.

Serve warm.

LAMB AND LEMON SOUP
Mageritsa (Greece)

This is the soup served all over Greece at midnight on Easter Sunday – a joyful breakfast, taken when the church bells have rung out to celebrate the resurrection of our Lord. Traditionally the soup is made with the innards from the lamb or kid which is to be roasted the next day – the broth can be left to simmer on the hob while the family is in church.

Quantity: Serves 6.
Time: About 2 hours intermittent attention.
Equipment: A large saucepan. A small frying pan. A small bowl and whisk.

1lb/500g lamb's liver and heart
4 pints/2.5 litres water
6 spring onions, trimmed and chopped
3 tablespoons chopped dill

2lb/1kg neck and/or breast of lamb, roughly chopped
salt and pepper
1 tablespoon olive oil
3oz/75g rice

To finish

5–6 leaves of spinach or Cos lettuce, shredded 2 eggs
juice of 2 lemons

Wash the liver and heart thoroughly, cutting out veins and gristle. Put them in the saucepan with the neck or breast of lamb and pour in the water. Bring to the boil, skim, and add a teaspoon of salt. Simmer for 1 hour, until all the meat is perfectly tender and the stock is reduced to 3 pints/1.5 litres.

Take out the meat and discard all gristle and bones. Chop all the meat into small pieces. Return the meat to the stock in the pan. Sauté the spring onions lightly in the oil, and add them to the soup. Bring back to the boil, add the dill and sprinkle in the rice. Season. Simmer for 20–30 minutes, until the rice is cooked.

When you are ready to serve the soup, reheat it, stir in the spinach or lettuce, and whisk the eggs with the juice of the 2 lemons until frothy. Just before you are ready to serve, add a ladleful of the hot soup to the egg mixture and whisk it well in. Add another ladleful and whisk that in. Draw the soup to the side of the fire and whisk the egg and soup mixture into the rest.

Serve the soup warm – if you reheat it now it will curdle, and anyway the Greeks do not approve of serving food piping hot.

Scarlet-dyed eggs, a salad of onion and Cos lettuce with a few leaves of wild mustard, *vrouva*, and cheese pies make a festive supper of this delicate but rich soup.

EASTER SUNDAY

The day starts with red eggs of course, either on their own or buried in the *tsoureki*, the plaited sweet loaf which is baked as the Easter treat right round the Mediterranean – and is to be found as far north as Austria, imported by the Greek tax collectors and traders employed by the Ottoman Turks. The recipe is very similar to the egg-bread of Spain (see p. 137). For a Greek version, flavour it with *masticha* (see the cheesecake recipe on p. 152).

Very early on Sunday morning, the lamb or kid goes on to the spit over a specially-dug ditch filled with hot coals. In the big cities, the rich employ special lamb-roasters to organize their barbecues. Appetites are appeased until the meat is ready – around two or three in the afternoon – with little dishes of olives and salted nuts, almonds and pistachios, which the Greeks love. Salt-pickled vegetables, cheese – doubly welcome after the long deprivations of Lent – cheese pies and bread fill the empty corners.

Outside Athens, there is a whole district of tavernas devoted to the roasting of the Easter lambs – and it is reported that several people die every year of over-eating. On Patmos, the holy island on which I spent Easter in 1989, the meat was sent to the baker or the local restaurant to be cooked – the pagan exuberances of the mainland being considered an open invitation to secular excesses. The only exception was a group of piratical sailors who had moored their small fishing vessel on the quay at Skala, the island's only harbour. They set up their own home-made barbecue at the stern of the vessel, and spent the morning filling the streets with the rich scent of roasting kid, and the afternoon feasting and carousing and inveigling the local girls aboard with gifts of titbits. Ulysses' sailors must have behaved in much the same fashion.

GREEK OFFERING BREAD
Prosforon (Greece)

Vilma Liacouras Chantiles gives chapter and verse, in her book on the food and folkways of Greece (Food of Greece, Avenel Books, New York, 1979) for this loaf, which plays a vital part in both the spiritual and the physical celebration of the Greek Easter.

An important contribution women make to the Orthodox Liturgy is to bake a *prosforon*, which means 'offering', which is blessed and cut at the altar by the priest during the church service. The custom began among early Christians, who brought bread and wine as an offering, and continues in modern times with sweet wine, oil and incense used for traditional church ceremonies. The bread is stamped before baking with a religious seal or *sfragida* which is often hand-carved in the monasteries. The seal is divided into nine sections, and the centre one is the most significant, with the symbols IE XR NI KA, Greek initials for 'Jesus Christ Conquers'. During the Transubstantiation service, this part of the bread is the Host and is mixed with the blessed wine for the Communion cup. Aside from the indispensable seal, the only other unusual treatment of the bread is the total lack of fat or oil during preparation.

Quantity: Makes a 2lb/1kg loaf.
Time: 3 hours intermittent attention.
Equipment: A mixing bowl, sieve, and board. A baking tray. A seal (the *sfragida* described above can sometimes be bought in Greek grocers).

2lb/1kg flour
1oz/25g fresh yeast (½oz/12g dried)

1 teaspoon salt
1 pint/600ml warm water

Sieve the flour and salt into the warm bowl and put it in a warm place while you start the yeast working.

Mix the fresh yeast with a cup of the warm water and give it a sprinkle of flour to feed on. (If you are using dried yeast, follow the packet directions.) When the yeast starts to seethe and bubble – it will take longer than usual, 10 to 15 minutes, as you have not included any sugar – make a well in the warm flour. Pour in the mixture gradually, working it into the flour with your hand, and add the rest of the warm water until you have a soft ball of dough – you may need more or less water.

Work the dough on a floured board, kneading, pushing and pulling until it is smooth and elastic. Put the dough back in its bowl, cover with clingfilm (over the bowl, not constricting the dough) and leave it in a warm place for 1½ hours, until it has doubled in size.

Knock the dough down to distribute the air bubbles, cut it in half, and knead each piece into a smooth flat round cushion. Damp the top of one cushion and set the other on it, to give you a double-layered, circular, flat loaf. Transfer it to the well-floured baking tray. Flour the seal and press it into the middle of the dough. Put the bread to rise once more – this time it should take only about 40 minutes.

Preheat the oven to 375°F/190°C/Gas 5. Put a tray of water on the base of the oven so that the crust crisps nicely.

Remove the seal from the bread, and put it to bake in the hot oven for the first 15–20 minutes. Then turn the oven down to 350°F/180°C/Gas 4 and bake for another 35–40 minutes, until the loaf is well risen and crusty.

OVEN-BRAISED LAMB WITH POTATOES
Arni psito (Greece)

The more devout communities of Greece, such as those of the monastery-dominated island of Patmos, do not like to make too much of the feasting at Easter. Not for them the whole lamb carcasses turning on the spit in the open air. The celebration Sunday lamb is shared quietly with family and friends, with the outdoor picnics and general jollity kept for Easter Monday.

Early on Easter Sunday morning, the housewives of Hora can be seen staggering up the narrow streets which ring the Monastery of the Theologian, weighed down under big double-handled roasting trays. They are heading for the village bakery, which has been working day and night throughout Easter week, baking egg-studded wreath breads, cheese pies and big round cross-stamped loaves of bread for the different Masses of the week – with time taken out to boil the red-dyed eggs to be handed out by the Metropolitan after midday Mass. These duties completed, there is space in the cooling ovens for the big dishes of meat which break the long fast of Lent.

Quantity: A 5lb/2.5kg joint of meat on the bone will feed 6–8 people.
Time: 2½ hours intermittent attention.
Equipment: A large roasting tin.

1 leg of lamb, chopped through to the bone in 6–8 places
4–5 cloves of garlic, skinned and halved
3lb/1.5kg old potatoes, peeled and quartered
1 glass water

¼ pint/150ml olive oil (the first for 46 days)
salt and pepper
1 handful rosemary sprigs
1 tablespoon oregano
juice of 1 lemon

Rub the meat well with 2 tablespoons of olive oil, salt and pepper. Slip the garlic and bits of rosemary into the gaps between the meat and the bone.

Pour 1 tablespoon of the oil into the roasting tin, and put in the meat, the potatoes and the rest of the garlic and rosemary. Sprinkle with more salt and pepper, the remaining oil, the oregano, the water and the juice of the lemon. Cover with foil (in rural Greece, this might still be a bed and blanket of vine twigs).

Cook in the oven at a high heat 400°F/200°C/Gas 6, for the first 15 minutes. Then turn the oven down to 300°F/150°C/Gas 2 and leave to braise gently for 2 hours at least. Uncover for the last 30 minutes to brown the meat and the tips of the potatoes. Sprinkle in more water as needed.

Serve with quartered lemons, bread, and a salad of bitter leaves – radicchio and dandelion are favourites, and, if Easter is late enough, the first broad beans of the year, to be eaten raw with salt.

If you are by the sea, serve grilled sardines while you are waiting – the first finned fish since Carnival.

ST. MARK'S FEAST: APRIL 24TH

In central Europe, April 24th, St Mark's Feast, was the day set aside by the Church for the blessing of the wheat crop. 'It has therefore,' explained the pre-war writer Gyula Illyes, 'a great importance and meaning in Hungarian life. It is at the end of April: there is hope of life. The people go in procession to the chosen wheat field, where under God's free sky, the future bread is blessed. Each person returns to his home with one ear from the field which has been blessed.'

The Eve of St Mark in medieval Britain was the day a young woman might learn who she was to marry, by waiting in the church porch at midnight. Then she would see a ghostly wedding procession pass through, and might count the bridesmaids for the months before she herself would be wed. The risk was that she would see a funeral procession – which would mean she was to die an old maid.

The funeral procession had other significances. Folklorist Christina Hole quotes a letter from an old Yorkshireman to the *Evening Standard*, printed on April 24th, 1929:

I remember very well hearing folks talking about it years ago. I never watched myself, but there was one old fellow used to sit in the church porch to watch the dead march into the church every St Mark's Eve. He had to do it, he couldn't help himself. He'd done it once, and he had to go on with it. They said he used to see the spirits of all the people who were going to die in the next year. Of course it happened at last that he saw himself in the procession. At any rate, he was dead and buried before another twelve months were out.

DUMB CAKE
(England)

Those maidens too timid to brave the church porch, but anxious to discover who their future husband was to be, could choose to bake a dumb cake. At midnight the spirit of the maiden's future spouse might be expected to enter and turn the cake. Then it had to be broken and eaten, still in silence, and the ghost of the future husband would follow the prospective bride up the stairs. Failing this, a group of young ladies might meet to bake and share a dumb cake – all in silence, of course – after which each can expect to dream of her bridegroom-to-be.

Quantity: Serves 4.
Time: 1 hour.
Equipment: A mixing bowl. A griddle or a heavy frying pan.

8oz/225g plain flour	8oz/225g barley flour
1 teaspoon caraway seeds	6oz/150g lard
¼ pint/150ml warm water	1 egg, lightly beaten
1 tablespoon rough salt	

Mix the two flours, stir in the seeds, and cut in the lard roughly with a knife. Pour the water and the egg into a well in the flour and mix with your hands into a soft dough. You may need extra water. Work the dough well. Pat it out into a thick round pancake, press rough salt into both sides, and prick all over with a fork – maintaining silence, naturally.

Preheat a griddle or heavy-bottomed frying pan and grease it lightly – or better still, rake out the embers of a fire into a nice flat bed.

Bake the cake, turning it once, until well-blistered and cooked through (about 15 minutes a side). Now you're on your own.

St George's Day is the traditional start of the summer transhumance of Europe's domestic herds of sheep and cattle. This pattern of seasonal movement from plains to mountains – the Pyrenees, the Alps, the Carpathians, the highlands of Scotland, Wales, and Scandinavia, the many smaller ranges which punctuate the contours of Europe – is very ancient. It ensured that the animals could crop the high pastures as the snows and frosts of winter retreated, leaving plenty of fodder available below for the winter months.

Where the summers are very short, as in northern Scandinavia, the lower slopes would be harvested of their hay while the animals were in the uplands, so that the cattle could overwinter in their barns along with their fodder. Young herdsmen and shepherds, male or female but without the responsibilities of family, were usually those detailed to accompany the herds. The young people lived in primitive bachelor huts, their chief work being the daily milking and the making of cheese to be brought back down in the autumn and stored for winter.

These summer farms were usually self-sufficient in food. Fish and small game, berries and wild greens could be cropped from the wild, and a potato patch was often planted on arrival – the remnants of self-draining 'lazy-beds' can still be seen on Scotland's peat and heather uplands, marked by the ruins of a small dry-stone bothy or sheiling. A network of these transhumance pathways criss-crosses Europe, a few of them still well trodden by the herds of today, from the dusty plains of the Mediterranean to the icy uplands of the Arctic tundra. I have seen the dusty streets of Arles, once capital of Roman Provence, echo with the bleating of the thousand-strong flocks from the stony Crau, on their way from or to the flowery uplands of the Alpilles some fifty miles distant.

Traveller Mary Eyre witnessed the departure of one such group in the French Pyrenees in 1865.

The shepherds of the ancient county of Foix still revere the fountains of their valleys and bring them mysterious offerings. When the winter snows disappear, they all meet together at a very early hour, ascend to the top of the hill, place themselves in a circle, and await in silence the rising of the sun. As soon as it appears, the oldest man present recites a prayer, to which the others listen with the deepest devotion. There seems to me something beautiful in this custom of thanking God for the return of spring. The assembly of shepherds then proceed to portion among themselves the different mountain pasture, and the summer huts erected upon them, forming, as it were, small tribes, and then every tribe selects its own chief. After this the chiefs swear to love God, to show the right path to travellers who have lost their way, to offer them milk, water, and fire, the use of their mantles and the shelter of their cabins.

In lowland Germany the *Viehaustrieb* – driving out the cattle – was organized strictly on a co-operative basis, with the cowherd returning home every evening. A cattle-owner in a pre-war German village would have expected to be wakened by the blast of a horn at six in the morning, warning him to get his beasts ready for driving out to the summer pastures. Each homestead took it in turn to supply the cowherd's lunch. Eggs, bread and butter went into the cowherd's satchel, left hanging on the door along with his staff of office by the cowherd the night before. An East Frisian cowherd was paid in cash, clothes, boots and food – and his was an important enough position to warrant his election each year by the parish council.

The herdsmen and milkmaids of the mountains of central Europe trekked up and down from their villages throughout the summer. The milk from their charges had to be treated before it was carried back, and an indigenous wild plant rennet was often used to turn the curd. James Fenimore Cooper, novelist of the Wild West, visiting Switzerland around 1836, traced his favourite cheese, *Schrabzieger* – very popular in his native United States – to its source in the summer pastures of the Alps:

The curds are formed on the mountains, the milk of goats and cows being used indifferently. Indeed, so far as I could hear or see, the cheese, in this respect, differs from no other, except that it is made of the whey left after a churning. When formed, the curds are brought down to the valley in bags. I met a waggon loaded with them, as we entered the place. In this state, there is nothing peculiar in the taste; nor does the material seem at all rich. It is pressed as dry as possible, and then put into a mill, resembling a small cider-mill; the one I examined being turned by water. There might have been a hundred-weight of curds in this mill. I presume the consistency of the cheese is owing to this thorough kneading, and the subsequent pressure, though those I questioned pretended that there is a virtue in the particular pastures. The peculiar colour, scent, and flavour are imparted by the herb *Trifolium meliot*, a blue pansy, which is grown in the valley, dried, pulverized and incorporated with the mass in the mill. The odour of the powder was strong, and its taste vegetable; but I like it less pure, than in the cheese. The latter is thought to attain perfection in a twelvemonth, though it will keep a long time.

The herdsmen of Scandinavia move their herds somewhat later – trekking up to the berry-clad uplands from early May to as late as mid-June in the far northern provinces. Travelling in midsummer of 1986 across the high spine of mountains which divides Norway from Sweden, I paid a visit to Birgitta Olsson, who runs single-handed one of the last of Norway's working *setors* in the high pastures above Roros, an old copper-mining town. Most of these summer dairy farms have long since been converted into holiday cottages, their hay meadows steadily climaxing into woodland scrub and pine forest.

Birgitta, in her mid-sixties and ten years a widow, still ran her family *setor* in tandem with her winter farm in the valley below – its log-built farmhouse dwarfed by the cathedral-high barns in which the cattle were cosily over-wintered with their hay. Like all mountain people, she was wiry and tough, and well able, with the help of a mechanical milker, to see to the six milk cows and four calves which formed her small herd.

Although Birgitta told me that she had been able in recent years to supplement her income by offering hospitality in the summer in a converted *setor* barn to the hikers who base themselves on Roros, her main interest is, and always has been, her dairy cows. The *setor* consisted of a little enclave of low wooden huts perched on stilts, with a stream of clear water running through the buildings. A supply of fresh water is very necessary for the dairy, for washing the cheese and cleaning the equipment. Birgitta drove her cows the twenty miles to their summer pastures in early June, as soon as the grass, dormant under snow all winter, had enough new growth to be ready for cropping. The journey was leisurely – twenty hours at one mile an hour. She left again in September, when the long Arctic nights set in. In the old days, she explained, the family stayed put until Christmas – the mountains of south-central Norway do not get their real snow until January.

The old house was heated by a heavy ornate iron stove and equipped with simple but beautifully-crafted furnishings. All was neat, scrubbed and dry. By the open hearth stood the kitchen utensils: a heavy iron griddle for baking *flatbrod*, the wafer-thin crispbread made with barley and oatmeal; a great iron pot for making oat porridge and soups; three plates, three cups, three spoons; a kettle for making coffee; a frying-pan – all that is needed for a summer sojourn.

Across the stream was the cowshed, a long low building of dark red logs, its window frames picked out in white. Inside it was dark, with the scent of warm animals and sweet hay heavy in the air. After the visitor's eyes became accustomed to the dark, it was possible to make out the outlines of the sturdy wooden stalls which lined the walls. The six cows were waiting to be milked. Two of the stalls were occupied by twin calves, anxiously waiting for their share – the buttermilk from the butter-making, or the whey from the cheese.

In the dairy, housed in a separate wooden building, the butter-churn had been scrubbed and was ready for use. A big wooden cask of soured cream, viscous and thick and cool, stood ready to be taken down to the farm at the head of the lake for sale to the local milk-product processors. Birgitta arrived with the pails of the day's milk. As she tipped the milk into a wide shallow wooden pan for the cream to rise, she smiled. 'It is a good pan, that one. It will turn the cream quickly and well. The secret is in a good pan – it has all the necessary microbes in its old wood to do it. We scrub it and scald it of course, but there is still something in that wood.'

Denmark, Norway's ex-colonial power, also relied heavily on dairy farming to supply much of its diet, either directly as milk and its derivatives, or indirectly through pigs fattened on the whey and waste products. Beryl Miles visited Denmark's rugged northern coasts and remoter islands soon after the last war, and gave her hostess a hand in the dairy:

Fru Hedegaard Andersen of Nørre-Lyndelsed was in the little stone scullery preparing smoked cheeses, the rygeost. She had already prepared for tomorrow's cheeses by adding buttermilk and a little salt to two churns of sour milk; the mixture standing in a covered barrel would be quite thick by morning.

'Before we go to bed,' she said, 'I must prepare about twenty cheeses so that they can be smoked at once when we get up.' We set up rows of aluminium sieves. She covered each with a piece of muslin, then dipping a ladle into the barrel of white blancmange-like mixture, she filled each one and left it to drip...

The tall brick chimney had an aperture at the bottom, and another half-way up. I fetched in an armful of barley straw and she stuffed it into the chimney and lit it, then poured on a little water. A cloud of white smoke filled the second hole. She turned a cheese upside down on to a blackened wooden grid and pushed this in till only the handle was visible; smoke rushed up between the bars of the grid and I lost sight of the cheese. After exactly two and a half minutes she pulled it out, shining and yellow on top, striped brown underneath. She turned it, striped side up, on to a plate, a few straws still sticking to it, and sprinkled it with caraway seeds.

The making of storeable cheese has long been a way of conserving the riches of summer for the winter larder, and the requirements of transhumance produced some of Europe's finest matured cheese. The substance used to curd the milk varied from place to place, and significantly affected the flavour and texture of the final product. In Andalucia, I have seen the rennet-rich curd from the stomach of a milk-fed kid used to turn the milk, and I have had the curd-making properties of blue thistle flowers demonstrated in Greece. The most delightful of all, though, is the delicate little glaucous-leaved, violet-flowered butterwort Pinguicula vulgaris, used in the old days in rural Britain, which curdles the milk into wonderful long strings – still remembered in Scandinavia by those who, as children, enjoyed the magic of the miraculous transformation.

RHUBARB FOOL WITH BROWN-CRUSTED CREAM
Frugtgrød med flud (Denmark)

Beryl Miles, on the Danish island of Mando in 1958, admired her dairy-farming hosts' modern methods and equipment:

> In the mejeri, a low brick building with a tall chimney – always the most prominent thing in a Danish village – everything glittered with cleanliness. A chromium container like a gigantic acorn was swinging back and forth by centrifugal force. Going up to it the dairyman opened it cautiously and I saw the yellow contents slapping up against the side. He scraped some out for me; it was like eating yellow cream. 'We have only a hundred and fifty cows on the island,' he explained, 'but we make twenty-two tons of butter a year – a lot goes to England. We fill two casks like that every day.'

Her supper that night she described as Denmark's national passion, a fruit porridge, served with the naturally-soured cream or milk, here crusted with brown breadcrumbs and sugar, which is Scandinavia's other passion. Fruit porridges are made with rhubarb in the spring, gooseberries in the summer, and apples in the autumn. When made with the juice (only) of strawberries, redcurrants and raspberries – scarlet berries which seem to ripen to perfection in the long summer days of northern climes – it becomes rødgrød, red porridge.

Quantity: Serves 4.
Time: Start 1 hour ahead. 15 minutes.
Equipment: A saucepan. 2 bowls.

The fool
1lb/500g rhubarb, trimmed of leaves, washed and cut into short lengths
4–5 tablespoons cornflour

1 pint/600ml water
4oz/100g sugar (more if you like it sweeter)

The cream
½ pint/300ml soured milk or cream (or fresh cream mixed with a spoonful of fresh cream cheese)

4 heaped tablespoons toasted brown breadcrumbs
4 heaped tablespoons brown sugar

Bring the rhubarb to the boil with the water and sugar. Simmer for 4–5 minutes, until the fruit softens. Then for each 1½ pints/900ml of the mixture, take 3 tablespoons of cornflour slaked with a little water, stir it into the boiling saucepan, and instantly remove it from the stove. (It is this 'instantly' which determines whether you finish up with frugtgrød or fruit glue.) Pour it into a bowl to cool.

Serve with a bowl of soured milk or cream sprinkled with a brown crust of breadcrumbs mixed with the sugar. Who could deny that such simple things are the best?

CHERRY JELLY
Rødgrød (Denmark)

Horace Marryat delighted in his visit to the 'Meiri', home of his friend Baron Adeler in Veighøi, in 1860. He admired the Baron's newly constructed dairy:

Highly ornamental, with water running, hot and cold, in all directions. Three hundred and forty cows form the establishment; to each milkmaid is allotted twenty cows; and the servants, farm dependants, and all, sit down to dinner each day, a hundred in number. One hundred and twenty pounds of butter is made every morning in summer; pats as big as cart-wheels, yellow as saffron, though none is added. Near the doorway stood, colossal, a turn of cream – not quite as large as the Heidelberg, but fit to bathe a Roman empress or to drown some milk-and-water Clarence.

We return to our inn, one storey high – like all its neighbours, it ducks away from wind and blast; find bow-pots of honeysuckle in our room; the table laid with silver knives; and they give us *rød-grød*, a national dish, a species of red jelly . . . to be met with in all villages in Jutland, and excellent it is.

1lb/500g cherries (fresh or bottled, or raspberries or redcurrants, or all three)
2oz/50g sugar
1oz/25g powdered gelatine

1 pint/600ml water
3oz/75g ground rice
1oz/25g ground almonds

Stew the cherries, stones and all, with the water until the juice has all run out. Press through a fine sieve to give 1½ pints/900ml juice.

Bring the juice back to the boil and stir in the ground rice, slaked with a little water, and the sugar. Bring back to the boil again, stirring for 20 minutes as it thickens. Sprinkle in the ground almonds and gelatine and give it a good stir.

Pour into a mould set into cold water, and serve it, when turned out, with thick cream round the dish.

TOASTED CHEESE
Croûtes au fromage (Switzerland)

The Swiss have dozens of these bread-and-cheese recipes – they belong to the same family and are as variable as the Welsh rarebit. They make a perfect light summer supper.

Quantity: Serves 4.
Time: 15 minutes.
Equipment: A large roasting tin.

1lb/500g hard cheese (at best, *Gruyère* or *raclette*)
2 cloves garlic, peeled and crushed
salt
8 thick slices bread

2oz/50g softened butter
½ teaspoon cayenne pepper
1 glass white wine

Slice the cheese thinly. Work the butter with the garlic and pepper and enough salt (if the butter is unsalted) to give an edge. Spread this garlic butter on the bread.

Preheat the oven to its maximum – continental ovens can be heated to 280°C – or preheat the grill.

Pour the wine into the roasting tin and lay in the bread, butter-side up so that the other side drinks the wine. Cover the bread with the slices of cheese. Bake for 10–12 minutes until the cheese is brown and bubbling – it may be necessary to finish the slices under the grill if your oven is not hot enough.

Serve piping hot, with more of the white wine to cool your burning tongue.

POOR MAN'S CHEESE
Raclette du pauvre (Switzerland)

Potatoes (the bread of the poor) were often cropped in a corner of the mountain pasture by the herdsmen – sometimes in dug-out beds, which took advantage of the underlying layer of rich loam by the wholesale removal of a layer of heather shrub and roots from the top of the soil. The scars of these 'lazy-beds' can still be seen.

Quantity: Serves 4.
Time: 1 hour intermittent attention.
Equipment: A baking tin.

6 baking potatoes (choose long thin ones for this dish)
salt and white pepper
1 teaspoon ground cumin

1oz/25g butter
1lb/500g matured soft cheese (such as Vacherin or a St Paulet)

Scrub the potatoes and bake them in their jackets in the oven at 400°F/200°C/Gas 6 for 40–50 minutes until they are almost cooked. Peel them as soon as you can handle them. Cut them in half lengthwise.

Butter the baking tin and arrange the potatoes in it in a single layer. Cover each potato with slices of cheese. Finish with salt, pepper and a sprinkling of cumin.

Turn the oven up to its maximum and bake the potatoes for 10 minutes, until they are quite soft and the cheese is bubbling and brown.

Serve with small pickled cucumbers and pickled onions.

May

May Day has a special significance for northerners, since it marks the real beginning of spring. Of all our festivals, this is the one which can be seen most clearly in its pagan finery, combining as it does three central pre-Christian rituals: the maypole, the vestal virgin, and the sacred fire. Timing is a little confusing, as May Day's trappings pop up at other times of year. The maypole and the white-crowned Queen dance again at Whitsun and at some of the rituals of midsummer. Bonfires appear at every seasonal rite of passage, including the midsummer fires of St John's Night, the celebration of All Hallows Eve, and the burning brand of the midwinter festival which became Christmas.

The eve of May Day – Walpurgis Night in central Europe, the Feast of Valborg in Scandinavia, Vapunaato in Finland – was the favourite time for the expelling of witches. On this night, too, Scandinavian students put on their white summer caps and have all-night parties punctuated with songs and speeches and splashing about in the town fountains. In Finland there are huge bonfires, and the white-capped students have their new status as adults marked by their parents with a ritual 'Now you have your white cap, take care that you keep it clean.'

Celtic Europe, at the mercy of its inclement climate, was much concerned with the propitiation of the angry gods who ruled wind and weather. The Scotsman James Frazer, examining the traditions of his own native turf, suggested that the bonfires of Beltane, still kindled with attendant ceremony until well into the eighteenth century, were themselves a relic of the sacrificial bone-fires of even earlier times:

> In the parish of Callender, a beautiful district of western Perthshire, the Beltane custom was still in vogue towards the end of the eighteenth century. Upon the first day of May, all the boys in the township or hamlet meet in the moors. They cut a table in the green sod, of a round figure, by casting a trench in the ground of such circumference as to hold the whole company. They kindle a fire, and dress a repast of eggs and milk in the consistence of a custard. They knead a cake of oatmeal, which is toasted at the embers against a stone. After the custard is eaten up, they divide the cake into so many portions as similar as possible to another in size and shape, as there are persons in the company. They daub one of these portions all over with charcoal. They put it in a bonnet and each one blindfold draws out a portion.

Whoever drew the black bit was then considered 'devoted' – sacrificed to Baal – and had to leap three times through the flames. In earlier times he might not have got away so lightly.

Once the witches were out of the way, May Day could be greeted with a light heart – from the dawn gathering of dew-laden may-blossoms to the robust symbolism of the maypole. Primitive religions share a common interest in phallic symbols – least mysterious and most easily identifiable of all reproductive activities – of which the maypole is an unvarnished example. In Germany, particularly Bavaria, the maypole was always in danger of being stolen by the neighbouring parish. Reports of maypole thefts go back to the twelfth century. The sapling for the pole was selected in February, the bark was peeled off in a pretty spiral pattern, then the pole was hung with carved figures and crowned with a fat beribboned garland.

The Saxons worshipped a stone phallic symbol: a column called Irminsul. A few reminders of its ancient ceremonies can still be found in the Ram Fairs of southern England, such as that of Kingsteignton, Devon – now moved from May Day to Whit Monday – when a live young ram (latterly a less obviously barbaric carcass) decked with ribbons and flowers was paraded through the town and then killed, roasted and eaten at a festival of games and dancing. In 1882 George Gomme recalled the May Day ceremony which preceded it:

> In the centre of the field stands a granite pillar or menhir, six or seven feet high. On May morning, before daybreak, the young men of the village used to assemble there, and then proceed to the moor, where they selected a ram lamb, and after running it down, brought it in triumph to the Ploy Field, fastened it to the pillar, cut its throat, and then roasted it whole, skin, wool and all. At midday a struggle took place, at the risk of cut hands, for a slice – it being supposed to confer luck for the ensuing year on the fortunate devourer. As an act of gallantry the young men sometimes fought to get a slice for their chosen young women, all of whom, in their best dresses, attended the Ram Feast. Dancing, wrestling and other games, assisted by copious libations of cider, prolonged the festivity until midnight.

Gomme points out that all the elements of sacrifice are present: the killing and roasting of the victim by the villagers at a place of sacrifice, the sharing of raw flesh and the magic properties of the meal, rounded off with a drinking-party.

Leo Allatius's recollections (written circa 1630, and translated by classical anthropologist John Lawson) of his native Chios trace the lineage of our May Queen back to flighty Artemis, virgin goddess of childbirth, huntress-queen of the Nereids, whose capricious moon-led nature distinguishes her from the mature beauty of Demeter, her sunny sister-goddess of the harvest:

> He whom Artemis' sudden anger has once smitten may regain her favour by offerings of honey and other sweetmeats on the scene of his calamity. On the first of May, the good women are obliged to make crosses on their doors, saying that the goddess of their mountains is due to come and visit them in their houses, and that without this mark she would not come in; likewise they say that she would slay any one who should go to meet her. And so they give her the name of 'good'; being obliged by the fear in which they hold her to give her this title of honour.

Artemis/Diana took on the trappings of a many-breasted eastern nature-goddess at Ephesus, where her cult caused St Paul and Bishop Nicholas a great deal of trouble (see p.14). In central Italy, Artemis shared many characteristics with Flora, who brought fertility to the earth, fecundity to the flocks, and success to the hunters, and whose festival was held annually from April 28th to May 3rd. The cult of Flora was brought into Britain by Belgic tribes around the first century BC.

The May Queen – her regal dignity confirmed as she sits on her flower-decked throne and watches her subjects dance – is Flora personified: May Day is Flora's holiday. In medieval times, the Queen, according to the custom of Shakespeare's day, was often a young man beribboned and beflounced in the guise of a pretty girl. In modern times we have come full circle, and the consort is sometimes the previous year's May Queen, dressed as a boy: the pantomime prince. There used to be a Lord of the May as well, magnificent in ribbons and silk handkerchiefs. Spring itself was represented by a Jack-in-the-Green or Bush who danced around inside a wooden archway frame decorated with greenery. In other parts of Europe he appears as Green George or the Wild Man of the Woods. He can still be seen as the Green Man on pub signs; his carved face framed with leaves, he peers from the top of church columns, or grimaces from under the choir stalls.

The Puritans denounced the pagan rituals of May Day – with pamphleteer Philip Stubbs as grand inquisitor:

> But their chiefest jewel they bring from thence is their maypole, which they bring home with great veneration, as thus: They have twenty or forty yoke of oxen, every ox having a sweet nosegay of flowers tied on the tip of his horns, and these oxen draw home this maypole (this stinking idol rather) which is covered all over with flowers and herbs, bound about with strings from the top to the bottom, and sometimes painted with variable colours, with two or three hundred men, women and children following it, with great devotion. And thus being reared up with handkerchiefs and flags streaming at the top, they strew the ground about, bind green boughs about it, set up summer halls, bowers and arbours hard by it. And then they fall to banquet and feast, to leap and dance about it, as the heathen people did, at the dedication of their idols, where of this is a perfect pattern, or rather the thing itself.

The embargo was short-lived, although the festival was never appropriated by the Church, unless it be for the branches to decorate the church building at Easter. The maypole, once a living tree but now a painted pole, was reinstated after the Restoration – in old Cavalier strongholds it is often erected and decorated on Restoration Day, April 29th. The maypole gradually became a fixture on the village green – a sapling elm, pine, larch, birch or ash which would last about fifteen years before it needed replacing. In England, the young men and girls would go a-maying before dawn, rising soon after midnight and going out into the woods and hedgerows to bring home the flowering branches of hawthorn – the may-tree – with more than a little dalliance on the way. When the calendar was changed in 1752, May Day was placed eleven days later – too late for the fragile may-blossom in southern Britain. Instead the young people brought back green-budded branches with blossoms tied to them. Unpopular villagers would wake to find their houses decorated with nettles and elder. In the north, May-birchers used to visit neighbours and leave a token appropriate to each householder – a plum for the sour, a pear for the fair whether of face or nature, an alder for the scolder.

Rodney Gallop found relics of similar customs in Portugal in the 1930s:

> The Alenteho and Algarve were the provinces in which the custom endured longest of electing a Maia or May Queen. Adorned with flowers she was set in a decorated chair at a door or window looking out on to the street, while satellites, with improvised song, collected money from passers

by. In front of the house stood a mast bedecked with flowers and myrtle. Not only each village, but each street had its Maia, and it was the frequent battles between the supporters of rival queens which led to the prohibition of this custom in the 1870s.

The Etruscan village of Marta, on the third Sunday in May, reported Thomas Ashby in *Some Italian Scenes and Festivals* (1929), has a festival on the third Sunday in May where the May Queen is the local Madonna herself.

It is indeed a festival unique, so far as I know, in the whole of Italy. Everything points to its being the representative of an ancient pagan spring festival.

At last the Mass was over and the 'passate' began. The representatives of the various industries passed into the church, out by a side door into the monastery, through the cloister, and back into the church again. The round was made thrice, and each time they called out loudly the name of their trade, as they made offering of its emblems or tools to the virgin. Pride of place was by common consent given to the *contadini*, the *bifolchi* (ploughmen), coming first with ox harness of various descriptions; the goatherd carried a live black kid decked with red and yellow ribbons; the haymaker, a net used for collecting hay; the shepherd, a small net with ropes and pickets for sheep pens; the vine-grower, a tiny ladder; the house servant, a tray with loaves of bread and two bottles of wine. In the third came the fishermen with nets and fish on a tray, including several squids and a large live eel in a net. We noticed especially two women with baskets of large ring loaves on their heads, covered with a white cloth, and a girl with a flat wooden tray of cakes, similarly covered.

When all was over, the horsemen assembled and gave their shout once more, and led the way down the straight steep road to the village. At intervals they halted and called out once more their salute to the Madonna. We noticed that on the return all carried rings of bread upon their arm. As the procession passed through its narrow streets, every window was thronged with girls who leant out and threw handfuls of petals of yellow broom and white acacia upon the heads of those below, until the street was carpeted with gold and silver. The effect of the rain of blossom against the houses was extremely beautiful...

The more remote areas of central Europe held to the old ways well into the twentieth century. In 1932 Hungarian Gyula Illyes offered an unsentimental glimpse of the spring rituals of the poverty-stricken *puszta* where he was born:

Laughter had its own traditional festivals. On the first spring day everybody had to smile and whistle. Everybody was prepared for this day, and on the first sunny morning whistling and singing echoed everywhere, as if by magic.

In May the maypole was danced out. It was a strong, slender poplar, with all the branches stripped from its long trunk except for a little foliage left at the very top, about the size of an umbrella . . . Custom demanded that it should be set up during the night of the first of May.

For weeks the maypole stood in all its glory in front of the stables. It was brought down on Whit Saturday, when its real decoration began. Now every unmarried girl had to tie a ribbon to it. It was also the duty of every craftsman on the *puszta* to put something on it. The cooper made a little wooden tub about the size of one's hand, the smith a horseshoe decorated with brass, the vinedresser a raffia garland, the shepherds each gave a piece of cheese. The farm officials would contribute a bottle of wine or two, if they happened to be in a good mood. Then the tree was set up again. We were burning with excitement.

After lunch on White Monday the festival began. Those who possessed zithers and mouth-organs formed themselves into a band. They played just one overture, the latest hit-tune, and they had to play it really well. Then came the tree-climbing. Everybody except the children had the right to climb to the top of the tree and bring down whatever he wanted, but only one article, of course.

The function of May Day as a day on which the whole population, and particularly the young people, troops out into the countryside still holds in Denmark, where May 1st is the day for the opening of Copenhagen's Tivoli gardens, and the whole population, whether urban or rural, goes out into the nearest open space to picnic. Andrew Hamilton, chronicling *Sixteen Months in the Danish Isles* around 1850, left an account of such an outing in all its nineteenth-century elegance. Artemis might have recognized her nymphs, but Baal would have had trouble recognizing his Beltane fire:

As the weather was favourable, it had been arranged that the whole party should go that evening to drink tea-water in a wood about an English mile from the house. A carriage was ordered to convey the infirm or indolent and the tea-things, while all who were young and strong walked. The road led through a series of avenues and plantations all the way, till it brought us to a deep, dense forest, forming the boundary of the estate on this side; and here in the midst of its primaeval darkness, on the side of a steep acclivity, had been formed a small grotto with table and benches and fire-place, all in the open air. A servant had gone before to light the fire and tidy up a little; the wood was blazing merrily when we arrived, and the kettle soon after began to sing.

Some young ladies clambered up the bank and placed themselves at the root of an aged tree, where they drank their beverage, and looked, at the little distance and in the vibratory light of a summer eve, like nymphs of the forest or priestesses of a sacred grove. In summer, in Denmark, people are very loth to leave the open air in the evening; they keep going about the doors, out and in, until it is time to sleep, like children afraid to quit some pleasant game, as if they were not to return to it any more.

Although now redesignated the May bank holiday or Labour Day, the ancient festival and its rituals remain close to our hearts; young girls still long to be crowned Queen of the May. Whether the encircling diadem is white blossom or diamanté, lilies of the valley or tinsel, whether her title is Prom Queen or Miss World, she continues to twist and preen, as at home on the TV screen as she was on the village green. We cannot help delighting in her mystery: eternal virgin yet goddess of childbirth, she holds out the promise of our own immortality.

The Victorians, those diligent excavators of pagan treasure exemplified by their Poet Laureate, held up the misty mirror of sentiment to the wild heathen sprite.

> You must wake and call me early, call me early mother dear;
> To-morrow 'ill be the happiest time of the glad New-year;
> Of all the glad New-year, mother, the maddest merriest day;
> For I'm to be Queen o' the May, mother, I'm to be Queen of the May.

Many-breasted Diana would have found her image hard to recognize in Tennyson's coy maiden, weaving her pretty satin ribbons round the oldest phallic symbol in the world. We live now in more robust times:

the delicate creature had her veil ripped off without ceremony in a traditional rhyme gathered by the poet Christopher Logue:

> Hooray, hooray, the first of May
> Outdoor fucking starts today.

That, perhaps, was the whole story all along.

HONEYCAKES
Melomakárona (Greece)

Here are sweets to tempt capricious Artemis – moon-led goddess of the woods, eternal virgin yet patroness of childbirth. Those who offend her can regain her favour only by such delicious offerings. The modern version has only butter and flour, although the original mix was a *halva*-like sweetmeat made with semolina and olive oil. Here is a recipe which combines the old with the new.

Quantity: Serves 10.
Time: Takes about 1 hour.
Equipment: 2 bowls, a whisk and a sieve. An electric mixer would be helpful. A 7 x 9in/15 x 22cm baking tray and a cooling rack. A saucepan.

The cake

4oz/100g softened butter
4oz/100g caster sugar
grated rind and juice of 1 orange
4oz/100g flour
knifepoint of salt
½ teaspoon grated nutmeg

2 tablespoons olive oil
3 eggs, separated
2oz/50g fine-ground semolina
1 teaspoon baking powder
½ teaspoon ground cinnamon
¼ teaspoon ground cloves

The honey syrup

8oz/250g honey
juice of 1 lemon

¼ pint/150ml water

To finish

3–4 tablespoons chopped almonds

Beat the butter with the oil until light and fluffy, then beat in the sugar – easiest in an electric mixer. Beat in the egg yolks, then the orange juice and peel. Fold in the semolina, the flour sifted with the baking powder, the salt and the spices.

Preheat the oven to 350°F/180°C/Gas 4.

Whisk the egg whites until they hold soft peaks and fold them into the mixture. Line the baking tray with buttered greaseproof paper and spread in the cake mixture.

Bake for 30–35 minutes, until the cake is beautifully brown and bounces back when you press the surface with your finger. The buttery, spicy scent is quite irresistible, so make sure you leave it for long enough.

Meanwhile make the syrup. Bring the honey and water gently to the boil in a saucepan. Skim off the froth which rises, remove the pan from the heat and stir in the lemon juice. Leave to cool.

Take the cake out of the oven and cut it into diamond shapes with a sharp knife. Pour the cooled syrup over all, and finish with a sprinkling of chopped almonds.

BUTTER BISCUITS
(Denmark)

'Tea is a very talkative herb; whoever saw tea drunk in silence? And the smoking cups, and the plates of bread and butter, cakes, chicken, radishes, and all the other substantial incidentals of a Danish tea, kept making an incessant circuit.' (Andrew Hamilton's account of May Day in Denmark, *circa* 1850.)

Here is a classic rich Danish butter biscuit.

Quantity: Makes about 3 dozen.
Time: 1 hour intermittent attention.
Equipment: A bowl and sieve. A baking tray and cooling rack.

6oz/150g softened butter	4oz/100g caster sugar
4oz/100g ground almonds	4oz/100g flour
a knifepoint of salt	1 teaspoon baking powder
scraping of vanilla pod or 2 drops vanilla essence	

Beat the butter with the sugar and work in the almonds sifted with the sieved flour, salt and baking powder until you have a softish dough. Stir in the vanilla. You may need a tablespoon of milk too.

Preheat the oven to 350°F/180°C/Gas 4.

Butter the baking tray. Cut off nuggets of the dough and roll them into ropes about as long and thick as your middle finger. Arrange these on the baking tray in the shape of a horseshoe.

Bake for 15 minutes until light and golden and firm to touch. Transfer them to a baking rack to cool and crisp. The biscuits store beautifully.

CURLED FRITTERS
Piirakka kivertää (Finland)

May 1st is a students' festival, explained Peggy Benton in *Finnish Food* (Faber, 1960).

Singing and carrying banners, the students form processions and march through the town and out into the country to their favourite inns. Everyone who has been a student joins them and even old men in faded caps link arms with the rest and sing. Having arrived at an inn, they sit at long tables under the trees and drink Sima and eat dropped cakes.

Sima is a fermented honey-drink – I can vouch for the size and energy of the Finnish bees which produce the raw material, having been dive-bombed by a fierce cloud of them on the shores of central Finland's Lake Inari.

Quantity: Makes 2 dozen fritters.
Time: 1 hour ahead for the fritters, plus 30 minutes to make them.
Equipment: A bowl and a whisk. A deep-fryer and draining spoon.

4 eggs	1 pint/600ml warm milk
1oz/25g fresh yeast (½oz/12g dried)	1 tablespoon sugar
1lb/500g flour	frying oil

Whisk together the eggs, the milk and the yeast liquidized with the sugar. Beat in the flour. Cover loosely and put to rise for 1 hour in a cool place.

Heat the oil in the deep-fryer until the surface is lightly hazed with blue smoke. Trickle in the batter, a tablespoon at a time, to make a pretty curl. Let the fritters gild underneath, and turn them to cook on the other side. Do not fry too many at a time or the oil temperature will drop. (You could cook them like pancakes, in a frying pan.)

Transfer them with a draining spoon to kitchen paper. Sprinkle them with sugar and serve them hot, with a glass of Sima (see p. 249). Think of the joy of the Finns when the sun lifts over the horizon after the winter-long night.

MAYDAY CAUDLE
(Scotland)

Thomas Pennant, travelling through Perthshire in 1769, recorded:

On the first of May, the herdsmen of every village hold their Bel-tien, a rural sacrifice. They cut a square trench in the ground, leaving the turf in the middle; on that they make a fire of wood, on which they dress a large caudle of eggs, butter, oatmeal and milk; and bring besides the ingredients of the caudle, plenty of beer and whisky, for each of the company must contribute something. The rites begin with spilling some of the caudle on the ground by way of libation: on that every one takes a cake of oatmeal, upon which are raised nine square knobs, each dedicated to some particular being, the supposed preserver of their flocks and herds.

The closest modern approximation to a caudle is probably Horlicks or Ovaltine. In *Food in England*, scholar cook Dorothy Hartley wrote:

The mixture of eggs and cereals and malt etc. is very ancient. We who do not normally go long periods without a meal, expect refreshments when we travel, and do not realize the need of the caudel type of 'soup wine' or 'ale meal'. After long hours of travel, hot wine, or spirits on an empty stomach were not too good, and yet often you were too tired to eat. Thus, the compromise of a caudel, which warmed you, fed you and 'kept you going' till you could obtain a solid meal.

That is why this type of 'food drink' has survived in working-class and rural circles, where the same physical need still occurs. Hot gruel with whisky and lemon is a type of caudle. Genuine caudles were made in so many ways it is difficult to choose the most popular.

Quantity: Serves 2.
Time: 20 minutes.
Equipment: A saucepan. A whisk.

2 tablespoons fine oatmeal	2 pints/1.2 litres creamy milk
1 curl lemon peel	2 eggs
2 tablespoons brown sugar	

To finish

1 tablespoon butter	a dram of whisky
cream	brown sugar

Whisk the oatmeal into three-quarters of the milk and bring it all to the boil with the lemon peel. Turn down the heat and simmer for 10 minutes, stirring regularly until the milk has thickened. Remove the lemon peel.

Whisk the eggs in a bowl with the rest of the milk and the brown sugar. Whisk the thickened hot milk into the eggs and milk. Return to the heat and bring back to just below boiling. Stir in the butter and the whisky and pour into pint mugs.

Finish with a dollop of cream and an extra sprinkling of brown sugar. Serve with oatcakes.

THE BELTANE BANNOCK
(Scotland)

After kindling the bonfire with the *tein-eigin*, the company prepared their victuals – as soon as they had finished their meal, they amused themselves a while in singing and dancing round the fire... Towards the close of the entertainment, the person who officiated as master of the feast produced a large cake baked with eggs and scalloped round the edge, called *am bonnach bealtine* – the Beltane cake...It was divided into portions, and distributed – there was one particular piece of whom the recipient was held in great opprobation. (J.G. Frazer, *The Golden Bough*, quoting John Ramsay)

The old recipe would not have included a chemical raising agent, and would probably have been made with a mixture of fine-ground barley and oatmeal – native grains in the Highlands.

Quantity: Serves 6.
Time: 15 minutes.
Equipment: A mixing bowl and a sieve. A wide gridle or large heavy frying pan. A ladle.

8oz/250g flour	1 teaspoon bicarbonate of soda
2 teaspoons cream of tartar (only 1 if the milk is soured)	1 large egg
scant ½ pint/300ml milk, fresh or soured	1 tablespoon honey

Sieve the flour into the bowl with the bicarbonate and the cream of tartar. Work the egg, honey and milk into a well in the flour, drawing in the dry flour from the sides. Don't beat it – just make sure it is smooth and thick enough to hold a deep edge when poured out.

Preheat the gridle or frying pan and grease it lightly.

Drop ladlesful of the batter on to the hot surface, starting with one in the middle, letting this one set and brown a little, and adding on satellites round the side. Do this slowly enough to make sure that each dollop retains its original shape, so that you have a single large pancake, but one in which the separate rounds are clearly visible. After 4–5 minutes, when the bubbles on the upper side break to leave a dry surface, turn the pancake carefully. Cook it on the other side.

The first, middle pancake will be darker than the others on the reversed hidden side, as it has been longer on the heat: this is Baal's portion. Next year, pour one of the satellite pancakes first, so that no one knows which is the blackened one.

CORPUS CHRISTI: END OF MAY–EARLY JUNE

This important Catholic festival (la Fête-Dieu in France), which falls on the Thursday after Trinity Sunday, commemorates the institution of the Eucharist – the Sacrament of Holy Communion – of its nature a celebration, but which cannot be suitably enjoyed on Maundy Thursday, in the dark days of Easter week. The festival was established in the thirteenth century by Pope Urban IV, and the story was soon marked by processions and tableaux vivants throughout Catholic Europe – an ambulatory celebration which, close as it was to the old midsummer festivals, quickly took on some of the trappings of the Carnival.

In fifteenth-century Provence, good King René – credited with many of the Midi's jollier occasions – officially instituted the Jeux de Fête-Dieu, a five-day period of games and public amusements which the people had in any event declared for themselves. Frédéric Mistral, arch-folklorist and reviver of Provence's traditions, glorified the games in 1851 in his passionate poem, Calendau. Jean-Paul Clébert described in 1982, in Les Fêtes en Provence, the traditions Mistral re-instituted:

> The Jeux are celebrated on two separate occasions, the Saturday night which precedes Trinity Sunday, and the Thursday of Corpus Christi itself. It all begins with the passado, the preliminary tour of the town streets by the beadle – or another official – ringing his bell to announce the procession and alert the citizens to decorate their streets and set up platforms from which local dignitaries might watch in comfort. Bunting and flags are the preferred decorations, with lights after nightfall.

The celebrations included the choosing of a Boy Bishop, the abat de la jouinesso – selected from their own number by the young men of the town, a ritual which was quite common in medieval Britain – whose reign, and voice in local affairs, lasted only as the celebrations. The abat was attended by a bodyguard of young men whose duties included letting off musket-fire to alert the populace to his passage. A cavalcade of mounted soldiers, the municipal band and the town's dignitaries and various guilds were all represented in the processions. Angels and devils, the 'Big Heads', stiltwalkers, clowns and, most important of all, the idiosyncratic biblical tableaux vivants – Adam and Eve, Noah and the Flood, Moses dividing the waters of the Red Sea – all had their strict order of procession culminating in the high-spot: the magnificently arrayed Queen of Sheba on her way to visit Solomon. Representatives of the Old Testament occupied the first festival, with the New Testament starring on the second, the eve of Corpus Christi.

Gaston Grégoire, observing the pre-Revolution festivities around 1770, described one of the more unusual representations: the journey to Bethlehem of the Three Kings – more in the guise of merry clowns than wise men:

> First comes a man in a long white robe carrying a gilded star on the end of a long white and gold stick. The Kings come next, in brightly-coloured robes with brilliantly beribboned cloaks, crowned and sceptred. Each is preceded by a page wearing a conical hat and the diamond motley of harlequin in the colours of his particular king. Each page carries a pyramid-shaped box containing the traditional offering of his own Magus. All follow the star-carrier, who meanders from side to side of the street. When he stops, all stop. The nearest page to the star then makes an obeisance, hopping first on one foot, then on the other five or six times, then makes a grand flourish with the gift. The page then minces over to his own King, his buttocks exaggeratedly switching from side to side. The King accepts similar homage from the second page – and so on until the third King has received all his due.

Black-costumed, skeleton-painted Death brought up the rear with his attendant demons, threatening the crowd with his skull-topped staff. Each town had its own special pageant. Marseilles's procession was headed, as befitted a prosperous bourgeoisie, by the butchers guild parading a fattened ox – the *boeuf-gras* – garlanded with flowers and ridden by a young boy dressed as John the Baptist. Behind him tripped the vestal virgins – young girls dressed as female saints, a living link between the pagan May Queens and the majorettes of our modern processions.

Rodney Gallop, researching folklore in Portugal in the 1930s, found similar traditions, although he reported that many of the characteristics appeared to have been transferred to the midsummer processions and *romerías* held on St John's Day:

> The responsibility for furnishing the various features of the Corpus Christi procession devolved in the Middle Ages upon the Guilds, which came in this way to form a link between the pagan mummer of the past and the stylized survivals of today. In Coimbra in 1517 these Guilds furnished an item in the processions: carpenters, potters, tailors, weavers and shoemakers. At Oporto in 1621, pastrycooks, tanners, smiths, masons, hatters, vintners, merchants and shopkeepers are also mentioned.

In 1932, reported Gallop, most of the dances were suppressed by the bishop, leaving only a *Mourisca* – a battle acted out by young men armed with shields and lances, led by their king – as well as these two dances to provide a reminder of the old sacred dances:

> In Braga the procession retains two interesting features, the *carro das ervas* or *dos pastores*, and the *dança do Rei David*. The *carro dos pastores* is an elaborately decorated lorry, drawn by oxen, on which was erected a large stage rock, with a fountain in a niche and a small boy dressed in silks and velvets leading a beribboned live lamb. At intervals the Baptist sang in a forced voice a conventional hymn, while a group of children dressed as shepherds and shepherdesses danced a simple country dance. The top of the rock fell apart and a child angel shot up unsteadily and blessed the audience. King

David and his courtiers wore a costume resembling the medieval artist's idea of Eastern dress. Every now and then they stopped, formed up in two lines, and continuing to provide their own music, began to dance.

BREAD AND MINT SOUP WITH BACALHAU
Sopa de pao com hortelã bacalhau (Portugal)

This soup, one of many such frugal but delicious suppers made by the thrifty housewives of Portugal, is the favourite party dish of the villages round Viseo in central upland Portugal. The dish is quickly made with bread from the store-cupboard and mint from the garden when friends and relations call in after the festivities. Its consistency can be nearer porridge than a soup, although everyone has their own preference. Some like it smooth, and some like it lumpy – people in Portugal are just as particular over their bread soups as the Scots with their porridge. A little salt cod, the great standby in Portuguese households, makes it all special.

Quantity: Serves 4.
Time: 20 minutes.
Equipment: A large saucepan. A potato masher.

8 slices day-old country bread, dried in the air overnight
2 pints/1.2 litres cold chicken broth
4oz/100g salt cod, soaked for 24 hours and torn into shreds (*optional*)
2 hard-boiled eggs, chopped (*optional*)

1–2 garlic cloves, skinned and chopped
2 tablespoons chopped salt-cured ham or gammon
2 tablespoons freshly chopped parsley leaves
4 tablespoons freshly chopped mint leaves
salt and pepper

Tear the bread into small pieces. Put them in the saucepan with the chopped garlic. Pour in the cold broth, give the mixture a stir, and leave to soak for 10 minutes. Stir in the ham or gammon and the optional salt cod. Bring it all to the boil and simmer for 10 minutes – 20 minutes if you have included salt cod. Mash with a potato masher to get rid of any lumps.

Stir in the chopped parsley and mint just before serving. Taste and add seasoning. Finish with a sprinkling of herbs and the optional chopped hard-boiled eggs.

If you have any dry bread left, cube it and fry it in olive oil to serve as hot little *croûtons* – lovely as texture variation.

CORPUS CHRISTI BUNS
Gimblettes de la Fête-Dieu (Provence)

The recipes which stipulate boiling and then baking are among the most ancient of Europe, forming a bridge between the cloth-dumplings of days when ovens were, at best, available only in the nearest village, and the baked cakes of today.

Quantity: Makes 2 dozen buns.

Time: Start 2 hours ahead.

Equipment: A mixing bowl and a sieve. A board and rolling pin. Biscuit cutters. A large saucepan and draining spoon. A baking tray and cooling rack.

1lb/500g flour	pinch of salt
2oz/50g butter	1oz/25g fresh yeast (½oz/12g dried)
2oz/50g sugar	1 teaspoon aniseed
6 eggs	warm water

To finish
1 egg, lightly beaten with 1 tablespoon milk

Sieve the flour with the salt into the bowl. Rub in the butter, yeast, sugar and aniseed with the tips of your fingers.

Fork the eggs together and pour them into a well in the flour mixture. Work all together, first with the fork and then with your hands – adding warm water if you need it – until you have a soft, elastic dough. Form it into a ball and put it back into the bowl, covered with a clean cloth. Put it to rise in a warm place for 2 hours, until it has doubled in bulk.

Knock it down to distribute the air bubbles, and roll the dough out on the floured board with the rolling pin to about the thickness of a finger.

Using biscuit cutters, stamp out an army of crowns, stars, crescents, suns – whatever reminds you of Corpus Christi and its processions.

Bring a large pan of water to the boil and throw in the buns – no more than a few at a time or the water temperature will drop too much. When the buns rise to the surface, fish them out with the draining spoon, dip them immediately in cold water, and transfer them to a buttered baking tray.

Preheat the oven to 475°F/240°C/Gas 9.

Paint the buns with a brushful of egg and milk. Bake them for 20 minutes, until well risen and golden. Transfer to the rack to cool – they're lovely warm, with a little glass of anis or sweet orange wine.

June

WHITSUN/PENTECOST: SEVEN WEEKS AFTER EASTER

This is the feast of early summer at which, all over Europe, sacred embraces profane: goblin fingers toy with holy bread. The festival, celebrated on the fiftieth day after Easter, marks the descent of the Holy Spirit to the disciples, gathered together to break bread at Pentecost – the Jewish Harvest Thanksgiving Festival. The blessing of fire and the gift of tongues, administered by the Holy Ghost in the shape of a dove, was too complicated a concept to slip easily into the vocabulary of heathen Europe. Otherwise known as Whitsun or White Sunday, it nevertheless ranks as the third most important festival in the western Church's calendar.

Various elements combine in the celebrations, of which the Whitsun distributions of food may be in direct line of descent from the early church's festival of Agape, the feast of sacred love, charity and chastity, distinguishing it from the riotous banquets of Eros, whose preoccupations were somewhat different. At these feasts, the early Christians came together to break bread, confirm their faith and, almost more important in such difficult times, to exchange news. The rich were expected to provide enough good victuals to feed their poorer brothers. Charity remains a characteristic of the Whitsun celebrations, including, in England in the old days, the custom of collecting for the Whitsun Ales, promoted with enthusiasm by the Stuart Kings and chronicled by John Aubrey. By the nineteenth century the Whitsun Ales had become Club Feasts and Club Walks – retaining their charitable purpose but becoming more exclusive. Various survivals or revivals of the Whitsun doles – the competitive award of the Dunmow Flitch, cheese rollings and distributions in Gloucestershire – still take place on Whit Sunday or Monday.

In addition, Whitsun was the time for performing miracle plays – of which the most famous were the cycles of Chester and York. Presented on a wheeled double-decker stage with the actors' dressing rooms underneath, the whole outfit could be trundled around the town and be seen by the whole population. The plays shared many characteristics with the nativity plays proscribed by the Catholic Church in the Middle Ages, including that descent into farce which so upset the medieval Popes. Devils and villains such as Herod provided burlesque comic relief, Christ and the Holy Family alone remaining aloof. In Chester in 1600 there were twenty-five guilds covering the whole story from the Garden of Eden to Armageddon, a *tour de force* which earned the disapproval of – and suppression by – the stern fathers of the Reformation.

The morris dancers – modern revivals of the relics of pagan theatre – perform at Pentecost. Whit

Sunday morris dancing has become a regular popular event at Bampton in Oxfordshire, where the performers are followed round the town by a dancer bearing a ritual cake stuck on a sword. Spectators should perhaps be grateful that the victim is merely a cake and not, as it may well have been in the old days, a creature of flesh and blood. George Long, a keen student of folklore in the 1920s, was in little doubt of the ceremony's origin as a hunting ritual, confirmed by the presence of the hobby-horse, alternating with a fertility dance:

> At Bampton there is a swordsman who carries a naked sword, impaling a cake, brightly beribboned; this – if I mistake not – related to the victim of the hunt. One learned gentleman whom I encountered at Bampton told me that the cake was no doubt the Host. I do not believe it. To the Catholic mind the Host was so sacred as to be untouchable – the very Person of the Deity. Some of the dances undoubtedly have to do with seed-time; the Bean Dance, with its thumping and clashing of staves, mimics the action of the dibbler who makes a hole in the soil to take the seed. Simple rites were performed to ensure the safety of the harvest, the fertility of the flocks and herds, or the success of tribal hunting. Hence the prevalence in nearly or quite all pagan religions of that bi-sexual dualism – the male and female deity, identified with the sun and earth or moon – the former requiring to be propitiated by human or animal sacrifices, and the festivals of the latter associated with the removal of sexual inhibitions.

Morris dancers, although they make their first appearance on May 1st, take their prolonged bow at Whitsuntide. This purely rural peasant dance was in its heyday at the end of the sixteenth century, falling casualty to the disapproval of the Church – a process completed naturally by the drift from the countryside during the Industrial Revolution. The morris men owe their revived popularity to Cecil Sharp's English Folk Dance Society, founded in 1911. The dancers include the androgynous Betty, or Betsy or Moll, who is a man dressed as a woman. There is also a Fool, who carries an inflated pig's bladder on a stick and belabours the other dancers and watchers. His mythology is particularly mysterious – some authorities identify him with the pagan King-Priest who both sacrificed and was sacrificed – and whose death might ensure the survival of the community. The ritual of death and revival can be traced back to the ancient Egyptian cult of Osiris: no wonder the Church suppressed such beliefs, so perilously near the knuckle of Christianity.

In the sixteenth century the mummers' cycle of Robin Hood plays were mixed in with the dances of the morris men. Robin himself has a murky past – some authorities reckon he is a Christianized version of the witches' familiar, Robin Goodfellow or Puck. In any event, Robin became interchangeable with the Fool – and like him dies and comes back to life. His consort Maid Marian doubled up with the Betsy. The Midlands remain the morris men's stronghold.

The dancers can be seen in force on May Day and at Whitsuntide – and also at country fairs and rural celebrations. They sometimes reappear with their close associates the mummers at Christmas. Some authorities see the dances as of Moorish origin – pointing to blackened faces and discounting the fact that this was the usual method of disguising oneself (see Carnival, p.89) and that real Moorish or morisco dancing is quite different. Palmer and Lloyd, in British Calendar Customs, prefer the simplest explanation: that 'morris' is a corruption of 'Moorish' and merely meant any foreign dance. Possibly, they suggest, the dance was brought over by Eleanor of Castile, Edward I's queen – or by John of Gaunt on his return from Spain in Richard III's time. There are records of such dancing in the thirteenth century in Belgium and France – so it may have drifted over the Channel informally. But Robert Graves in The White Goddess proposes that 'morris men' is an elision of 'Mary's Men' – and is a reference to Aphrodite's predecessor Marian the Moon-goddess.

The morris men would be perfectly at home on the pilgrimages of southern Europe, where Whitsun has borrowed the trappings of the outdoor feasts of midsummer. Christian charity and pagan revelry still meet and embrace each year at the gypsy pilgrimage to Les Saintes-Maries-de-la-Mer in the Camargue, and in the week-long pilgrimage to the Andalucian shrine of the Virgin of the Rocío (see p.185) – an exuberant singing, dancing, open-air picnic in the dunes of the Guadalquivir's delta, during which food and drink and, not infrequently, other tributes more suitable for Agape's brother Eros were – until the new road was built and the fast-food vendors moved in – shared by all.

The ceremony shares certain characteristics with Whitsun celebrations, still extant in the 1930s, in central Europe. Károly Viski reported that in the Hungarian province of Transdanubia, a Whit-King was chosen by means of a horse race which tested the participants' cunning as well as their physical strength.

Whitsun's Kingdom lasted for a year – its perks were power and the right to eat and drink at the expense of the other lads. In mountain areas, too, there are historical records of the election of a shepherd boy who was given a sleeping draught and settled on his throne while comatose. A year later, he was returned in the same drugged state to his former obscurity.

It must be added that other less squeamish authorities suggest that prior to this the mock king's reign was more permanently terminated.

Gyula Illyes described the election *circa* 1920 of the Whitsun Queen in Rácegres, one of the brutal farm ghettos of the Hungarian *puszta*:

Four older girls held a sheet over a younger one as they went singing from house to house. At the end of their song, the four girls ran to the middle, snatched up the little girl in the sheet, and then they ate whatever they were given – fried doughnuts and cake-bread. These were days when half the *puszta* dressed up as animals or devils, with fur caps and cloaks turned inside out just for a good laugh. At other times they dressed up as ghosts, with sheets and candles stuck in scooped-out pumpkins, to frighten folk. We laughed and trembled as ancestral custom demanded. The lads and youths and sometimes even the older folk also turned their occasional big feasts into a kind of mass entertainment, by improvising verse, dancing and cutting capers, like the Attic Greeks at their goat-festivals. They would act whole scenes which made no kind of sense whatsoever; why did the *puszta* roar with laughter as if they were having an outing?

No doubt Greece's scatterbrained goat-gods, or the contrary goblins of the Celts, could explain the matter – or, as is their habit, further complicate it all.

Pagan undercurrents also swirled beneath the Whitsun celebrations at Tarascon in the Roussillon, southern France. The underlying purpose of the spring processions of Mediterranean Europe – including those of the four Rogation Days on April 25th and the three days preceding Ascension Day – was to ask the gods' blessing on the young crops. Simultaneously, evil spirits must be chased away so as not to risk their destruction of the good work. When Christianity took on responsibility for the welfare, both spiritual and practical (for what use was there for theory without reality?) of Europe's farming communities, the local saint or Virgin, processed in effigy, was considered sufficiently potent to deter potential spoilers of the harvest. But in high-risk areas, such as Tarascon, beneath whose ramparts the waters of the Rhône constantly threatened inundation, the dangers from flood and other water-borne disasters were personi-fied by the water-dwelling fire-belching dragon, the tarasque.

The earliest description of the progress round the town of Tarascon's own dragon, a six-metre-long, man-powered creature of painted wood and cloth, was supplied in 1787 by Claude-François Achard:

> At the festival of Pentecost, a joy verging on madness takes hold of the inhabitants, together with those visitors drawn by curiosity to the city. The long-tailed Tarasque creaks and sways as it hurls itself into the crowds, threatening the spectators with instant mutilation. Those who transport the creature from beneath, charging across the street from one side to another, swing the tail with such force that it sometimes breaks the arm or leg of a spectator not agile enough to escape. Then a disaster which elsewhere would have brought the procession to a halt, merely serves to whip the public into a frenzy of delight. As soon as creature lands a blow, the crowd immediately yells encouragement – 'Elle a bien fait! Bien fait!'

The blood on the monster's carapace is now dried and crusted: she last killed a man in 1891. She allows herself to be led, docile as a lamb, on a ribbon by a young girl, her dual role, both as visible reminder of possible disaster and hostage to future fortune, all but forgotten. The procession has expanded to include a carnival of trade guilds and rural occupations – vintners, shepherds with a child on a donkey to indi-cate the transhumance, carpenters, fishermen – whose representatives ape good-humouredly the old aggression of the tarasque. Until the end of the nineteenth century there were games to accompany the monster's appearances – although her outings were as irregular as the disasters she was supposed to avert. Whitsun charity, recalling our own Whitsun Ales, was supplied, whether or not the tarasque paraded, by the annual Whit Monday procession of brotherhoods and guilds which carried offerings of butter-enriched breads to the church of St Martha to be blessed – from where the largesse was distributed to the beggars and poor of the town.

At Whitsun in Loreto Aprutina in the Abruzzi, the curious festival of the fattened ox and San Zopito was reported by J.A. Spranger in the Journal of the Royal Anthropological Institute (Iii, 1922).

> The actual festival lasts three days; it begins with the unveiling of the handsome silver urn con-taining the ashes of the saint, on the morning of Whit Sunday. On this same morning the ox is led through the streets of the village, while a house to house collection takes place. It is also led into the church and made to kneel before the image of the saint. I was informed that the ox is offered spontaneously by one of the peasants of the district. The same ox continues in office until for any reason – illness, death or sale – it ceases to be available.
>
> On Whit Monday a bagpipe player must go immediately before the ox, piping continually dur-ing the whole time that the ox is marching slowly along in procession. The ox is adorned with ribbons, horns and tail are gaily decorated, and a bright red cloth laid over its back. On the ox's back a boy child rides in the procession. For the procession, the child is dressed in white, with arms left bare, while two wings and a veil are added to give him the appearance that justifies his name of 'l'angioletto'.

The animal is led round the town, and into the chapel of San Zopito, where it is made to kneel before the holy effigies. When this part of the ceremonies is over, the animal is taken to the house of the local landowner, where his peasant companions and the piper adjourn to the kitchen and eat a large cake, washed down with plenty of wine.

In Germany, most Whit custom is based on the pagan rites of spring – an open-air festival complete with maypoles and the Green Man, and not easy to disentangle from May Day itself. In Swabia there is a tradition of young people going round the village with empty buckets, begging food – eggs, bacon, pretzels, sausages, and wine – for their Whitsun feast, as children in France beg eggs for the Shrove Tuesday omelette. Among the devout communities of the Tyrol, the churches have a round window in the roof through which, on Ascension Day, the effigy of Jesus Christ is drawn, and, ten days later at Pentecost, down which the Holy Ghost spirals as a carved dove perched in the centre of a gilded wheel.

In the far north of Europe, the festival raids the Easter store-cupboard. Northern Norway, Finland and the northerly Baltic states enjoy their egg feast at Whitsun to coincide with the return of the migratory birds for the nesting season: hen's eggs were, in the old days, food for the rich – everyone else raided the wild for their seasonal treat. Denmark's northern Protestants, Beryl Miles remarked in 1958, celebrate Whitsun with hard-boiled gulls' eggs and mustard sauce, washed down with mulled beer.

The roots of the Whitsun/Pentecost celebration remain well buried beneath the forest floor – keeping the secrets of an essentially mysterious festival. Gentle Agape consummates a shotgun wedding with her ruffian brother Eros. Eostre sprawls on her flowery couch at the solemn Feast of Passover.

WHITSUN BRIOCHE
Coque de Pentecôte (France)

These rings of butter-enriched breads were taken in procession, looped over sticks and shown around for the edification of the populace by the rich townsfolk of Tarascon as charitable offerings for distribution to the poor of the city on Whit Monday. They would do fine for the morris cake-dance, too.

Quantity: Makes 1 ring.
Time: Start 2½ hours ahead. About 1 hour intermittent attention.
Equipment: A sieve and bowl. A baking tray and cooling rack.

1lb/500g flour
4oz/100g sugar
7oz/200g butter
8fl oz/200ml milk
4–5 tablespoons orange-flower water or extra milk

1 teaspoon salt
grated rind of 1 lemon and 1 orange
2oz/50g fresh yeast (1oz/25g dried)
1 whole egg

To finish
1 egg yolk, forked with 1 tablespoon milk

4oz/100g crystallized fruit

Sift the flour and salt into the bowl. Mix in the sugar and the grated rinds. Rub in the butter and yeast with the tips of your fingers, as if making pastry. (If using dried yeast, follow the packet instructions.)

Fork together the milk and the whole egg and pour it into a well in the flour mixture. Work the flour in gradually, adding enough orange-flower water or extra milk to give you a soft, slightly sticky dough. Work it well, pulling and pushing with the ball of your hand, until the dough is smooth and elastic.

Put the dough back into the bowl, cover loosely with a cloth or clingfilm, and put it in a warm place to rise for about 1½ hours.

Knock the dough down and knuckle it well to distribute the air. Roll it into a long fat sausage, and form it into a crown 10in/25cm in diameter. Transfer to a well-greased baking tray. Paint it with the beaten egg and milk, and press the crystallized fruits into the surface: no sense in hiding your generosity inside the bread.

Put it back in the warm place to rise once more. This should take about 1 hour – the dough is ready when it has doubled in thickness and bounces back when you press a fingertip into its surface.

Preheat the oven to 350°F/180°C/Gas 4.

Bake the crown for 25–30 minutes. It will be ready when it is well risen and brown and sounds hollow when you tap the base. Be careful taking it out – the sugar burns.

Transfer to the rack to cool.

WHITSUN DOUGHNUTS
(Hungary)

These cream- and egg-rich doughnuts were prepared in Transdanubia as a present to the little white-flounced Whit Queen and her attendants when she came calling under her white canopy. They ensured the giver good fortune in the coming year. This recipe for carnival doughnuts is recommended by Hungarian Vera Levai.

Quantity: Makes 2 dozen.
Time: Start 2 hours ahead. 40 minutes.
Equipment: A sieve and 2 bowls. An electric mixer would be useful. A pastry board. A 3in/7cm diameter biscuit cutter and 1–2 large baking trays. A deep fryer and a draining spoon.

2oz/50g fresh yeast (1oz/25g dried)
2 tablespoons sugar
3oz/75g softened butter
oil for frying

8fl oz/200ml cream, lukewarm
1lb/500g flour
5 eggs, separated

To finish
vanilla-flavoured sugar

apricot jam

Dissolve the yeast in the lukewarm cream with a little sugar. Sieve in enough of the flour to give you a thick batter. Cover and put to rise in a warm corner, until the dough has doubled in size.

Beat together the butter and the sugar until light and fluffy. Whisk in the egg yolks one by one. Incorporate the mixture into the risen batter. Whisk the egg whites and work them in, alternating with the rest of the flour, until you have a soft, smooth, well-blistered dough.

Press the dough out with your hands into a thick layer on the board, well dusted with flour. Cut out rounds with the 3in/7cm biscuit cutter and transfer them to the baking trays. Paint with oil and put back again to rise for another 40–50 minutes, until doubled in size and firm to the finger.

Heat the frying oil – not too hot, as the doughnuts must be given time to bake right through.

Slip in the doughnuts one at a time – not more than 4 or 5 in a large pan, or the oil temperature drops. Fry them first on one side with a lid on, then on the other side without. They are at their best, says

Vera Levai, when they turn out with a white stripe round their middles. Transfer each to absorbent paper sprinkled with vanilla sugar, to drain.

Serve the doughnuts warm, with apricot jam.

GULL'S EGGS WITH MUSTARD SAUCE
(Denmark)

Beryl Miles observed in 1958 that throughout May the fishermen of Revsore collected gull's eggs and sent them to Copenhagen – 'perhaps as many as 600 a day' – for use in omelettes and cakes, rather than as the gourmet delicacy they are considered today. Two years ago, finding myself in Tromsö in northern Norway at Whitsun, I bought and cooked some huge snow-white 'gull's eggs' which I think were in reality wild goose eggs. It might have been more instructive, but less delicious, to have hatched them out instead. Wild-gathered goose, duck and gull's eggs all have a delicate sea-flavour and translucent bluish whites – more rubbery than a hen's egg. They need thorough cooking.

Quantity: Serves 4.
Time: 15 minutes.
Equipment: A saucepan. A soup-plate and a fork.

Allow at least 2 gull's eggs per person

The sauce
1 tablespoon mild mustard, German or Dijon
3–4 tablespoons vinegar
salt and pepper

1 teaspoon sugar
scant ¼ pint/150ml seed oil
1 heaped tablespoon chopped dill or chives

Put the eggs in warm water and bring them to the boil. Turn the heat right down to simmer, lid the pan, and leave for 8–12 minutes, depending on the size of the eggs. Take them out and plunge them into cold water. The eggs should be served just cool.

Meanwhile make the mustard dressing. Drop the mustard into the soup-plate and work in the sugar and vinegar with the fork. Add the oil slowly, as if for a mayonnaise, forking it gently in until you have a thick liaison. Season and fork in the chopped dill or chives. That's it. Don't work it any more or keep it waiting – it separates. Restaurants usually rely on an extra stabilizing of egg, when it becomes a mustardy mayonnaise – not the same thing.

Hand the dressing separately in a small bowl, with the eggs served in their shells, accompanied by black bread, unsalted butter, radishes and mulled beer.

WHITSUN BREAKFAST
Pfingstenfrühstück (Germany)

This is the egg-and-sausage breakfast traditionally begged, borrowed or stolen by the young people of Swabia for their alfresco Whitsun feast. Refusal would be unwise, for, as with the collections of Shrove Tuesday and the trick-or-treaters of Hallowe'en, Christian charity, begging-bowl in hand, door-knocks in thieving pagan company.

Quantity: Serves 4 hungry scavengers.
Time: Start collecting the ingredients at daybreak. 20–25 minutes.
Equipment: A large frying pan.

1lb/500g pure pork sausages
1 onion, skinned and chopped
1oz/25g lard
salt and pepper

8oz/250g cubed bacon
1lb/500g cold sliced potatoes
6 eggs

Heat the pan. Prick the sausages and put them to fry with the bacon and the onion, in the lard. Let them fry until the sausages are well browned, the bacon is crisp and the onion is soft and nicely caramelized. Push to one side and fry the potatoes in the drippings.

Fork the eggs lightly together with salt and pepper. Pour the eggs into the hot fat around the other ingredients. Turn over once or twice for the uncooked egg to firm.

Take it off the heat and eat it all straight from the pan with forks. This is a secret feast and no trace must be left. Enjoy it with salty pretzels and a bottle of one of the Rhineland's delicious flowery white wines.

MAYBUTTER
(Austria)

The Tyrolese in the Austrian Alps manage without a maypole, but at Whitsun it is traditional to eat this rich spiced butter-cream, after which the young men make their way to the fields and hold whip-cracking competitions until midnight – a mirror of the witch-scaring ceremonies which preceded fertility festivals, when the populace went into the fields and made a great din to scare away witches and goblins. A fine dish of clotted cream would do well enough instead.

Quantity: Serves 2–4.
Time: 5 minutes.
Equipment: A bowl. A whisk or electric mixer.

1 pint/600ml whipping cream
2–3 tablespoons brown sugar

2oz/50g unsalted butter, softened
2 tablespoons powdered cinnamon

Whisk the cream with the softened butter, sugar and cinnamon until the mixture is thick and light – don't overbeat or it will separate into butter. Finish with an extra sprinkling of cinnamon and sugar. Very rich, but lovely with lemon biscuits and the first strawberries of the year.

WHITSUN PILGRIMAGE OF THE ROCÍO: SPAIN

Of all the pilgrimages Catholic Europe undertakes, none has quite the magic of the long trek across the marshes and dunes of Andalucia's Guadalquivir estuary to worship at the shrine of the Virgin of the Dew. So potent was her magnetism that, at Whitsun in 1498, she delayed Columbus's sailors for a full week from embarking from nearby Sanlúcar de Barrameda on their third voyage of exploration.

The Virgin's legend resembles that of many other such pilgrimages. In the early thirteenth century a hunter from the little village of Almonte on the edge of the Guadalquivir delta, some thirty kilometres south of Seville, was out with his dog, scouring for nesting birds in the spiny cistus scrub. The dog pointed at a thicket. The hunter, following his dog's instruction, found to his surprise not a brooding water-bird, but a carved wooden statue of the Virgin. He pulled the statue free, shouldered it and set out for home. Very soon, exhausted by the increasingly heavy burden and the midday heat, he lay down and fell asleep. When he woke, the Virgin had vanished. Returning to her hiding place, the hunter was amazed to find the Virgin re-installed.

The next day the bewildered man returned with companions from the village. They too fell asleep, once again waking to find the Virgin was back in her thicket. The village priest took the matter up through the Church's hierarchy to the Bishop of Seville, who eventually decided that the Virgin had selected her own home, and that there she should have her shrine. The village which grew up around her chapel in the dew-laden marshes was called El Rocío – the dew – and the reputation of the Virgin of the Dew, and the Whitsun pilgrimage which the villagers of Almonte made to her, grew over the centuries. The little pueblo of El Rocío, its sandy streets lined with hitching posts for the horses which were the only transport until the new road opened the way through the marshes, is occupied only for the week of Whitsun. The rest of the year it lies dormant, inhabited only by the cloud of white doves who quickly colonized the chapel's bell-tower and have given the Virgin her pet-name, *La Blanca Paloma*.

Gradually the White Dove was acknowledged as the purest of all Virgins (with the tacit consent of the Church), and the neighbouring villages and towns, and even Mother Seville herself, joined the pilgrimage to her shrine, carrying with them their own local Virgins to receive the benediction of the Sinless One. The pilgrims, faced with the usual dangers which awaited travellers in medieval times, compounded by an inhospitable landscape, joined together for safety. Some had to cross as many as seven rivers and make a journey of many days. The groups soon formed themselves into brotherhoods or *hermandades*, each of which built, in the village of El Rocío, a chapterhouse and shrine to accommodate their own visiting Virgin.

These days each group has a separate identity, reflecting the preoccupations and affluence of the membership. There are the foot-soldiers of nearby Almonte, the privileged original sponsors of the White Dove. The red-faced farmers of Vejer de la Frontera canter in on their sturdy working horses. The horsemen and women of Jerez, severely tailored in their dark *traje corto*, the flat Sevillian hat tilted over fine-boned aristocratic faces, ride through the dunes on their Arab stallions, tooled leather chaps protecting legs against sharp-thorned sage brush. The magnificently outfitted Sevillanos prance by, their elegant gypsy-dressed ladies side-saddle behind, in the vanguard of a parade of huge ox-drawn covered wagons, the interiors brilliant with a palace-wardrobe of shimmering silk shawls, and more and more richly flounced skirts. The grandees of Seville change their outfits twice a day – annually there is a new fashion to be followed: this year the trimmings are of *broderie anglaise*, last year the sleeves were puffed and sprigged with tiny flowers.

It is to the *manzanilla*-makers of Sanlúcar de Barrameda, Columbus's home port, that my family owes special allegiance. In the early seventies their cheerful brotherhood – more homely than the aristocrats of Jerez, to whom they sell much of their sherry production – took my young family under its wing and made us, for three consecutive pilgrimages, members of their *hermandad*. We crossed with their horses and carts and carriages on the rickety ferry which links Sanlúcar with the wild hunting grounds on the other side of the Guadalquivir's wide mouth, slept under the stars for two magical nights, danced and sang and drank the dry salty *manzanilla*, and finally paid homage, with the rest of the huge company of mounted and foot pilgrims, at the shrine of the Virgin of the Dew.

My husband Nicholas recorded the pilgrimage we made together in *Andalucía, a Portrait of Southern Spain*:

The provisions were simple. The food was Andalucian country fare – huge round loaves, asparagus-and-potato omelettes, chickpeas, black pudding and chorizo for stews to be cooked over open fires, endless tapas of olives and *jamon serrano*.

About clothes there was little choice. The pilgrimage is also a major social occasion, as grand and formal as any full-dress ball with the difference that it goes on continuously for seven days and nights and the setting is the watery and open-skied Guadalquivir delta. All true *Rocieros*, as the pilgrims are called, are on display from dawn to dusk and then from dusk through to dawn again. To be superbly turned out throughout the week is not merely a matter of convention, it is a duty to the Virgin in whose honour the pilgrimage is being made.

That night we slept fitfully. All round us fires burned, guitars played, whirling figures danced in the light of the flames, rockets soared into the sky, and the night was full of the monotonous beat of drums and the haunting chant of flutes. As the sun rose the next morning the party continued uninterrupted as it would for the next five days. A bottle was opened, a young girl in a shining swirling dress paused to wash her face, and then with the beads of water still gleaming on her skin spun into a dance, a man joined her briefly, caught up the reins of his horse, vaulted into the saddle and cantered away singing.

On the Sunday morning Mass is celebrated in the open with the pilgrims attending on horseback and looking in their uniform of *traje corto* like massed regiments of cavalry gathered in prayer before battle. Next day comes the Rocío's climax. The Virgin is brought out from her chapel on a wooden float and carried in procession through the village. The task of carrying her belongs by tradition to the men of Almonte, but the honour is considered so great that every red-blooded man in Rocío battles to share it for at least a moment. Bobbing and swaying in a haze of dust above a throng of frenziedly struggling figures, the Virgin slowly makes her way through the packed streets. In spite of the exhaustion, the drink and the intense passions aroused by the occasion, fights during the procession or at any time during the whole pilgrimage are almost unknown. The Paloma Blanca is the white dove of peace and permits no violence during her festival. Whenever an argument breaks out which looks like ending in blows, a shout instantly goes up, '!Viva la Paloma Blanca!' The quarrellers are then honour-bound to stop and shake hands. Throughout the Rocío the Virgin's wishes are paramount.

For the *hermandad* of Sanlúcar there was the two-day return journey across the marshes to the mouth of the Guadalquivir. The atmosphere of the journey back was subtly different from the outward trip. The singing and dancing, the guitar-playing and drum-beating went on as before, but it was less clamorous and insistent. A mood of contentment, almost of gentleness had settled over the column. Things had been done properly and with due ceremony. The white dove had been honoured not as a formality, an excuse for a wonderful week-long fiesta, but with faith and love and belief. She stood at the very centre of life. She gave meaning to the year and the passing seasons, to birth and death and all that filled the road between the two. Now she had been revered the pilgrims could return safely to their ordinary existence, sure in the knowledge that spring would come again and the grave-faced little wooden lady would be waiting for their adoration in the white shrine in the marshes.

GRILLED PRAWNS
Gambas a la parilla (Spain)

The mouth of the Guadalquivir has wonderful shellfish and crustaceans. The housewives of Columbus's point of departure, Sanlúcar de Barrameda, have the pick of the catch, although supplies last only for the first day or two of the pilgrimage – horses have no built-in fridge. Andaluz housewives test the freshness of raw prawns by shoving an inquiring finger into the whiskery pile and tasting the juice to see if it is overly salty – which would indicate that the fish has been stored too long with ice and salt.

El Rocío is only a few miles from the Atlantic, and in the old days enterprising fishermen would load their donkey-baskets – or their own broad backs – with the night's catch, and race each other inland to sell fresh fish to the arriving pilgrims: first one in does the business.

Prawns for grilling should be raw when you start. Ready-cooked ones are at their best served cold, with mayonnaise or a squeeze of lemon.

Quantity: Serves 4.
Time: 10 minutes.
Equipment: A hot grill or barbecue.

1lb/500g large raw prawns, fresh or frozen   1 tablespoon oil
1 tablespoon rough salt

To finish
1 quartered lemon   bread

Rub the whole prawns, unpeeled and with the heads left on, with a slick of oil. Salt them heavily – plenty of salt on the skin enhances the natural sweetness of the flesh inside.

Heat the grill or barbecue till it is sizzling hot. Slap on the prawns and let them cook, turning once – 2–3 minutes a side should be enough.

Serve them with quarters of lemon, and plenty of bread – an edible napkin for fishy fingers.

POTATO OMELETTE
Tortilla española (Spain)

If Spain has a national dish, it is this egg and potato pancake. Not the frothy frivolity of the French omelette, it is a thick juicy cake which any Spanish housewife seems to be able to turn out to perfection. It is the ideal all-purpose picnic food, either cooked ahead and taken ready-made, or quickly assembled from the raw materials over a small camp-fire. Children take it to school for lunch. Grannies thrive on it.

Every household has its own special way of making it, the person who makes it best, and the perfect pan to cook it in. On the Rocío, I would always watch out for edible greens to add to my dishes – particularly, in spring, the bright green shoots of asparagus which grow wild all round the Mediterranean. The closest to this gypsy-gathered crop is the slender green asparagus sold as sprue. Other favourite nibbles included sugar-cane shoots, crisp and sweet – delicious chopped fine and tossed in with a salad.

Quantity: Serves 3–4.
Time: 20 minutes.
Equipment: An omelette pan. A bowl. A sieve.

1lb/500g potatoes (allow 1 medium potato per egg)
4–5 asparagus sprue stalks (*optional*)
½ teaspoon salt

4 tablespoons good olive oil
1 thick slice Spanish (mild) onion, finely chopped
3 eggs

Peel and cut the potatoes into thin slices or fat chips. Put the oil to heat in the omelette pan. Fry the potatoes and the onion gently in the oil until the potatoes are quite soft but have not taken colour. Add the optional asparagus sprue, chopped into pea-sized lengths.

Transfer the potato, onion and sprue to a sieve placed over a bowl to catch the oil as it drains.

Beat the eggs lightly with a little salt. Add the drained potato mixture from the sieve. Pour most of the oil out of the pan, leaving only a tablespoon or two. Return the pan to the heat and tip in the egg-potato mixture. Fry gently until the eggs begin to look set. The heat should be low or the base will burn before the eggs are ready. With a spatula, push the potato down into the egg so that all is submerged.

As the *tortilla* cooks, neaten the sides with a metal spatula to build up a deep straight edge. When it looks firm, slide it out on to a plate, then invert it back into the pan to cook the other side. Don't overcook it – the centre should remain juicy. A little more oil in the pan may be necessary. Reverse it on to a plate. Pat off excess oil with kitchen paper.

Serve the *tortilla* warm or cool. There is nothing more completely Andaluz than a good *tortilla* made with barnyard eggs and thick virgin olive oil.

GYPSY TRIPE
Menudo gitano (Spain)

This is my own favourite outdoor stew – it's better made with untreated tripe, as the juices are richly flavoured and deliciously gelatinous. If you can get unblanched tripe (hard to find in modern butchers), scrub it well with salt, water and vinegar – as if you were a washerwoman doing the sheets by hand.

Quantity: Serves 4–6 – it depends whether you have been on a horse all day.
Time: Start a day ahead.
Equipment: A large saucepan.

1lb/500g tripe, cleaned and blanched
1lb/500g chickpeas, soaked overnight
1 onion, skinned and chopped

1 pair pig's trotters, split and washed
1lb/500g tomatoes, scalded, skinned and chopped
   (or 1 large tin)

3 garlic cloves, skinned and halved
1 teaspoon paprika
1 short piece ham or gammon bone, or 2
  rashers bacon, chopped
salt and pepper

1 bay leaf
1 sprig mint
8oz/250g small spicy sausages – preferably *chorizo*
4oz/100g black pudding in one piece

To finish
4 tablespoons olive oil

Put the tripe, cut into small squares, into the saucepan with the pig's trotters. Cover with 2 pints/1.2 litres of plain water and bring all to the boil. Skim off any grey foam and add the rest of the ingredients, keeping back the sausages and the black pudding – and no salt yet.

Bring back to the boil, turn down the heat a little, and leave it all at a low boil for 1½–2 hours. It should not be allowed to drop below a simmer which breaks the surface. Stir the pot every now and again, and if you need to add water, make sure it is boiling.

When the chickpeas are tender, remove the trotter and sort the bones from the gelatinous meat. Chop up the trotter meat if it is tender enough, but don't bother if it isn't – it was there primarily for its gluey juices. Return the chopped trotter meat, with the chorizo and black pudding, to the stew. Bring everything back to the boil and simmer for another 15 minutes uncovered, to reduce the juices to a lovely thick shiny sauce. Season.

Finish with a seasoning of olive oil, stirred well in. If you prefer you can finish the stew with a *soffrito* instead: fry a chopped garlic clove, a chopped small onion, and a peeled and chopped tomato in the oil, and stir that in when you are ready to serve. You will be on your own, though: I confess to a taste for good raw olive oil.

GYPSY EGGS
Huevos a la flamenca (Spain)

Travellers are not long enough in one place to grow fresh green vegetables – so tinned vegetables are a standard item in the Rocío pilgrim's stores. Nowadays this dish is usually presented in the shallow single-portion earthenware casseroles which are standard equipment in the Andaluz kitchen. Out in the *campo*, though, the whole dish is cooked in one pot.

Quantity: Serves 4.
Time: 40 minutes intermittent attention.
Equipment: A lidded saucepan. 4 one-portion shallow casseroles (*optional*).

1 onion, skinned and chopped
6 tablespoons olive oil
4oz/100g salt-cured ham or gammon, diced small
8oz/250g green beans (fresh or tinned)
8oz/250g peas (fresh or tinned)

2 garlic cloves, skinned and chopped
1 tablespoon chopped parsley
1lb/500g tomatoes, scalded, skinned and chopped
  (or 1 tin)

To finish

8 eggs

4oz/100g spicy, *thin*, cured sausage (*chorizo* for preference)

Fry the onion and garlic gently in the oil until they soften, then add the parsley, ham and tomatoes and bring all to the boil. Add the beans and peas, lid tightly, and turn down to simmer for 10 minutes.

Divide the vegetable stew between the 4 shallow dishes, if you have them. Crack 2 eggs on each portion, and finish with a few slices of spicy sausage. Bake in a hot oven, 425°F/220°C/Gas 7, until the white is set. Serve immediately. The casserole should be so hot when it is served that anyone who likes their egg well set can stir it in and it will finish cooking.

Alternatively, make 8 hollows in the vegetable stew with the back of a ladle and drop an egg into each hollow. Lid the pan and return it to the heat until the egg white has set. Serve ladled in portions, with a pair of eggs in each.

LENTILS WITH BLACK PUDDING AND CHARD
Potaje de lentejas con morcilla y acelgas (Spain)

Lentils are the great standby of the pilgrim. Needing no preliminary soaking, they soften in an hour – which makes them the fast food of Spain's basic store-cupboard of dried pulse vegetables. The Andaluz housewife makes an imaginative variety of these lovely one-pot soup-stews with haricot beans, chickpeas or lentils soaked with whatever meat and green vegetables are available, well spiced and enriched from her larder-stores with olive oil, *chorizo*, ham bone and *morcilla* – black pudding spiked with paprika, garlic and marjoram. On the Rocío, it is possible to gather wild greens instead of the chard: maybe *tagarnina*, the base-bud of a large thistle stripped of its spikes, a gypsy-gathered crop which looks like a pile of vegetable octopi, to be found in Andalucia's markets in the spring.

Quantity: Serves 4.
Time: 1 hour.
Equipment: A saucepan.

1lb/500g green lentils
4oz/100g black pudding, cut in chunks
3–4 garlic cloves, singed over a flame
1 short length ham bone or a bit of gammon
1 teaspoon dried marjoram or oregano
1 large potato, peeled and chunked
salt and pepper
2 tablespoons olive oil

2 pints/1.2 litres water
2oz/50g *chorizo* or spicy dried sausage
1 carrot, scraped and chopped
1 tablespoon paprika
1–2 bay leaves
3–4 stems of chard – leaf and stalk, chopped (or spinach)

Put all the ingredients except the potato, chard, seasoning and oil in the saucepan. Bring to the boil, turn down to simmer, lid and leave to bubble gently for 1 hour. Give it a stir every now and again. 15 minutes before the end of the cooking, add the potatoes (and extra boiling water if necessary). After 5 minutes, stir in the chard.

Taste and add salt and pepper. Make sure the potatoes are quite soft, and then finish with a stir of olive oil.

Serve in deep bowls with spoons. A slice of cheese and a juicy orange complete the feast.

AUBERGINES WITH GARLIC
Berejenas con ajo (Spain)

Aubergines are much prized in Mediterranean lands by those who cannot afford or have little access to meat. They provide good strong sustenance to line the stomach of a hungry man – and cooked like this they have a rich, strong, earthy flavour. The spices are an optional extra – southern housewives, with access to their own native, sun-ripened aubergines, can afford to do without them. I include spices only when preparing the dish back in my northern kitchen.

Quantity: Serves 4.
Time: 1 hour intermittent attention.
Equipment: A colander. A large saucepan with a lid.

2lb/1kg aubergines, hulled and cubed
½ pint/300ml olive oil
1 teaspoon powdered coriander
1 tablespoon powdered cumin

salt and pepper
6 cloves garlic, peeled and halved
1 teaspoon paprika

To finish
Cos lettuce leaves

lemon quarters

Salt the cubed aubergines and leave them in the colander to sweat while you warm the oil in the saucepan. Add the garlic and fry gently until it softens.

Rinse the aubergine cubes and shake them dry. Stir the spices into the hot oil and tip in the aubergine cubes. Aubergine drinks oil like a sponge. Fry steadily, turning the cubes over with a wooden spoon, until the aubergine softens and caramelizes a little at the edges. Add salt and pepper, lid, and leave to cook very gently in its own juices for 15–20 minutes, until the aubergine is a thick soft purée, speckled with its own beautiful deep purple skin.

Serve with Cos lettuce leaves to act as scoops, and lemon quarters to cut the richness.

ROCÍO RICE
Paella rociera (Spain)

Tradition has it that a *paella* is an outdoor dish to be cooked by men only. It seems that every red-blooded southern Spanish male has his own method of preparing the *paella*, and enjoys cooking it, with the usual Andaluz flair for theatre, for family and guests whenever there is an alfresco party. The shallow *paella* pans are too wide to be used on anything but a bed of coals – unless you have, as some restaurants do, a very broad gas ring specially designed for the purpose. Wild-snared ingredients – a brace of partridges or fine plump rabbit, crayfish from the stream, snails from the bushes, wild asparagus – are probably out of bounds now that the approaches to El Rocío are through the Coto Doñana nature reserve.

Designed to take the rice in a single layer, *paella* pans come in many sizes, from a small one for 3–4 persons to a huge one for 14, and are so proportioned that the water required to cook the rice comes up to the edge of the pan handles. The volume of rice to liquid is in the ratio of 1:2, which makes it easy to measure, using anything from a breakfast cup, to a pint mug, to a sherry *copita*.

If the Spanish housewife cooks the same dish in her own kitchen, using an ordinary wide frying pan, she will usually describe it as un *arroz* – a rice dish, which neatly sidesteps any argument about its proper preparation.

Quantity: Serves 6.
Time: 40 minutes.
Equipment: A large frying pan or *paella* pan.

8–10 strands saffron
4 tablespoons olive oil
4oz/100g salt-cured ham or gammon, diced
1 pint/600ml round rice
1 large tomato, scalded, peeled and chopped (use the scalding-water as part of the *paella* liquid)
8–10 stalks asparagus sprue, chopped into pea-sized lengths (or 4 tablespoons peas)

2 partridges, a wild rabbit or a small chicken
2 garlic cloves, skinned and chopped
1 green pepper, hulled, de-seeded and chopped
2 pints/1.2 litres water
salt and pepper
8oz/250g raw prawns or fresh-water crayfish
1 pint/600ml mussels or clams in the shell (or snails), well-rinsed

Put the saffron to infuse in a little boiling water.

Divide each partridge into 8 joints. A rabbit should yield 12–14 pieces, including the head, split; and if you are using a chicken cut it into 16 bits, including the back and neck, gizzard and liver, and chopping each drumstick and thigh in half. It is amazing how many people can feast on one small scrawny chicken in rural Spain – or Greece or Italy too.

Heat the pan. Pour in the oil and stir in the garlic and ham. Let them soften. Add the chopped green pepper and the game or poultry pieces. Fry them gently for 8–10 minutes, until they take a little colour. Stir in the rice and let it fry for a minute or two until it turns transparent and has taken up all the oil. Pour in the water. Add the tomatoes and the saffron crushed into its water, and season with salt and pepper. Bring everything to the boil and simmer uncovered for 18 minutes exactly from the time the liquid starts to boil. 5 minutes before the end, throw in the prawns and asparagus bits, and lay the shellfish on the top to open in the steam. Test the rice – it should not be quite soft but should retain a little nutty kernel, like an Italian risotto.

Remove the pan from the heat, cover with a clean cloth (or newspaper), and leave at the side of the fire for 10 minutes to allow the rice to swell.

Eat the *paella* straight from the pan with a fork or spoon, with a bit of Cos lettuce as a pusher.

HANGOVER CURE
Panacea (Spain)

Andrés Diego, master of horse at the Terry sherry *bodegas*, rides to the Rocío with the *hermandad* of Jerez. The journey on horseback takes six days, with plenty of stops for dancing, singing and gulping down the half-bottles of dry *fino* sherry which fuels everyone throughout. Stores – *chorizo*, paprika-pickled pork fillet, olives, salt-dried mountain ham, dense-crumbed 4lb/2kilo loaves of pointy-ended *pan tellera* – are as custom-dictated as the traditional bum-freezer jackets and leather chaps of the horsemen.

Quantity: Cures one hangover.
Time: 5 minutes.
Equipment: A saucepan.

½ pint/300ml very strong broth   1 glass *oloroso* sherry

Oloroso – the matured dry dark sherry which is the preferred tipple of the sherry connoisseur – is regarded as the fortifying pick-me-up of the morning after.

When the going gets really rough, take a cupful of boiling hot *caldito de feria* – home-made meat and chicken broth strengthened with plenty of beef marrow bones and chickens' feet – and spike it with a generous slug of *oloroso* sherry. Andrés swears it clears the head in no time, and he, as a veteran of more *Rocíos* than he cares to remember, should know.

ROSE HARVEST:
FIRST SUNDAY IN JUNE

This is the date for the official Festival of Roses in Karlovo, near the Shipka Pass in Bulgaria. A modern festival, it features rose-picking and folk dancing. The damask roses, planted in the 1600s by the Ottoman Turks, are deep red and sweet-scented. They are cropped to make attar of roses for export – with rose-water, much used in Middle Eastern cookery, as the secondary product.

The Ottoman Turks occupied Bulgaria for 500 years, and bequeathed both their culinary habits and their etiquette to the nations they conquered. By the end of the nineteenth century the Ottoman Empire was crumbling fast – de-stabilizing the whole of eastern Europe. In 1912 British Naval Intelligence compiled a *Handbook to Bulgaria* – with a view to possible invasion. The compilers identify the Bulgarians themselves as a hard-working, early-rising nation of peasant proprietors who dine frugally on wholemeal bread, hard cheese, soft or sour curds, and vegetables, with only occasionally meat and eggs.

> From the Turks he has acquired a liking for sweetmeats. But also he is a Slav and likes a glass of wine on Sundays and feast days. His chief drink is water, with now and again tea made in the Russian fashion, or coffee in the Turkish fashion. The principal amusement on Sundays and holidays is the dancing of the *khoro* on the village green to the music of the *gaida* or bagpipe, and the *gulsa*, a rudimentary fiddle. Many ancient superstitions linger among the peasantry, such as a belief in the vampire and the evil eye, and witches and necromancers are numerous and much consulted.

Five years earlier, intrepid journalist Henry de Windt of the *Westminster Gazette* had fought his way *Through Savage Europe* to the rose fields:

> The Shipka Pass is nearly 5,000 feet above sea-level, and it took us several hours to reach the summit, for the road was very rough. From here there is a magnificent view, and this is perhaps the only object to be gained in ascending the fatal Pass where, in 1877, almost as many perished from

blinding blizzards and the ferocious cold as from shot and shell. From here you may discern to the north the Danube river – a tiny thread of silver over a hundred miles away – and southward, the pretty red-roofed village of Shipka, nestling in gardens and fruit orchards, in the centre of a vast forest of rose trees. The town of Kazanlik, hard by, furnishes the most costly attar of roses in the world, and I was told that 60oz of the essence is worth £100.

So powerful is the scent of the roses in summertime that it extends for many miles around, and may be smelt at the very summit of the mountain. Everything around the spot, the cosy home-steads in the valley, the teams of oxen ploughing in the fields, and tinkling cow-bells, now wore an air of rustic peace ad prosperity.

ROSE-PETAL PRESERVE
(Bulgaria)

The Bulgarians make a rose-petal preserve as a by-product of their rose industry. Rather than spread it western-style on bread, the inhabitants of eastern Europe love it neat, eaten with a spoon and a glass of water. This jam is served to visitors as a gesture of welcome: sweets for the sweet. It's lovely with the thick yogurt which seems to be richer and more delicious in Bulgaria than anywhere else – and which the Bulgarians have a good claim to having invented.

Quantity: Makes about 3lb/1.5kg jam.
Time: Start a day ahead. 30 minutes.
Equipment: A large bowl. A saucepan. Jam jars.

1lb/500g damask rose-petals, picked on a
   dry day when the roses are in full bloom
juice of 4 lemons

2lb/1kg granulated sugar
1½ pints/900ml water

Pick over the rose-petals, clip off the white bases, and put the petals in the bowl with half the sugar, well stirred in. Leave overnight for the juices to run.

Next day, put the rest of the sugar into the saucepan with the water and the lemon juice and heat gently, stirring, until the sugar has dissolved. Stir in the sugared rose-petals. Heat again until it is nearly boiling. Turn down to simmer and cook gently for 10 minutes. Bring up to the boil – keep it there for 10 minutes until a dab of jam on a saucer looks set.

Pot in small sterilized jars. Cover and seal. Offer it to your friends to keep them sweet.

ROSE-WATER PASTRIES
Banitsa (Bulgaria)

The scented water left when the oily attar of roses has been skimmed is bottled and exported all over the Middle East, where it is used to flavour and perfume pastries as well as being used as a delicate skin fresh-ener. The Bulgarians learned the art of making paper-thin filo pastry during their many centuries under the Ottoman Turks – these are one of the most delicious of a larger repertoire of sweet and savoury pas-tries made for special occasions.

Quantity: Serves 4–6.
Time: 40–45 minutes.
Equipment: 2 small saucepans. A clean kitchen cloth. A pastry brush (a new ½in/1cm painting brush is fine). A baking tray.

8oz/250g filo pastry (6 sheets)
4 tablespoons rose-water
3oz/75g butter, melted

8oz/250g sugar
8oz/250g walnuts or almonds, crushed

To finish
2 tablespoons rose-water

Keep the filo pastry covered while you make the stuffing.

Melt the sugar gently with the 4 tablespoons rose-water until you have a clear syrup. Stir in the crushed nuts and leave the mixture to cool.

Lay a sheet of filo on the cloth. Paint it with melted butter. Top with a second sheet and paint that with butter. Top with a third sheet. Spread half the stuffing on the top layer, leaving a finger-wide margin all round. Tuck two opposite margins over the filling. With the help of the cloth, roll up the pastry and its stuffing into a long bolster and lay it on a buttered baking sheet. Repeat with the rest of the pastry and the stuffing.

Bake in a very hot oven, 450°F/230°C/Gas 8, for 15–20 minutes, until the pastry is crisp and brown. As soon as you take it out of the oven, sprinkle it with the rest of the rose-water.

Serve cool, cut into short lengths, with a tiny cup of Turkish coffee and a glass of water.

FESTIVAL OF ST ANTHONY: JUNE 12TH-13TH

June 12th is the eve of the Festival of St Anthony, patron saint of Portuguese lovers, who was born in Lisbon's old Moorish quarter, the Alfama. On his festival, the steep cobbled alleyways of the Alfama are decorated with pots of basil and carnations, and young men traditionally present the girl of their choice with a basil plant as a love-token. Dancing and singing goes on all night, and the revellers feast on grilled sardines bought from kerb-side braziers. The Portuguese – and their neighbours in Andalucia – love freshly grilled sardines. The little silver fish, canned in olive oil as a major export for Portugal, are at their best and fattest from May to October.

Portugal's inshore fishing fleet depends on the sardine shoals – immature pilchards, but, to my mind, firmer and better-flavoured than their northern brothers – for its daily bread.

Sacheverell Sitwell remembered, as Hitler's battalions isolated Britain in 1940, the sardine fishermen of his beloved Portugal:

The Phoenician fishermen of Nazaret in Portugal have sardine boats which transcend their men and women – barefoot fishermen in check trousers – red, blue and yellow, no two alike – stocking caps of the tarantella dancers, their women immobile in black, heads shawled in black over the water-carrier's flat hat, level for amphora. The boats are square and flat-bottomed at the stern, then narrow and curving up to a prow, painted in bright patterns. Here is all that remains of Tyre and Sidon, on the way to the tin mines of the Cassiterides.

GRILLED SARDINES
Sardinhas assadas (Portugal)

Sardines are the perfect fish for grilling – fat enough to need no extra oil, small enough to crisp and cook through at the same time. Fresh sardines have a lovely viridian sheen to their flanks, and will still be shedding their large scales. Andalucian housewives test for freshness by poking the fish with a finger – if the flanks keep the print, the fish is not fresh enough.

Quantity: Serves 4.
Time: 10 minutes.
Equipment: A hot grill or open fire and a grid.

1½lb/750g fresh sardines   2–3 tablespoons rough salt

Gut the sardines – easily done with your index finger through the soft bellies, although if the fish are sparkling fresh, they need not be gutted at all. Leave the heads and scales on, and sprinkle the fish with plenty of salt.

Heat up the grill or barbecue until the metal is really hot. Lay on the fish. Grill them fiercely, turning once, till the skin blisters black and bubbly. The thicker the fish the longer they will need – 3–4 minutes a side should be ample.

Pick the sardines up by the tail and eat them off the bone – first one side, then the other, or sandwich them whole in thick-cut slices of sweet golden Portuguese cornbread (see next recipe).

CORNBREAD
Broa (Portugal)

The busy trade between the seafaring Portuguese and the New World ensured early acceptance of American staples such as maize in the kitchens and vegetable patches. More than any other nation of Europe, the Portuguese look west for their culinary inspiration, and this bread is also a staple in Mexico. The Portuguese alone in Europe, with the exception of Cyprus, use fresh coriander in their dishes – a herb beloved of the cooks of China, Japan and India as well as of South America.

Quantity: Makes 2 loaves.
Time: Start 3½ hours ahead. 20–25 minutes intermittent attention.
Equipment: A mixing bowl. 2 baking trays and a cooling rack.

1lb/500g stone-ground yellow cornmeal   2lb/1kg strong white flour
1½ tablespoons salt   4oz/100g fresh yeast (2oz/50g dried)
1 teaspoon sugar   1 pint/600ml warm water
2 tablespoons corn oil

Sift the cornmeal into the bowl with the flour and salt. Liquidize the yeast with the sugar and stir it into a cupful of the warm water. Pour the yeast mixture into a well in the flour and sprinkle some flour over the top. Put it in a warm place for 20 minutes or so to start the yeast working. (If using dried yeast, follow the packet directions.)

Work in the yeast liquid, drawing in the flour from the sides with your hand, and then work in the rest of the warm water and the corn oil until you have a sticky dough. Knead the dough vigorously on a well-floured board until it is smooth and elastic and developed enough to have lost its stickiness – an electric mixer is a bit light for this heavy dough, so the kneading really has to be done by hand.

Cover the dough and put it in a warm place to rise for 2 hours, until it has doubled in size. Knead thoroughly to distribute the air bubbles. Divide the dough in half and knead each piece into a round cushion. Transfer to the oiled baking trays and put back into a warm place to double its bulk again – about 1 hour should do the trick.

Preheat the oven to very hot, 475°F/240°C/Gas 9. Put a shallow tray of boiling water on the base of the oven. Portuguese brick ovens, still in common use in rural areas, are damped throughout the baking with a bucket of water, and it is the resulting steam which gives the bread its thick brown crust.

Bake the loaves for 35–40 minutes, turning the oven down a little after the first 25 minutes. When the bread is well risen and deliciously browned, and sounds hollow when you tap the base, transfer to the rack to cool.

Cut the bread into thick slices: perfect to accompany the sardines of St Anthony's Eve, but almost as good with a slick of virgin green olive oil and a rub of garlic.

MIDSUMMER EVE AND MIDSUMMER DAY: THE FEASTS OF ST JOHN, JUNE 24TH–26TH

The festival of high summer, a celebration of ripening corn and maturing harvest, is traditionally marked throughout Britain and Europe with sun-strengthening bonfires, a scattering of well-blessing rites, with a few simple courting rituals to encourage general fertility; measures such as herb-burning and beating the boundaries with flaming brands were designed to scare away destructive spirits who might undo the good work. The oldest festivals are the ones which all Europe shares: the rituals characteristic of midsummer are echoed from the North Cape to the Pillars of Hercules.

The date of the old summer solstice, July 4th, was changed with the calendar in 1752, when it landed cheek by jowl with June 24th, the feast of the Nativity of St John the Baptist. The firebrand saint, who said of his Master: 'He must increase, and I must decrease,' inherited the festival intended to give the waning sun extra muscle for its long roll downhill into winter. Perhaps the water-blessing and well-dressing rituals which – although also celebrated throughout the summer from Ascension Day onwards – attach to the festival are equally appropriate to the Saint's celebrated labours in the same element.

In Britain our traditional midsummer rituals fell foul of the Reformation. The Protestant Church has never looked on the old gods with as kindly an eye as the Roman Catholics. Sixteenth-century historian John Stow – himself suspected of secret sympathy for popery – noted in his survey of the ancient customs of London that on the vigil of St John the Baptist 'every man's door was shadowed with green birch, long fennel, St John's Wort, white lilies, and garlanded with beautiful flowers, and had also lamps of glass, with oil burning in them all the night'. All the plants he listed were believed to have magical properties, especially St John's Wort, a sun symbol because its golden flower suggested protective and fertility-inducing powers.

At the extremities and on the offshore islands of Britain the old ceremonies were not so easily suppressed, many surviving until the Second World War. On the Isle of Man, bonfires were built to windward so that the smoke would fertilize the fields. People used to run round the boundaries of their fields with lighted brands or straw-bundles to ensure a good harvest. In Cornwall, one of the last bastions of pre-Christian custom, Midsummer Eve was considered the best time for combating witches. In Penzance young men marched through the streets swinging round their heads flaming torches attached to chains. At St Cleer a huge bonfire, crowned with a witch's broom and hat, was lit on a hill as a warning to witches to steer clear and forty varieties of herbs and flowers were sprinkled into the flames. The custom of lighting a chain of bonfires was revived in Cornwall in the 1920s: the first bonfire is lit at St Ives, and a chain of fires then flares from one coast to the other. A Lady of the Flowers is chosen to toss in a sickle-shaped bunch of blossoms – a gentle reminder of the magic plants and the wooden sickle cut from an oak tree which were tossed on in the old days, and which some believe to be a relic of human sacrifice.

Just across the Channel, Holland has a relic sacrificial ceremony – a St John's procession during June in the woods near Laren, which ends at the Old Cemetery – supposed to have been the site for sacrifices. In Belgium the eve of St Peter's Day, June 29th, is the chosen day – and there is a tradition that the fires of St Peter are lit to drive away dragons. In North Africa aromatic plants are burnt on the midsummer fires: giant fennel, thyme, rue, chervil, camomile, geranium and pennyroyal. In Germany *Johannistag* is held unlucky or lucky according to the district. In most places it is traditional to light bonfires or empty tar barrels, and sweethearts jump over the fire hand in hand for luck. All other fires – cooking and hearth – had to be extinguished when the midsummer fires were burning, the ritual associated with the Beltane need-fires of the Celts (see p.164).

Throughout rural Europe, people danced round the midsummer bonfires, young men and girls leapt over them for strength and good fortune, and cattle were driven through the embers in a purifying rite to protect them from disease. In Brittany the custom of the midsummer bonfire was kept up with most of its old rituals until well into the twentieth century. The rituals still take place annually all over Spain, when, on the eve of the feast of San Juan, fires are lit in the streets so that youth can prove their bravery by running over the coals. The best known of these festivals is held in San Pedro Manrique, Soria, where the streets are decorated with branches and flowers, and the young men walk barefoot across burning charcoal.

In Provence the midsummer fires still burned until the Second World War. At Aix a nominal king, chosen from among the youths for his skill in shooting at a popinjay, presided over the midsummer festival, leading the processions and reigning for a year. Paulette Villedieu remembered, in 1988, the pre-war bonfires of upper Provence:

> In my grandfather's time there were fires everywhere – even in the streets of Avignon. It all changed with the war of 1939. Now it is a matter for the folkloric societies – we have our fire on the hill in Vaison-la-Romaine. The young people used to court at the fires – there were rituals attached to jumping over the coals. We would take with us the first summer fruits – strawberries and cherries, the first peaches and apricots.

In searching for the tangled roots of these customs, it can be instructive, as so often with our ancient festivals, to look to eastern Europe. Károly Viski mused, in 1932, on the midsummer rituals of his native Hungary, where the festival was known as Flowery St Ivan's (John's) Day:

> The day of the summer solstice is at the time when Hungarian wheat, St Ivan's apples, and cherries ripen; in the midst of the season of white bread, green apples and red cherries. The day on

which the calendar of the church fixed St Ivan's day used to be the feast of love in the calendar of ancient man. The ancient pagan feast, held at the same time as the Christian festival of Pentecost, is the feast of the internal fire which burns for ever in man. A tall tree trunk is set up on top of the nearest hill, or a suitable tree is chosen for the occasion; a number of old baskets are placed on it, and a girl's wreath is laid on top of them. When this is done, the tree is set on fire at sunset. Sometimes a number of St Ivan's fires flame up at a smaller or greater distance from each other. If the wreath also catches fire, it is a good sign: its owner will soon be married! This form of the custom is merely a small fragment of the ancient fire feast. We can find this feast nowhere in its original form.

The Transylvanian Calvinist scholar-priest Peter Bod, writing in the mid eighteenth century, highlighted the elements of St Ivan's Night which he felt were throwbacks to the pagan festival. He noted that children collected all kinds of rubbish and bones and made smoky fires round the wells to prevent snakes from multiplying around the water, a frequent occurrence at the time. He continued disapprovingly:

The Christians in their ignorance, made fires about that same time and leapt over them, wishing that all their sadness might get burnt. They carried hot embers along the boundaries of their land, hoping that the harvest of the fields would thus be blessed. In some places they rolled wheels on that day, meaning that the sun had already reached the top of the horizon, and that everything was on the eve of change.

In Portugal, at the other extremity of Europe, the old customs took an equally long time to vanish, and the festivities reported in the 1930s by Rodney Gallop concentrate on the spirit-scaring and fertility-celebrating aspects of the event. He explains that there is a traditional link between the dead and the buried seed from which presently the crops will spring:

Folklorists would probably agree in seeing representatives of the spirits of the dead in the young men with blackened faces, wrapped in white sheets, who run about the country round Oliveira de Azemis on St John's Night, howling dismally, and in the figures wrapped in sheets, who hiding their faces and disguising their voices, break up the *desfolhada*, the communal stripping of the maize, and are rewarded with apples by the girls. Dr Wolfram of Vienna suggests that the custom of masked men or children going around importuning and threatening for gifts, the wild-hunt, is no other than the army of the dead.

Northern Scandinavia, in semi-darkness all winter, greets Midsummer Eve with unparalleled pleasure: huge bonfires blaze across northern and eastern Finland, through northern Sweden and down the fjords and valleys of Norway. The time of the longest day and the Midnight Sun dictates these northerly midsummer celebrations, which are much like May Day celebrations further south. In southern Sweden and western Finland, everyone decorates their houses, offices and cars with leafy and flowering branches. A maypole is raised in the afternoon in the village square in rural areas, and everyone dances in a ring around the pole – and later moves on to a barn or a harbour warehouse to share a meal.

City dwellers try to go out to the country for the celebrations. Dalarna in central Sweden, where pagan and Christian rituals, including church-boat races – small Viking-type boats – once used to ferry people to church, which accommodate ten oarsmen and their passengers in full traditional dress. Midsummer morning, too, is the traditional time to collect dew and special plants to cure illnesses. And if you sit up all night you may have a chance to see the ferns bloom, and gather the seeds which protect the possessor from all evil – the magic fern seed was familiar to medieval necromancers in Britain too. Swedish and Norwegian girls who want to find out the identity of a future husband pick a bunch of midsummer flowers, tuck them under their pillow and hope to dream of the man they will marry. The alternative is to eat very well-salted 'dream herring' or 'dream porridge' to dream of their bridegroom. Salt seems to sharpen the focus of dreams.

Horace Marryat, travelling in Denmark with his aristocratic host Baron Adeler around 1860, found evidence of both fire and water festivals:

> We drove to the Veirhoi, one of the biggest points in Zeeland, where my eyes fell on a blackened stone. 'That,' said Baron Adeler, 'is the stone on which the bonfire is lighted by the peasants on St John's Eve – an old custom handed down to us from the earliest time. It is a beautiful sight; on every hill a fire is lighted. We can from this spot count eighty or ninety at a time.' How this bonfiring escaped the anathemas of the Reformed Church I know not. The sacred well of St Helena, near Tidsvilde, whose waters effected most marvellous cures, was a favourite place of pilgrimage to the simple peasantry on St John's Day – a custom which, as well as the erection of small crucifixes by the well's side as thank-offerings, continued long after the Reformation was finally established in Denmark. In vain the prelates forbade, under pain of punishment and fine, the continuation of such Popish practices: it was of no use. 'Why,' exclaimed the Boers, 'should we pay for doctor's stuff when good St Helena furnishes us with water much more efficacious, free of all expense?'

There we have it: fire, water and earth all rejoice in the sun's zenith, and each population seems to have found one aspect – perhaps those which best reflect its most pressing needs – more worthy of preservation than others. When I was a child at school in the Malvern Hills in Worcestershire, on Midsummer Night we would all climb in the long soft twilight to the top of the beacon. We always stopped half-way up at St Anne's Well. Beside the well-spring which bounded from a cleft in the rock, there was a cup on a chain, and we would queue to sip the clean clear water and drop a penny in the pool below – the modern face of well-dressing. The view from the summit of the beacon – bald these days from many pounding feet – is famous: seven counties can be seen on a clear day.

We were more interested in our own ritual: the performance of well-rehearsed midsummer plays of our own devising, each class in competition with the others. Sometimes we wrote our own scripts, sometimes – in sight of Shakespeare's birthplace in the vale below – we would perform *Pyramus and Thisbe* or scenes from *A Midsummer Night's Dream*. Then we would sprawl on the flowery grass and eat our midsummer picnic: sausage rolls and cake and apples and maybe crisps and chocolate, wonderful treats in the days when we still had post-war rationing.

SALT-COD FRITTERS
Bolhinos de bacalhau (Portugal)

For Lucinda Oliveira, *bacalhau* was both her livelihood and her feast-food, and these fritters were the proper way to celebrate the festival of St John. Born and bred in the little village of Boa Aldea near Viseu in the highlands of central Portugal, she remembers the long hardships and short pleasures of her young womanhood forty-five years ago:

My family was poor, so money had to be earned. When I was fourteen I went to Lisbon, and stayed there until I was twenty-five and married, working on the fishing boats, like a man . . .

We were three girls and two boys in my family, and all except the youngest went off to earn money. I first went to Lisbon with my elder sister – she was only thirteen when she first went – because there was work to be had in the *bacalhau* trade, salting and packing cod for sending away to other countries. We went in the little boats to the big boats to fetch the cod back to the factory. Then we unloaded the fish in big baskets you carried on your head. And we cleaned the fish with big hard brushes. And then salted it and laid it out in layers on flat racks in the open air. And every evening, unless it was high summer, we had to bring the fish back in and put it in the hot room so that it went on drying. There was one wage for men, another for women, and another for children. We all did the same work though. Often the little children worked harder than any of us.

When I buy *bacalhau* now, I look at it carefully. To be good, the flesh must be pure white. If it has a yellow tinge, that is not good. And if you can see pink down the spine, that is because it was not properly dried before it was packed and sent away.

In my village we had many festivals. Christmas and Easter, and one in the middle of August. And the festival of São Joao on June 24th. The people went in procession from the church, and we'd take a picnic. Big round cheeses and bread. Fruit and wine. And the real treat was *bacalhau* fried in batter. We all really liked that.

Quantity: Serves 4.
Time: Start 24 hours ahead. 30 minutes.
Equipment: A bowl, wooden spoon, whisk and a deep fryer.

1lb/500g salt cod (or 1½lb/750g smoked
    haddock, which will not need soaking)
¼ pint/150ml water
1 garlic clove, minced finely
frying oil

1 egg
4oz/100g self-raising flour
1 teaspoon olive oil
1 tablespoon chopped parsley

Put the salt cod to soak in plenty of clean water for 24 hours, changing the water at least twice.

Cut the fish into bite-sized pieces and put it into a roomy saucepan with enough fresh cold water to cover.

Bring the water up to a fast simmer – do not let it boil – and poach the fish for 5 minutes. Drain the cod, let it cool a little, and carefully remove all the skin and any stray bones.

Make the batter. Separate the egg. Sieve the flour into a bowl, make a well in the middle and work in the egg yolk, water, oil, garlic and parsley until you have a batter which will coat the back of the spoon. When you are ready to fry, whisk the egg white and fold it into the batter. No salt is necessary, as there will be enough still in the cod. Heat the frying oil until you see a faint blue haze rising.

Drop the cod chunks into the batter, and slip them, a few at a time, into the hot oil. Fry until puffed and golden. Transfer to absorbent paper to drain.

Continue until all the batter is used up. Serve with quartered lemons.

MIDSUMMER SMÖRGÅSBORD
Midsommar smörgåsbord (Sweden)

Sweden has officially decided to move the midsummer celebrations to the closest weekend to June 24th. The meal always features pickled herrings – the passion of Scandinavia – served with new potatoes boiled with dill, and concludes with the first strawberries of the year: wild-picked ones if summer arrived good and early. Scandinavia has a wonderful wild larder of berries, the only fruits which have time to ripen in the short summers of the Arctic circle, including several peculiar to the area, such as the succulent golden cloudberry, which will not be ripe until well into July. Wild strawberries grow everywhere – even conveniently transplanted to the turf-roofs which topped out the old birch-log cowsheds.

Quantity: Serves 6.
Time: Start 1–2 hours ahead. 20 minutes.
Equipment: 3 serving dishes.

First dish

1 pickled herring, chopped
1 tablespoon spring onion, chopped
3 tablespoons vinegar
1 tablespoon sugar

2 apples, cored and chopped
1 teaspoon ground allspice
3 tablespoons water
salt and pepper

Second dish

1 pickled herring, chopped
1 tablespoon pickled gherkins, chopped
½ teaspoon crushed mustard seeds
3 tablespoons water
salt and pepper

2–3 large beetroots, cooked, skinned and chopped
2 tablespoons chopped chives
3 tablespoons vinegar
1 tablespoon sugar

Third dish

1 pickled herring, chopped
1 tablespoon chopped dill
1 small piece fresh horseradish, grated
3 tablespoons vinegar
1 tablespoon sugar

3–4 large new potatoes, cooked, cooled and sliced
2 spring onions, chopped
1 hard-boiled egg, sliced
3 tablespoons water
salt and pepper

Combine each group of ingredients in its own dish and leave to marinate for 1–2 hours – the fish and the other ingredients should more or less equal each other in bulk. Serve with a bowl of soured cream, crispbread and unsalted butter, and hot boiled new potatoes cooked with a head of dill.

Fresh strawberries complete the meal. Offer tiny glasses of ice-cold aquavit to toast the glorious midnight sun, with beer to wash it down.

GRILLED LAMB WITH HERBS
Agnello arrosto con odori (Italy)

Michaela, the cook at the *pensione* in Florence where I lived as a young student, loved any excuse to barbecue. Sometimes, on special days such as the feast of St John, she would take me with her to her village in the hills above the town – it was a busman's holiday for her, as she always prepared all the family's food at home as well as at work.

When she cooked over the open fire she did not like to spend too long standing over the hot coals, so she would always split open and flatten out the chicken or de-bone the joint first so that it took the heat faster. In fact, this is an excellent way to deal with large joints – the butterflied meat crisps and caramelizes over a much wider surface than a round joint – and I have followed her lead ever since. The bone was put on the grill to brown at the same time, and then it went to flavour the soup-stock. Michaela's mother grew her favourite herbs in pots, and the meat went into an aromatic marinade for as long as it took the charcoal to heat up in the brick barbecue at the end of the vine-trellised courtyard.

Quantity: Serves 8.
Time: Start 1 hour ahead. 30–40 minutes intermittent attention.
Equipment: A shallow dish. A red-hot grill or barbecue.

4lb/2kg boned leg or shoulder of lamb
rock salt and roughly ground pepper
2 tablespoons chopped fresh mint (Michaela used
  wild mint)
1 tablespoon chopped rosemary
1 garlic clove, skinned and chopped

2 tablespoons olive oil
1 tablespoon strong wine vinegar (*aceto balsamico*,
  or sherry vinegar)
2 tablespoons chopped parsley
1 tablespoon chopped thyme

Light the barbecue well ahead – it should be a well-settled bed of hot charcoal, showing no flames, by the time you are ready to cook.

Meanwhile, lay out the meat on a large dish, skin side down. Rub the cut side with 1 tablespoon of the oil, salt, pepper and vinegar, and work in the herbs and garlic. Roll up roughly, cover, and leave to marinate for at least 30 minutes.

When the barbecue is well heated, unwrap the meat, flatten it out and smack it on the hot grill. Let it sizzle for 10–12 minutes on one side, then turn it and do the other. Stab it to check whether the juices are as pink or clear as you like it. If no juices run, then the lamb is not yet cooked through at all. How long it needs depends on the heat of the barbecue and your own taste.

Serve speared on big slabs of bread, with a bowl of plump ripe tomatoes handed separately.

ELDERFLOWER FRITTERS
Hulasträubla (Germany)

Water-loving elder is sacred to St John, and the fragrant blossoms are in full bloom on St John's Day in the Egerland, where they are frittered to celebrate the Saint's birthday. Pick the large creamy flowerheads well away from crop-sprayed fields, on a dry day, and shake them gently to dislodge insects. Do not de-stalk or wash them, but separate the heads into manageable bunches ready for dipping.

Quantity: Serves 4.
Time: 40–45 minutes.
Equipment: A bowl and a whisk. A deep-fryer and draining spoon.

4–5 elderflower heads, separated into sprigs
1 teaspoon salt
¼ pint/150ml light beer
sugar

4oz/100g flour
1 egg
frying oil

Prepare the elderflowers as described above.

Sieve the flour and salt into a bowl. Work in the egg and the beer and whisk until you have a smooth, thickish batter.

Heat the oil in a deep-fryer. When it is just lightly hazed with blue, start cooking. Dip each sprig in the batter and fry until crisp and golden. Don't add too many at a time, or the oil temperature will drop and the fritters will be heavy.

Drain the fritters well on absorbent paper, pile them high, and serve them sprinkled with sugar.

SAUSAGE ROLLS
(Britain)

This was the special treat in the picnic-bag issued to each school-girl before we set up to climb the Malvern Hills for our midsummer picnic. We were not allowed to open the bags until we reached the top, but we always knew what was inside – we could smell the warm herby sausage rolls.

Quantity: Makes a dozen rolls.
Time: 1 hour intermittent attention.
Equipment: 2 mixing bowls and a sieve. A rolling pin and board. A baking tray.

The pastry
3oz/75g lard
1 teaspoon salt

4oz/100g plain flour
2–3 tablespoons cold water

The filling
½oz/12g lard
8oz/250g good sausage meat
½ teaspoon dried sage

1 medium onion, peeled and chopped
1 teaspoon dried thyme
salt and pepper

To finish
1 tablespoon egg

First make the pastry. Cut the fat roughly into the flour sieved with the salt, using a sharp knife. Cut in the water until you have a firm but soft dough, finally working it together with the tips of your fingers. Leave the dough to rest for 15–20 minutes, while you make the filling.

Melt the lard in a small pan, and fry the chopped onion until it is soft. Work the onion into the sausage meat with the herbs and seasonings.

Preheat the oven to 400°F/200°C/Gas 6.

Roll out each piece of pastry on a floured board to a thickness of about ¼in/0.5cm. Cut the pastry into 3–4 strips about 3in/7cm wide and lay ribbons of spiced sausage meat down the middle. Damp one of the long sides and fold it over to enclose the meat. Cut each into finger-length sausage rolls and transfer them to a baking tray. Paint the tops with lightly beaten egg for a shiny glaze.

Bake for 40 minutes, until the pastry is crisp and golden and the sausage meat is cooked right through.

HARVEST BREAD
(Britain)

As a child in the 1950s I used to summer-holiday at my stepfather's home near Newark in Nottinghamshire. The house and garden were protected from the farmland and the munching cows by a ha-ha – a dry moat walled with stone on the house side, with a gentle grassy daisy-starred slope on the other. The cows grazed the nearest meadow, then there was a field of corn, and beyond, most exciting of all, a lake with two heavily overgrown islands – which might be reached in the punt by an enterprising and disobedient child who had come by a key to the boathouse door. My grandmother's cook, who knew all about my habits, would slip me an elevenses for my pocket: a thick slice of harvest bread, the cut-and-come-again cake which she baked in a single enormous batch each week to send out to the field-workers. Although by my day the old traditions were no longer remembered, such cakes used to be taken to the fields and eaten there – the crumbs to be scattered among the swelling ears to encourage the corn to ripen.

Quantity: Makes a 2lb/1kg loaf.
Time: Allow 10 minutes to prepare, 1 hour 45 minutes to bake.
Equipment: A mixing bowl and sieve. A small saucepan. A large loaf tin.

12oz/350g self-raising flour	1 teaspoon bicarbonate of soda
8oz/250g caster sugar	8oz/250g sultanas or raisins
1 egg, lightly beaten	8 fl oz/200ml water
2oz/50g butter	2 tablespoons golden syrup

Mix together the flour sifted with the bicarbonate of soda, the sugar and the dried fruit. Stir in the beaten egg.

Heat the water with the butter and the syrup until all is melted. Stir the mixture into the rest of the ingredients.

Preheat the oven to 325°F/170°C/Gas 3.

Grease a loaf tin and line the base with greaseproof paper. Spread in the mixture.

Bake for about 1 hour 45 minutes, until the cake is well risen and a skewer pushed into the middle comes out clean.

ST JOHN'S HERB LIQUOR
Liqueur aux herbes de St Jean (France)

A sovereign remedy in Provence, every herb merchant knows the composition of this bundle of aromatics, traditionally gathered on St John's Night, which gives its name to the herb-flavoured liquor. Here is an infusion of the basics – for the rest, you will have to find a Provençal herb merchant and twist his arm.

Quantity: 2 pints/1 litre.
Time: Start 4 months ahead.
Equipment: A 1 litre bottle.

1 sprig rosemary
1 sprig marjoram
1 sprig sage
2 tablespoons sugar, melted in 2 tablespoons
  hot water

1 sprig thyme
1 sprig hyssop
1 litre white alcohol (vodka or gin will do)

Cram the herbs into the bottle. Pour in the sugar syrup and top up with the liquor. Seal and store for at least 4 months. It will keep for years.

WEDDINGS: JUNE

June is the traditional month for weddings – timed for the birth of the first child in the spring, the proper season for new life to enter the world. The mother could then suckle her infant and regain her own strength on summer's plenty. Modern paediatrics suggest that this old wives' tale may have some practical truth in it: statistics indicate that children born in the spring thrive and grow faster than babies born at any other time of the year.

Old wives' tales dominate this – as every other – important rite of passage, and all Europe shares many of the basic traditions designed to ensure the happy couple's acceptance in the group and the fertility of their union. As a first step, there are the symbols of betrothal to be observed, from the engagement ring to the wedding invitations: in Germany this was done either in person by the young couple bearing presents for the invitees, or by the *Hochzeitslader* – a formal wedding-inviter dressed in his best clothes, with a fine buttonhole and a garlanded stick.

In those parts of Britain where the Celtic traditions hold, the first warning of a betrothal was given when two spoons lay together, lover-like, in the same dish: sweethearts exchanged spoons as love tokens – particularly in Wales, where beautifully carved wooden cawl-spoons were, until the last century, the proper engagement gift. On the practical side, aphrodisiacs were held in great esteem: in Britain these included lettuces for their soporific qualities, mushrooms for their mysteriously rapid growth, carrots and eggs for their more obvious symbolism, and herbal infusions such as henbane, myrtle and mandrake root – the forked man-like tuber was considered particularly efficacious. Northern bridegrooms, observing the cod's stupendous capacity for egg-laying, added fish to the list of aphrodisiac substances – but in the Catholic south, where the monks, the intellectuals of the Middle Ages, ate fish on fast days, it was considered brain-food – not at all suitable for an innocent maiden. Anaphrodisiacs also had their place:

unwilling brides might demonstrate their reluctance by strewing the bridal chamber with rue.

The traditions of Germany, too, offer a clue to the origin of the rowdy stag-parties which are now a near-universal feature of the modern wedding. The night before a marriage in rural Germany, tradition requires the holding of a *Polterabend* or ghost-chasing: an all-night party to drive away evil spirits with much banging and smacking and cracking of whips.

Throughout most of Europe, white is considered the proper colour for the bride, although pink and blue are acceptable; green is unlucky, as it summons ancient and far from benevolent gods. In the low-lands of Scotland, no green vegetables were served at a wedding feast – perhaps less to avoid the attentions of the Little People than because no one could stand any more kale.

Celebration food was, until the current century, defined by that which was not available every day: dairy farmers left the cheese in the larder, fishermen killed a pig and staple foods – beans, lentils, rice, oats, potatoes – were avoided. Sweetmeats and sugary desserts, never available every day even in the richest households, were essential to the success of the party. The north made its porridges with fine white flour and cream, the south baked bread with refined wheat flour enriched with eggs and butter – eschewing the whole-grain rough stuff of every day. Wholemeal bread and vegetarian dishes, including salads, would have been quite unacceptable at a medieval wedding table – a prejudice which remains in many rural districts. Pot-roast kid was the chosen wedding dish of my Andalucian village neighbours when I lived there in the 1970s – although the Sunday treat was rice-and-rabbit *paella*. Meat has always been the most desirable and the hardest to come by of all foodstuffs. In Britain, wild game – venison, wild boar, hare, pheasant – was the preferred centrepiece of the wedding banquet, replaced on the modern table with roast turkey and baked ham.

French ethnologist Arnold van Gennep, in his massive study published in 1946, *Manuel de Folkore Français Contemporain*, outlined the pre-war French wedding feast:

> The food was always as plentiful and rich as possible. Those preparing the menu would generally try to avoid the dishes of every day such as stews of beans, potatoes – in fact, all vegetables – concentrating instead on as much meat as possible, a luxury not often enjoyed by the peasantry. Wedding menus from the Middle Ages to the eighteenth century always included plenty of game – untrammelled by modern seasonal strictures. There is a record of a country wedding meal in the Vendée which consisted of an 'opener' of sixty chickens and capons; elsewhere gatherings of from 100 to 500 would feast on joints of mutton, haunches of veal, legs of pork and even whole carcasses of beef.

Arnold van Gennep's research offers wider illumination than the narrow confines of political boundaries suggest: France's geographical position and the extent of her cultural and culinary exchanges with her neighbours ensures that much of the custom he observed, and its variations, was common to the rest of Europe.

> If the church establishes the union of the betrothed, so the wedding meal unites the two families, obeying the ancient ceremonial of sharing food. However, it cannot be assumed that all customs are shared by all. In those areas, for instance, where the bride and groom's cortège returns separately from the church, so the meal which follows is taken in the appropriate house. The families do not share a meal until the evening. In areas where the two meals are taken in the same house, there is often a period of rest in the middle, when the bride and groom might visit relations, or friends who had not been guests at the wedding itself. The first meal is called the diner, the sec-

ond the souper. It was in order for guests to bring their own knives.

Whether the cost was borne by both families, or one alone, a gift-toll, either in money or in kind, ensured that the prudent and careful Frenchman was not usually out of pocket from the exercise – and some might even manage to turn a profit. Breiz-Izel gives a revealing account of a wedding in Brittany, where festivities would sometimes last for three days:

When the revellers have finished and gather themselves to return home, they find the young couple and their parents waiting at the exit to collect – usually an ecu, sometimes two, never less than thirty sous. The father pays for his wife and children. In addition, the guest is expected to slip into the groom's hand an additional few sous – for which he is rewarded with a farewell glass of wine or a nip of eau de vie. The following morning, the two sets of parents meet and apportion the receipts according to moneys received and number of guests invited by each family. To the total must also be added the presents offered before, during and after the feast – food supplies such as butter, pancakes, and cakes, and more long-lived assets such as pots and pans, ribbons and pins and household goods. Enough profit is anticipated for this to be a genuine family speculation. And the guests, knowing this, do not feel inhibited in criticizing the arrangements and provision.

It was always unusual for the party to be held in the house itself – hence the modern transition to restaurants. The table was laid in an outhouse or barn – maybe in the open-sided granary-cum-wagonhouse adjoining the house. Van Gennep continues: 'The place is always decorated with garlands and bunches of flowers and the walls gaily draped with snowy white sheets starred with flowers and little pinned-on posies.' I remember in 1978, when my brother married the daughter of a Normandy farmer, we spent a whole day arranging just such a room, with pink rosebuds and white gardenias pinned to the sheets.

In other areas where such barns and storehouses were not common a tent supplied by the wine merchant would be pitched in the courtyard – in the old days the tent used to be made from the sails of shipwrecked vessels. The whole of the interior would be occupied by the nuptial table, draped in the best linen and decorated with ribbons, with a crown of flowers suspended over the bridal couples' chairs. The food was cooked in huge dishes set over the heat from a long trench dug at the entrance to the tent, and filled with red-hot charcoal. At Saint-Goueno, in the Côtes-du-Nord, when the weather was fine, two parallel trenches were dug in the back yard, deep enough for a man to sit in with his legs comfortably resting on the ground.

The space between the trenches served as a table, an arrangement which recalls the turf-dug tables of the spring fire festivals of Scotland (see p164).

Some traditions, particularly those expressed in the formal patterns of the dance, are mystery plays in miniature, with a moral content as well as entertainment value. At São Tiago da Cruz in Minho, Portugal, a lemon and an apple are hung on an arch under which the bridal couple dances: the bride plucks the lemon, the groom the apple, and then they exchange them: the lemon guarantees that married life may retain its savour for the groom, and he in return is given safekeeping of the apple, so that his bride may be exposed to no temptations.

The need for each young person to emulate the bridal pair and play their part in the survival of the community is underlined by the universal popularity at weddings of ring-dances which mix up the young guests – from the polite excuse-me dances of Britain, to the formal partner-exchanging reels of Scotland, to the wild bride-purchasing waltzes of eastern Europe.

The symbolism of the wedding minuet was not lost on journal-keeper James Boswell, attending a nuptial in Berlin on July 20th 1764:

> At six in the evening I went in our family coach to Herr Splitgerber's garden, where the young couple gave a fine ball and most excellent supper. I danced a great deal and was in true, gay, vigorous spirits. I must mention a particular circumstance or two in a German marriage. There is a poem of hymeneal guise composed, and every guest receives one. The bride stands in the centre of a ring of gentlemen, and they dance around her. She is blindfolded, and holds in her hand an emblematical crown of virginity, which she puts on the head of what gentleman she pleases, and he is considered as marked out to be the first married of the company.

Boswell's 'excellent supper' would certainly have been a stupendous feast – unmatchable in quantity anywhere in Europe. German traditions of hospitality put generosity and plenty right at the top of the list. Some remarkable records have been set: in 1907 a Pomeranian wedding party hundreds strong consumed thirty-two hundredweight of flour, four whole pigs, two calves, three sheep, thirty-two geese, eight hundredweight of large fish, ten hundredweight of small fish, fifty-four barrels of beer, 500 bottles of wine and 300 litres of brandy. Some relief must have been felt by the guests that whatever was left could be taken home in a napkin provided by the hosts – in Bavaria, this is traditionally in blue and red check. In rural districts, too, it was customary for everyone to pay an entrance fee with a present, except the pastor, the schoolmaster, the magistrate, and, presumably, Mr Boswell – not a man noted for his willingness to open his purse.

Rural Germany has many traditions rationalized as designed to chase away or outwit evil spirits, but with the proviso that some of the tricks seem to make little differentiation between the groom and malingering gremlins. In some areas, the bride hid and had to be found by her groom. In Bavaria the bridegroom might expect to be greeted outside the church by a bearded man in a wedding dress. Round Bruckenburg the bridesmaids dress exactly the same as the bride, ostensibly to confuse evil spirits. The whole ceremony was ringed with pitfalls: those driving to the church in a wedding cart were customarily obliged to bribe the young men of the village not to steal the horse. Presumably the modern custom of tying old tin cans and shoes to the back of the honeymoon couple's car is from the same stable.

However Hungarian Károly Viski, observing in 1932 a line of virtually unbroken tradition, casts another light on the matter. He suggests that such rituals, and the payment of money for dancing with the bride, are relics of the two most ancient forms of acquiring women – kidnapping and buying them.

> The purchase price of a woman was as much as her were-geld in case she was kidnapped. Innumerable symbolic memories of the purchase of women are still alive in Hungarian weddings. They attempt to kidnap, or for fun even actually kidnap, the bride; they besiege her house, all kinds of obstacles are placed before the wedding procession, even shots are fired.

Gyula Illyes described, in 1932, the rowdy weddings on the puszta, one of the huge farms worked by Hungary's impoverished landless peasantry:

> The wedding-feasts were always prodigally extravagant. On the long bean-shelling tables bor-

rowed from the estate there were vast quantities of wine and dripping, and in the pots which had been collected from three *pusztas* there were rows of fried chickens and ducks. This gorging was as indispensable a part of the wedding as the priest's blessing. Indeed, it was even more important, for while there were plenty of couples who got married without the blessing of the church, there was not a single instance of a marriage in church before they had found some way of holding a 'proper' wedding-feast. They would never have lived down the shame of a barefoot-wedding.

According to custom, it is not proper for a bride to eat or drink at the wedding-feast. She just pecks at the food, merely to give her strength for the wild whirling of the bridal dance which lasts for hours. In this all the guests who have brought presents – a salt-cellar, an enamelled jug, a pair of slippers, or a fork with the monogram of some aristocrat or restaurant roughly scored out – dance her dizzy and shout themselves hoarse shouting 'The bride is mine!' But the bridegroom, happy man, can eat and drink, and so he does, for propriety bids him feast as never before in his life. He is stuffed like a goose. Meanwhile the bride has partnered all those who have obtained the right to her by paying money instead of giving presents.

Henry Wolff, in *Rambles in the Black Forest* (1890), participates in a German wedding feast.

A Black Forest wedding dinner is a huge feast, to which none but a cast-iron stomach would be equal, were it not that the time is deliberately spun out and a fresh appetite is got up by a general dance between each two courses. Here is the regulation menu: Two soups – one invariably vermicelli. Next, boiled beef with horseradish. After that the *pièce de résistance* of every wedding meal, 'macerated beef' – something like *boeuf à la mode*, garnished with vermicelli and light paste gugelhopf. The next course is pork with sauerkraut, with sausages added – for peasants throughout Germany love their fat. After that roast veal and salad, a favourite Black Forest dish. After that baked calves' feet with prunes. This is reckoned a particular delicacy. And last the courses are brought to a close by a fresh supply of soup, for which, however, recently coffee has come to be substituted. This is without counting cake and 'knopfle' and light baker's ware. Drink is proportioned to the food. And a good deal has to be consumed. This generally involves going home half-seas-over. When all the guests have gone, the bride addresses herself at once to the consumption of a regulation dish of sauerkraut for good luck.

Northerners seem more decorous in their nuptial celebrations. Maturin Ballou, a popular American travel writer, attended a marriage in the far north of Norway in the 1880s:

A wedding feast in Norway is always looked upon as a grand domestic event, and is everywhere made the most of by all parties concerned; but at Hammerfest and the north part of the country generally, it becomes a most important and demonstrative affair. No expense is spared by the bride's parents to render the event memorable in all respects. The revels are sometimes kept up for a period of three weeks, until at last every one becomes quite exhausted with the excitement and with dancing, when the celebration by common consent is brought to a close. During the height of the revels, street parades constitute a part of the singular performance, when bride, bridegroom, family and friends, preceded by a band of musicians, march gaily from point to point; or a line of boats is formed, with the principals in the first, the musician in the second, and so on, all decked with natural and artificial flowers and bright-coloured streamers, the diaphanous dresses of bride and bridesmaids looking like mist-wreaths settled about the boats. It was easy to distinguish the bride from her attendants, by the tall, sparkling gilt crown which she wore.

After the wedding, modern bridal couples, wherever they are and whoever legitimizes their vows, can still expect to be showered with the tiny symbols of fertility: rice, sugared almonds, rose-petals – roses conveniently bloom in June – or their modern replacement, confetti. All such demonstrations are the bane of registry offices and the cause of many an undignified scuffle as officialdom explains its unwillingness to clear up the mess. The tradition of sharing out cake – sometimes the guests had to be literally showered with its crumbs – is part of the general preoccupation with fertility. And that, after all, was the whole purpose of the exercise.

FRENCH WEDDING LUNCHEON

Paulette Villedieu recalled for me in 1988 the wedding feasts of her pre-war childhood in upper Provence:

> One ate a great deal – but each family to their own taste. The marriage would be celebrated in the church at eleven o'clock. Aperitifs were taken at midday or one. Then the meal was served – finishing with a *pièce montée*. I remember the one at my aunt's wedding. It was a great pyramid of choux stuffed with *crème pâtissier*, stuck into place with crisp caramel. The cake would be broken with a blow from a hammer, and the children would scramble for the flying sugar pieces. Then at seven, people would start dancing. And around midnight everyone would eat the leftovers. There might be a soup – but that was more usual in other places than round here.

Ethnologist Arnold van Gennep gives more historical detail:

> Everyday rough bread was replaced by bread made with fine white flour, enriched and decorated and twisted into elegant shapes – this became a positive passion by the end of the nineteenth century. Noteworthy, too, is the quantity of sweet dishes – *tartes*, *tourtes*, *rougasses* and *pâtisseries*; sugar lumps, sweets and all manner of sweet things; highly sweetened wine for the ushers and the bridal couple. To this basic provision would be added local variations. Salt-pastured lamb, goose, ducks, turkeys; in the Dauphiné, guineafowl; there is no particular record of cheese and milk products, probably because such things were everyday fare and did not deserve to appear on a festival menu. As for the drink, that was expected to run as copiously as the guests could imbibe it – and keep on running until the cider kegs and wine vats ran dry and the guests were as drunk as they might be.

ROAST GUINEAFOWL WITH MOREL SAUCE
Pintade aux morilles (France)

The guineafowl is my own favourite bird for a wedding. I like its natural independence. Native of the wild plains of Africa and a relative newcomer to the barnyard, the guineafowl does not take kindly to factory-farming methods and gives all kinds of trouble when kept indoors. My farming neighbours when I lived for a year in the Languedoc kept a small flock of the near-wild birds for their own table, and I had an arrangement with them to supply mine. When the daughter of the house was married that year, a dozen roast guineafowl starred as the *pièce de résistance*, memorably sauced with the morel mushrooms we all gathered in spring from the rough pastures where the sheep grazed – it was an icy spring, but they didn't seem to mind that, and we had a fine crop for drying. Chanterelles and other wild edible fungi are possible substitutes for the morels.

Quantity: Serves 6–8.
Time: 1 hour intermittent attention.
Equipment: A lidded casserole which will accommodate the birds. A small frying pan.

2 young guineafowl, with their livers
sprigs of thyme and marjoram
2 bay leaves
3oz/75g butter

6oz/175g morel mushrooms (or 2oz/50g dried,
    soaked for 30 minutes in a splash of warm water)
3–4 garlic cloves, halved but not peeled
2oz/50g fat bacon, diced

To finish
1 small glass *marc* or brandy
1oz/25g cold butter

½ pint/300ml cream (the French slightly
    soured *crème fraîche* is perfect)

Wipe the birds inside and out and singe off any stray little feathers. Shake any earth off the morels (the honeycomb is terrible for holding grit) and trim off the stalks. Reserve the morel caps with the guineafowl livers. Stuff the cavities of the birds with the herbs, the morel stalks and the garlic.

Heat 2oz/50g of the butter in the casserole. Turn the birds in the foaming butter until they take a little colour. Toss in the diced bacon. Lid tightly and transfer to a medium oven, 375°F/190°C/Gas 5.

Cook the birds for 30–35 minutes, until they are tender enough for the leg to pull away from the body without resistance.

Meanwhile toss the reserved morel caps and the livers, roughly chopped, in the rest of the butter – if the fungi are large, cut them in half, but do not chop them up or the beauty of the patterned hollow caps will not be so easily appreciated. They need 8–10 minutes over a gentle heat.

Joint the birds – French housewives don't usually send an uncarved joint to table – and return them to the pan (remove the herb twigs) with their juices. Pour the *marc* or brandy over the joints and set fire to it – this evaporates the alcohol and caramelizes the birds' skin a little. Reheat the joints for a moment, and transfer them to a warm dish.

Stir the morels and livers and their cooking liquor into the pan juices, and pour in the cream (if you have no *crème fraîche*, a squeeze of lemon juice can be added to ordinary cream). Bubble up and simmer to thicken a little.

Hand the creamy aromatic sauce separately.

ROAST LAMB WITH GARLIC AND ROSEMARY
Gigot d'agneau à l'ail (France)

Here is intrepid Victorian lady walker Mary Eyre's instruction for the classic French celebration joint:

Sheep constitute a great part of the wealth of the Pyrenees, and a pastoral life is here no fiction. The mutton of these sheep is generally very small, and excellent in flavour. I have bought legs whose bones were not thicker than a lady's forefinger. It is common here to *piquer* a leg of mutton with garlic, that is, small holes are drilled into it before roasting, and a small kind of garlic resembling a very young onion, inserted therein. When my first tiny leg of mutton came up dressed in this manner, I ate it without thinking about it, and found it to be a decided improvement, giving the whole joint a high gamey flavour. Another way of dressing a leg of mutton here is to stew it whole in *vin ordinaire*, together with some ham, a little butter, a little garlic, mushrooms or ceps, and a little salt; a little burnt sugar is added to colour it, and it comes up to table a rich brown colour, like a roasted hare, and is a capital dish.

Here is my own version of the dish, using a well-grown leg of lamb.

Quantity: Serves 6–8.
Time: Start a few hours ahead. 1 hour 45 minutes intermittent attention.
Equipment: A lidded casserole large enough for the whole joint.

1 leg of lamb – 6–7lb/3–3.5kg	8 cloves of garlic, skinned and slivered
1 wine glass olive oil	salt and pepper
a large bunch rosemary sprigs	2 glasses dry white wine

Wipe the joint and make deep incisions all over it with a narrow-bladed sharp knife. Push slivers of garlic into these incisions. Rub the meat with some of the olive oil, season with salt and pepper, and leave it to absorb the flavours for an hour or two – overnight is best.

Pour half the remaining olive oil into the casserole and sauté the joint until it takes a little colour – enough to produce the caramelized effect admired by Miss Eyre. Tuck the rosemary all around and above. Trickle on the rest of the oil. Pour in the wine and bring it all to the boil on top of the stove.

Transfer to a hot oven, 425°F/220°C/Gas 7, for 1½ hours – allowing 15 minutes to the pound. Shove a skewer into the thickest part – if the juices are still delicately pink, it is ready. Leave the meat to settle for 10 minutes before carving and sending it to table, sauced with its own juices.

CHOUX-BUN WEDDING CAKE
Croquembouche (France)

France likes its wedding cakes as sugary as possible – as with this sophisticated caramel-drenched pyramid of choux. Its ancestor was the magnificently baroque marzipan creations seen and admired at the public banquets given by the monarch to entertain visiting royalty – until the Revolution put a stop to such culinary theatre.

At the turn of the century the *pièce montée*, so called because it was built up with more than one tier, was subject to many regional variations. Anjou had a large single-tier cake, called the *fouace* or *chantenau*, which was presented with a special dance – and was supplied by the godfather or godmother: today the name remains, but the cake is now a gift of silver. In Bourgogne and the Bourbonnais the cake is traditionally a Savoy sponge, decorated with a small figurine of the bride. Gascogne, unable to make up its mind, had two cakes, a plum-cake and a tiered cake, the *gâteau à la broche* – a spit-roasted cake which requires much time and great manual dexterity. In Lorraine custom dictates that pieces of cake are distributed with the invitations. Around Orléans in the last century, it was customary to make a cake in the shape of one of the famous châteaux of the area, or even of the church in which the marriage was celebrated. In Savoie, a young girl danced in with the cake balanced on her head. The cake was then passed from one young woman to another until it was all broken up and could be taken home for good luck.

Nowadays the *croquembouche*, a glorious tribute to the skill of the bakers of Paris, has taken over as the universal *pièce montée* of family celebrations: baptisms, first communions, and of course, weddings.

Quantity: Makes one wedding cake.
Time: Allow 2 hours intermittent attention.
Equipment: A large and small saucepan. An electric mixer would be useful. Baking trays and a cooling rack.

The choux buns

6oz/175g flour	½ pint/300ml water
4oz/100g butter, cubed	1oz/25g sugar
½ teaspoon salt	5 eggs

The *crème pâtissier*

6 egg yolks	6oz/175g sugar
1½oz/40g flour	½ pint/300ml milk
1 tablespoon rum	

The caramel

12oz/350g caster sugar	1 tablespoon water

Make the choux first. Preheat the oven to 400°F/200°C/Gas 6.

Sieve the flour.

In the large saucepan, bring the water, butter, sugar and salt to the boil. When the butter has melted, remove from the heat and stir in the flour. Return the pan to a low heat and beat the mixture until it is smooth and does not stick to the sides of the pan (7–8 minutes). Leave it to cool a little.

Beat in the eggs, one by one – easy with an electric mixer. How many the paste will accept depends on the size of the eggs – when it is shiny and slides off the spoon, but still holds its shape, it is ready for baking.

Grease the baking trays and, using 2 teaspoons (or a piping bag), drop on well-spaced-out nuggets of dough about the size of a hazelnut.

Bake for 15–18 minutes, until the little buns have puffed up to 3–4 times their size, and are well crisped and firm. Nick each one to let out the steam before you put it to cool on the rack.

Next, make the *crème*. Beat the egg yolks with the sugar and work in the flour. Heat the milk in the small saucepan to just below boiling and then whisk it into the egg mixture. Return the custard to the pan and beat it over the heat until it thickens – no more than 2 minutes just on the boil, or the yolks will curdle. Beat in the rum. Dot with butter to avoid a skin forming, and leave it to cool.

Stuff the choux buns with the custard as soon as it is cold.

To make the caramel, melt the sugar very gently in a small saucepan with the water, stirring constantly until it is a light golden brown. Remove from the heat and use the caramel to stick the choux buns into a pyramid.

Pour the remaining caramel over the pyramid. If it solidifies in the pan while you are working, melt it down again over a low heat.

The bride should be provided with a hammer to crack the caramel: very exciting, as the pieces are bound to fly all over the place.

Don't forget to put out bowls of sugared almonds – particularly silver ones for a prosperous married life, with plenty of children to keep you out of the old folks' home.

ENGLISH WEDDING BREAKFAST

In Britain the usual time for the church ceremony is Saturday morning – obeying the dictates of the modern work-pattern – with a wedding breakfast to follow. The couple are then left free to leave for their honeymoon at around four o'clock. If there is to be an evening dance, the wedding ceremony is often moved to the afternoon, with a tea featuring the cake-cutting, toasts and speeches merging into a supper-dance. My younger sister Marianna was the last one of my family to be married; and she had poached salmon as the centrepiece of her Nottinghamshire wedding buffet, with dancing to follow. The party didn't break up until 2 a.m. – short night for the honeymoon.

POACHED SALMON WITH CUCUMBER CREAM SAUCE
(Britain)

It would be hard to get further from the sea or a salmon river anywhere in Britain than Newark, Nottinghamshire, so perhaps my family unwittingly conformed, in serving this at my sister's wedding breakfast, to the old traditions which valued scarcity in its festival food above all else. The most noble of fish is in any event the best of feasts – at its most succulent served plain-poached à l'anglais, with the lightest of sauces.

Quantity: A 10lb/5kg salmon serves 12–14 people.
Time: Start a few hours ahead. 20 minutes.
Equipment: A large fish-kettle. A grater, whisk and bowl.

The fish

1 whole salmon	water
salt	

The sauce

1 pint/600ml double cream	½ cucumber, grated with its skin
2 tablespoons vinegar	salt and pepper

To finish
½ cucumber, sliced thinly

Scale, clean and gut the salmon, leaving its head on. Put it in the fish-kettle. Cover with enough cold water to submerge the fish. Add enough salt to make the water into a brine about as strong as sea-water.

Bring to the boil, allowing a single belch. Lid, and leave to cool in its water. The fish will take as much time to come to the boil as its own mass dictates – the larger the fish, the longer it takes. When it is cool, the fish will be succulent and perfectly cooked. Transfer it to a large long platter and remove the skin on the top.

Arrange cucumber slices down the dark stripe which runs down the centre of the fish's flank.

To make the sauce, beat the cream until it is stiff. Fold in the cucumber and the vinegar. Season with salt and pepper. Serve the cucumber cream with the salmon: simple but perfect.

ICED WEDDING CAKE
(Britain)

The bride herself must cut the cake, or she risks there being no children of the marriage. In Yorkshire a plate of cake was tossed from an upstairs window as the party returned from church – the more pieces it broke into, the better the luck. Saxon brides had to bake such cakes to prove their marriage skills, and their descendants have baked cakes to mark special celebrations ever since. The icing is a rather more recent addition.

Quantity: Makes a 3-tier cake. About 100 servings.
Time: The basic cakes are best made 1–2 months ahead: about 6 hours intermittent attention. To decorate it, allow as much time as you please.
Equipment: 2–3 mixing bowls. 3 baking tins with removable bases, in decreasing sizes. They can be round or square – if the latter, the largest to be approximately 10in/25cm square, the next 7in/18cm, and the smallest 5in/12cm. To get diameter of the round tins, add 1in/0.5cm. A cake rack, 6 pairs of supporting pillars for the cakes (you can use pretty egg-cups at a pinch). A board and rolling pin. Piping equipment (*optional*). 3 cake bases.

The cakes

12oz/350g whole almonds	1lb/500g prunes
1lb 4oz/600g sultanas	1lb 4oz/600g raisins
1lb 4oz/600g currants	1lb/ 500g crystallized peel
8oz/250g crystallized cherries	2lb/1kg plain flour
1lb 12oz/800g butter	1lb 8oz/750g soft brown sugar
6 tablespoons molasses or dark honey	12 eggs
2 teaspoons salt	6oz/175g ground almonds
4 teaspoons powdered cinnamon	4 teaspoons grated nutmeg
2 teaspoons powdered cloves	1 glass brandy or whisky

The marzipan

5lb/2.5kg marzipan (see p.121)	icing sugar for dusting
1 jar apricot jam	

The royal icing

4lb/2kg icing sugar	6 egg whites (use the yolks in the marzipan)
4–6 tablespoons lemon juice	

Chop the almonds roughly. De-stone and chop the prunes. Pick over the dried fruit, checking for little bits of stalk and pips. Sprinkle a tablespoonful of the flour into a bowl and toss the fruit in it (this helps prevent the fruit sinking to the bottom of the cake). Beat the butter and sugar together until light and fluffy – the more you beat, the easier it is to incorporate the eggs without the mixture separating. Beat in the eggs one by one – if the mixture does curdle, stir in a spoonful of flour. Sieve the flour with the salt and fold it in. Fold in the chopped and the ground almonds, the fruit, the molasses or honey, and the spices. Stir in enough brandy or whisky to give a soft mixture which drops easily from the spoon.

Butter and line the cake tins with butter-paper. Divide the cake mixture between them. Smooth the surface of the cakes and leave a slight dip in the middle so that the cake rises evenly. Leave them to one side for 30 minutes so that the fruit can swell.

Bake the largest cake for about 5½ hours, the next largest for 3½ hours, and the smallest for 3 hours. Start the cakes at 300°F/150°C/Gas 2, reducing to 250°F/130°C/Gas ½ half-way through. Bake until the cakes are well browned and firm to the touch. If they brown too fast, cover them loosely with foil. Test if they are done by thrusting in a skewer – when it comes out clean the cake is ready.

Allow the cakes to cool in the tin, then turn them out on to a rack to cool. Store in an airtight tin until you are ready to ice them a few days before the wedding (not too long before, or the marzipan tends to discolour the icing).

To finish, divide the marzipan into 3 proportionate pieces. Roll out each piece into a round lid and long thin piece for the sides, using a board and rolling pin well dusted with icing sugar. Spread the jam over the sides and on the top of each cake, and cover neatly with marzipan. Transfer to the cake bases.

To make the royal icing, sieve the icing sugar if it is lumpy, and work in the egg whites and the lemon juice. Beat steadily until you have a smooth paste.

Spread the icing smoothly over the cakes, using a knife dipped in hot water.

When the icing is set, balance the cake in tiers on its pillars.

Decorate with white ribbon bows, a tiny posy of fresh flowers, and a miniature bride and groom – or if you are skilful with the icing-bag, do something magnificently baroque with your usual piping mix.

The bride and groom should cut into the bottom layer together. Slices of this should be distributed to the guests. Send slices of the second away to absent friends and relations – you never know, you may get a wedding present in return. Save the top tier, the smallest, for next year's christening – take off the icing and marzipan for storage, and re-ice it when you need it.

SICILIAN WEDDING FEAST

Eliza Putnam Heaton, a young American journalist, 'marooned in Sicily by ill-health' in the 1920s, was invited to a wedding of fisherfolk – who naturally served anything but fish for the feast: 'Brigida's mother was dishing roasted kid and spaghetti to be sent to the neighbours. Brigida's sister served wine and Spanish bread, which is a powdery sponge cake.' Eliza noted that there was much Spanish in the native patois – not surprisingly, since the Spanish noblemen ruled here in the old days.

One guest, an old fisherman, felt it necessary to explain the sugary delights of the banquet to the young guest: '"The rich strangers who visit our country pick a little of many things, but we eat all we can get of one or two things – bread and macaroni, or bread and beans. It is only at weddings," he finished confidentially, "that we arrive at sweets."'

ROAST LAMB OR KID WITH SPAGHETTI
(Sicily)

If you are roasting a whole lamb or kid, well and good. Use the oil, lemon juice, herbs and seasonings to baste the meat as it turns on the spit – there should be a metal tray underneath to catch the drippings. Otherwise, this is an easy way out.

Quantity: Serves 6.
Time: About 1 hour intermittent attention.
Equipment: A roasting tin and a large cooking pot.

The meat
2lb/1kg lamb steaks	salt and pepper
6 tablespoons olive oil	4–5 garlic cloves, skinned and sliced
juice of 2 lemons	1 glass warm water
1–2 bay leaves	3–4 sprigs oregano
3–4 sprigs rosemary	

The pasta
water	salt
1lb/500g spaghetti	

Wipe the meat and season it with salt and pepper.

Heat the oil in the casserole and put in the meat and the garlic. Turn the pieces in the hot oil until they take a little colour. Squeeze in the lemon juice. Add the water, herbs and seasonings. Lid tightly and cook in the oven, 325°F/170°C/Gas 3, or on a gentle heat on top of the stove, for 35–40 minutes.

10 minutes before the end of the time, bring a large pan of water to the boil with 1 teaspoon of salt – you need about 5 pints/3 litres of water for this amount of pasta.

Add the pasta, pushing it down into the water as it softens. Bring it back to the boil and cook until it is soft but still retains a central bite – *al dente*.

Meanwhile, transfer the cooked lamb pieces to a dish and keep them warm. Stir up the juices in the pan, scraping in the delicious sticky bits.

Drain the pasta quickly (don't let it dry too much, it should retain a few drops of moisture), transfer it to a deep warm bowl and toss it immediately with the oily lamb juices.

Serve the pasta first, with the meat to follow.

CASSATA ALLA SICILIANA
(Sicily)

Sicily has its Arab conquerors to thank for the art of making sherbets and ice-creams, originally with snows from the summit of Etna – when it wasn't about its other business, of course. The Arabs also introduced lemons, oranges, jasmine, cotton, aubergines and palm-trees: quite a basketful. The Madeira cake which lines the mould is known locally as Spanish bread. The chocolate did not make its appearance in Europe until the *conquistadores* learned its secrets from Montezuma. The *cassata* is in fact an assembly of all things Sicilian.

Quantity: Serves 8–10.
Time: Start a day ahead. 1 hour intermittent attention.
Equipment: Mixing bowls. A Swiss roll tin and an 8in/20cm diameter cake tin with a removable base. A cooling rack.

The cake
6oz/175g butter

6oz/175g caster sugar

3 eggs

6oz/175g flour

The ice-cream
1lb/500g fresh ricotta (or a soft white curd cheese – ricotta is made with whey)

4 tablespoons fresh cream

2 eggs, separated

4oz/100g caster sugar

4oz/100g mixed candied peel, roughly chopped

1oz/25g candied cherries, roughly chopped

2oz/50g pistachios, shelled, husked and roughly chopped

2oz/50g bitter chocolate, roughly chopped

1 teaspoon powdered cinnamon

juice and grated rind of 1 orange

2 tablespoons orange-flower water

To finish
8oz/250g icing sugar

4 tablespoons hot water

1 drop green colouring

1 tablespoon ground pistachios or almonds

Make the cake first. Butter and line the Swiss roll tin with greaseproof paper.

Preheat the oven to 375°F/190°C/Gas 5.

Cream the butter with the sugar until the mixture is white and fluffy. Beat in the eggs. Fold in the flour. Smooth the mixture into the prepared tin.

Bake for 20 minutes, until well risen and firm. Transfer to the rack to cool. Peel off the paper, cut the cake into thin slices, and use them to line the cake tin – save enough slices to cover the top.

Next, make the ricotta ice-cream. Sieve the ricotta into a bowl and work in the cream, egg yolks and sugar. Stir in the peel, fruit, nuts, chocolate, cinnamon, orange juice and grated rind, and the orange-flower water. Fold in the egg whites, whisked stiff.

Tip the mixture into the sponge-lined cake tin. Freeze until stiff, and then cover with a thin layer of the reserved sponge. Return the tin to the freezer and freeze until solid. Slip a knife round the sides to loosen it, and turn it out on to a pretty dish when you are ready to serve it.

To finish, mix all the icing ingredients until smooth, and cover the sponge with pale green icing. It needs no further embellishment.

Serve cut in wedges like a cake, and accompany with a glass of moscato di Trani, or golden Strega, the most delicious of aphrodisiacs. For children, the Sicilians make an iced infusion of crushed almonds called orzata – much like the tiger-nut infusion of Spain, horchata, sold from kiosks in every village in summer.

MARZIPAN FRUITS
Fruta di pasta di mandorle (Italy)

Sicilian pastry-cooks are maestros of the art of making the most beautiful hand-tinted marzipan fruits – and salami and sandwiches too – and serve them at all their family festivals. Use your dexterity and ingenuity to make your own, rolling the basic shape out of marzipan as if it was plasticine, and painting the shapes with a palette of food colours. For a wedding, peaches, strawberries and figs – ancient symbols of fertility – would be appropriate. Pile them on their own real leaves, and no one will know the difference until they bite into the delicious sweetmeat.

Quantity: Makes 1½lbs/750g marzipan.
Time: 20 minutes to make the paste.
Equipment: A bowl. A small paintbrush, and a plate for mixing.

1lb/500g ground almonds
4 egg yolks

½lb/250g icing sugar
1–2 tablespoons orange-flower water

To finish
extra icing sugar for dusting your hands

food colouring

Mix together the ground almonds, sugar and egg yolks, adding enough orange-flower water to make a firm but workable paste. Knead it, then shape small nuggets into the fruits of your choice, dusting your hands with icing sugar as you work.

Let the fruits firm in a warm dry place. Paint them with all the skill you can muster, using food colouring diluted with water as you need it. Pile them prettily on their own natural leaves.

QUINCE PASTE
(Mediterranean)

Native to Persia and one of Europe's earliest known cultivars, the quince was Venus's prize when Paris delivered his judgement. It was also the fatal fruit with which Eve is alleged to have seduced Adam: not the apple, that crisp rosy-cheeked fruit of a northern orchard, as translators would have us believe, but its sweet soft cousin from Venus's garden. Medieval Europe served quinces at all its wedding feasts, and a gift of quinces was a declaration of love. Catholic Europe, migrating Venus's secular banquet to the sacred feast of Christmas, still offers quince paste to celebrate the Virgin birth.

Quantity: Makes about 4lb/2kg paste.
Time: Start the day before. About 1 hour intermittent attention.
Equipment: A heavy saucepan. A baking tray.

5lb/2.5kg quinces
approx. 3lb/1.5kg preserving sugar

water

Peel, core and slice the quinces. Put them in the saucepan with just enough water to cover them. Bring to the boil, cover, and turn down to simmer for about 25–30 minutes, until the quinces are quite pulpy.

Weigh the pulp and stir in the same weight of sugar. Warm gently, stirring as the fruit dissolves. Stir it over the heat until the paste is as thick as firm mashed potato.

Spread the paste in a lightly oiled baking tray and leave in a very low oven to dry out overnight. Cut into squares, wrap loosely in wax paper, and store in a cupboard. The paste darkens and hardens as it matures – a process which can be halted by keeping it in an airtight tin.

HUNGARIAN WEDDING SUPPER

How fine they were at these feasts in the stupor produced by wine and happiness, how angelically innocent and childlike after the first glass! How triumphant and ceremonious was the procession of guests as it made its way on foot to the church in one of the nearby villages, ankle-deep in the autumn dust or winter mud! They sang the whole way. The lads, even if they could not prance around on horseback like the sons of village farmers, danced around on their feet, kicking up the dust and leaping over ditches and bushes, even whinnying in their merriment. They stopped everybody who happened to be passing through the puszta, stuffed them with cakes and begged them to have a drink. (Guyla Illyes, People of the Puszta, 1932)

Illyes's contemporary Károly Viski offers further illumination on the correct way to celebrate a Hungarian wedding:

In the evening comes the banquet. This time the whole household of the bride's family is asked. They come along provided with all kinds of goodies, sweets and the inevitable symbolic nuts and fruit fertility symbols. Last of all walks the bride's mother, who brings a stuffed chicken and a bottle of very sweet wine. All the good food they bring is put into the loft – the place designated for the wedding night.

The menu of the banquet is: noodle soup with chicken or beef, cabbage with mutton or pork, and lastly some kind of sausage. Plenty of wine. Everyone eats freely, only the bride and bridegroom are not allowed to touch anything. It would be a great disgrace to eat, although, poor things, they are already faint with hunger.

Among the cakes should be mentioned the multitude of wedding cakes and biscuits, the most interesting of all being the cock and hen of sugar cake in Boldog which is placed in front of the bridegroom and the bride. This is a more refined form of the custom, prevalent in other districts, whereby a live cock and hen is the due of the young couple, or a cock is led at the head of the wedding procession, or the bridegroom carries one in his hand. Or cocks are made of sugar or sweets.

WEDDING CHICKEN SOUP
Tyúkleves (Hungary)

Károly Viski, 1932; 'Snail pastry is cooked with the wedding chicken soup. Friends, relations, companions all come together to make the enormous amount of snail pastry required, and each person brings his or her own implement.' The instrument is a flat piece of grooved wood or china in which the egg-noodle dough is deftly twisted. In default, buy the most snail-like pasta you can find – small fusilli or conchiglie are probably the closest. Soup is essential to the midday meal in Hungary – the reverse of the French custom, where it is the nominate dish of the evening. If you make your own egg-noodles, 1lb/500g flour will take about 4 medium eggs to make 1½lb/675g fresh dough.

Quantity: Serves 8.
Time: Start 2 hours ahead.
Equipment: A large soup-pot.

The soup

1 boiling fowl	6 pints/3.5 litres water
2–3 celery sticks or a piece of celeriac	3–4 large carrots, scrubbed and chunked
1 turnip, scrubbed and chunked	1 parsnip, scrubbed and chunked
2 large leeks or 2 onions, washed and roughly chunked	3–4 sprigs parsley
	1 heaped teaspoon salt
12 peppercorns	

To finish

1lb/500g twist pasta – small fusilli or conchiglie	flat-leaved parsley, chopped

Joint the chicken into 8 pieces and put it into a big soup-pot with the water. Bring to the boil and skim off the foam which rises. Add the vegetables, salt and peppercorns. Bring to the boil again, allowing a single belch, then turn down to a barely perceptible simmer.

Leave for 3–4 hours on a very low heat, until the chicken and vegetables have given everything to the soup. Strain the broth, without pressure as you want it to be as clear as possible, and return it to the pan (the solids would be fine for the pig). Skim off the fat – easy to lift off if you have the time to let it cool. Save the chicken-fat, it makes lovely pastry.

Reheat the broth to a rolling boil, and stir in the pasta. Cook it for the 8–10 minutes it needs to soften.

Taste, and add salt and pepper if necessary. Finish with a stirring of chopped flat-leaved parsley.

STUFFED CABBAGE
Töltött kel (Hungary)

Gyula Illyes, *People of the Puszta*, 1932: 'The labourers crammed themselves with stuffed cabbages the size of a child's head, and topped them off with loaf.' Stuffed cabbage is a very good dish for every day, let alone weddings – delicious, cheap and pretty.

Quantity: Serves 4 as a main dish.
Time: About 2 hours intermittent attention.
Equipment: A large lidded saucepan. A colander. A small frying pan. String.

1 large Savoy cabbage (about 3lb/1.5kg)	1lb/500g cooked pork or ham
2 tablespoons lard or goose fat	1 large onion, skinned and finely chopped

2 cloves garlic, skinned and finely chopped
8 tablespoons milk
salt and pepper
1 pint/600ml home-made stock or plain water
2–3 sprigs thyme

8 tablespoons fresh breadcrumbs
2 tablespoons raisins
3 eggs
2–3 sprigs marjoram

Trim the cabbage, and cut a cross in the stalk end. Put it into a large saucepan of salted cold water. Bring the water to the boil and then lift out the cabbage. Drain in a colander, then cut out the heart-leaves and chop them.

Finely chop the pork or ham.

Melt 1 tablespoon of the lard in a small pan and fry the onion and garlic gently until they soften.

Crumble the bread, soak it in the milk and then squeeze out the surplus liquid. Make a stuffing with the ham, onion and garlic, soaked bread, chopped cabbage-heart, raisins, salt and pepper. Bind the mixture with the eggs, lightly beaten together. Form the mixture into a large dumpling, and put this into the empty heart of the cabbage. Fold the leaves over the stuffing.

Truss the cabbage with string, parcel-fashion. Settle it in a lidded casserole which will just accommodate it comfortably. Pour in the stock and dot with the rest of the lard. Tuck the herb sprigs round the cabbage. Bring it all to the boil, then lid tightly and transfer to the oven at 350°F/180°C/Gas 4. The total cooking time will be 1½–2 hours, depending on the size of the cabbage. Take care towards the end to see that it does not stick and burn.

Transfer the cabbage carefully to a serving dish and undo the string. Cut into segments as if it were a cake.

Serve, if you like, with a bowl of soured cream.

STUFFED PAPRIKA CHICKEN
Csirke paprikas (Hungary)

After the supper the new couple and the matrons of honour and bridesmaids who have been waiting at table go up into the loft, and all but the poor bride – who might permit herself a nut perhaps – can eat. After midnight the bride's household go home with the bride and groom. The bride's hair is put up, ready for the bonnet of matronhood to replace the flowing hair and flower garland of her maidenhood. The best man brings out the bride and the groom accepts her. The gypsy band begins to play and the party dances. At about 2 or 3 in the morning a dish of paprika chicken is served and eaten. After that comes the bride's dance and all who dance with her must pay for the honour. (Károly Viski, 1932)

The Hungarians put the stuffing under the skin rather than inside the cavity of the chicken – this keeps the flesh moist and juicy.

Quantity: Serves 5–6.
Time: 1 hour 30 minutes intermittent attention.
Equipment: A mixing bowl. A lidded casserole which will just accommodate the chicken.

3lb/1.5kg chicken   salt and pepper

3 tablespoons fresh breadcrumbs	2oz/50g minced pork
1 egg	1 tablespoon chopped parsley
1 tablespoon lard	1 large onion, peeled and chopped finely
½ tablespoon paprika	1 small glass water

To finish

8 fl oz/200ml soured cream	salt, pepper and paprika

Wipe the chicken inside and out and loosen the skin of the breast and thighs, working with your finger and taking care not to puncture the skin. Salt the cavity of the chicken.

Work the breadcrumbs with the minced meat, eggs, parsley, salt and pepper until smooth.

Stuff the mixture under the skin of the chicken, and truss the bird neatly.

Melt a tablespoon of lard in the casserole and sauté the chicken on all sides until it takes a little colour. Remove the bird and add the rest of the lard. Sauté the onions gently until they soften and gild. Sprinkle in the paprika and settle the bird on to its bed of onions. Sprinkle in salt and pepper. Pour in the water, bring it all to the boil, and turn down to simmer.

Lid tightly and leave to cook gently for 1–1½ hours, until the chicken is tender and the juices are concentrated to a few tablespoons – add more water during the cooking if necessary, but only a little at a time.

When the chicken is ready, remove it from the casserole, joint it, and keep it warm while you finish the sauce.

Pour the soured cream into the pan juices, and allow it all to bubble up. Taste and add extra salt and pepper. Pour the sauce over the chicken. Finish with a sprinkle of paprika.

WEDDING MILK BREAD
(Hungary)

This braided loaf is one of many of the enriched bread bride-cakes of Europe. It is moulded in the shape which means most to the population – the plait has a double significance, marking the moment when the young girl's garland is put away and her loose tresses must be put up and hidden under a head-kerchief; and also calling to mind the rebirth ceremonies of Easter. Mould the loaf to the shape which is most appropriate to you. Travelling through bread-rationed Romania in 1986, I followed a wedding-cart which trailed the delicious scents of these butter-rich loaves all down the village street, past the frescoed church, to the bride's house. The wedding party acting as guard to the fragrant mountain invited me to taste a piece of the rich golden crumb – it was like manna from heaven after the deprivations of the rest of the trip.

Quantity: Makes 1 loaf.
Time: 2 hours intermittent attention.
Equipment: A sieve and a large bowl. A small saucepan. A small bowl. A clean cloth. A baking tray and cooling rack.

12oz/350g flour	1oz/25g fresh yeast (½oz/12g dried)
2oz/50g sugar	¼ pint/150ml milk
4oz/100g butter	3 egg yolks

To finish

1 egg

Sieve the flour into a large warm bowl and make a well in it. Liquidize the yeast with a little of the sugar and the milk. Pour this mixture into the flour, sprinkle with a little loose flour and leave it for 10 minutes for the yeast to bubble up. (If using dried yeast, follow the packet directions.)

Melt the butter so that it just oils but does not fry.

Beat the egg yolks lightly together in a bowl with the rest of the sugar. Work all the liquids, including the melted butter, into the flour until you have a soft dough. Pummel the dough until it is a smooth soft ball. Cover with a clean damp cloth (or tie it into a plastic bag – as a miniature greenhouse) and leave to rise in a warm place for 1 hour.

Beat down the dough to distribute the air bubbles. Cut the dough into 3 pieces and work each piece into a long thin sausage. Plait the dough into a thick braid, pinching the ends together. Transfer to a baking tray. Put the bread to rise again for 30 minutes.

Preheat the oven to 350°F/180°C/Gas 4.

Paint the plait with beaten egg. Let the egg dry for 5 minutes. Bake the bread for 35–45 minutes, until well risen and brown.

Serve the wedding bread surrounded with little dishes of jams, nuts and fruit.

July

The urge to escape into the countryside – anywhere, as long as the grass under the trees is dappled with sunshine and the meadow-grass is sweet – grips the population of Europe like a fever every July. This is nothing like the May Day flirtation with flighty young Artemis: rather it is a full-blown love affair with the voluptuous sun-goddess Demeter. Her worshippers, although they could no longer call her by name, renew their devotion every year as they flock to the southern beaches – propelled by a universal urge to feel the sun on the skin and the earth beneath naked feet.

The inhabitants of the south, more blessed by climate than their northern neighbours, do not have so far to travel to Demeter's shrine, and so have retained some of the letter as well as the spirit of the old summer pilgrimages. In the Catholic Mediterranean, country people made sure that their local Virgin, usually following some miraculous manifestation, was housed in a little shrine a few miles up in the hills, which somehow coincided with the sacred grove of an earlier, more wanton sprite. In medieval times the great courts of Europe, too sophisticated to content themselves with the simple *romería*, held magnificent outdoor feasts, developing during the course of the eighteenth century into the extravagant *fêtes-champêtres* of Versailles, with the simple dancing, singing and story-telling of the peasantry formalized into lavish entertainments and plays. The bourgeoisie aped its betters, wore a shady hat, set up decorous tables and chairs and tea-urns under the trees, and told itself it had only come to admire the view. Meanwhile many a young lady wandered out of sight in the trees with the gentleman of her choice: the goddess of fecundity is not so easily diverted. She has always been as at home in the leafy bowers of the city's pleasure gardens as in the shady woods of her rural devotees.

The peasantry of the Mediterranean, uninhibited by courtly manners or bourgeois niceties, continued to make its annual summer pilgrimage, selecting the day appropriate to its custom and declaring a local holiday to enable the population to down tools and pack its picnic. The outing is a festival, so everyone put on their best – flowers and ribbons for the girls, a smart new hat for the boys. Garlands and votive gifts must be taken to please their special Madonna, so neglected for the rest of the year. In Italy *circa* 1915, Norman Douglas joined just such a party as it wound its way between San Severino and Castrovillari to the mountain shrine of the Madonna di Pollino for a celebration as ancient as the hills of his beloved Old Calabria.

Very few foreigners, they say, have attended this annual feast, which takes place on the first Saturday and Sunday of July, and is worth coming a long way to see. Here the old types, uncontaminated by modernism and emigration, are still gathered together. The whole country side is represented; the peasants have climbed up with their entire households from thirty or forty villages of this thinly populated plain, some of them marching a two days' journey. It is a vast picnic in honour of the Virgin. Two thousand persons are encamped about the chapel, amid a formidable army of donkeys and mules whose braying mingles with the pastoral music of reeds and bagpipes – bagpipes of two kinds, the common Calabrian variety and that of Basilicata, much larger and with a resounding bass key, which will soon cease to exist. A heaving ebb and flow of humanity fills the eye; fires are flickering before extempore shelters, and an ungodly amount of food is being consumed, as traditionally prescribed for such occasions – 'si mangia per divozione'. On all sides picturesque groups of dancers indulge in the old peasants' measure, the pecorara, to the droning of bagpipes – a demure kind of tarantella, the male capering about with faun-like attitudes of invitation and snappings of fingers, his partner evading the advances with downcast eyes. And the church meanwhile is filled to overflowing; the priests are having a busy time of it . . .

One is struck with the feast of costumes here, by far the brightest being those of the women who have come up from the seven or eight Albanian villages that surround these hills. In their variegated array of chocolate-brown and white, of emerald-green and gold and flashing violet, these dames move about the sward like animated tropical flowers.

Night brings no respite, on the contrary, the din grows livelier than ever; fires gleam brightly on the meadow and under the trees; the dancers are unwearied. Certain persons have told me that if you are of a prying disposition, now is the time to observe amorous couples walking hand in hand into the gloom – passionate young lovers from different villages, who have looked forward to this night of all the year on the chance of meeting, at last, in a fervent embrace under the friendly beeches . . . Festivals like this are relics of paganism.

Regarding the origin of this festival, I learned it was 'tradition'. It had been suggested to me that the Virgin had appeared to a shepherd in some cave near at hand – the usual Virgin, in the usual cave; a cave which, in the recent instance, no one was able to point out to me. The truth, I imagine, is that [the priests] have very sensibly not concerned themselves with inventing an original legend.

Ethnologist Rodney Gallop joined the July celebration in pre-war Portugal:

For all its Brazilian gold, for all its imitation of the sophisticated modalities of Versailles, the eighteenth century in Portugal was never completely divorced from the real country side. Country life, in consequence, never quite lost the Theocritan charm of the romería, to degenerate into the stilted mannerisms of the fête champêtre . . .

Another of the essential features of the merenda or picnic meal eaten in the open, links it with pagan festivals at which offerings of food were eaten in common by all the participants, who thereby hoped not only to accomplish an act of propitiation [to the gods of harvest and fertility] but also to acquire strength against evil influences.

The romerías of the North are most numerous in July and August. Who shall say when or how these pilgrimages began? The romería of Nstra Sra da Guia, at the mouth of the Ave, has been held continuously since the eleventh century. They are frequently mentioned in the lyrical verse of the troubadour period. A romería falls into two distinctive sections, the purely religious celebrations, and the secular arraial, a name given to the fair in the precincts of the church and to the revelry held there ion the eve of the festival. These saintly vigils have provoked scandals at intervals ever since the re-conquest. Round Braga, in its time a great Roman settlement, they were known till well into the Middle Ages as Kalendas. Gama Barros' *History of the Public Administration of Portugal* (1922) records that in the Middle Ages the people ate and drank in the churches, setting up tables, and sang and danced there on the pretext of the vigils of Saints, or on the day of some festival; and the very parish priests kept corn, barley, wine, olives, chickpeas, onions, garlic and other similar products in the churches for more than a day. The primitive concept of the expulsion of evil is maintained in the ceremonial cleansing of a romería. Fire and noise are the means most usually employed to drive out evils, and there is plenty of both at romerías – including rockets and fireworks.

The pilgrimages have swollen in recent years with the influx of tourists in beach-hats and sunglasses, curious to find out what lies at the end of the road. Cars and motor-bicycles now join the foot-travellers, horsemen and loaded donkeys as they wind slowly inland, and visitors are surprised to find nothing much but a little shrine, maybe with a spring rising nearby. The whole population of my local part of Tarifa, a Phoenician-founded trading post hard by the Pillars of Hercules turned out to pay their respects to their own beloved Virgin of the Palm Tree on her allotted day each year. It was quite natural that my family, with the children attending the local school, should join the pilgrimage.

The three little girls dressed in their stiffly-flounced Sevillana dresses, made by the local dressmaker with plenty of turnings to allow for growth, and which all the local children wore in feria, the boy proudly sporting a small version of the hard black sombrero always worn by the Andaluz horsemen, and we all went to pay our respects at the shrine of the Virgin of the Palm Tree. After Mass had been celebrated, the Virgin, dressed in her best and richest robes, was taken out and paraded round the meadows, through the tall stems of the wild asphodel and spiky blue thistles, so that she too could enjoy the sunshine and the admiration of her people. Then the occasion turned into one huge open-air picnic.

The urgent rhythms of the guitar called up the formal patterns of the Sevillana dances – performed, in these blossom-starred pastures, with a sinewy elegance which is the birthright of every true Andaluz. Grannies and toddlers, young girls and matrons, all form the square and call the number of the sequence, waiting motionless, tranquil as the carved wooden figure of the Madonna, for the moment dictated by the music and the sharp rhythmic handclaps of the spectators. The great dancers are known and called forth, admired for the seductive grace of their arms, the passion of their movements. The belles of the ball are often not the slender young girls, but the plumpest of matrons, the most spinsterly of aunts – the seductive Sevillana is the dance in which plain women come into their own.

Here are my favourite romería treats. Not the simple everyday fuel-food taken by the labourer in his pocket, but the best of what is available, prepared with love and care. These recipes are a traveller's miscellany, picked up and adapted on my own family romerías throughout Europe. Most of them owe allegiance to no particular country – a spice from here, a pie from there – as is proper to the peripatetic feasts of golden Demeter, by whatever name we call her.

LEMON-ROAST CHICKEN
(Mediterranean)

Chicken is the celebration dish of the peasantry of Europe. Food-laying hens, most productive and valuable members of the household, never went into the pot until they were stringy old grandmothers – and even then the children would not like to eat her who had become a personal friend. A young cockerel, on the other hand, would be fattened up for this special day. This is how I like my picnic chicken – roasted not long before the time to leave so that it is still juicy and warm, oil-drenched and perfumed with the scents of the Mediterranean hillside, and cooked till it drops off the bone.

Quantity: Serves 4–6.
Time: 1 hour 15 minutes.
Equipment: A roasting tin.

1 chicken	rough salt
1 lemon	2–3 cloves garlic, roughly chopped
2–3 healthy sprigs rosemary, marjoram and thyme	4–5 tablespoons olive oil
1 tablespoon chopped rosemary	1 tablespoon chopped thyme
1 tablespoon chopped marjoram	

Wipe the chicken inside and out and singe off any stray feathers. Salt it inside.

Cut the lemon in half and rub the chicken skin all over with it, squeezing in the juice. Chop the remains of the lemon and stuff the pieces into the chicken with a bit of garlic and the sprigs of herbs. Rub the chicken all over with a tablespoon of oil, the rest of the garlic and a good sprinkling of salt.

Pour a little oil in the roasting tin and put in the chicken, breast down. Pour the rest of the oil over the bird and sprinkle it with the chopped herbs.

Roast at 400°F/200°C/Gas 6 for 1¼–1½ hours, turning it first on one side and then on the other, and finishing up with the chicken on its back, until it is deliciously, stickily brown and so tender the meat falls off the bone. The generous amount of olive oil ensures that the meat does not dry out.

Take a napkin full of lettuce leaves to wrap the chicken pieces in as you eat them. If I serve this chicken at home, I use the juices to dress a plain lettuce salad.

ELIZABETHAN PASTIES

There has never been better finger-food than the pasty – and the whole world knows it: everyone has their own version of this unleavened bread pancake stuffed with a tasty filling, from the Turkish börek, to the Indian samosa, to the Chinese spring roll, and full circle to the Cornish tin-miner's favourite snack.

Quantity: Serves 6.
Time: 20–25 minutes. 45 minutes to bake.
Equipment: A mixing bowl and a sieve. A bowl, rolling pin and board. A baking tray and cooling rack.

The pastry

8oz/250g flour	2oz/50g butter
2oz/50g lard	4–5 tablespoons cold water

The filling

8oz/250g raw chicken, roughly chopped	8oz/250g minced pork
2–3 dried apricots, finely chopped	1 tablespoon sultanas

grated rind and juice of 1 orange

1 teaspoon cinnamon

½ teaspoon powdered cloves

2 tablespoons blanched almonds, roughly chopped

½ teaspoon powdered nutmeg

salt and pepper

To finish

1 egg, lightly forked

Make the pastry first. Sieve the flour with the salt and roughly chop in the butter and lard, using a knife. Mix in enough water to give a soft but firm dough. Leave the pastry under cover in a cool place to rest while you prepare the rest of the ingredients.

Mix all the stuffing ingredients together. Leave them to marinate for 10–15 minutes.

Preheat the oven to 400°F/200°C/Gas 6.

Cut the pastry into 6 pieces. Knead each one swiftly into a small ball. Roll out each to the size of a saucer and dampen the edges with water. Drop a tablespoon of stuffing on one half of each round and fold the other over to enclose the stuffing in a half-moon.

Press the edges together with your thumbs and index fingers to give a wavy crimp, as for a Cornish pasty. Transfer the pasties to a baking sheet. Brush the tops with beaten egg yolk to make them shine.

Bake the pasties for 40–45 minutes, turning the oven down to 350°F/180°C/Gas 4 after the first 10 minutes.

Transfer them to a rack to cool, and carry them to the picnic in a cloth-lined basket or open tin – not in an airtight box, or the pastry will lose its crispness.

SPICED MEAT CIGARS

(Turkey)

No doubt primitive man spread a bit of marrow and a scrap of meat on to the dough cake he had slapped on his bakestone, flipped it over to enclose the filling, and had himself a fine huntsman's piece for the pocket. These sophisticated delicately-spiced Ottoman börek, slender as a houri's beckoning finger, are about as far away as it is possible to get from the rough original.

Quantity: Makes about 3 dozen.

Time: Allow about 45 minutes – it's fiddly business.

Equipment: A small saucepan. A pastry brush. A frying pan and draining spoon.

The filling

1 tablespoon butter

1 clove garlic, chopped finely

1 teaspoon powdered coriander

8oz/250g lean minced meat

2 tablespoons finely chopped mint

1 glass water

1–2 tablespoons fresh breadcrumbs

1 small onion, chopped finely

1 teaspoon powdered cumin

1 teaspoon powdered cinnamon

1 tablespoon finely chopped parsley

1 tomato, scalded, skinned and chopped

salt and pepper

The pastry

8oz/250g filo/strudel pastry   4oz/100g melted butter

To finish

frying oil

Make the stuffing first. Melt the butter in the pan and fry the onion and garlic gently until they soften. Stir in the spices and let them feel the heat, then add the meat and let it fry until it seizes and changes colour. Stir in the herbs and the tomato. Let it all bubble for a moment. Pour in the water and bring it back to the boil. Season with salt and pepper, turn down the heat, cover, and leave to simmer for 8–10 minutes to marry the flavours and tenderize the meat. Remove from the heat and leave the mixture to cool. Stir in enough breadcrumbs to take up the juice.

Cut the sheets of filo into strips about 3in x 10in (7cm x 25cm). Cover the filo until you are ready for each piece – it dries out fast. Paint a layer of butter on one strip and lay another on top. Lay a narrow cigar of filling along the short side. Turn in the long sides, and roll up the filo on itself like a miniature cigar. Continue until all the filo and filling is used up.

Heat the frying oil in the pan. When it is lightly hazed with smoke, fry the cigars, a few at a time so that the oil temperature does not drop.

As soon as the pastry is crisp and brown, remove the cigars and drain them. Serve warm – lovely with a little dipping sauce of creamy yogurt liquidized with a generous handful of mint.

VEGETABLE OMELETTE
Tortilla a la payesa (Spain)

This is a fine solid omelette, a meal in itself. The *tortilla* is the picnic food of Spain – no one goes on a *romería* without it. With a loaf of bread, a bottle of cold dry sherry, and a handful of olives, it makes the perfect picnic. The ordinary *tortilla* has potatoes only – the ham and vegetables make it special.

Quantity: Serves 4.
Time: 20–25 minutes.
Equipment: An omelette pan or small deep-sided frying pan, and a spatula.

4-5 tablespoons olive oil
2oz/50g salt-dried ham or lean bacon, diced
1 slice onion, chopped
4oz/100g green beans, top-and-tailed and
   chopped into short lengths
salt and pepper

1 large potato, peeled and sliced finely
1 garlic clove, peeled and chopped
1 small tomato, chopped
4 tablespoons shelled peas (fresh or frozen)
4 eggs

Heat 3 tablespoons of the oil in the pan.

Add the sliced potatoes and cook them gently until tender. Remove and drain in a sieve over a bowl to catch the drippings.

Reheat the oil. Throw in the ham or bacon, garlic and onion. Fry gently until it all softens and takes colour. Add the tomato, beans and peas and bubble up to evaporate extra liquid.

Beat the eggs lightly with salt and pepper and mix in the cooked ingredients, including the contents of the pan.

Add the rest of the oil, including the drippings. Tip in the egg mixture and cook as a thick pancake. The heat should be low or the base will burn before the eggs are ready. With a spatula, push the potato down into the egg so that all is submerged.

As the *tortilla* cooks, neaten the sides with a metal spatula to build up a deep straight edge. When it looks firm, slide it out on to a plate, then invert it back into the pan to cook the other side. Don't over-cook it – the centre should remain juicy. A little more oil in the pan may be necessary. When the *tortilla* feels lightly set and firm, remove it and pat it dry with kitchen paper.

Serve the *tortilla* warm or cold, cut into bite-sized cubes, each pierced with a toothpick.

SCOTCH EGGS

I used to take a big box of these on our Sunday *romerías* when I lived with my young family in a cork-oak forest in Andalucía. Our Spanish friends found the name hilarious: eggs have an inescapable double meaning in Spain, and negotiations for a dozen of them in the local market were fraught with pitfalls. In the bull-running Andaluz countryside, where manliness is the most desirable of all virtues, the Scotch eggs were greeted with hoots of delight.

Quantity: Serves 6.
Time: Allow 40 minutes.
Equipment: A small saucepan. A mixing bowl. A frying pan and draining spoon.

6 small and 1 large egg	1lb/500g pure pork sausage meat
1 teaspoon crushed sage	1 teaspoon powdered cumin
½ teaspoon mustard powder	1 teaspoon freshly ground pepper
1 teaspoon celery salt (ordinary salt will do)	home-made dried breadcrumbs
oil for frying	

Hard-boil the small eggs. Start them in cold water and bring it to the boil. Take the pan off the heat. The eggs will be perfectly cooked in 8 minutes. Drain them and run them under cold water to loosen the shells, then peel them.

Mix the sausage meat with the herbs and spices and the lightly-beaten large egg. Divide the mixture into 6 balls. With wet hands, flatten them into flat patties so that you can wrap each egg in a jacket of spiced sausage. Roll the Scotch eggs in the breadcrumbs.

Heat the oil in a frying pan. When it is hot enough to fry a cube of bread brown immediately, put in the eggs. Fry them gently on all sides – they will take 8–10 minutes for the sausage meat to cook through.

Drain on paper and leave them to cool. Don't put them in the refrigerator – they never recover their crispness.

BELGIAN CHEESE STRAWS

These delicious biscuits from the beautiful medieval city of Bruges are the richest of self-indulgences – so light they vanish on the tongue. The Belgians have wonderful pastry shops and prodigious appetites.

Quantity: Makes about 3 dozen.
Time: 25–30 minutes.
Equipment: A mixture bowl. A rolling pin and board. A baking tray and cooling rack.

8oz/250g plain flour
8oz/250g well-matured hard cheese, grated
¼ teaspoon cayenne pepper

8oz/250g softened butter
1 teaspoon salt

Sieve the flour. Beat the softened butter with the cheese. Work in the flour, salt and cayenne. It should form a soft dough without any water – add a splash of water only if absolutely necessary. Chill for 30 minutes.

Preheat the oven to 375°F/190°C/Gas 5.

Roll out the dough gently on a lightly floured board to a thickness of ¼in/0.5cm and transfer to a baking sheet. Cut the dough into finger-length batons, pulling each finger gently apart.

Bake the biscuits for 12–14 minutes, until golden but not yet brown. Transfer them to a baking rack: they will crisp as they cool. Store in an airtight tin.

LITTLE INDIANS

These are very nutty American brownies – perfect with summer strawberries. The recipe comes from diplomat Sir Harry Luke's *The Tenth Muse*, a lovely idiosyncratic collection of recipes published in 1954. The source for the Indians is given as Alexandria, Virginia.

Quantity: Makes about 12.
Time: 45 minutes intermittent attention.
Equipment: A mixing bowl. A 10 x 8in/25 x 20cm baking tray and a cooling rack.

2oz/50g bitter chocolate
8oz/250g caster sugar
2oz/50g flour
6oz/175g chopped nuts (walnuts, almonds, hazelnuts – even peanuts)

4oz/125g butter
2 eggs
vanilla to flavour

Melt the chocolate and butter together over hot water. Remove the mixture from the heat as soon as it creams. Mix in the sugar, eggs, flour, vanilla and nuts, in that order. Spread the mixture in the buttered baking tray.

Bake for 25 minutes at 400°F/200°C/Gas 6.

Cut them into squares while still hot. They will look raw inside, but pay no attention: they will be perfectly done – moist and chewy.

ITALIAN MELON SHERBET

This is so much my favourite water-ice that I cannot resist including it, even if it is not usually my habit to lug an iced thermos with me on a picnic. To make it you need the ripest of melons – bargain with the greengrocer for an over-ripe fruit.

Quantity: Makes about 2½ pints/1.5 litres of sherbet.
Time: Start a few hours ahead, unless you have an instant ice-cream machine.
Equipment: A saucepan. A bowl and whisk. A liquidizer or sieve. An ice-cream maker would be useful.

2lb/1kg cantaloup melon, yielding 1½ pints/900ml juice juice of 1 lemon	8oz/250g sugar ½ pint/300ml water 1 egg white

Examine the melon and cut out any bad bits. De-seed, peel and pulp the flesh through a sieve or in a liquidizer.

Make a syrup with the sugar and water: bring them to the boil, take the pan off the heat and allow the syrup to cool before you use it.

Mix the syrup into the melon juice with the lemon and egg white. Taste and add extra lemon if necessary – cold food needs to be more highly flavoured than warm food.

Freeze the mixture – in an ice-cream maker if possible. If you use the ice-making compartment of the fridge, take the ice out when it is solid, beat it thoroughly, and re-freeze.

SHEEP-SHEARING SUPPER

Sheep have long been a mainstay of Britain's farming communities – grazing the rich southern meadows as well as the colder pastures of the north and western uplands. Journal-keeper Celia Fiennes, travelling side-saddle through her native land around 1690, noted the flocks grazing among the 'prodigeous' ancient stones of Stonehenge on the Salisbury plain: 'This country is most champion and open, pleasant for recreations; its husbandry is mostly corn and sheep, the finest wool and sweet meat though but small.' Later she visited the greatest sheep market in the country, that of Weyhill, where in Defoe's time 500,000 sheep were traded in a single day. Defoe held the wool from the sheep of Leicestershire in the highest esteem – the fleece having the longest staple, the animals being 'without comparison, the largest, and bear the greatest fleeces of wool in their backs, of any sheep of England'.

A century and a half later, Sir Henry Ellis, Librarian of the British Museum, recorded in 1841 that the shepherding communities of England could still throw a good shearing party: 'In England on the day they began to shear their sheep a plentiful dinner was provided for the shearers and their friends. A table also, if weather permitted, was spread in the open air for the young people and children. The washing and shearing of sheep is attended with great mirth and festivity.'

A hundred years later, the rural pattern was changing and the sheep-farmers were retreating to the more marginal land. Dorothy Hartley noted in 1935, in her chronicle of *The Countryman's England*, that it was still customary in mountain districts to hold large sheep-shearing parties in turn at each farm. 'Usually a barn is cleared, or some sort of shelter put up, straw stacks are thrown down on a clean rick cloth, and there's a regular set-to with beef sandwiches, fresh mustard, cheese, beer jokes, the news of the district and some courting.'

The second of the two world wars swept up the remnants of the shepherding communities. In 1940, Welsh sheep-farmer Thomas Firbank looked back with longing from the regimentation of a Caterham barrack square to the 'wild freedom' of his farm in the hills of Wales:

Shearing-time is upon us at Dyffryn almost as soon as the washing is finished. We need forty men to shear the Dyffryn flock in one day. At shearing time the kitchen is full of food. In a slow oven a huge round of beef is roasting against the hungry morrow. There are bowls and bowls of fruit jellies and custards. There are more jam tarts than the Knave of Hearts could ever have tackled. A stack of home-baked loaves is on the window-still. Carrots, ready scraped, and peeled potatoes stand waiting in crocks of water. A big pan of porridge is slowly simmering for the gatherers' breakfast. It is often eleven o'clock by the time we have eaten, and in another four hours we must be on top of the Glyder to clear the remaining half of the mountain.

Frequently it is nearly nine when the last sheep is carried out, and everyone is too tired to joke about it. The cart will have caught up with the accumulation of wool, and as it goes off with the final fleeces the men plod stiffly up the hill to the house for supper.

ROAST BEEF WITH HORSERADISH
(Britain)

Beef is the traditional sheep-shearing meal all over Britain – never lamb or mutton. Maybe after a long day wrestling with heavy fleeces no one wants to face up to another sheep, not even a roast one. Choose the Yorkshireman's favourite cut, a fine sirloin on the bone, with the undercut left in place. The beef is roasted the day before, left to cool, sliced and made into thick sandwiches to be taken out to the shearers in huge flat baskets with a pot of mustard tied to the handle. More would be served up in the farmhouse after the day's work, with a sideboard of good old-fashioned sweets to follow.

Quantity: A 10lb/5kg joint on the bone serves 12–15 people.
Time: Start a few hours ahead to allow the joint to cool.
Equipment: A roasting tin. A whisk and bowl.

The meat

a 10lb/5kg sirloin, with its fat curled round the undercut

1 tablespoon dry mustard
1 tablespoon freshly ground pepper

The horseradish sauce

8oz/250g grated fresh horseradish
1 tablespoon made mustard

½ pint/300ml cream, whipped

To finish

salt

Rub the joint with mustard and pepper – add no salt until the end of cooking.

To cook a joint rare to eat cold (it cooks a little more as it cools) allow 15 minutes a lb, with 15 minutes extra: this piece will need 2 hours 45 minutes at 350°F/180°C/Gas 4 for the first 2 hours, with oven turned up to 425°F/220°C/Gas 7 for the final 45 minutes to crisp the fat. Start it with the fat and undercut on top, and reverse it after 30 minutes when the fat has begun to run.

Salt the joint and leave it to cool.

Mix the grated horseradish with the cream and mustard.

Serve the meat carved into generous slices, sandwiched in thick slices of bread spread with horseradish cream.

After the shearing, the beef can be served with baked potatoes, pickled onions and cucumber slices soaked overnight in malt vinegar, with good strong beer to wash it down.

CUMBERLAND CLIPPING-TIME PUDDING
(England)

Milk puddings enriched with beef marrow were the great treat of clipping time in the shepherding communities of the fells. These days they have virtually dropped out of the culinary repertoire of Cumberland – people find them too rich and heavy, and in any event there is not the same reason for a party, as the shearers now come over from New Zealand for the season and will be on to the next job by tomorrow. Rice puddings, if made with a lighter modern hand and with cream to replace the marrow, are quite delicious and certainly don't deserve to drop into obscurity. Rum is a favourite flavouring and nutmeg a widely-used spice in Cumberland, which had access through its Atlantic ports to the spice trade and the sugar-cane products of the West Indies.

Quantity: Serves 6.
Time: 15 minutes to prepare. 3 hours in the oven.
Equipment: A saucepan. A bowl and whisk. An oval oven-proof pudding dish.

4oz/100g raisins
1 glass rum
1½ pints/900ml milk
½ pint/300ml cream
4 tablespoons soft brown sugar

4oz/100g sultanas
12oz/350g short-grain (round or pudding) rice
a curl of lemon rind
4 egg yolks
¼ teaspoon salt

To finish
1oz/25g butter
1 teaspoon grated nutmeg

2 tablespoons soft brown sugar

Soak the raisins and sultanas in the rum.

Put the rice into a saucepan and pour in enough cold water to cover it to a depth of one finger. Bring to the boil, remove the pan from the heat and drain the rice. Return the rice to the pan with the milk and the lemon rind. Bring to the boil and remove from the heat.

Stir in the cream, egg yolks, sugar, salt and the soaked fruit with its rum. Tip the mixture into the pudding dish and spread the rice evenly. Sprinkle the top with nutmeg and brown sugar and dot with butter. Bake in a low oven, 300°C/150°F/Gas 2, for 2½–3 hours, until the rice is tender.

The delicately mottled golden skin was my favourite treat as a child.

CHEESECAKES
(England)

These were the great favourites of Yorkshire farmhouse teas – made with curd from the rich milkings of summertime. No one makes a cheesecake like a Yorkshirewoman.

Quantity: Serves 6.
Time: 1 hour.
Equipment: Two mixing bowls and a sieve. A rolling pin and board. A sheet of patty tins – the ones used for individual Yorkshire puddings are perfect.

The pastry
6oz/175g flour
½ teaspoon sugar
2oz/50g butter

½ teaspoon salt
2oz/50g lard
3–4 tablespoons cold water

The filling
1lb/500g curd cheese, well drained
2 tablespoons cream
6oz/175g caster sugar
1 tablespoon sultanas, plumped in a splash of tea

grated rind of 1 lemon
6 eggs (omit 1 of the whites)
1 teaspoon grated nutmeg

First make the pastry. Sieve the flour with the salt and sugar into a bowl. Chop in the lard and the butter and rub together lightly with your fingers. Work in enough cold water to give a soft but firm dough. Roll out on a well-floured board, cut out 12 rounds with a biscuit-cutter, and use them to line the patty tins. Put aside in a cool place.

Preheat the oven to 425°F/220°C/Gas 7.

Work all the filling ingredients together thoroughly. Drop a spoonful of the mixture into each lined patty tin.

Bake for 15–20 minutes until the pastry is crisp and the filling set.

Serve them warm, with a good strong cup of Yorkshire tea.

SHERRY TRIFLE
(Britain)

This is the old favourite celebration pudding from Land's End to the Borders. Sponge cake and custard are the two invariables – for the rest, each family has its own particular recipe which may include peaches, tinned or fresh, bananas, and cherries.

Quantity: Serves 6.
Time: Start a few hours ahead. 40–50 minutes.
Equipment: A mixing bowl, a Swiss roll tin, greaseproof paper and a cooling rack. A small saucepan, a bowl and a whisk for the custard. A pretty glass bowl to assemble the trifle – no point in hiding its light under a china bushel. An icing pipe with a thick nozzle for cream (optional).

The sponge cake

3oz/75g butter

2 small eggs

3oz/75g caster sugar

3oz/75g self-raising flour

The custard

¾ pint/450ml milk

3 tablespoons sugar

1 small nut butter

3 eggs

1–2 drops vanilla essence

To finish

6 tablespoons strawberry jam

1lb/500g raspberries

1 tablespoon chopped nuts or whole almonds

1 glass of sherry or Madeira

8 fl oz/200ml cream, whipped

Make the Victoria sponge first. Butter the Swiss roll tin and line with greaseproof paper.

Preheat the oven to 375°F/190°C/Gas 5.

Cream the butter with the sugar until the mixture is white and fluffy. Beat in the eggs. Fold in the flour. Divide the mixture between the two tins. Bake the cake for 15–18 minutes, until well risen and firm. Transfer to a cake rack to cool.

Make the custard next. Put the milk to heat in the small saucepan. Whisk the eggs with the sugar and vanilla. When the milk is just up to the boil, pour it slowly into the eggs, whisking furiously. Return the pan to a very gentle heat, and beat until the custard coats the back of the wooden spoon. Remove from the heat, float a knob of butter on top so that it doesn't form a skin, and leave to cool.

Now assemble the trifle. Cut the sponge cake into squares. Sandwich the squares together in pairs with jam, and lay them in the bottom of the trifle bowl. Soak the sponges with the sherry or Madeira.

Cover with a layer of raspberries (save a handful for the finishing touch), then spread in the custard, and top with a smooth rich layer of whipped cream. Decorate with a few perfect raspberries and the chopped nuts or whole almonds.

August

SWEDISH CRAYFISH FESTIVAL

August 8th is the day the Swedish freshwater crayfish season opens – and everyone tucks into their crayfish feast at midnight on the night of August 7th. This new festival commemorates an old habit – Sweden's streams no longer yield enough of the delectable crustaceans to satisfy her population's appetites, and more crayfish is now farmed or imported than was ever caught.

The crayfish never liked its streams too Arctic, and does not thrive further north than the central lakes. Northern Sweden has an alternative food festival: the third Thursday in August marks the release of the *surströmmings* – the day on which the year's supply of soured herring, lightly salted and fermented herring, a very strong and peculiarly Swedish taste, is ready for sale. *Surströmming* is served with very thin *tunnbröd*, chopped raw onion, *mandlpotatis*, almond-shaped new potatoes with a deliciously sweet flavour, and strong *västerbotten* cheese – made into a wrap-around sandwich inside a slice of *tunnbröd*. Soured milk is the traditional accompaniment.

No Swedish festival is complete without its story-telling. First the sagas of family and travels, then, as the moon rises, there may be someone who can retell for the children the myths of gods and trolls, giants and dwarfs – tale-telling skills are finely honed in the long dark northern winters.

DILLED CRAYFISH
Kräftor (Sweden)

Crayfish turn a wonderful brilliant crimson when they are cooked: a visual celebration to gladden the heart as well as the palate. The creatures are all too easily trapped in the wild – which probably accounts for their virtual disappearance from the streams of Europe. A piece of rotten meat dragged through the stream on the end of a string brought them up by the dozen in the old days when there were crayfish there at all: they seem, like the dodo, to have no natural sense of preservation. My children used to catch them in southern Spain – they could be found lurking under the stones in the bright little stream which ran behind our house. The children held that the pleasure of eating them – cracking the succulent little claws and sucking out all the juices – was well worth the painful little nips the creatures could inflict. The dill weed indispensable to the dish grows in every ditch – by this time of year it is 3 feet / 1 metre high and in full flower. Allow at least a dozen live crayfish per person – this, after all, is a feast.

Quantity: Serves 6.
Time: Prepare 1–2 hours ahead. 10 minutes.
Equipment: A large saucepan.

6 dozen freshwater farmed crayfish (about 4lb/2kg)
1 generous bunch of dill with the flowering heads

7 pints/4 litres water
6 tablespoons salt

Check that the crayfish are alive – they can survive for a long time out of water, but once dead, like all crustaceans, they instantly deteriorate.

Bring the water to the boil with the salt and half the dill, and boil for 2 minutes. Remove the dill. Throw in the crayfish. Bring the water back to the boil as fast as possible. Cook the crayfish for 5–6 minutes after the water has reboiled. Remove from the heat and add the rest of the dill – reserving a few heads for decoration. Let the crayfish cool in the pot liquor.

Drain them and pile them up on a plate. Decorate with dill heads.

Serve with plenty of bread and cheese, beer and aquavit.

Now is the time for songs and speeches, to allow full rein to the heirs of the story-tellers and myth-spinners. Who knows what wild night spirits might be called up in the moonlight?

THE GLORIOUS TWELFTH

August 12th – the Glorious Twelfth familiar to all British sportsmen – is the day the grouse season begins. A great deal of time and energy has gone into studying the habits of the most prized of European game-birds, *Lagopus scoticus*, a species endemic to the heather-clad uplands of Britain and Ireland. A diet of young heather shoots and insects, supplemented by moorland delicacies – bilberries, wild raspberries, the delectable golden cloudberry – makes up the daily menu of the adult bird.

For their first ten days, the pullets are wholly insectivorous, exercising their infant leg-muscles scuttling through the heather cropping the undergrowth for their high-protein prey. Thereafter, their inclination is to rely on fast legwork and low bushes for cover, taking to the air only when absolutely necessary. When they get air-borne, however, no bird is faster on the wing – as the hunter with his eye on the pot knows well. As ground-feeders, the birds do not need the muscular breasts required to power sustained flights, and their breast meat remains pale and tender, even in older birds.

There are those who hang their grouse in the feather for a fortnight – and there are those who pluck and cook the birds straight from the heather. Both are entirely respectable schools. A clean-shot bird, unplucked and ungutted (and therefore free from our destructive human-carried microbes) can be hung in a current of air in a cool larder for a week or ten days to ripen – a mummifying process which develops the flavour and tenderizes the meat.

ROAST GROUSE
(Britain)

If you eat your grouse on the Glorious Twelfth itself, you will be keeping knowledgeable company: Veronica Peel, wife of Earl Peel, owner of a considerable stretch of Yorkshire's grouse moors, plucks her birds straight from the butts and roasts them that evening. She explains that if you don't hang them, the birds must be plucked while they are still warm: once they have stiffened up the feathers are far harder to pull and the job takes twice as long.

Quantity: Serves 6.
Time: 1 hour.
Equipment: A roasting tin.

6 fresh young grouse
2 tablespoons butter
6 slices smoked streaky bacon

12 juniper berries
salt and pepper
water

To finish
butter
stock or water

flour

Pluck the birds and remove the innards. Tuck a couple of juniper berries, a small piece of butter, and a pinch of salt inside each cavity. Trim the rind off the bacon rashers. Cover the breasts with bacon. Transfer the birds to a roasting tin – don't squash them together. Pour in a finger's width of water.

Heat the oven to 450°F/230°C/Gas 8.

Roast the birds for 45 minutes. Don't forget that a full oven takes longer than a half-full one (8 birds will need 50 minutes – add on 5 minutes per extra brace).

Take out the birds and put them to keep warm while you make a gravy. Reserve the pan juices and melt a knob of butter in the roasting tin. Sprinkle in a teaspoon of flour and fry it for a moment or two to take colour. Pour back the pan juices and allow the sauce to bubble up while you scrape in all the sticky brown bits from the pan. Add enough stock or water to make the gravy up to ¾ pint/450ml – don't use a stock cube – but do use a drop of gravy browning if you like a dark gravy.

BREAD SAUCE AND FRIED BREADCRUMBS
(Britain)

These two dishes are the required accompaniments to a Yorkshire grouse. Scots might think of an oatmeal skirlie instead.

Quantity: Serves 6.
Time: 20 minutes.
Equipment: A saucepan. A frying pan.

1 small stale white loaf	1 pint/600ml milk
1–2 bay leaves	1 onion
3–4 cloves	small piece mace
4oz/100g butter	salt and pepper
1 teaspoon dried thyme	

Trim off any dark pieces of crust and breadcrumb the bread. Bring the milk to the boil with the bay leaves. Remove from the heat and add the onion stuck with the cloves, and the mace. Leave to infuse – on the side of the cooker all day is best.

To finish the sauce, sprinkle in as much of the breadcrumbs as the milk will take up. Bring to the boil, turn down the heat and simmer for 10 minutes until thick. Remove the onion, cloves and bay leaf. Beat in a large knob of butter. Taste and add salt and pepper.

Fry the rest of the breadcrumbs in butter and toss in the thyme.

GAME CHIPS
(Britain)

These are much better if you make them at home, and are easy if you have a food-processor to take care of the slicing.

Quantity: Serves 6.
Time: 25–30 minutes.
Equipment: A deep-fryer and a draining spoon. A slicing mandolin, or a food processor with a slicing attachment, would save a great deal of time.

2lb/1kg potatoes	salt
corn or vegetable oil for frying	

Peel and slice the potatoes very thinly. Sprinkle them with salt.

Heat the oil in a deep-fryer until the surface has a faint blue haze. Scatter in the chips, a handful at a time: they should gild and crisp within moments. Remove them with the draining spoon and transfer them to kitchen paper to drain. Serve with red cabbage (see p. 35).

COLD GROUSE PIE
(Britain)

Make this with old birds – test the flexibility of the claws and beak, and the length of the flight feathers, to give you an idea whether what you have to cook is this year's bird or one from the season before. This dish is excellent for a shooting lunch.

Quantity: Serves 6–8.
Time: 45 minutes preparation. 2 hours cooking time.
Equipment: A rolling pin and board. A mixing bowl. A small loaf tin.

2 old grouse
6oz/175g thickly sliced cooked tongue
1 medium onion
8oz/250g pig's liver
2 bacon rashers, finely chopped
1lb/500g pastry – hot-water crust or shortcrust
   (see p.204)

1 bay leaf
salt and pepper
2 cloves garlic
8oz/250g minced pork or sausage meat
1 teaspoon thyme
1 tablespoon milk

Remove all the meat from the raw grouse and shred it. Put the carcass on to simmer with the onion trimmings and a bay leaf, in enough water to cover. Slice the tongue into strips and mix it with the grouse meat. Season with salt and pepper.

Peel the onion and the garlic, and mince them well with the liver. Work in the minced pork, chopped bacon and thyme.

Line a loaf tin with pastry, leaving enough to make a lid to enclose the meat. Spread on a layer of the minced meat mix, then a layer of grouse/tongue, then minced meat again, then grouse, finishing with meat. Damp the edge of the pastry and lay on a lid. Crimp the edges together with a fork, and decorate with pastry leaves cut from the trimmings. Cut a hole in the top to let out the steam. Paint with a brushful of milk.

Bake the pie in a medium oven, 350°F/180°C/Gas 4, for 2 hours until thoroughly cooked.

Meanwhile, strain the stock, boil it down to a good strong ¼ pint/150ml, taste and add salt and pepper, and pour into the pie when you take it out of the oven.

Serve the pie cold, with a pickled onion or two.

EVE AND FEAST OF THE ASSUMPTION OF THE VIRGIN MARY: AUGUST 14TH/15TH

Catholic Europe – both Roman and Orthodox – celebrates this feast with delicious sweetmeats: a graceful tribute to the femininity of the Mother of God. Such confections were the special skill of the convents, particularly in areas where egg whites were used to refine wine, leaving plenty of egg yolks available for the sweet custards and marzipans the nuns loved to prepare.

The Feast of the Assumption is a major public holiday over much of Mediterranean Europe. The Panayia is second only in the Orthodox calendar to Easter, and is preceded by a fast of fifteen days, beginning on August 1st, for which the same fasting rules apply as for Lent. The fast is interrupted half-way through by the Feast of the Transfiguration, which commemorates the day when Christ appeared to the disciples as a fisherman, and when fish is permitted.

No fishing boats leave the harbour during that day, as the wind blows ill. But on the evening before, everyone pushes out the boats and races each other – old and young. People dip their hands in each passing wave and sprinkle their heads with the spray. Later, everyone goes home for the big meal: a fish soup (see Palm Sunday, p.148). In some areas people take baskets of grapes to church to be blessed as at harvest festival – the priest sprinkles the fruit with holy water and distributes it to the congregation.

Then it's back to Lenten fasting to prepare for the great celebration of the Assumption of the Virgin. On the eve of the feast, everyone leaves the cities and makes for the hills: the islands are the favourite place to pass the festival, particularly Tinos in the beautiful Cyclades, where an icon of the Virgin is believed to have performed many miracles; or St John's holy island of Patmos, where the nuns of the convent below the monastery of Hora make beautiful honeyed sweetmeats for such celebrations. The nuns of the sister convent to the Monastery of the Theologian on Patmos also make wonderful honeycakes (see p.169) and Easter twist-biscuits, as well as fruit preserves and orange-blossom water. For the Greeks the feast marks the end of the summer. Afterwards everyone drifts back to the cities, wishing each other a good winter and leaving the beaches to the last of the tourists.

James Frazer, the author of *The Golden Bough*, did not have far to search for a pagan blueprint for the Christian celebration:

> At Diana's annual festival, which was celebrated all over Italy on the 13th of August, hunting dogs were crowned and wild beasts were not molested; young people went through a purificatory ceremony in her honour; wine was brought forth, and the feast consisted of a kid, cakes served piping hot on plates of leaves, and apples still hanging in clusters on the boughs. The Christian Church appears to have sanctified this great festival of the virgin goddess by adroitly converting it into the festival of the Assumption of the Blessed Virgin on the 15th August.

In rural Portugal the holiday can run for a week. The most famous Assumption *romería* is at Viana do Castella, capital of the province of Minho. The whole population is woken at 4 a.m. on the eve of the feast by the *alvarados* beating their drums and pumping their bagpipes – we are here bordering on Galicia, the southernmost land of the Celts. The following day the whole population leaves home to picnic outside the town on the banks of the Lima, where bars, booths and kiosks have been set up for their amusement – and, in time-honoured fashion, to relieve the population of some of its hard-earned wages. Bonfires and fireworks ensure that everyone remains wide awake throughout the celebration, and the music provided by ukeleles, accordions and guitars keeps everyone on their toes for the dance.

In Germany, the post-Assumption thirty days were known as Lady's Thirty, and were the proper time for gathering herbs to dry for the winter – seventy-seven herbs were collected, tied into a bunch and taken to church for blessing.

Great feasts are traditionally preceded by a fasting eve – with dishes of fish or vegetables, cheese or eggs, depending on local habit. This brief deprivation heightens pleasure in the delicious sweet treats which mark the festival itself.

TARAMOSALATA
(Greece)

Serve this – the favourite food of Greece – on the Eve of the Assumption. The strict rules of Orthodoxy prohibit eggs, cheese and olive oil in fasting periods, which limits the diet of the faithful to plain vegetables and bread. *Taramosalata* is the dish which makes it all tolerable. The salted, dried fish-roes which from the basis used to come from the grey mullet – now largely replaced with cod's roe. Choose a firm 'wing', well-salted and innocent of scarlet dye – not at all proper to a fast day. You can include a tablespoon of grated onion if you like – although if you do, the salad will not keep, and this is essentially a dish to make in quantity and dig into over several days.

Quantity: Serves 8.
Time: 15 minutes.

Equipment: A *goudi* (pestle and mortar) if you have one. A food processor makes it all much easier, although it gives a fluffier result than the old hand-pounding.

8oz/250g salted cod's roe
juice of 2 lemons
salt and pepper

2 slices day-old bread
½ pint/300ml corn or sesame seed oil (no olive oil in fasting time)

To finish
a handful of black olives

Remove any hard bits from the cod's roe – don't skin it, there's plenty of flavour there, and the slightly rough texture is lovely. Put the bread to soak (cut off the crusts if they are hard) in a splash of water. Squeeze it dry.

Pound all the ingredients together – either in the mortar or in a liquidizer (you may need a little extra water) – until you have a smooth purée.

Serve spread on a plate, dotted with olives, and accompanied by bread for scooping.

VANILLA BISCUITS
(Greece)

This is a basic Greek rich biscuit dough – you can perfume it with grated orange or lemon rind, nutmeg and cloves, cinnamon, anything you please. Make several batches in different flavours to honour the feast – the delicate rich scent of vanilla is particularly appropriate to Our Lady.

Quantity: Makes 3 dozen.
Time: 1 hour intermittent attention.
Equipment: A sieve. 2 mixing bowls and a beater. An electric mixter would be helpful. A baking tray and cooling rack.

12oz/350g flour
8oz/250g butter (the Greeks use concentrated
  butter, which does not go rancid in the heat)
2 egg yolks
2–3 tablespoons water

1 teaspoon baking powder
6oz/175g sugar
1 short length vanilla pod
1 tablespoon brandy

Sieve the flour with the baking powder. Soften the butter and beat it to a fluffy cream with the sugar, the contents of the vanilla pod scraped out, the egg yolks and the brandy. Mix in the flour with your hands, and add enough water to give a soft workable dough.

Preheat the oven to 350°F/180°C/Gas 4.

Break off walnut-sized nuggets of dough and roll them into short ropes, which can be joined with a dab of water into rings, or figures of eight, or lovers' knots.

Arrange the biscuits on a baking tray, leaving them enough room to expand, and bake them for 20–25 minutes, until pale gold. Transfer them to a baking rack to cool and crisp.

SOFT MERINGUES WITH EGG CUSTARD
Suspiros com ovos moles (Portugal)

The Feast of the Assumption is a lady's feast, to be celebrated with sweet delicacies. There are innumerable Portuguese recipes for these *doces de ovos*, sweets made with eggs, originally made by nuns. *Ovos moles* are special to Aveiro and are packed in little wooden barrels; there is thick rich caramel custard, *touçinho do ceu*, *trouxas* and *lamprias de ovos* from Portalegre and Caldas da Rainha; *fios de ovos*, *aletria* from Abrantes; *doces de amendoa*, *doce podre* of Evora, *morgado* and *dom rodrigo* of Algarve; *tijelinhas* of Santo Tirso; *pasteis de nata*, sweet cakes of Tentugal; *paes de lo*, gingerbreads of Fafe, Ovar, Figeiro, Alfeizerao; *cavacas* of Caldas, Felguiras, Resende; the *morcela* of Arouca; marzipan of Poretalegre; *arrufadas* of Coimbra; fig or almond cakes of Freixo de Espada of Moncorvo; and there are dozens more. These creamy meringues filled with a rich egg custard (the nuns made them with egg yolks only, very rich indeed) are among the easiest to prepare – such recipes need great skill and patience, and the Portuguese queue for them in the local bakeries on feast-days – sometimes eating them then and there, standing gossiping by the counter and wiping sticky fingers on little squares of tissue paper.

Quantity: Makes about 6 dozen.
Time: Start 2–3 hours ahead. About 1 hour – the custard needs attention throughout.
Equipment: A saucepan. A bowl and whisk – electric mixer would be a godsend. Several baking trays, foil or rice-paper, and a cooling rack.

The custard

12oz/350g sugar	¾ pint/450ml water
1 curl lemon peel	6oz/175g rice flour
9 egg yolks	

The soft meringues

1¾lb/850g sugar	¾ pint/450ml water
9 egg whites	1 tablespoon lemon juice
½ teaspoon salt	

First make the custard. Put the sugar and ½ pint/300ml of the water in the saucepan and bring it to the boil with the lemon peel, stirring as it dissolves into a syrup. Remove the peel and boil the syrup until it reaches hard-ball stage – 246°F on the sugar thermometer.

Meanwhile slake the rice flour with the remaining water. Whisk the egg yolks until light and frothy. Whisk the boiling syrup into the yolks, pouring steadily with one hand and whisking with the other. Stir in the slaked rice flour. Return all to a gentle heat and simmer very gently, stirring all the time with a wooden spoon and paying particular attention to the base of the pan, for about 30 minutes, until the custard is so thick that it holds the trace of the spoon. Pour into a bowl or a jar, cover with clingfilm, and leave to cool and thicken. You can store it in a screwtop jar in the fridge for a couple of weeks – it's lovely just with biscuits.

Next make the meringues. Preheat the oven to 300°F/150°C/Gas 2.

Dissolve the sugar in the water and boil steadily until it reaches the soft-ball stage – 236°F on the sugar thermometer. Meanwhile whisk the egg whites with the lemon juice and salt until they are stiff.

Whisk in the hot syrup, pouring steadily but gradually with one hand, and beating with the other. Go on beating it until it is stiff and beautifully white.

Line the baking trays with foil or rice-paper, and drop on rounded tablespoons of the meringue. Bake for 30 minutes. Leave them in the turned-off oven for 1 hour to dry out.

Sandwich the meringues together with the custard. Serve with a deliciously refreshing cold fruit syrup – lemon or mint, orange or grenadine, or the iced coffee recipe which follows.

ICED COFFEE
Cariocca gelato (Portugal)

Portuguese coffee is excellent – not surprisingly, since the Portuguese were the colonial power of Brazil and still retain strong links. Coffee is served in the *pastelarias* and *cafés de cha* (tea-shops) which serve as meeting places for the town housewives. When you order a coffee in a Portuguese café, a small hour-glass-shaped pot is brought to the table and set over its oven burner – the scent curls down the street, seducing more customers. A *galao* is a tiny cup of strong coffee poured into a glass of hot milk. A *cariocca* is the same tiny strong cup cut 50–50 with water – normally hot, in this case iced.

Quantity: Serves 2.
Time: 10 minutes.
Equipment: A coffee maker. 2 glasses.

2 tablespoons sugar
¼ pint/150ml iced water

¼ pint/150ml freshly-made strong coffee
ice, cubes or crushed, whatever you like

Dissolve the sugar in the coffee. Add the iced water. Fill the glasses with ice and pour in the coffee. Give it a good stir – it will immediately ice down into a lovely refreshing drink, and the coffee-flavour will still be fresh.

LEMON ICE
Gelato di limone (Italy)

Innumerable were the cakes and sweetmeats for which the different convents of Palermo were famous. They prepared them for the various feasts and festivals of the church, and for weddings and receptions. The nuns were among the first to make the ices and sorbets from the snow of Etna. It was the same in Messina, that destroyed centre of seventeenth-century life with its palaces and convents, and in every small town of Sicily and southern Italy. (Sacheverell Sitwell, *Sacred and Profane Love*, 1940)

Quantity: Makes about 2 pints/1.2 litres of sorbet.
Time: Start a few hours ahead, unless you have a *sorbetière*.
Equipment: A saucepan and mixing bowl. A lemon squeezer. An ice-cream maker would be useful. A freezing tray.

| 6 lemons | 8oz/250g granulated sugar |
| 1 pint/600ml water | 1 egg white |

Slice 2 of the lemons and put them in a saucepan with the sugar. Pour in 1 pint/300ml of boiling water and stir until the sugar is dissolved. Strain it after 10 minutes and bring to the boil. Simmer for 8–10 minutes and then put aside to cool.

Squeeze the other 4 lemons and add their juice to the cool syrup. Freeze the syrup until it begins to harden. Beat in the egg white. Freeze it again. When it is once again hard, give it another thorough beating – this time it will nearly double in volume.

Freeze the sorbet until you are ready to serve it.

I like a few mint leaves included with the initial infusion of the lemon in this recipe – it makes it doubly refreshing, and the ice can be prettily decorated with a few mint leaves dipped in water and frosted with sugar. This is a basic water-ice, which can be adapted to any other well-flavoured fruit – if the flavour is not strong enough, include a good squeeze of lemon.

HONEY HARVEST:
ST BARTHOLOMEW'S DAY, AUGUST 24TH

This was the traditional day for collecting honey from domestic bees – when the combs are full of the summer's harvest and the bees are drowsy. In the old days, until the introduction during the course of the sixteenth century of the double-tiered hive, the survival of the swarms was not of paramount interest. Bee-keepers would collect the honey each year by breaking open the hives – clay, wood or straw were the usual materials – and removing the honeycombs, leaving the bees to overwinter without food or shelter. One hive was always left untouched, so that the swarms had some chance to renew themselves the following spring.

Until around 1500, when the more easily storable sugar began to be imported in quantity by town and city dwellers, honey was the only sweetener available to most of Europe. It remained so in country households until well into the nineteenth century. Landowners took part of their rent in honey, and prodigious amounts were used to preserve fruit for the winter, a formula which led to our modern jam-making.

Until the last war, bee-keeping was very much a natural activity of country households – even the smallest kept a hive or two. Sixty-five years ago Dorothy Hartley remembered the honeycombs of her childhood:

Honeycomb taken from the straw skep hives used to be sold in Abergelly market in great bowlfuls. I remember my father bringing in a brown earthenware bowl full of rough chunks of bright yellow comb, glistening and crumpling in deep golden-brown honey, dark as a wall-flower, and rich with perfume; the comb was set at all angles – and had rounded pendulous shapings, large as apples, where the comb had hung down, heavy, within the rounded skep. Such would be the medieval honey, probably set to drip clear into jars and the wax used to harden the candle wax. The same wax, melted and rubbed on, glazed the wood-work, was used to stopper bottles, and had a hundred other uses. The honey was used in the kitchen where we would use sugar, and also for its preservative properties. It was soon known that it would seep through wet parchment, and this system of osmosis was used to make pickles strike through the skin of hams, as well as soften my lady's hands and form a base for her toilet creams and for medical use.

Mead – fermented honey water – was a by-product of bee-keeping and the rituals of honey-production, often a speciality of the medieval monasteries. It was made with the water used to wash the sticky honeycombs after they had been squeezed of their honey – the wax was very valuable and had many domestic uses including candle-making and waterproofing. The fermentation which converted the sugar in the rinsing syrup to alcohol happened spontaneously through the action of a yeast fungus which formed naturally on the straw of the hives, which might survive from one brewing to the next in the wooden utensils – the same ones which were used for beer and cider making. In addition a bit of 'bee-bread', a curious substance made up of plant pollen partly digested by the bees, was added to start the yeasts working.

Central Europe, Britain and Scandinavia – all the populations too far north for vine-growing – brewed mead as well as cider and beer as part of the ordinary store-keeping of the household until well into the nineteenth century. The popularity of fermented honey drinks in seventeenth-century Britain is confirmed by scholar-cook Sir Kenelm Digby, who gives 100 recipes (about half the total) for meads, metheglins and hydromels in his *The Closet Open'd*. Sir Kenelm also had something of a reputation as a necromancer, so perhaps it was a subject which interested him more than most.

The drinking of mead has always been something of a ceremonial occasion, where beer, cider and wine were more of a dietary staple. In classical Rome, which had access to more than enough of Bacchus's favourite brew, it was the libation poured to the gods of love and fertility. In Britain and throughout the Celtic nations, it was part of the stock-in-trade, along with a selection of hallucinogenic mushrooms, of the pre-Christian priesthood.

Cornwall is the last stronghold of the English mead-drinker – the rest of the country having long since succumbed to alternative alcoholic refreshment, their sweet tooth satisfied in other ways. Gulval on St Mount's Bay has recently introduced a Blessing-the-Mead Ceremony to mark the honey-harvest of St Bartholomew's day. It was traditionally drunk from a *mazer*, a carved bowl made from pickled bird's-eye maple, the rim mounted with silver.

Isolated homesteads in northern Finland, about as far north as it is possible to get in Europe, still make mead as part of the normal domestic arrangements – the Finns are in any event relative newcomers to the art of making fermented drinks.

LEMON MEAD
Sima (Finland)

Modern bee-keeping methods are far too sanitized to allow any spontaneous fungi growth, so yeast must be added to the honey syrup to start the action – although I have recently seen some wicker hives in the Greek hinterland which might well harbour the right stuff. Choose your mead-honey with a careful eye to the end result. Heather honey is perfect; failing that, use one of the dry-flower honeys – thyme, rosemary, lavender.

Quantity: Makes 10 pints/6 litres of mead.
Time: Start 3 weeks ahead.
Equipment: A sterilized bucket and lid. A strainer. Bottles.

10 pints/6 litres of water
2oz/50g hops
2oz/50g brewer's yeast

rinds of 2 lemons
1lb/500g honey
1 tablespoon sugar

Bring the water to the boil with the lemon rinds and the hops. Let it cool. Stir in the honey and the yeast dissolved in the sugar.

Pour the mixture into the bucket, lid, and leave for 3–4 days to ferment. Strain, bottle and seal. Leave to mature in a cool place for 3 weeks.

HONEY CHEESECAKE
Melopitta (Greece)

Honey-sweetened curd cakes are the most ancient and primitive of festival foods. Sweetmeats are always the ladies' portion, so it was perfectly appropriate that they should be offered at the shrines of Europe's many goddesses of fertility in pre-Christian days. Greece is famed for its honey, and the island of Siphnos is famed throughout Greece for its skill with this pie, a speciality of feast days – of which the Orthodox calendar has a considerable number.

Quantity: Serves 6.
Time: Start 1 hour ahead. 50 minutes intermittent attention.
Equipment: 2 mixing bowls and a sieve. A rolling pin and a board. A 8–9in/20–22cm diameter pie tin – the Greeks use cheap aluminium pie tins as picnic containers as well, so need to worry less about transporting their pies on alfresco meals.

The pastry
8oz/250g flour
6oz/175g cold butter

½ teaspoon salt
2–3 tablespoons cold water

The filling
1 tablespoon raisins
1lb/500g white curd cheese
3 eggs, lightly forked together

juice and grated rind of 1 orange
6 tablespoons orange-blossom honey
1 teaspoon cinnamon

Sieve the flour with the salt and cut in the butter with a knife. Finish rubbing it in with the tips of your fingers. Work in enough water to give a smooth soft dough. Wrap it up and leave it in the refrigerator for 1 hour. Put the raisins to soak in the orange juice at the same time.

Work all the filling ingredients well together, including the soaked raisins and orange juice – but keep back a little cinnamon to sprinkle on top at the end.

Preheat the oven to 350°F/180°C/Gas 4.

Roll out the pastry on a floured board and use it to line the pie tin. Spread in the filling.

Bake in the oven for 30–35 minutes until the filling is set and the pastry is crisp.

September

OYSTER HARVEST

Although the shellfish season used to open on St James's Day (August 5th in the old calendar), September 1st is now the first day of the oyster season in Britain: the day on which the famous beds of Colchester are ceremonially inspected by the mayor. The royal grant of fishing rights of 1256 is read out, and the mayor and town dignitaries eat gingerbread and drink the reigning monarch's health in good English gin – the only drink to accompany a fine Colchester native. The Oyster Festival itself – a banquet in the town hall, when oysters are eaten – is held on October 20th. Until 1752 the feast took place on October 8th.

To be consumed live and raw, an oyster must be fresh. Hence the strictures against eating them in the summer, when there is no 'r' in the month. Although modern refrigeration methods now make such precautions unnecessary, the custom of seasonality still prevails in Britain. France sees the matter differently and carries on eating oysters in large quantities all year round. The mollusc does its breeding in warm weather, which gives summer oysters rich milky juices. The French call them *laiteuses*, and much appreciate their buttery flavour. Oysters can remain alive for as long as they can keep water in their shells – ten days is perfectly reasonable. The Romans used to carry them, tightly packed to prevent the shells from opening, from the shores of Britain to the tables of the imperial capital.

Oyster-chronicler Hector Bolitho described his visit to the Colchester beds *circa* 1929:

The most splendid ceremonies dedicated to the oyster take place every year at Colchester where the season is opened by the Mayor, who himself goes out in a small boat to help in bringing in the catch. This is followed by a small feast, the merest incident compared with the great Oyster luncheon which is given a little later in the season. For this occasion, famous and clever people are invited to the chamber in the Town Hall, the stained glass windows of which are dedicated to the Roman Emperor and other Royal personages who have smiled on the oysters of Colchester. The fine new plate which appears at the annual Oyster feast spells wealth, and one is able to sigh and rave before a tremendous silver mace into which a felonious Corporation melted all the precious old plate, a hundred years ago. Colchester oysters are so fat, so monstrous fine in taste, their shells so neat and white and sound, that the names of all other fisheries are second thoughts.

The rival beds, across the estuary at Whitstable, found a eulogizer in an anonymous contributor, quite possibly Charles Dickens, to *All the Year Round* for November 1859, which goes some way to explaining the role of the freemen of the town hall in the whole undertaking:

> Whitstable, in Kent, the port of Canterbury, on the estuary of the Thames, exists upon one idea. Its one idea is oysters. It is a town that may be called small, that may be considered well-to-do, that is thoroughly independent, and that dabbles a little in coals, because it has got a small muddy harbour and a single line of railway through the woods to Canterbury, but its best thoughts are devoted to oysters. Its flat coast is occupied by squat wooden houses, made soot-black with pitch, the dwellers in which are sturdy freeholders, incorporated free-fishers, or oyster-dredgers, joined together by the ties of a common birthplace, by blood, by marriage, capital and trade. It has always been their pride, from time out of mind, to live in these dwarfed huts on this stony beach, watching the happy fishing-grounds that lie under the brackish water in the bay, where millions of oysters are always breeding with marvellous fertility, and all for the incorporated company's good. How can the free-dredgers, and the whole town of Whitstable, help thinking of oysters, when so many oysters seem to be always thinking of them?

Two species of oyster are farmed round Europe's shores: the long narrow-shelled Portuguese *Crassostrea* and our own more expensive, finer-flavoured native, *Ostrea edulis*. Oysters have been a staple of the European diet since prehistoric times. They remained the food of the poor until the middle of the nineteenth century, when the beds, including those of Essex, succumbed to over-fishing and pollution – a legacy of the industrial revolution. Even though stocks were slowly replenished and refrigeration made transportation easier than it had ever been, the oyster became a luxury from then on. Today cultivated oysters are fattened in tidal river mouths, where they are alternately washed by sea and fresh water. Wild-gathered oysters, which spend their entire lives in salt water, have a stronger sea flavour. Oysters are graded for sale by size and place of origin. The prized 'green' oysters of Marenne get their emerald tinge from feeding on a particular algae, which also give them a superb flavour.

The opening of the shell-fishing season coincides with the end of the Atlantic fishing season, when the deep-sea boats return to harbour. On the second Friday in September at Musselburgh, Midlothian, and at other fishing ports throughout Scotland, the townsfolk traditionally celebrate the safe homecoming of the seamen by decorating the streets with flowers and bunting, and turning out at midday to cheer a Fishermen's Walk, finishing on the games field with sports – a formalization of a celebration which was as much a part of Europe's annual rhythm as the farmers' harvest festival.

OYSTERS IN THE HALF SHELL
(Britain)

Here is oyster-specialist Hector Bolitho's recommended way with the do-it-yourself feast:

> Let me sketch the scene. In the centre of the table, covered with a clean white cloth up to the top hoop, stands the barrel of oysters. Each gentleman at table finds an oyster-knife and a clean coarse towel by the side of his plate, and he is expected to open oysters for himself and the lady seated by his side, unless she is wise enough to open them for herself. By the side of every plate is the *Panis ostrearius*, the oyster-loaf made and baked purposely for the occasion, and all down the centre

of the table are plates filled with pats of butter, or lemons cut in half, and as many vinegar and pepper castors as the establishment can furnish. As the attendance of servants at such gatherings is usually dispensed with, bottled Bass or Guinness, or any equally unsophisticated pale ale or porter, is liberally provided. Of spirits, only good English gin, or Irish or Scotch whisky are admissible.

From the Romans to the Romantics, however it is served, the oyster holds to its amorous legend. Here is the stuff with which to seduce coy young maidens, to bounce new life into flagging old gentlemen. Oysters, until the native beds gave out, was the Englishman's Christmas Eve feast – whether rich or poor.

Quantity: Allow 6–12 oysters per person.
Time: As long as it takes you to open the oysters.
Equipment: An oyster knife, or a small sturdy kitchen knife, and large plates.

6–12 oysters per person
lemons
spiced chilli vinegar
pepper

bread and butter – thinly cut and buttered
    wholemeal, or crusty chunks
tabasco
crushed ice or rough salt to bed the oysters
    (optional)

An oyster knife, a short dagger-like instrument with a fist-guard, is invaluable for opening the tight-clamped shell. A strong kitchen knife will also do the job – but make sure you have some sticking-plaster handy just in case. Hold the oyster firmly in a clean cloth, and slip the point of the knife in round the side of the hinge. It will open with a gentle pop. Slide the knife across parallel with the top shell and sever the connector muscle, taking care not to lose any of the delicious juices. Then slide the knife under the oyster and sever the bottom muscle.

Serve the oysters – in a bed of ice or rough salt if you have it – in the deep half-shell, with their accompaniments.

Gingerbread for dunking, and a toast drunk in gin should follow.

OYSTER SOUP
(England)

The oyster's aphrodisiac reputation is hard to pin on any single attribute. Everything about the creature contributes. One species is transexual – virile male to ovulating female and back again at the drop of a moon phase. There is, too, its physical appearance: the sharp-ribbed shell rough as chipped granite, enclosing soft smoke-pale flesh. There is the texture – like smooth cold velvet. To clinch it all, there is the scent when the creature is prised open – a heady whiff of seaweed and tide-washed salt-flats. It all adds up to a potent mix.

If the oysters are to be cooked, as here in a soup, the lightest of poaching is all that is necessary – just enough to plump them up and warm them through.

Quantity: Serves 6.
Time: Allow 1 hour intermittent attention.
Equipment: An oyster knife. A large soup-pot. A bowl and a whisk.

24 fresh oysters or 1lb/500g frozen oyster meat	3–4lb/1½ - 2kg white fish bones and heads (try to get a cod head)
2½ pints/1.5 litres water	
1 glass white wine	1 onion, quartered
1 stick celery, washed and roughly chopped	1 carrot, washed and roughly chopped
1 bay leaf	2–3 crushed peppercorns
salt and pepper	2 egg yolks, beaten up with 2 tablespoons thick cream
½ teaspoon nutmeg	

To finish

bread   lemon quarters

De-freeze or shuck the oysters, saving all the liquor.

Put the soup ingredients – fish bones and heads, water, wine, onion, celery, carrot, bay leaf, peppercorns and 1 teaspoon salt – into a large saucepan. Bring to the boil, turn down the heat, lid, and simmer for 30 minutes. Strain out the solids, return the soup to the pan, and boil until reduced to a concentrated 1½ pints/900ml.

Slip the oysters and all their juices into the hot soup. Simmer for 2 minutes only. Take off the heat and beat a ladleful of hot broth into the egg and cream. Stir this mixture into the soup. It will turn pale cream and velvety. Taste and add salt, pepper and nutmeg. Serve the soup immediately, with hot bread and lemon quarters.

SPICE HARVEST

Europe lacks indigenous spices. There are plenty of herbs, but the closest Europe can come to those magic ingredients which transform plain everyday fare into festival food is a handful of aromatics – the seeds of a few familiar umbellifers: dill, caraway, cumin, fennel and celery; plus mustard seed, juniper and a few other lesser home-grown berries. All are replaced with eastern spices at the drop of a merchant's hat.

The Bosphorus was for many centuries the funnel through which the spices of the Indies flowed – a trade which so enriched the pashas of glittering Constantinople and their partners, the merchants of Venice, that in their heyday their palaces rivalled those of their suppliers, the princes of the East, in splendour. It was to feed Europe's hunger for spices, to break the monopoly of the cartel, that Iberia's sailors risked falling off the edge of the world: Vasco da Gama, Magellan and the Genoa-born Columbus were all searching for the way to the spice-wealth of the East Indies when they stumbled into the New World. The West Indies did not yield what they sought, but added chocolate, vanilla, allspice and the vast range of capsicums – from the sweet mild red pepper to the fiery chilli – to Europe's treasure chest.

The housewives of Europe bought their spices from travelling salesmen, who set up their stalls at the autumn markets and the massive medieval fairs at which country people sold their cash-crops and replenished their stores of the goods they could not produce themselves. Salt was bought in the spring, spices before the winter season – in time for the autumn pig-killing and the Christmas baking. Pepper was the most important spice, used in prodigiously large quantities as a preservative, and so highly valued it was an alternative currency and could be used to pay rents. The spice merchants (often called Turkish merchants, whatever their ethnic origin, and who included carpets as part of their stock-in-trade) made the trip to Venice or Istanbul to deal directly with the wholesalers, buying from the quayside as the flat-bottomed barges glided in from the Asian shore of the Bosphorus.

Today the spice-market of Istanbul – since 1930 no longer Constantinople – is still an Aladdin's cave of sensual delights. Ginger-root and grain-of-paradise, fenugreek and cubes, rose-water and jasmine tea, long pepper and liquorice twigs: name your potion, the spice-merchants of Istanbul have been supplying it to their customers since Scheherazade filled the Sultan's nights with her thousand tales. The interior of the market, known as the Egyptian Souk, is arched and dim as a gothic cathedral. Sunlight slants across the shadows of the graceful alleyways. Scented dust is everywhere, drifting from the honeycomb of cells which accommodate the merchants' wares, spiralling into the white domes which tent the vaulted aisles.

The market's business is conducted at leisure. A pair of chess players perch on their pyramids of baskets and tourist souvenirs, oblivious of customers. The game they play made its way from Asia to Europe through this very trading post more than 1,000 years ago: there is no hurry to finish the ancient contest. At a neighbouring stall, loose-robed black-clad peasants and veiled housewives wait patiently for slivers of paprika-crusted dried beef sandwiched between slabs of yellow dense-crumbed bread. It makes a deliciously spicy mid-morning snack – a pleasure completed by a tiny cup of bitter coffee milled to order, brewed in a brass briki and sweetened to the customer's special preference.

But the real business of the Egyptian Souk gleams from every second kiosk, glowing from shadowy shelves, spilling out on to the pavement in open sacks. Even the colours are as rich as jewelled carpets from Isfahan – topaz and tiger's eye, amethyst and onyx – shapes as delicate as the borders round a Persian miniature. The few kiosks which deal in gold jewellery and wedding rings and silks cannot compete with the treasure in the spice-merchants' glass-stoppered jars. Here are all the teas in China stored in wooden boxes, all the herbs of the Mediterranean heaped in baskets, bags of scented rose-petals from Bulgaria, trays of raisins, currants, sultanas and dried figs from Smyrna, jars of sweet and bitter almonds from the Jordan valley; nuts and pulses of every kind; olives and vegetables in a dozen different brine pickles.

The precious spices are weighed out on graceful little brass scales to each customer's order, tiny quantities twisted into scraps of brown paper. Some aromas are familiar, some so odd and ancient it seems impossible they can find buyers: curious twisted roots for medicinal potions, unidentifiable aphrodisiacs for the sultan's mistress.

Trade in the everyday flavours of the Turkish kitchen is brisk: Turkish housewives buy their spices as regularly as they bargain for fruit and vegetables – here is no corner-cupboard hoarding of spice-jars. Cumin seeds are essential for the kebabs on sale on every street corner. Coriander spices eastern marinades and stews (northern Europeans add it to the aquavit). Cardamom perfumes the coffee without which no Turkish conversation is complete. Cinnamon sticks and cassia bark (the poor man's cinnamon), powdered or whole, scent the delicate pastries which are the treats and feast-dishes of the Ottoman kitchen.

There are three kinds of saffron on offer. The most expensive by far is Turkish saffron – the true saffron, the dried stamens of *Crocus sativus* – soporific and aphrodisiac: infuse it in a splash of boiling water for 10 minutes, and use it to perfume rice dishes and fish soups and stews (I also love it in English saffron bread). Turmeric, India's favourite colouring spice, is sold under the name of Indian saffron. Marigold petals, the poor man's saffron (much used in Elizabethan England to colour jellies and puddings) are sold cheaply under the label of Mexican saffron.

Istanbul's spice trade has always been worth a sultan's ransom. The Egyptian Souk itself was built by the beautiful wife of a seventeenth-century Ottoman sultan to endow her new mosque, the Yeni Valide Camii, with a royal tax revenue. The steps of the market lead past the mosque directly to the ancient quays. Here, before bridges spanned the channel which divides the continents, the wooden caiques unloaded their aromatic treasure, to be haggled over and priced before being packed on to donkeys and mules bound for Europe's market-places. Perhaps it was on this same wharf that Alexander's soldiers first acquired a taste for the saffron which their king complained made them so sleepy they could not do battle. Here Vikings traded sea-dried cod for the spices to enliven a dull northern diet. From here Richard Lionheart's Crusaders took home sugar, oranges and spices for English Christmas pies and puddings.

By the sixteenth century the traders of Istanbul had received their first supplies of New World vegetable seeds from their business partners of Venice. Courtesy of the Ottoman conquerors, Hungarians had paprika pepper to plant for the *goulash*; maize flour replaced dried chestnuts in the *mamaliga* of Romania; and the green-fingered Bulgarians, acknowledged master-gardeners of eastern Europe, cultivated all the new vegetables for the stew-pot *ghivetch*: potatoes and squash, haricot beans and pumpkins.

The spice-traders of Istanbul can still sell you the very perfumes Helen chose to scent her marriage bed at Troy, that same incense Cleopatra burned to conquer Caesar. They have traded such goods ever since founding-father Byzas, on advice from the Delphic oracle, first pitched camp on Homer's Threshold of Felicity.

SPICE MIXTURES

Make up your own spice mixtures each autumn – keep them no longer than a year. Store them in tightly-stoppered ceramic jars. If you use glass, keep them in a dark cupboard – spices lose their colour in the light.

Quantity: approx. 8oz/250g each mixture.
Time: 10 minutes.
Equipment: Storage jars.

For the peppermill
3oz/75g black peppercorns
1oz/25g allspice (sometimes called Jamaica pepper)
1oz/25g grains-of-paradise

3oz/75g white peppercorns (these are mature berries stronger in flavour than black pepper)

Mixed spice for cakes
3oz/75g powdered cinnamon
2oz/50g powdered allspice
pinch of ground black pepper

2oz/50g powdered ginger
1oz/25g powdered cloves

Mixed spice for marinades
1oz/25g ground cloves
1oz/25g ground white pepper
½oz/12g ground cumin
½oz/12g ground cardamom
1oz/25g powdered thyme

1½oz/40g ground coriander seeds
½oz/12g cayenne pepper
½oz/12g ground ginger
½oz/12g powdered lavender
1oz/25g powdered rosemary

Mix each group of spices together, bottle and label.

STUFFED BONITO
Bonito domasi (Turkey)

The striped bonito or skipjack tuna migrate down the Bosphorus to and from their spawning grounds in the Sea of Marmora. When the churning shoals are sighted in spring or autumn – indigo and emerald backs humping high above the waves, silvery white flanks flashing as they hurl themselves through the narrow waters – every able-bodied man and boy in Istanbul and the teeming villages beyond drops everything and grabs a rod and line, not to return to his office, shop, bank or building site until he has a bucketful of the fish. The old men who sit shucking mussels under the Galata bridge, hard by the spice market, will tell you that it was for this rich harvest that the Golden Horn was named, not for any romantic talk of sunsets on ochre stones, or sunken treasure ships of Byzantine emperors.

At other times, the tuna's cousin the mackerel – also plentiful in the Bosphorus – is used for the dish. But the pink-fleshed bonito is the best of all.

Quantity: Serves 6.
Time: About 1 hour intermittent attention.
Equipment: A baking dish which will accommodate the whole fish. Aluminium foil.

1 whole middle-sized bonito (about 2lb/1kg cleaned weight), or a salmon trout	salt and pepper
	3 tablespoons butter or oil
1 medium onion, skinned and finely chopped	1 clove garlic, skinned and finely chopped
2oz/50g pine kernels	4oz/100g rice
2oz/50g raisins	1 teaspoon powdered cinnamon
½ teaspoon powdered ginger	1 tablespoon chopped parsley
½ pint/300ml fish stock or plain water	

Wipe the bonito and trim off the sharp fins. If you are feeling spirited, remove the backbone – press down on the bone to loosen it before you slip in a sharp filleting knife. Take care not to cut the skin of the back. Sprinkle the fish inside and out with salt.

Melt the butter or warm the oil in a frying pan. Stir in the onion, garlic and pine kernels, and fry gently for a few minutes. Stir in the rice and fry until it is no longer opaque. Stir in the raisins, spices, and parsley, and pour in the stock or water. Allow it all to bubble up, turn down the heat and leave to simmer gently for 15 minutes, until most of the liquid has been absorbed. The rice should still have a firm bite.

Stuff the belly of the bonito with the rice pilau. Wrap it in aluminium foil and bake it in the oven at 350°F/180°C/Gas 4 for 35–40 minutes.

FROZEN SALEP
(Turkey)

This delicately scented ice-cream is made with vanilla-flavoured milk thickened with the dried powdered root of ground orchids – salep. The preparation used to be Europe's universal pick-me-up – Charles Lamb wrote an essay in praise of it, and it was the Victorian cab-driver's preferred hot drink. Western Europe's ground orchids are now largely protected species, so it is only in eastern Europe that the plants are still gathered – and only in their markets that salep is on sale. The fresh root has a higher protein content than fillet steak. Salep is expensive, but a teaspoonful will thicken and flavour a pint of milk.

Quantity: Serves 4.
Time: Start a few hours ahead.
Equipment: A medium saucepan. A whisk. An ice-cream maker would be useful.

1 teaspoon salep (potato starch or cornflour might substitute)
2 tablespoons runny honey

1 pint/600ml rich milk
½in/1cm vanilla pod

To finish
powdered cinnamon

1 tablespoon crushed pistachios (*optional*)

Slake the salep powder, starch or flour in a splash of milk. Pour it into a saucepan with the rest of the milk, add the vanilla pod, and bring to the boil. Turn the heat down and simmer for 3–4 minutes, until the milk thickens. Stir in the honey, and let the mixture cool. Remove the vanilla pod, scrape out the little black seeds, and mix them back in. Freeze the mixture quickly – it can separate if you leave it too long. Take it out when it firms up and give it a good whisking. Refreeze.

To serve, spoon it out and mound it up prettily, sprinkled with cinnamon and – if you like – crushed pistachios, a very Turkish pleasure.

MAIZE HARVEST

Mary Eyre, impecunious Victorian foot-traveller in the south-east of France, visited Bagnères-de-Bigorre in the autumn of 1862. She was intrigued by the many uses of maize – a New World import, which took happily to the Old World climate and is now a staple throughout the Mediterranean and the Balkans.

When the cobs of Indian corn are gathered, they are plaited together while the stalks and leaves are pliant, and suspended from the balcony roofs, exposed on one side to a current of air. They keep better thus than in a closed granary, and look very ornamental and pretty besides. As they are wanted, the strings of maize are taken down and the cobs cut off them, and the plaited band left serves to make mats, which when new, are white-looking and pretty, and wear well. Every part of the Indian wheat seems valuable; the tender leaves are stripped off the plant while it is yet growing, as fodder for the cattle, and the ears seemed to ripen best when thus exposed to the sun and air. The mattresses throughout France are made of the inner husk, or soft leaf, enveloping the cob. They make the cleanest and softest mattresses I ever slept on; and even poor people usually have the case washed, and refilled with fresh leaves, once a year. The very refuse of the cob is serviceable, and is sold after the grains have been shelled off with a knife, under the denomination of *charbon blanc*. It burns out very rapidly, of course, but throws out great heat, and is very useful in lighting a reluctant fire.

MAIZE CAKE WITH RAISINS AND PRUNES
Millassou perigourdin (.France)

This is the celebration cake of the Périgord, where maize has been grown since the sixteenth century. The cobs are harvested when fully ripe as a grain for milling – they are not usually eaten young as sweetcorn. Cornmeal dough is used to fatten geese for *foie-gras*, a cottage industry in the area, a delectable winter treat which keeps fine company with the other speciality of the Périgord, the black truffle. For the rest, the cornmeal is made into porridges in most areas. In the Périgord there is a dumping, *la mique sarladaise*, which is served with rich stews such as *civet de lièvre*. Provence uses it as an alternative to chickpea flour in the *panisso*. The Franche-Comté has its *gaudes*, a cornmeal porridge; and the Pyrenees has a bread, the *broyo*.

Quantity: Makes 1 cake.
Time: Start 30 minutes ahead. 45 minutes cooking time.
Equipment: 2 bowls and a whisk. A cake tin.

1lb/500g cornmeal	8oz/250g flour
½ teaspoon salt	8 fl oz/200ml warm milk
1 oz/25g softened butter or goose-fat	4oz/100g raisins, pipped
4oz/100g prunes, stoned and chopped	1 small glass eau-de-vie or brandy
3 eggs, separated	4oz/100g caster sugar

Toss the cornmeal with the flour and the salt and mix in the warm milk and the softened butter or goose-fat. Leave the mixture to swell for 30 minutes. At the same time put the dried fruit to soak in the eau-de-vie or brandy.

Whisk the egg yolks with the sugar until white and fluffy. Fold the mixture into the flour with the dried fruit and its soaking liquor.

Whisk the egg whites until stiff, and fold them in.

Preheat the oven to 350°F/180°C/Gas 4.

Butter a cake tin and spread in the mixture. Bake it for 45 minutes, until golden and spongy. Serve warm, with a glass of sweet white wine.

CHESTNUT HARVEST

Where there are mountains and pigs in the uplands of Europe, there are likely to be sweet-chestnut groves. The tree was introduced to Britain by the Romans, and it has long been an important food item in Mediterranean countries – both as the whole nut and ground into flour, as well as for fattening the wild-foraging pigs who were turned out into the groves each autumn when the gathering was complete. After the arrival of the New World vegetables, the chestnut gave ground on the peasant table to the more prolific and more easily cultivated Indian corn, which replaced it in many recipes.

Sacheverell Sitwell, in pre-war Spain, visited the little town of Jabugo in the mountains to the west of Seville, where the pigs were still foraging free.

Jabugo is famous for two products, chestnuts and dried hams, the one of which feeds the other. The chestnuts ripen at the end of the summer, and are then shaken with long poles from the trees which are planted on steep slopes so that their round prickly-cased nuts roll down-hill. The nuts can then be easily gathered by the women and children who wait with spread cotton sheets at the bottom. The nuts are exported fresh, or dried locally for winter use. The lean red pigs of Andalusia are taken to forage in the gleanings, and their hams are salted and dried in the cold clean air of the Sierra Morena. These are the 'black' hams, the most prized hams of Spain.

The chestnut harvest he described was still being gathered in much the same way when I visited Jabugo a few years ago. The inhabitants dry the chestnuts and add them to their winter *potajes* and stews, and mill it into flour to make a thick winter soup flavoured with ham bones.

The French are not so easily content, and confect delicious *pavés* and *marrons glacés* with the harvest. Mary Eyre, button-booted Victorian lady traveller, took a walk in the chestnut groves of southern France on October 13th 1862:

I have taken my last long walk at Argèles. A little lane near the church soon leads one into an upper road parallel to, but above, that which leads to Pierrefitte; this led me into a noble chestnut wood, nearly three miles long, and some of the trees were really majestic. The chestnut crop was already gathered, and a drove of pigs and a few merry children were contesting for the stray fallen ones hidden under the leaves. It is customary here to drive the pigs into the chestnut woods after the gathering is over, and the refuse fattens them well. Every commune seems, as at the English lakes, to have a certain portion of uncultivated land on the mountain side belonging to it, where the wood for the district is procured. The acorns are considered a crop, and the pigs from one village must not eat acorns off the lands belonging to another commune. Chestnuts are also *a récolte*, they are not considered fruit, but as an article of food, and are commonly sold ready roasted and stripped of the husk in the markets. They are also often parboiled; the rich adding a small quantity of vanilla to them in boiling.

CHESTNUT CAKE
Castanhet (France)

This vanilla-scented cake was traditionally served at the conclusion of the festival meal which marks the gathering in of the chestnut harvest in the Ardèche, famous for its hams and sausages, and the neighbouring Cévennes on the southern edge of France's high central plateau.

Quantity: Serves 8.
Time: 1 hour.
Equipment: A saucepan. A food processor or sieve. A bowl and whisk. An 8in/20cm cake tin.

2lb/1kg chestnuts (fresh, or dried and soaked overnight)
2–3 drops vanilla essence
2 eggs

½ teaspoon salt
1oz/25g butter
6oz/175 sugar

To finish
icing sugar

Peel the chestnuts and put them to boil in plenty of lightly salted water. Drain them when they are soft – being fresh, this should not take more than 20 minutes. Drain and peel off the soft inner skin as soon as they are cool enough to handle. Pound them to a paste in the food processor – otherwise you will have to push them through a sieve. Beat in the butter while they are still warm and add the vanilla essence.

Whisk the eggs with the sugar and stir them into the purée. Tip the mixture into a buttered cake tin. Bake the cake for 30 minutes at 350°F/180°C/Gas 4, until firm.

Tip the cake out on to a plate, and leave it to cool overnight. Dust it with icing sugar before serving.

It's lovely with *crème fraîche* or whipped cream soured with a spoonful of thick yogurt. Accompany the cake with a small glass of Chartreuse.

CORK HARVEST

The stripping of the cork-bark was a major event in the rural Andalucian community in which I and my young family lived for many years. Smuggling, cork-harvesting and tuna fishing had been the main industries for centuries. Only the cork remained by the mid-seventies: cigarettes and contraceptives, the smugglers' moneyspinners under Franco's puritanical regime, were more readily available as restrictions on imports were lifted, and the tuna shoals had succumbed to the deep-sea trawlers long before they reached the inshore fleet of my local port of Tarifa.

The cork was harvested in rotation every seven years, and the skilled strippers moved from one area to the next. Since my house was buried in the middle of the handsomest and largest cork-oaks in the valley, my turn inevitably came round. The strippers were contracted, the price agreed, and the men appeared at dawn one autumn morning, in company with the local herd of semi-wild pigs of the small nimble Iberian breed, which left no juicy acorn nor tender-rooted fruit tree unturned in my garden each year.

As the cork was stripped, the landscape underwent a surprising change: suddenly we were surrounded not by the familiar thick-trunked silver-barked giants which protected us from the *levante*, the wild wind from the east which the locals swore caused all miscreant behaviour – but by a crowd of brick-red naked boles, their upper branches clad in pale cork-bark – limp-wristed as débutantes in white gloves. The cork grew back, of course, slowly and steadily, each year thicker and more silvery, but it took the next seven years to do so.

The ancient cork-oak forests of Spain, Portugal, and Provence between them satisfy Europe's appetite for cork. In 1926 Douglas Goldring watched the cork-strippers at work in the forest of Les Maures, near St Tropez:

The cork-tree, which the Saracens are said to have introduced to Provence, retains its leaf for two years. It has a double covering of bark, and it is only the outer covering which can be removed without destroying the life of the tree. The cork-oak is first skinned when it is from twenty to twenty-five years old. From five to ten years later it is then peeled a second time. The third and best harvest takes place when the tree is from forty to forty-five years old. The bark is cut from the ground to a height of about six feet, leaving visible the dark red inner bark. What is cut off is plunged into boiling water for half an hour and then cut into strips and squares. It is again boiled for a quarter of an hour, and then dried slowly. After that it is not touched again for six months. At the end of which time it is cut into the shapes desired. The waste pieces are ground into powder, which is then spread upon sailcloth and made into cork carpet.

Rodney Gallop followed the cork-stripping gangs in southern Portugal, *circa* 1936:

Like all poor folk in Portugal the Alentejan peasants live with great simplicity. Only on feast days do they eat meat, chicken or eggs. All that they can produce is sold in the market. In the *Serra de Monfurado* a labourer's dinner or supper consists of vegetable soup and a scrap of garlic sausage varied with macaroni or beans, kept in home-made Thermos containers of cork. Throughout the Alentejo, work in the fields, olive groves and cork woods is organized on traditional lines. The cork-stripping, in particular, is a highly skilled operation. With easy virtuosity, the *tiradores* hack through the bark with their double axes without injuring the tender core of the tree and peel it off as clean as a cast-off snakeskin. Their foreman (*Maioral* or *menageiro*) is obeyed with the strictest discipline in his administration of the rules, some of them very curious.

An elaborate ritual centres round the midday meal. This is served in a huge cauldron. The men stand round with their hats on and spoons in their hands. The *maioral* takes the first spoonful, after which the place where he had dipped his spoon is left to the last. The others advance in turn, help themselves, take three steps backwards and eat. No complaints are allowed, and every scrap must be finished.

CORK-STRIPPER'S POTTAGE
Sopa de grão (Portugal)

The province of Alentejo, to the south and east of Lisbon, covers half the total area of Portugal. The cork-oak forests are in the south, abutting on my own cork-oak forests of Andalucía. Portugal and Spain share a skill in constructing these delicious thick pulse and vegetable stews – this version comes from the Alentejana province. The cork-stripping gangs in my area doubled up as charcoal burners, and their midday soup was put to stew gently over the charcoal fire while the men completed the morning's work. The local baker made them special 6lb/3-kilo loaves to take into the hills – often they had to travel great distances without roads, and were away, sleeping in the forest, for four or five days at a time. Wild greens were often stirred into the soup at the end – wild cabbage, thistle rosettes and turnip tops. The flavour of wild plants is stronger than their cultivated cousins.

Quantity: Serves 6–8.
Time: Start the night before. 15 minutes to prepare, 4–5 hours slow cooking.
Equipment: A large soup-pot.

1lb/500g chickpeas, soaked overnight
1 whole head of garlic
½ teaspoon coriander seeds
1–2 short lengths ham bone or 1 bacon knuckle
1 stick celery, chopped
4oz/100g cured Portuguese *chourico* or any
  paprika-spiced dried sausage, sliced
2 tablespoons chopped mint

3 pints/2 litres cold water
1 bay leaf
6–8 black peppercorns
1–2 onions, peeled and roughly chopped
1 carrot, washed and chopped
4 tablespoons chopped fresh coriander (in Europe
  only Portugal and Cyprus use it) or parsley
1 tablespoon chopped oregano or marjoram

To finish

2–3 large potatoes, peeled and chunked

salt and pepper

8oz/250g spinach, washed and shredded

2 tablespoons olive oil

Drain the chickpeas and put them in a pan with the water. Bring all to the boil. Skim off the grey foam.

Singe the garlic head in a flame until the papery covering blackens at the edges and the air is filled with the fine scent of roasting garlic. Throw it in with the chickpeas. Add the bay leaf, coriander seeds, peppercorns and ham bone or bacon – the onions, celery, carrot, sausage, and herbs can go in after the first hour. Bring to the boil, turn down the heat, lid and cook for 2–3 hours, until the chickpeas are quite soft.

Keep the soup at a gentle boil – don't let the temperature drop – and don't add salt, as if you do the chickpeas never seem to soften. If you need to add water, make sure it is boiling. 30 minutes before the end of cooking, add the potatoes. 10 minutes before the end, stir in the spinach.

Just before you are ready to serve, add salt and pepper and stir in the olive oil.

Pour the richly scented stew into a beautiful cork-thermos, and take it out into the forest. Accompany with thick chunks of dense-crumbed country bread and plenty of the dark strong red wine of rural Portugal. A big piece of watermelon completes the autumn pleasure.

MICHAELMAS: SEPTEMBER 29TH

The feast of St Michael and All the Angels should rightly be celebrated with a fine roast goose, and with many of the nut-cracking and fire festivities now shifted to Bonfire Night. The festival has dropped out of fashion in recent years in Britain – maybe because the mail-clad fist and hell-fire of the Lord's principal strong arm is no longer the way the Church likes to present itself. The day remains a quarter-day – on which, in law and commerce, rents are collected and contracts fall due – for the non-Celtic people of Europe.

St Michael is the patron saint of Germany, and his feast-day coincides with the date on which the ancient Germans held their annual gathering, the Thing, at which laws were made and disputes settled.

The goose with which the holy day was celebrated remains an obdurately seasonal bird. Modern husbandry and test-tube farming have no power over its reproductive cycle – whatever the weather and hormones, the bird cannot be persuaded to breed out of turn. A goose, you can bet the tar-and-gravel boots in which it once marched to market, is five months old at Michaelmas.

The Michaelmas goose fairs which survive in Britain – Palmer and Lloyd, writing in 1972, list fairs at Nottingham, Abingdon, and Bedford – are often held a week or so into October since they acknowledged the old calendar. They are now recreation days, and lack the star turn itself.

ROAST GOOSE WITH QUINCES
(Britain)

A Michaelmas goose will weigh from 9–12lb/4.5–6kg (the bones are heavy, but the meat is rich). Medieval cooks included quinces and garlic in the stuffing, and served the bird with a strong garlic sauce spiked with sour grape juice. The stuffing in the cavity keeps the bird moist during the long cooking, and, served as a sauce, provides a counterpoint to the richness of the meat.

Quantity: Serves 8.

Time: 20 minutes attention. 3½–4 hours to cook.

Equipment: An oven rack and a large roasting tin. A small saucepan.

1 goose	salt and pepper
1lb/500g cooking apples	2–3 quinces
1lb/500g onions	2–3 garlic cloves
1 sprig sage	

To finish

sugar	4 tablespoons breadcrumbs
1 tablespoon chopped sage	redcurrant jelly, port (*optional*)

Wipe the goose and trim off excess fat from the interior cavity. Salt and pepper the bird inside and out, and tie two pieces of the fat over the breast.

Heat the oven to 350°F/180°C/Gas 4.

Peel, quarter and core the apples and quinces. Peel and quarter the onions and the garlic. Stuff the goose with the apple and quince in one end, and the onion, garlic and sage in the other end. Sew up the cavity, and put the bird breast down on a rack in the oven, over a dripping tray. Pour a mug of boiling water over the bird and into the tray.

After 30 minutes, turn the bird breast up. Prick the skin (not through to the flesh), particularly round the throat and the base of the wings to let the fat run. The goose will need 3½–4 hours total roasting, depending on its weight, which includes the stuffing. Pour out the goose-fat regularly – basting the bird when you do so.

Splash a little cold water over the bird 10–15 minutes before the end of the cooking – this will crisp the skin. When you judge your goose cooked, thrust a skewer into the base of the thigh – if the juice runs pink it is not yet done, if it runs clear, it is ready.

Remove the goose and take out its stuffing – don't mix the apple-quince with the onion-garlic. Transfer the goose to a warm serving dish and leave it to rest in a turned-off oven for 20 minutes for the meat to firm up. Heat the fat from the roasting tin in a small pan, sprinkle in a little flour, and splash in ½ pint/300ml well-flavoured stock to bubble up and make the gravy – a tablespoon of redcurrant jelly and a splash of port will do wonders for it.

Mash the apples and quinces into a purée. Taste, add a little sugar if necessary and transfer them to a pretty dish. Chop the onion and garlic and mash with the breadcrumbs and chopped sage. Taste, add salt and pepper and transfer the mixture to another dish.

Carve the bird in long thin slices parallel to the breastbone. Serve with the apple sauce and sage-and-onion handed separately.

STUFFING BALLS

(Britain)

Savoury stuffing balls, cooked under the roast, serve the same function as the old bread-puddings and dumpling (including Yorkshire pudding) – to make the meat go further. They are so good – rich and fragrant with the meat juices – that they now appear in their own right.

Quantity: Serves 8.
Time: Start 1 hour before the end of cooking. About 15 minutes.
Equipment: A small frying pan. A mixing bowl.

4–5 slices bread
1 small onion
1 tablespoon goose dripping
grated rind of 1 lemon
½ teaspoon salt

the goose liver, gizzard and heart, cleaned and
  trimmed
1 egg
2oz/50g blanched almonds
pepper

Soak the bread in a little water and squeeze it dry. Chop the goose lights and the onion finely, and fry both lightly in the goose dripping.

Work all the stuffing ingredients together well and roll the mixture into small balls. Drop them into the pan under the goose to roast in the drippings for the last 40 minutes of the cooking time, turning them so that they brown all over. Serve with the goose.

POTATOES IN GOOSE-DRIPPING
(Britain)

Goose-fat is snowy white and very pure – the Romans valued it more highly than butter. It's lovely for frying. In Britain in the old days, the drippings were saved, purified, and used, lightly perfumed with home-distilled flower-fragrances, for face-creams.

Quantity: Serves 8.
Time: About 40 minutes intermittent attention.
Equipment: A saucepan. A colander. A heavy frying pan.

3lb/1.5kg old potatoes   6 tablespoons goose dripping

Peel and quarter the potatoes. Boil them in plenty of salted water until they are soft but still whole. Drain thoroughly.

Melt the dripping in a heavy frying pan. Sauté the potatoes over a gentle heat, turning regularly, until they are beautifully crisp and brown.

SWEDE PURÉE
(Britain)

Yellow turnips or rutabaga have been known as Swedish turnips since they arrived in Britain from Sweden at the end of the eighteenth century. Unlike the white turnip, they do not go woody in the middle: the Scots continue to call them turnips or neeps, and love them mashed up with potatoes.

Quantity: Serves 8.
Time: Allow 45 minutes intermittent attention.

Equipment: A saucepan. A potato-masher. A baking dish.

3lb/1.5kg swedes	3oz/75g butter
¼ pint/150ml milk (cream is even nicer)	2 eggs
salt and pepper	

Peel the swedes and cut them into large chunks. Boil the pieces in plenty of salted water until soft – about 20 minutes.

Drain the swedes well and put them in a liquidizer with the butter and the milk. Process thoroughly until everything is reduced to a purée. Add the eggs and process again. If you have no liquidizer, push the swedes through a sieve and then beat in the butter, milk and eggs. Season with salt and freshly ground pepper.

Fill a straight-sided soufflé dish with the mixture – it should come two-thirds of the way up. Put the dish in the oven (with the goose) for 15–20 minutes: this will set the purée and allow it to rise like a modest soufflé.

PEASE SOUP
(Britain)

The goose carcass springs to new life in an old-fashioned pea soup for the day after Michaelmas. Pease soup and pottage – thickened with flour or breadcrumbs and boiled in a cloth – was a popular poor man's food until the eighteenth century, when potatoes largely replaced it as a belly-warmer.

Quantity: Serves 4.
Time: Allow 1 hour intermittent attention.
Equipment: A large saucepan with a lid.

the goose carcass	1 onion
3 cloves	2 carrots
2 sticks lovage (a rather neglected herb) or celery	8oz/250g split peas
black peppercorns	salt
2 large potatoes	1 slice cabbage or greens

Put the stripped carcass in a deep saucepan. Cover with cold water. Add the onion, peeled and stuck with the cloves, and the carrots and lovage or celery, scrubbed and cut into short lengths.

Bring to the boil, turn down the heat and leave for 1½ hours at least to simmer to a strong stock. Strain out the bones and return 2½ pints/1.5 litres of stock to the pan.

Stir in the split peas, add the peppercorns, and bring back to the boil. Simmer until the peas are soft – 50–60 minutes should be plenty. Add the peeled, diced potatoes after 30 minutes and the cabbage or greens, washed and chopped, 10 minutes before the end of the cooking time. Season before serving.

GRAPE HARVEST: SEPTEMBER–OCTOBER

Whoever can claim credit for the discovery that the fermented juice of the grape is the perfect antidote to an excess of reality, the wine harvests of Europe have been the occasion for a celebration for 3,000 years – at least since Homer's time. The early wine-makers of Greece had a powerful ally in Zeus's favourite son Dionysus, who, as a suffering god who died and was resurrected for the sake of his worshippers, was expected to relieve man of his sorrows – particularly in the guise of his *alter ego*, Bacchus.

The consensus of the ancient world was strongly in favour of liquor, whatever the religious allegiance of its devotees. King Solomon recommended his cellar's restorative qualities to the fathers of the Old Testament, particularly those who had come to the end of their allotted five-score-years-and-ten: 'Give strong drink unto him that is ready to perish, and wine unto them that be of heavy hearts. Let him drink, and forget his poverty, and remember his misery no more.'

Plato, schooling his pupils in the shade of an Athenian olive grove some 400 years before Christ celebrated the first Eucharist of bread and wine, agreed with the King on the fortifying virtues of the nectar of dreams:

When a man is verging on the forties, we shall tell him, after he has finished banqueting, to invoke the gods, and more particularly, to ask the presence of Dionysus in that sacrament and pastime of advancing years – I mean the wine cup – which he bestowed on us as a comfortable medicine against the dryness of old age, that we might renew our youth.

The Romans adopted Bacchus and his riotous youth-giving festival, and the soil of Italy was so well suited to the growth of the vine that its wines rapidly outclassed all others. Pliny, who disapproved of the effect of wine on his contemporaries, nevertheless devoted one whole volume of his *Historia Naturalis* to the matter of wine-making – listing in the first century BC the best wine-making areas, in order of merit, as Italy, Greece, Egypt and Gaul. The Romans took their wine-making skills with them wherever they colonized – Spain and Britain, Germany, Austria, Hungary, Romania, Bulgaria. The Christian Church, anxious to convert the heathen outposts of Europe and administer her Sacrament of Holy Communion, completed the circle – taking her chalice to the cold north of Scandinavia, the misty islands of the Celts, and eventually to win souls in the New World. At home, the monasteries, perceiving the minor sins of the flesh as preferable to the major sin of the spirit, concentrated on improving the quality of life, and distilled the products of their vineyards into eaux-de-vie. Dionysus would have been well pleased.

Naturally the grapes of Europe are not all harvested simultaneously. The time of gathering depends on several factors – the type of wine to be made, the climate in which the grapes grow to maturity, the height above sea-level at which the vineyards have been planted.

In southern France the grapes are harvested early – between September 10th and 24th. But the wine co-operatives of the Midi, mindful of the tourist trade and the profitability of selling their wines *en vente directe*, have scheduled their wine-harvest celebrations to coincide with the summer season – they hold them in July and August, and the festival has become an organized commercially oriented event, rather than the merry *bacchanale* of the old days. The harvesters are nowadays seasonal workers, without the old traditions, so there is little continuation of the old celebrations – unless it might be in the vaulted kitchen of a peasant-farming household, where there is still a patch of vines among the sorgum plantations, and the grandfather still holds a licence to distil his own eau-de-vie. Then the *souper de vendange* – a magnificent *pot-au-feu* served with all its many relishes – still loads the long scrubbed kitchen table after the grapes have been gathered.

The dry straw-pale wines of Andalucía, particularly those of Jerez, have been a favourite British import since Sir Francis Drake made off, in 1587, with the supplies earmarked for the Spanish Armada. Shakespeare's Falstaff concurred with Plato and Solomon on the virtues of wine as a restorative:

> A good sherris-sack hath a two-fold operation in it. It ascends me into the brain; dries me there all the foolish and dull and crudy vapours which environ it; makes it apprehensive, quick, forgettive, full of nimble fiery and delectable shapes; which deliver'd o'er to the voice, the tongue, which is the birth, becomes excellent wit. The second property of your excellent sherris is, the warming of the blood; which, before cold and settled, left the liver white and pale, which is the badge of pusillanimity and cowardice; but the sherris warms it . . . If I had a thousand sons, the first humane principle I would teach them should be, to forswear thin potations, and to addict themselves to sack.

The official date for the start of the harvest of the Palomino vines which apron the whitewashed town of Jerez is September 8th – the Feast of the Nativity of the Virgin Mary. Nowadays the moment for the gathering-in is selected by more scientific methods. The date in early September for the official celebration of *vendemmia* is declared in advance: a merry occasion marked by a parade of horsemen – the Jerezanos' other passion – and a festival of *flamenco* and *cante jondo*. As for the festival's food, it is taken mainly as tapas, that peripatetic feast of little dishes – a square of potato omelette, a single plump pink prawn, a handful of olives, a plate of paper-thin salt-cured ham, a heap of juicy shellfish, a dab of the dish-of-the-day – which accompanies the glasses of cold dry wine in every bar in the town.

The German harvest, the *Weinlese*, is marked by wine festivals and public tastings up and down the Rhine, the Aar and the Mosel. In the Tyrol, as harvest approaches, the vineyards are traditionally guarded from malignant spirits – and light-fingered passers-by – by a watchman, the magnificently attired *Saltner*, resplendent in scarlet tunic, leather jerkin, white knit stockings and a huge tricorn hat decorated with peacock and cock feathers, with squirrels' tails and foxes' brushes dangling down: quite enough to scare the daylights out of the living, let alone the dead.

Further to the east in pre-war Hungary – still, in the 1920s, relatively untouched by the hand of commercialization which was soon to change wine-making methods everywhere – Károly Viski remembered the harvests of his youth. The grapes which produce Hungary's heavy honeyed sweet wines, including those of Tokay, are harvested late – well into October. The grapes need all the autumn sun they can gather. The grape harvest, the *szuret*, was also the time for celebrating weddings on new bread and new wine.

> Every peasant vineyard, even if only half an acre in size, has its own cellar built into a hill, before which is a porch with a fireplace. People go there very frequently to sit about, roast bacon, drink a few glasses of wine and smoke. In some places whole villages grow up in the vineyards, called hill-villages. Their laws are even more strict than those of the other villages. The Turks, in spite of Mohamed's prohibition on wine, did not interrupt these activities for the 250 years they were in residence.
>
> The vineyards, which are carefully guarded and deadly quiet in the late autumn, are seething with life at the time of gathering the grapes. The hills seem to move, coloured patches swarm about on them, songs resound, guns go off. The rattles and whips for frightening birds are now used to frighten the female part of the assembly. Today is the day of gaiety and unrestrained noise.

The gypsy fiddler plays.

The door of the cellar is open, the wine from last year and the year before takes effect. In the open space before the cellar the paprika stew simmers; the stuffed cabbage, brought from home, is warmed up, and those whose appetite has been taken away by the grapes can still put it right before dinner with wonderful fragrant peach brandy. The table is laid on grass on which blossom good appetite, toasts and later on discussions about politics. Sometimes the *szuret* continues at home and in more than one place it is followed by a hot supper, its end being well after midnight.

The owner of a large vineyard engages workers paid by the day. According to ancient custom they make an enormous grape bouquet, such a big one that two people have to carry it on their shoulders on a pole. Soon there is a whole procession. The gypsies go in front playing gay dance tunes, after come a few players, who do all kinds of comic turns, then the gatherers of the grapes, then a few girls dressed in white surrounding the enormous cluster-like grape bouquet. The girls wear wreaths made of wild flowers and pass through the village dancing, singing and shouting, drinking from flasks as they go. In the farmer's house they hang the grapes on the ceiling, and they are then given a good meal. The best ceremonies are to be had in the best wine-growing districts – the festivities of the district of Tokaj and the little town of Ma'd are famous.

Patrick Leigh Fermor helped at a modern Bacchanalia in pre-war Crete, pouring the wine into casks resinated to make them leak-proof:

Scores of skins exploded and the juice squirted between our toes . . . In a minute or two a mauve-pink trickle crossed the stone lip of the spout, and dripped into the waiting tub; the trickle broadened, the drops became a stream and curved into a splashing arc . . . We were handed glasses of the sweet juice which already – or was this imagination? – had a corrupt and ghostly tang of fermentation. When the stream slackened, the manhood of the treaders, shuffling calf-deep in a tangled slush by now and purple to the groin, was jovially impugned . . . For days the sweet heady smell of the must hangs over the village. All is sticky to the touch, purple splashes and handprints on the whitewash and spilt red rivulets between the cobbles and the clouds of flies suggest a massacre. Meanwhile, in the dark crypts of the houses, in huge grooved Minoan amphorae, the must grumbles and hits out and fills the house with unnerving fumes and a bubbling noise like the rumour of plots, a dark conspiracy of whispers. For as long as this vaulted collusion lasts, a mood of swooning and Dionysiac laxity roves the air.

By 1984 in Italy, when Eric Newby harvested his own Tuscan vineyard, he shared the vendemmia dinner with his neighbours.

We always help four families with the *vendemmia*. The harvesting of the grapes usually takes one or two days; the fermentation takes about ten days. To be asked to help is an honour because it means that we are regarded as hard workers, and therefore earn the prodigious quantities of wine and food that are served throughout the *vendemmia*.

At about a quarter to one we go back to the house for the midday meal, by which time we have, temporarily at least, had enough. Sometimes, if it is hot, we eat at a long table outside in the yard, but usually we are in the parlour with great black and white photographs of ancestors on the walls.

We eat *brodo*, broth, made with beef or chicken stock, with pasta in it, followed by *manzo bollito*, boiled beef, stuffed with a mixture of spinach, egg, parmigiano cheese and mortadella; and also roast or boiled chicken chopped up with a chopper and the bones broken, the chickens being the best sort that have scratched a living in the yard, roast potatoes, the bitter green salad called *radici*, mixed with home produced olive oil and vinegar, and plates of delicious tomatoes eaten with oil, salt and pepper.

BOILED MEATS AND STUFFED CHICKEN
Manzo bollito con pollo ripieno (Italy)

A boiled dinner is the traditional wine-harvest feast all over Europe. A cauldron full of good things is left all day to slow-simmer on the back of the stove, while everyone – father, mother, children, grandpa, granny, neighbours – helps with the precious harvest. It is a practical solution in a peasant community when every pair of hands counts. The herbs and flavourings change from region to region – France includes plenty of vegetables and little dishes of relishes, Austria adds delicate little dumplings, Hungary cannot resist spicing the dish up with paprika, the Romanians often roast the chicken after its preliminary poaching, the Bulgarians pop in a stuffed cabbage as well, Spain includes ham bones, Greece likes a lemon and a dish of pickled capers to accompany it– but the basic recipe remains a constant. The soup is served first, with the meats as the second course.

Quantity: Serves 8–10.
Time: Start a day ahead. 30 minutes to bone and stuff the chicken. 15 minutes to finish.
Equipment: A strong needle and thread. A large boiling pot. A mixing bowl. A rolling pin and board.

The broth

4lb/2kg shin of beef, with its own weight of bones, chopped and cracked
1–2 leeks, rinsed and roughly chopped with their green
8 black peppercorns

1 whole onion, halved and stuck with 3–4 cloves
3–4 celery sticks, washed and roughly chopped
1 small bunch parsley
2 bay leaves
7 pints/4 litres water

The chicken

1 roasting chicken, about 4lb/2kg
2 tablespoons olive oil
1lb/500g spinach, picked over and well rinsed
4oz/100g chopped prosciutto or gammon
4oz/100g fresh breadcrumbs
1 glass white wine
1 teaspoon marjoram
1 egg

salt and pepper
1 onion, skinned and finely chopped
2 tablespoons parmesan cheese
4oz/100g chopped salami, mortadella or any spiced sausage
2 heaped tablespoons parsley
1 teaspoon nutmeg

To finish

1lb/500g fresh noodles (half this quantity if dried)

Put all the broth ingredients into your largest stockpot. Bring all to the boil. Turn down to simmer, lid and leave to shudder quietly all day. The chicken should be added 2 hours before you are ready to eat.

To stuff the chicken, you will first have to bone it. Set the chicken breast-down on the table. With a sharp knife, cut the bird right down the back – the bone is very close to the surface here. Work the knife, angling it against the bone to avoid nicking the skin, so that the flesh is parted from the cage of bone. When you come to the leg and wing joints, sever them through neatly, and carry on round. When you have worked your way to the crest of the breast-bone, feel the gelatinous rib which joins it on to the skin. Cut it away cleanly – the cartilage will dissolve in the cooking anyway – leaving a flat butterflied chicken, with no central cage of bone. Throw the carcass bone into the soup, with the neck, gizzard and feet (if you can get them), well scrubbed, with the lower toe-nailed joint chopped off. Finely chop the liver and the heart for the stuffing.

Take up the sharp knife again, and push back the meat from the second joints of the leg and wing. Sever them neatly at the joint. Lay the chicken flat on the table, skin-side down, like a flattened frog. Sprinkle it with salt and pepper. Now you have an empty chicken to stuff.

Make the stuffing. Heat the olive oil in a saucepan and turn the onion in the hot oil until it softens. Put in the spinach, cover the pan, and shake over a high heat until the leaves wilt. Chop the spinach.

Mix the rest of the stuffing ingredients in a bowl. Work in the spinach and form all into a large oblong dumpling. Put the dumpling on the flattened chicken. Work the stuffing into the empty leg cavities, and draw the back up over the top to enclose the stuffing. Sew it up neatly and pat it back into a chicken shape.

Poach the chicken gently for 2 hours in the stock – you can take the bones out now if there is not enough room.

Take the poached chicken and the beef out of the broth, and keep them warm, well moistened with broth. Discard the remaining bones and soggy vegetables. If you have extra mouths to feed, poach new vegetables and potatoes to serve with the second course.

Meanwhile, set out a plate of thin-cut salami and prosciutto, a dish of last year's well-pickled olives, and a bunch of radishes rinsed but still sporting their bright green leaves, and call everyone to table while you attend to reheating the broth and carving the meats.

2–3 minutes is enough to poach the noodles in the hot broth (4–5 if the pasta is dried).

Serve the soup and the noodles first, with plenty of bread.

Then set out the meats, sliced – the chicken will cut beautifully, in thick rich slices – accompanied by a jug of good olive oil, salt and quartered lemons.

Follow with a salad of bitter leaves – radicchio, frisee, arugula, whatever you can find – left innocent of dressing, but with olive oil and wine vinegar for everyone to dress their own; and a dish of the last tomatoes of summer, sliced and dressed with a trickle of olive oil, a sprinkling of chopped oregano, finely sliced garlic and a generous grind of black pepper.

No sweets today – there's no time for such niceties. But when everyone has eaten their fill, serve a well-matured goat's cheese, salty and pungent, and a dish of the dark juicy figs which ripen at this time of year, laid on their own elegant green leaves. No grapes – everyone has their fill of them out in the fields.

Finish the meal with walnuts, sweet wine, and tiny cups of strong bitter coffee, brewed in one of the little two-tiered aluminium coffee-pots which simmer on every hob in Italy.

OCTOBER

KERMESSE, KIRCHWEIH AND VOLKSFEST:
END OF SEPTEMBER THROUGH OCTOBER

Autumn is festival-time in Germany. The celebrations of a rich agricultural people naturally took place at the end of harvest, when the store-cupboards were full, the goose-down covers restuffed, and the shutters put up against the coming winter. It is a time when families get together and elderly relatives are visited. Large rural households, the main business of the year completed, throw a party for family, friends and neighbours. Over the festival, custom dictates the eating of three large meals – including at least one roast goose (see German Christmas, p.35).

The Kirchweih or Kermesse, originally a service of annual rededication held on the feast day of each church's patron saint, is celebrated in Bavaria on the third Sunday and Monday in October. The churches are filled with flowers and the congregation might choose to wear traditional costume. Those who observe the old customs go to morning service, and return home for the big meal early in the afternoon. Traditionally, the women prepared the meal while the men went off together to the local inn, the Bierstube, for a Frühschoppen – early drink – and to eat the delicious little fresh sausages, Weisswürste, for which Bavaria is famous. The food is plentiful, the beer and sekt unlimited, as befits the appetites of the inhabitants of this lush and generous land. Custom dictates that each household decorates with flowers and ivy a corner of the farmhouse for the lares et penates – God's corner, the Herrgottswinkel. In the evening the climax is the Kirtatanz – a dance held in the local barn or church hall. Zithers, guitars and accordions provide the music for the dance, and the background to the songs.

The timing of these autumn celebrations – church festival, harvest-home and thanksgiving for the safe return of the cattle from the mountain meadows – coincides with the traditional autumn fairs, which grew to enormous size in medieval times, and subsequently degenerated into purely pleasure fairs – a transition which echoed the ancient secondary function of these gatherings, the arrangement and celebration of weddings. Germany is rich in such fairs, many of which were given formal shape in recent times. Cannstatt in Swabia has Volksfest, an agricultural show and cattle-market instituted on September 28th 1818 by William I of Wurttemberg to commemorate the famine of 1816–17; a huge pillar of fruit, the Fruchtsäule, serves as a talisman against similar disaster. Of most venerable ancestry is the Kerferloh Markt, a horse-market held just outside Munich on the first or second Sunday of September, instituted by the Holy Roman Emperor Otto in gratitude to his Bavarian cavalry for their victory over the Hungarians in

955 at the battle of Lechfelde. The fair continues to commemorate the spirit of the Bavarian irregulars, with fist-fights and the rowdiest behaviour in all Germany.

Munich's world-renowned *Oktoberfest* – now held in September to take advantage of fine weather – is another nineteenth-century normalization of an ancient custom: the fair was established in 1810, when Crown Prince Ludwig, heir to Max-Joseph of Bavaria, marked the occasion of his marriage to Thérèse of Schleswig-Hildburghausen with a huge open-air celebration. Since then the fair has grown annually, now covering hundreds of acres of meadow. Scholar-cook Hans Karl Adam described the festival of thirty years ago:

> Hardly is summer over before the *Oktoberfest* makes its appearance. This is a tremendous occasion, one of the world's great folk festivals. Here one is a human being, here one can achieve humanity. This great throng is proudly headed by heavy-laden beer wagons, often drawn by teams of eight horses. The horses' brasses are highly polished and at their destination the *Obergermeister* of Munich personally taps the first barrel of beer. Additional attractions are provided by oxen roasted whole on the spit, poultry roasted over charcoal fires, calves' knuckles, innumerable kinds of sausages, cheeses, roasted almonds, spiced breads, Bavarian malt cookies and all the other little bits and pieces contributing to the main event. Year after year people come from all over the world to see this show. They join in, they drink, they dance, they conduct the bands and are delighted to eat and drink to their hearts' content.

Henry Wolff describes a *Kirchweih* in Germany's Black Forest *circa* 1890:

> . . . the church supplies merely the pretext – the service is gone through in much the same spirit as Charles Lamb's 'grace before meat'. The main object of the feast is relaxation and merrymaking. It is the sociable part of a fair intensified and spread out. Wherever there is German speech or German descent, there people will have their *Kirchweih*. They have it in Prussia – where an inconsiderate Government make them keep it at Michaelmas, when all hands are wanted for lifting potatoes. They have it in Austria, they have it on the Rhine. Even the French-speaking Belgians so far remember their Flemish parentage as to stickle for their *Kermesse*. In the Black Forest it used to be kept at Martinmas. As St Martin's Day is expected to be celebrated by thank-offerings in kind – eggs, ham, butter, fruit, and the like – offered to the soldier-saint – the dedication festival becomes something very like a second harvest festival. Now it is mostly kept in October. Great preparations are made for it in the way of killing and baking. *Küchle* (small cakes), *strüwle* (cakes baked in stripes), *bache-moche* (pancakes) and *butternüdeln* (a German version of 'fat rascals'), and every variety of the local baked meat is got ready. One distinctive speciality of the season are 'snowballs', a sweetmeat made of flour, eggs, sugar, and sour cream or butter, strongly inflated by fermentation. At the *Kirchweih* itself there is no time for preparing anything. For that is a period of rest, above all, for men and maids. The *schlumperwoche*, which forms a leading feature of the festival, is a season of regular topsy-turveydom, during which servants keep holiday, and masters and mistresses serve. A variety of curious games are the order of the day. Dog and menageries races are very much in vogue. But the favourite race of all is the one in which the lads push their sweethearts along in wheelbarrows, the girls getting out and relieving their cavaliers at certain stages. Then there are dances such as the *Hammeltanz* – danced for the prize of a wether (*hammel*) to be won by the man, and a tin dish and flaming red ribbon for the lady.

BAVARIAN FAIRING SNACKS
Brotzeit (Germany)

There is such a huge variety of magnificent *würst* and cold meats to be bought just in the *charcuteries* of Germany, let alone in the streets at festival time, that it is hard to know where to begin. Here are the better-known specialities — always remembering that each little village has its individual recipes and their traditional accompaniments.

Quantity: Allow 8oz/250g per person.
Time: Moments to lay everything out.
Equipment: Plenty of large flat serving dishes.

Main ingredients

Weisswürst: white sausage served with pretzels and mild mustard

Schweinsbratwürstel: fried sausages served with sauerkraut

Würstsalat: sausage salad

Pressack: head cheese, served with vinegar and oil, and bread

Hirschgeräuchertes: smoked venison

Knackwürst: thick meat sausage served with vinegar and oil

Regensburg sausages: served with crescent-shaped buns (*Kipferl*) and hot mustard

Hackerbrotzeit (vintner's snack): smoked pork ribs, liver sausage and black pudding

Tellersulz: jellied pork

Tellerfleisch: boiled beef

Relishes

Fresh horseradish: grated on the diagonal in long thin strips

Horseradish with apple: short-grated horseradish, mixed with twice its volume of grated apple and a squeeze of lemon

Horseradish with cream: short-grated horseradish, folded into thick whipped cream and finished with a squeeze of lemon

Mustard sauce: Chop 2 hard-boiled eggs and 2 pickled gherkins and mix with 2 tablespoons mild mustard, 1 tablespoon cream or poaching broth, 1 tablespoon chopped chives, 1 tablespoon chopped dill and 1 tablespoon short-grated horseradish

Cranberry sauce: cranberries stewed with a little sugar and a slice of pear

Serve everything with large juicy white German radishes, trimmed and sliced vertically towards the root, left joined at the base, with fresh cold butter so that a sliver can be tucked inside each slit. Cold butter, too, should be spread on a slice of dark *Schwarzbrot* and sprinkled with chives. A little glass of *Obstler* – eau-de-vie – would aid digestion.

Raise your stein and drink the health of the happy prince of Munich and his lovely princess – or the Emperor Otto, or whomever you please.

CHURCH DOUGHNUTS
Kirchweihküchle (Germany)

Stretch the dough balls over your knees to form the dumb-bell shaped doughnuts. This has a double advantage: you will end up with snowy-white knees and the right shape of *Kirchweihküchle*.

Quantity: Makes about 18 doughnuts.
Time: Start 2 hours ahead. 45 minutes.
Equipment: A mixing bowl. A deep-fryer and draining spoon.

1lb/500g flour
1oz/25g fresh yeast (or ½oz/12g dried)
1 tablespoon sugar
2 tablespoons cream
frying oil or clarified butter

½ teaspoon salt
1 tablespoon butter
¼ pint/150ml milk
2 eggs

To finish
caster sugar

Sieve the flour with the salt. Rub in the fresh yeast (if using dried yeast, follow the instructions on the packet) and the butter, and mix in the sugar. Make a well in the middle and pour in the milk, cream, and beaten eggs. Work all in with your hand until you have smooth elastic dough. Work it some more. Put the dough to rise, covered with clingfilm, in a warm place, until it has doubled in bulk – about 1–1½ hours.

Knock the dough down and knead it to distribute the air bubbles. Cut it into 2oz/50g nuggets and work each into a ball. Either stretch them into a dumb-bell shape over your knees, or cut a cross on the top of each with kitchen scissors. Let the doughnuts rise again for 10–15 minutes.

Heat the clarified butter or oil in a deep-fryer. When it is hazed with blue, slip in the doughnuts, a few at a time, and let them fry gently, turning them once, until they are well-risen and brown as a walnut. Remove them and drain them on kitchen paper. Toss them in caster sugar. Of course they will all be eaten hot – this is festival time, and no one is on a diet at *Kirchweih*.

HARVEST-HOME:
NEAREST SUNDAY TO OCTOBER 1ST

These days it is only country-dwellers who are aware of an event which was for centuries the main preoccupation of the farming year – the gathering of the harvest. Throughout most of Europe, wheaten bread is the staple diet, and the end of the reaping signalled a great celebration to mark the victory of life over death: the filling of the granaries. Due homage had to be paid to the fickle gods and goddesses of harvest for this year's favour, and their spirit had to be in some way preserved for next year.

The Corn Dolly represented the goddess in rural Britain. The lady seems to have inherited her fine clothes from Ceres, the Roman harvest-goddess – although James Frazer, author of *The Golden Bough*, traces the origins still further back:

The corn-spirit is represented sometimes in human, sometimes in animal form, and in both cases he is killed in the person of his representative and eaten sacrificially. To find examples of actually killing the human representative of the corn-spirit we have naturally to go to savage races; but the harvest-suppers of our European peasants have furnished unmistakable examples of the sacramental eating of animals as representatives of the corn-spirit. In Wermland in Sweden, the farmer's wife uses the grain of the last sheaf to bake a loaf in the shape of a little girl; this loaf is divided amongst the whole household and eaten by them. As usual the corn-spirit is believed to reside in the last sheaf; and to eat a loaf made from the last sheaf is therefore to eat the corn-spirit itself. Similarly at La Palisse, in France, a man made of dough is hung upon the fir tree which is carried on the last harvest-wagon. The tree and the dough-man are taken to the mayor's house and kept there till the vintage is over. Then the close of the harvest is celebrated by a feast at which the mayor breaks the dough-man in pieces and gives the pieces to the people to eat.

In Britain the corn-spirit was known by several names: the Maiden, the Harvest Queen, the Kern Baby, the Neck – in Kent she was called the Ivy Girl. In Hertfordshire she was known as the Mare, and retreated into the last sheaf: the reapers all threw their sickles at the sheaf from a distance, so that no one would reap her anger along with the final bundle. In the north-east of Scotland she was a straw doll dressed as an old woman, the Cailleach, and she wore an apron to preside over the feast – afterwards the young men would take turns to whirl her around the floor.

Sometimes she was represented by the fattest and ripest stalks of corn. At the harvest supper, the culmination of the farming year, the goddess, however she was personified, was the guest of honour at the feast held in the farmer's biggest barn. Pies, ham and roast beef, vegetables, fruit and puddings, with an unlimited supply of beer and cider, were served by the farmer's wife and the young women of the village. Afterwards there were songs and games. When the party was over the dolly was taken to the farmhouse and kept until the next harvest supper – when she would be ceremonially burned, and the new one installed.

Our official church harvest festival dates back no further than the last century. It was predated by the harvest suppers and the rituals of Lammastide, which lapsed during the Middle Ages and were designed, not to celebrate a *fait accompli*, but to encourage the ripening of the corn. The service of thanksgiving is a Victorian innovation – instituted in 1843 by the Rev. R.S. Hawker, vicar of Morwenstow in Cornwall, who decided to revive the old Lammastide but moved it to the nearest Sunday to October 1st so that he might invite his parishioners to receive the Sacrament in the 'bread of the new corn'. In the chapels of Cornwall the harvest festival is still celebrated with enthusiasm – and is followed by the customary cream tea, to which the whole congregation contributes its own good baking. The produce offered for blessing and thanksgiving is sold immediately after the service, and the proceeds are given to charity – particularly sought after are the beautiful wheatsheaf-shaped loaves which are now a traditional thanksgiving offering. The Corn Dolly once again rides the last sheaf, and is still treasured from one year to the next.

In the rolling wheat fields of East Anglia it was customary to elect a Lord of the Harvest, usually a venerable and respected tenant, who acted as the head reaper. He paid no rents during his year, enjoyed various privileges such as eating at the manor and stabling his horse in the lord's yard, and presided over the harvest or Mell supper. The Mell or Meal – sometimes called the Horkey – was the last load, and it was brought home in style, with cries of joy, in a high wagon decorated with flowers and oak and ash boughs. Ronald Blythe found traces of the old rituals in 1969, when he interviewed eighty-eight-year-old farmer John Grout for *Akenfield*, his much-admired study of a Suffolk community.

The holy time was the harvest. Just before it began, the farmer would call his men together and say, 'Tell me your harvest bargain.' So the men chose a harvest lord who told the farmer how much they wanted to get the harvest in, and then master and lord shook hands on the bargain.

We reaped by hand. You could count thirty mowers in the same field, each followed by his partner, who did the sheaving... Some men mowed so quick they just fled through the corn all the day long. Each mower took eleven rows of corn on his blade, no more and no less. We were allowed seventeen pints of beer a day each and none of this beer might leave the field once it had been brought. What was left each day had to be kept and drunk before eight on a Saturday night.

The lord sat atop of the last load to leave the field and then the women and children came to glean the stubble. Master would then kill a couple of sheep for the Horkey supper and afterwards . we all went shouting home. Shouting in the empty old fields – I don't know why.

John Grout may not have known why he shouted, but modern ethnologists suggest that this cacophony – also called 'crying the neck' – was the mourning keening which greeted a death, and the shouting and dancing which followed captured the joy of resurrection.

Horace Marryat found the inhabitants of Liselund, on the Danish island of Møn, celebrating in similar fashion when he arrived at his host's huge rambling half-timbered farm on September 1st 1860, when harvest-home was being celebrated:

A cart drove into the court laden with sheaves of corn and peasants, male and female, shouting and singing. Horses, men, women all were decorated with garlands of leaves and flowers, the latter bearing in their hands large bouquets stuck upon the ends of long sticks. Then, later, other carts decorated and be-garlanded like the first, and a rustic Silenus, more horrid-looking than can be imagined, who approaching the farmer and his wife, according to ancient custom, sickle in hand, says:

'We have cut the corn; it is ripe; it is gathered in. Will you now that we cut the cabbages in the garden?'

'No thank you,' reply the *hunsbond* and *hustru*. 'We had rather not.'

'But we will; the corn is gathered in; we will now cut the cabbages in the garden.'

'No,' answers the master. 'As the corn is ripened and is gathered into the barn, we will give you a festival.'

And there follows a bacchanale of innocent jollity.

Andrew Hamilton travelled the same island road eight years earlier, when the harvest appears to have been celebrated a full month later – perhaps the weather was inclement that year:

About the end of September and beginning of October, the feast of harvest-home, *Höst-Gilde*, was celebrated. Everybody who had a harvest, had also a harvest-feast to finish it off with. We were invited in all directions at that time to help the merry-making along. It always took place in the granary, or largest room about the offices. The peasants had merry-makings as well as their superiors, for the benefit of their assistants and servants who had aided them upon the field. But at the great houses, harvest-homes were upon a grand scale. All the out- and in-door domestics, along with all the work-people, and many besides, assembled in this spacious apartment where they first dined, dinner consisting of salt fish and rice-*gröd* or porridge, the two dishes Danish peasants regard as their chief delicacies, after which they proceed to dance.

In rural Germany, the *Erntefest* or *Schelhenke* – sickle-hanging, as it is called in the south – is marked with similar traditions, albeit with different personifications. It was customary to leave the last sheaf of wheat standing 'for the white horse' – and children were warned to watch out for the bogeyman, the

Roggenmuhme, who hid among the tall stalks. In Bavaria it was customary to bake a loaf with the last sheaf, cut it in half, hang one half in the kitchen until next year, and take the other half, decorated with ribbons and cakes, to burn in the fields, while the young men jumped over the flames. In other areas, the last wagon out of the fields brought home the wreath, the harvest crown, which was hung in a place of honour at the harvest feast.

On the plains of Hungary the rural population were still celebrating their harvest festival in the 1930s in much the same way as they had for 1,000 years:

> In Transylvania the poor people, who had very little land or grow very little wheat, organize themselves into reaping bands, who look for work and go to the bigger estates to do the reaping. When the landowner appears for the time near the reaping ground the reaping girls and women meet him and tie him up with a straw rope. He is only released for a ransom! All over the country the feast which celebrates the end of the reaping has given rise to many customs. At the reaping we meet straw wreaths and peculiarly shaped, beautifully arranged wheat bouquets.
>
> In Transylvanian Calvinist churches it is the custom to make a biggish wreath on the occasion of taking new bread. It hangs from the ceiling just over the Lord's table until next year's new bread. Often a wreath is carried back stuck on the end of a pole, or the prettiest girl in the village is crowned with wheat ears. In many places, especially in Transylvania, it is still customary to wait in every gate for the crowned lad or lass with a pail of water, and to throw it over them to ensure a rich harvest for the next year. At the farmer's house there is a big meal, perhaps dancing as well. We must not forget the custom of presenting the reapers with cakes, the extraordinary cakes made for the occasion, and the particular and renowned cakes of certain towns. (Károly Viski, *Hungarian Peasant Customs*, Budapest, 1932)

These days it is comforting to find that the Corn Dolly, be she goddess or ancient sacrifice, has found her niche in the church's harvest festival decorations – and keeps her pagan eye on the Christian service of Thanksgiving from a vantage point at the end of each pew. It would be foolish, the Reverend Hawker would surely agree, not to make her welcome at her ancient feast.

FRESHLY SALTED COD
Grønsalted Torsk (Denmark)

Andrew Hamilton, Victorian traveller in the Danish islands, enjoyed a harvest supper:

> At our parsonage, we had also our harvest-party. There were altogether about sixteen in the servants' room. They had partaken of their *rice-gröd* and salt fish before we went out to pay our needful visit. I had seen Karen with the kitchen-maid (*kokkepige* is the euphonious Danish word for kitchen-maid) carrying large dishes of fragrant porridge, with its agreeable sauce of beer and sugar, across the courtyard, and returning for the fish shortly before she brought in the dining-room dinner. The rice-porridge is very commonly used in Denmark instead of soup, and an excellent dish it is, with the beer and sugar sauce inseparable from it, and the powdered cinnamon. We also partook of it that day in the parlour dinner, and I could not but own the peasants knew what was good.

The 'fragrant porridge' of the first course is a close approximation to the clipping-time pudding on p.236. This 'green-salting' is a common Danish way with fresh-caught fish – it is good with haddock, mackerel and herring too – and much improves the flavour and texture, particularly of the end-of-the-summer catches.

Quantity: Serves 4.
Time: Start 12 hours ahead. 30 minutes.
Equipment: 2 china plates. A large saucepan.

4 codling – one for each person
2–3 large carrots, scraped and thickly sliced
1lb/500g potatoes, peeled and cut into bite-sized
 chunks

salt and pepper
1–2 onions, skinned and sliced

To serve
4oz/100g butter, melted
whole-grain mustard

2 chopped hard-boiled eggs
thick cream and mild vinegar (*optional*)

Clean the fish and sprinkle them on both sides and in the cavity with plenty of salt. Sandwich the fish between the 2 china plates, and leave them overnight in a cool larder. The next day, rinse off the salt – don't let the fish soak or you will undo all the good work.

Half-fill the saucepan with salted water and put in the carrots and onions. Bring to the boil, lid, and simmer for 5 minutes. Add the potatoes, bring back to the boil, lid, and simmer for another 12–15 minutes, until the potatoes are nearly done. Lay the fish on top, bring all back to the boil, lid and simmer for 5 minutes – when the fish should be perfectly done.

Remove the fish and vegetables (save the delicious liquor for a fish soup, or as the basis for a white sauce for a fish pie) and arrange them on a warm serving dish.

Accompany with the melted butter with the chopped hard-boiled eggs stirred in, and plenty of whole-grain mustard – particularly good with this dish if you mix the mustard with an equal volume of thick cream and a little extra mild vinegar. Danish fishmongers sell mild fish-mustard, dipped out of a bucket, alongside their fish.

LAMMASTIDE LOAF
(England)

The Loaf Mass – Hlafmaesse – was the Anglo-Saxon Festival of First Fruits. Bread made from the first corn was offered in church: it was not a harvest-home but a vote of thanks to the gods for the promise of harvest.

Quantity: Makes 1 generous loaf.
Time: 2-2½ hours intermittent attention.
Equipment: A mixing bowl and sieve. A rolling pin and board. Any tools you please to help you model the sheaf. A large baking tray. A pastry brush and a cooling rack.

3lb/1.5kg strong unbleached flour

1oz/25g yeast (not too much, or the loaf will
   rise out of shape)

1 tablespoon salt

1 teaspoon sugar

1 pint/600ml warm water

To glaze

1 egg, lightly forked

Sieve the flour and salt into the bowl.

Cream the yeast with a teaspoon of sugar and mix in a cup of warm water. Pour the mixture into a hollow in the flour and let it froth. Work it, and the rest of the water, in with a fork – then you do not need to get your hands sticky.

When the dough is well mixed, get your hand in and knead it, adding more flour if necessary, until you have a soft elastic dough. Put it to rise by the fire in a bowl covered with a clean cloth. When it has formed a good sponge, knock it down and knead it well.

Now make the sheaf. This is easiest done in a well-floured mould, but then you would have to carve a reverse-image in a piece of wood (the loaf is put to prove in the mould, and tipped on to the baking sheet just before baking). Failing this, roll the dough out as thin as pastry and cut one half into a flat wheatsheaf shape to act as a base. Transfer it to the greased baking sheet.

From the remaining dough, cut out thin strips with spoon-shaped bulges at the top to represent the wheat stalks and ears. Make diagonal slashes down the sides of the 'ears', damp them and pull them over each other to make three-dimensional grains. Damp the base and lay on the wheat stalks, with the last stalk to tie up the bundle. Cut the trimmings into small diamonds, and stick them with a spot of water on to the ears to indicate the rest of the grains. Model a little mouse for one corner.

Preheat the oven to 375°F/190°C/Gas 5.

Put the sheaf-loaf back into a warm place to prove for 10 minutes – not too long, or it will pull totally out of shape.

Neaten up the wheat-ears with a sharp knife, and give the whole thing a final polish with a brushful of egg.

Bake for 30 minutes, until well risen and hollow when you tap the base.

Turn the oven off, and leave the bread to dry out for another 30 minutes.

Hold your breath – then take the loaf out and transfer it to the rack to cool. Take it to the harvest festival for the blessing, and sell it for charity to the highest bidder.

RABBIT PIE
(Britain)

The harvest suppers of East Anglia were held, Saxon-style, in a barn garlanded with flowers, and there were traditional songs with a toast to the farmer and the family by the seasonal workers. The main dish of the supper – along with the mutton and beef which was standard everywhere – was a rabbit pie, made with the plump little rabbits which ran out of the wheatfields ahead of the reapers. In the old days, reaping was done in formation, with a special rhythm and songs to keep the line advancing. The rabbits should be 'hulked' – paunched – as soon as they are shot. Skinning can wait – for two days in summer, three days in the autumn, a week in winter. Young rabbit skins easily – older beasts are harder.

Quantity: Serves 6.
Time: Start 1 hour ahead. 1 hour intermittent attention.
Equipment: A mixing bowl and sieve. A rolling pin and board. A pie dish.

The filling

2 rabbits, skinned and wiped
2 medium-sized onions
approx ¾ pint/450ml water
salt and pepper

8oz/250g belly pork
1 bay leaf, 3–4 sage leaves and 1 thyme sprig, tied
    in a faggot

The pastry

10oz/300g flour
5oz/150g lard

½ teaspoon salt

Start well ahead, as the filling has to cool before you can put on the pastry.

Joint the rabbit into 8 pieces. Dice the pork belly. Skin and chop the onions. Put the rabbit, pork, onions, herbs and water into a casserole or saucepan. Season lightly. Bring it all to the boil, turn down the heat, lid tightly, and leave to cook gently either on top of the stove or in a moderate oven, 325°F/170°C/Gas 3, for 1¼–1½ hours, until the rabbit is quite tender. Check every now and again, and add a little extra hot water if the stew looks like drying out.

Tip the rabbit into a pie dish (remove the herbs) and leave the stew to cool.

Make the pastry. Sieve the flour with the salt, and rub in the fat as lightly as you can, lifting to let the air in. Work in enough water to make a soft dough – only a tablespoon or two, the less water the lighter the pastry.

Roll the pastry out on a very lightly floured board, into a round of the correct size and shape to fit comfortably, without stretching, over the pie-dish. Damp the edges of the dish and lay on the pastry lid. Decorate with pastry leaves and paint the top with a brushful of milk to give a glaze.

Bake in a hot oven, 400°F/200°C/Gas 6, for 45 minutes, until the pie crust is crisp and golden.

Accompany with swedes and potatoes mashed together with butter and milk. The King of the Harvest's portion is the back legs of the rabbit.

POTTED PIGEONS
(Britain)

Pigeons competed with the hens in the fields after the gleaners had finished. As many of them as possible, and of the larks which flocked behind the harvesters, ended up in the pot for the harvest supper. If you don't care to pluck the birds, skin them (feathers and all) or just use the breasts. The stew is cooked on top of the stove – in East Anglia, even as late as the 1930s, many people did not have ovens, and the Sunday dinner would be carried to the baker for cooking.

Quantity: Serves 4.
Time: 15 minutes to prepare – longer if you have to pluck the birds. 3 hours cooking.
Equipment: A roomy lidded saucepan.

6 pigeons, cleaned and plucked

2–3 onions

2–3 smallish turnips

1 teaspoon thyme

1 level teaspoon salt

plenty of black pepper

3–4 mature carrots

1 tablespoon good beef dripping

½ teaspoon sage

To finish
2 tablespoons chopped fresh parsley

Split the pigeons in half, or leave them whole, as you please. Pepper them thoroughly. Peel and slice the onions. Scrape and chop the carrots and turnips.

Melt the dripping in a heavy casserole or stewpot, and turn the birds in the hot fat for a few moments. Push them aside and fry the onions till they soften and take a little colour. Pack in the rest of the vegetables, add the herbs and salt, and pour in enough water to submerge the birds. Bring it all to the boil, turn down the heat, lid tightly and leave to simmer gently for at least 3 hours, until the pigeons are quite tender. Check every now and again and top up with boiling water if necessary. Take off the lid at the end, and boil for a few minutes to concentrate the gravy.

Finish with a sprinkling of parsley. Serve the stewed pigeons with two kinds of potatoes – East Anglians love their potatoes. The first creamed with plenty of milk and butter, the second baked – big King Edwards with the crisp skins split open, and the floury insides well salted and buttered and peppered.

CORNISH PASTIES
(England)

Harvest festival is celebrated in the middle of September at Wendron near Helston in Cornwall. Everybody takes clotted cream of course, and apples, plums, turnips and daffodil bulbs, and the wheatsheaf bread, and the produce is auctioned off after Chapel Sunday school. Afterwards there is a supper; people bring pasties made with potato, turnip, onions and meat but no sweetened fruit pasties – sugar was blacklisted by Charles Wesley when he was preaching the abolition of the slave trade.

Quantity: Makes 4 man-sized pasties.
Time: 25–30 minutes to prepare. 1 hour to bake.
Equipment: A mixing bowl and sieve. A rolling pin and board. A baking tray and cooling rack.

The pastry
12oz/350g plain strong flour

3oz/75g frozen lard

4–5 tablespoons cold water

½ teaspoon salt

3oz/75g frozen margarine (it would have been all
   lard in the old days)

The filling
1lb/500g beef (skirt or chuck)

8oz/250g swede

salt and pepper

1lb/500g potatoes

1 onion

Make the pastry first. Everything should be as cold as possible. Sift the flour with the salt into a bowl and leave it in the fridge for an hour or two.

When all is really cold, grate the fat into the flour and stir it in with a knife. Mix in enough cold water to make a manageable dough. Knead it for a moment, but not for long. The fat should remain quite lumpy, to give a firm enough crust to hold the juices of the filling. Cover the dough ball with clingfilm and leave it in the refrigerator for at least 30 minutes.

Trim any gristle off the meat and cut it into thin pieces ¼in/0.5cm square, including some fat. Peel the potatoes and chip off thin slivers – the volume should be about the same as matchsticks. Do the same with the swede. Skin the onion and slice finely.

Quarter the dough and roll each piece out on a floured board into a circle the size of a dinner plate (about 7in/15cm diameter). Place the onion along the centre of each circle. Cover it with a layer of swede, and season with salt and pepper. Spread the meat over the swede, making sure the filling reaches right into the ends. Season the meat. Finish with the potato.

Moisten the top half-circle edge with water, and bring the sides together over the top to form a fat bolster. Seal firmly in a narrow edge, starting at the middle and working to the corners. With dry fingers, crimp the edges in a rope pattern. Transfer the pasties to a baking tray. Glaze with milk and egg if you like, but don't prick or slit them.

Bake in a hot oven, 400°F/200°C/Gas 6, for 30 minutes to crisp and brown the pastry. Turn the oven down to 375°F/190°C/Gas 5 and continue baking for another 30 minutes.

Strong sweet tea goes with these – as a rule Cornish people don't take sugar in their tea, except with a pasty, when almost everyone takes a little sugar.

HARVEST BEER
(England)

East Anglian farmer John Grout, born in 1880, but with his memory still sharp in his eighty-ninth year, gave this recipe for home-brewed harvest beer to Ronald Blythe:

You boiled five or six pails of water in a copper. Then you took one pail of the boiling water and one pail of cold water and added them together in a tub big enough to hold eighteen gallons. You then added a bushel of malt to the water in the tub. You then added boiling water from the copper until there was eighteen gallons in all in the tub. Cover up and keep warm and leave standing for at least seven hours, although the longer the better. When it has stood, fill the copper three parts full from the tub, boil for an hour and add half a pound of hops. Then empty into a second tub. Repeat with the rest. All the beer should now be in one tub and covered with a sack and allowed to cool. But before this, take a little of the warm beer in a basin, add two ounces of yeast and let it stand for the night. Add this to the main tub in the morning, then cask the beer. You can drink it after a week. And it won't be like anything you can taste at the Crown, either.

HALLOWE'EN, ALL SAINTS, ALL SOULS, BONFIRE NIGHT: OCTOBER 31ST, NOVEMBER 1ST, 2ND, 5TH

Hallowmass or Hallowe'en is celebrated on October 31st, the Eve of All Hallows (All Saints) – Samhain in the ancient Celtic calendar – which is in its turn followed by All Soul's Day. Hallowe'en is a Celtic festival, full of mystery and dark magic. This is the time when the little folk are abroad, a time of witches, ghosts, hobgoblins and lost souls. The uneasy truce between Christianity and paganism is as vulnerable in the three days which span October 31st and November 2nd as it is during the reign of King Carnival.

In the pre-Christian Celtic world, the Beltane fires, last lit in the spring, were rekindled with need-fire to mark the end of summer and the beginning of the Celtic New Year – a tradition which lasted longest in Ireland, and in Scotland's highlands and islands. Household hearth fires were re-lit from the Samhain blaze, and everyone took precautions on that day against malevolent spirits. The fathers of the northern Church, struggling with the ancient Druidical and Norse gods, managed to build on the embers of the pagan bonfires two of its own major holy festivals – the first of which is dedicated to those saints who have no day of their own, and the second sacred to all departed souls. In England, too, the state had some success – achieving the wholesale migration of Bonfire Night to the commemoration of Guy Fawkes on November 5th, which remains a re-dating of Hallowe'en, with little, apart from the identity of the sacrificial offering and the fireworks whose noise rightly belongs to the earlier festival, to distinguish it from the old Beltane fire-feast of Samhain.

A nineteenth-century correspondent of *Notes and Queries* commented on the Beltane traditions in Scotland:

> On the last days of autumn the children gathered ferns, tar-barrels and the long thin stalks called *gainisg*, and everything suitable for a bonfire. Each house had its bonfire on an eminence . . . Fey means the same as devoted: sacrificed or doomed. In Wales too the habit is not yet extinct, and men still living can remember at the end taking to their heels shouting the sacrifice: 'the cut black sow take the hindmost.'

The Beltane fires were lit twice: on the Eve of May Day and on the Eve of All Hallows. This timing does not coincide with the planting and harvest of the agriculturalist, but celebrates the approach of summer, when the herdsman drives his cattle out into the open to crop the fresh grass, and again at the approach of winter when he leads them back to the safety of the stall. Scottish ethnologist James Frazer suggests that these northern Celtic fire-festivals were timed – unlike those with a Mediterranean cultural base – without reference to the position of the sun, the farmers' preoccupation, but to mark the annual transhumance.

Seasonal games, with that strange reversal of reality, a delight in mirror-image nonsense, which is the hallmark of Celtic celebrations, mark the festival. Christian (McEwen) Hesketh remembers her childhood Hallowe'en at the family house, Marchmont, in the border country of Scotland.

> We had a bonfire party for everyone around – and of course we baked potatoes and roasted chestnuts in the ashes. There was a tub of flour with coins in it – you had to stick your face right in the flour and search for the coins – everyone was gasping for breath and covered in flour by the end. There was bobbing for apples in a barrel of water, with your hands behind your back and no pushing it against the side of the basin, which would be cheating. We hung turnip lanterns in the windows and on every gate-post.

Turnip lanterns – now often replaced by New World pumpkins – their grotesque carved grins made doubly hideous with candlelight, were designed to scare away the witches, ghosts and goblins who were about their business at Hallowe'en. Apples, too, are an essential ingredient of northern Hallowe'en festivals. Apple trees were the Celtic tree of Paradise – the Mediterranean-based Israelites gave the honour to the quince. Naturally, when the Bible was translated into the vernacular, the original quince of the Old Testament was translated as the fruit which had already established its sanctity under the preceding régime.

Robert Burns devoted twenty-eight stanzas to the saga of Hallowe'en – the night when the kale-patch was emptied. The poet supplied a note to explain how to read the kale roots:

The first ceremony of Hallowe'en is pulling each a stock or plant of kail. The people must go out in pairs, hand-in-hand, with eyes shut, and pull the first they meet with. Its being big or little, straight or crooked, is prophetic of the size and shape of the grand object of all their spells – the husband or wife. If any gird, or earth, stick to the root that is *tocher* or fortune.

In northern England, where Hallowe'en was known as Nutcracker Night, similar rituals were attached to the cracking of nuts, and all over Britain the ceremony is linked to making mischief – now formalized in the children's offer of 'trick-or-treat'. The 'treat' element comes from the custom of begging soul cakes or dole bread to send to the relatives of the dead, whose passing is commemorated on All Souls. Once the collection had become a children's game, the outlines quickly blurred: the soul cakes first turned into shop-bought biscuits and sweets, then into coin-of-the-realm, which in its turn has become the modern exhortation of a penny-for-the-guy of Bonfire Night.

The Eve of the Feast of All Saints – the day which follows Hallowe'en and All Souls – was celebrated throughout pre-Reformation England with pealing church bells. Henry VIII put a stop to such superstitious papist nonsense – although the custom was revived when the anti-Catholic witch-hunting was over.

As for Gunpowder Guy Fawkes – chief plotter of November 5th, who nearly, in 1605, reduced the entire Houses of Parliament to one gigantic bonfire – the Catholic conspirator provided a neat excuse for rekindling the need-fires of Samhain, which the Reformed Church had gone to considerable trouble to eradicate.

Up to the beginning of this century, Bonfire Night was known as Pope Day, still celebrated with fervour in the old Sussex town of Lewes. Here all the townsfolk belong to different brotherhoods, and on Guy Fawkes Night they parade round the town dressed up as pirates, Spaniards, Indians, Breton sailors – anything strange and foreign – brandishing lighted torches. The motley crew then wends its way through the half-timbered houses of the old town, past Lewes's famous fortress prison, and on to the hill behind, pausing at various pubs on the way, where each brotherhood lights its own enormous bonfire, burns its Guy (which some recalcitrant groups still call the Pope), quarrels with its rival brotherhoods, and lets off fireworks for half the night. In the old days, too, great fights, tugs-of-war and fisticuffs would take place over the ownership of the Guy – known as Smugging the Guy.

Humanity loves its fire-festivals. The lighting of ceremonial bonfires marks all our most ancient rituals – Midsummer, May Day, Hallowe'en, Christmas. Given an excuse for celebration, we mark it with conflagration.

LANG KALE
(Scotland)

Robert Burns recommended buttered sowans – oat-husk porridge – as the Hallowe'en supper, washed down with a dram of whisky, of course. This old Scots recipe, based on skirlie, combines the kale and oatmeal proper to the celebration. Skirlie is only worth making with good drippings from roasted meat.

Quantity: Serves 4–6.
Time: 30 minutes.
Equipment: A saucepan. A frying pan.

1lb/500g curly kale or green cabbage
salt and black pepper
1lb/500g medium oatmeal

2 medium onions
5oz/150g good meat dripping

Pick over, rinse and shred the kale. Skin and slice the onions thinly.

Cook the kale in a lidded pan over a high heat in the water which clings to its leaves, with a little salt and a tablespoon of the dripping.

Heat the rest of the dripping and fry the onions. When they are soft but not brown, turn up the heat, add the oatmeal, turn it in the dripping and brown it a bit. Throw in the kale and turn it well. Fry it for a minute or two. Add salt and black pepper to taste.

Serve it all hot, with a cup of strong tea and a dram of whisky against the cold night.

> Wi' merry sangs, an' friendly cracks,
> I wat they did na weary;
> And unco tales, an' funny jokes, –
> Their sports were cheap an' cheery;
> Till butter'd sow'ns, wi fragrant lunt,
> Set a' their gabs a-steerin';
> Syne, wi' a social glass o' strunt,
> They parted aff careerin'
> Fu' blythe that night. (Robert Burns, *Hallowe'en*)

HALLOWE'EN CHAMP
(Ireland)

This is a midland Irish dish, special to Bonfire Night because it has favours buried in it, and festival food because it has butter – a most extravagant luxury in the peasant community, where the butter went to pay the rent. In the old days everyone usually had buttermilk as a sauce for the potatoes – and if you didn't have the buttermilk, well, you put out the empty bowl and dipped in the potatoes just the same. The potatoes themselves were never peeled before cooking – you shook them over the heat so they split and showed their floury insides – and were dumped on the table in the middle of a strong cotton flour-bag, with the bowl of buttermilk alongside.

Quantity: Serves 4.
Time: 30 minutes.
Equipment: A large saucepan. A bowl.

2lb/1kg mealy potatoes
8 fl oz/200ml buttermilk or soured milk

approx. 4 shallots or 2 leeks
salt and pepper

The favours

a ring (for a wedding)
a blackthorn twig (for a husband or a wife who'd
  beat you)

a dried pea (for prosperity)

To finish
4oz/100g butter

Boil the potatoes, still in their well-scrubbed jackets.

While the potatoes are cooking, trim and slice the shallots or leeks into fine rings (including all the green parts) and put them to simmer in a small saucepan with the milk.

When the potatoes are soft, drain them. As soon as they are cool enough to handle, peel them, return them to the saucepan and mash them.

The shallots or leeks should be soft by now. Liquidize them with their milk in the food processor (if you have no processor, leave them as they are).

Reheat the mashed potato gently and beat in the onion and milk mixture – the potato will turn a delicate creamy green. Taste and add salt and pepper.

Stir in the favours and tip the potato into a hot bowl. Make a hollow in the middle.

Drop the softened butter into the hollow. Everyone should eat out of the same bowl, dipping into the melting butter with each mouthful.

SOUL CAKES
(England)

Soul cakes were given to the Soulers when they came to call on All Souls' Day. The custom of going round to the neighbours to sing souling songs – or as in Cheshire, performing a soul-caking play – was still extant in Shropshire and Cheshire in the late thirties. The custom dates back to the Middle Ages, when black-clad men went from house to house collecting money and gifts to pay for Masses for the dead. A man draped in white and wearing a horse's head accompanied them – a relic from pre-Christian days. The recipes for these most primitive spice-and-honey cakes varied from region to region – the uplands made oatcakes or parkins, the lowlands made wheat-based biscuits.

Here I give a recipe for a parkin, the Yorkshire soul cake: Harcake or Soul Har Cake, named for the Norse god Odin or Har. In Derbyshire they are known as Thor cakes, and coriander spices the mixture.

Quantity: Makes about a dozen portions.
Time: 20 minutes to make. 45 minutes to bake.
Equipment: A mixing bowl. A small saucepan. A meat roasting tin.

8oz/250g flour

1 tablespoon sugar

3oz/75g butter

¼ pint/150ml milk

1 teaspoon bicarbonate of soda

1lb/500g medium oatmeal

2 teaspoons powdered ginger

3oz/75g dripping or lard

10oz/300g honey, treacle or golden syrup

Mix the flour, oatmeal, sugar and ginger together in the mixing bowl.

Melt the butter and the dripping or lard with the milk and the honey, treacle or golden syrup, over a gentle heat in the saucepan. Stir in the bicarbonate of soda, and as soon as it froths, stir it into the dry ingredients. Beat it all well – the mixture should be soft enough to drop from the spoon, so add more hot water if necessary.

Preheat the oven to 350°F/180°C/Gas 4.

Grease the roasting tin and pour in the parkin mixture.

Bake it for about 45 minutes, until firm to the finger. Let it cool in the baking tray, and cut it into squares. It's nicest if you keep it in a tin for a week, when it matures and softens.

> Soul, soul, for a soul cake!
> I pray, good missus, for a soul cake!
> An apple or pear, a plum or a cherry,
> Any good thing to make us merry.
> One for Peter, two for Paul,
> Three for Him who made us all.
> Up with the kettle and down with the pan,
> Give us good alms and we'll be gone. (*Traditional souling song*)

BONFIRE NIGHT PIE-AND-PEAS
(England)

Meat pie with mushy peas is the traditional treat for Bonfire Night in Yorkshire and Lancashire. The rest of the year it is standard pub-fare all over the Dales – its accompaniment is immortalized in the children's rhyme: 'Pease-porridge hot, pease-porridge cold, pease-porridge in the pot, nine days old.'

Quantity: Serves 4.

Time: Allow 1½ hours intermittent attention.

Equipment: 2 saucepans with lids. A mixing bowl and sieve. A rolling pin and board. 4 individual pie dishes.

The peas

8oz/250 dried marrowfat peas, soaked overnight   salt and pepper
   in cold water

The meat filling

12oz/350g shin of beef, cubed by the butcher   1 small onion, peeled and chopped
   with a sharp knife   1 tablespoon chopped parsley

1 teaspoon dried crushed thyme
salt and freshly milled white pepper

½ pint/300ml water
1½lb/750g potatoes, peeled and cubed

The pastry

8oz/250g flour
4oz/125g lard

1 teaspoon salt
4–5 tablespoons cold water

Bring the peas to the boil in enough water to cover them. Turn down the heat, lid, and stew them gently until they are mushy. Season them at the end with salt and pepper – they should be quite wet and juicy, with the skins giving a rough texture to the near-purée.

While the peas are cooking, put all the filling ingredients except the potatoes in a saucepan – the water should not quite cover the meat. Season lightly. Bring to the boil, lid, and turn down the heat. Leave to simmer until the meat is very tender – about 1 hour. 15 minutes before the end of cooking, add the potatoes – and extra water if necessary. Remove from the heat, taste and adjust the seasoning, and leave the mixture to cool.

Meanwhile, make the pastry. Sift the flour with the salt. Roughly work in the lard with a sharp knife, finishing with the tips of your fingers. Work in enough cold water to give you a soft pliable dough. Leave the dough, covered with a cloth, in a cool place until the meat is ready.

Divide the meat among the 4 individual pie dishes. Quarter the pastry and roll each piece out to make a lid. Damp the edges of each dish and lay on the pastry lid.

Bake the pies at 375°F/190°C/Gas 5 for 20–25 minutes, until the pastry is crisp and brown.

Wait until everyone comes in from the bonfire. Serve the pies with a ladleful of mushy peas poured on to the lid.

Vinegar and mint sauce is the usual accompaniment – with a serving of pickled red cabbage, and slices of onion and cucumber soaked overnight in vinegar.

> Please to remember the fifth of November,
> Gunpowder treason and plot.
> We know no reason why gunpowder treason
> Should ever be forgot. (*Traditional since the seventeenth century*)

NOVEMBER

The hunting season in the forests and mountains of central Europe begins on St Hubert's Day, by the light of the hunter's moon. The organization of a hunting party and its dogs – boar, roedeer and hare are the main quarry – is traditionally conducted with great formality, with bugle-blowing and a Court of Honour which can award fines of a round of drinks or the supplying of a huntsmen's supper – the *Schusseltreiben*. The novice hunter had to serve a three-year apprenticeship to a master huntsman, and be able to recite the litany of the rules of conduct, before he was handed his hunting knife – and received a box on the ears just to concentrate his mind on his responsibilities. In the 1880s class restrictions were lifted and hunting became available to all – and Vienna's wild-meat market, the *Wildbretmarkt*, was able to supply the talented cooks of the bourgeoisie with a new pleasure. Austrian cooks love game and prepare it magnificently.

HAUNCH OF WILD BOAR WITH CRANBERRY SAUCE AND POTATO PANCAKES
Wildschweinebraten mit Presielbeersauce und Rösti (Austria)

The flavour of wild boar – called *marcassin* in France – is much like the best lean pork, but it has a firmer texture, darker colour and stronger taste. The saddle and the haunch are the best portion. Good pork can be used instead, naturally, but choose a small lean leg, and increase the amount of aromatics in the recipe – you will not need to lard it, either.

Quantity: Serves 6–8.
Time: Start a day ahead. 2 hours regular attention.
Equipment: A larding needle. A large lidded casserole. A saucepan. A frying pan.

The meat
1 haunch of young wild boar (about 4lb/2kg) or
   lean pork
6 peppercorns, crushed
1 bay leaf
2 tablespoons softened butter

2 glasses red wine
1 tablespoon juniper berries
2oz/50g fat pork, cut in strips
1 small glass brandy

The *Rösti*

2lb/1kg potatoes
salt and pepper

4oz/100g butter

The cranberry sauce

8oz/250g cranberries
1 glass water

2oz/50g sugar
1 teaspoon grated horseradish

The day before, put the haunch to marinate with the red wine, peppercorns, juniper and bay leaf.

Also the day before, boil the potatoes in their skins, but leave them slightly underdone. This pre-part-cooking is essential to the success of the dish, as the starch re-hardens overnight.

Next day, remove the haunch from the marinade, pat it dry, and lard it with the strips of pork fat. Spread the meat all over with the butter and put it in the roasting dish. Roast it at 425°F/220°C/Gas 7 for 10 minutes, then turn the oven down to 375°F/190°C/Gas 5 and roast it for another hour, basting regularly with the marinade.

Meanwhile put the cranberries, sugar and water into a small covered dish and put them in the base of the oven to soften as the meat cooks. Stir in the grated horseradish to finish.

Now turn your attention back to the Rösti. Skin and grate the potatoes through the grater's largest holes. Melt the butter in a large frying pan and spread in the grated potatoes. Sprinkle them with salt and pepper. Cook over a medium heat, stirring often. Pat out the softened potato into a large pancake and let it fry to a golden crust. Turn it carefully (sliding it out on to a plate first, or flipping it over – whatever comes easiest). Fry the other side. Slide the Rösti out on to a warm plate.

Test the meat with a skewer. When it is done, pour the glass of brandy over it and set light to the alcohol. When it has burned out, transfer the haunch to a warm serving dish, scraping all the brown sticky bits into the brandy juices in the pan. Reheat this gravy with the last of the marinade, and hand it separately with the meat after it has been allowed to set for 10 minutes ready for carving.

Serve the haunch of wild boar in all its glory, decorated with sprigs of evergreen and thyme, and accompanied by its own gravy, the Rösti and a bowl of cranberry sauce – with red cabbage and apple sauce on the side.

Carve the joint skilfully with your sharpened hunting knife, and serve generous portions. Do not stint the good red wine: this is not a time for restraint.

VENISON GOULASH WITH BUTTER DUMPLINGS
Paprika Rehbraten mit Butternockerl (Austria)

Roedeer, the main quarry in Austria, is paler-fleshed and less gamey in flavour than the red deer of the Scottish highlands – fallow deer venison is reckoned the best of all. If you have hunted your own, rub the meat with pepper, particularly around the bones, and hang it for 1–2 weeks, depending on the warmth of the weather. The only alternative is to cook and eat it then and there, straight from the hill and before the meat has had time to harden. A young animal will produce smaller and more tender joints than a mature beast with a fine set of antlers. With such a creature, it will need very long slow cooking indeed. For roasting, the shoulder is much esteemed in Austria, although it is often the most peppered with shot. The haunch and saddle-fillets are equally choice. Venison should be dark in colour, with firm white fat. All venison animals – including moose, elk and reindeer – are delicious cooked as a goulash.

Quantity: Serves 6–8.

Time: 1½ hours intermittent attention.

Equipment: A large lidded stewpan. A mixing bowl. A saucepan.

The goulash

2lb/1kg stewing venison	2lb/1kg onions
2 tablespoons lard	1 tablespoon wine vinegar
1–2 glasses water	2 tablespoons paprika
1 teaspoon marjoram	1 teaspoon caraway seeds
salt and pepper	

The dumplings

2oz/50g softened butter	1 egg
3oz/75g flour	½ teaspoon salt

Trim the meat into bite-sized cubes. Peel and finely slice the onions.

Melt the lard in the stewpan and throw in the onions. Turn them in the hot fat until they soften and turn golden. Push them to one side, and add the meat. Fry the meat until the outside seizes. Stir in the paprika, and fry for a few seconds only. Sprinkle in the vinegar, a splash of water, the marjoram and caraway, salt and pepper. Bring to the boil, turn down the heat, lid tightly, and leave to simmer very gently either on the top of the stove or in a low oven, 300°F/150°C/Gas 2 for 1–1½ hours, until the meat is very tender. Check every now and then and add a little more water as necessary.

Meanwhile make the dumplings. Cream the butter, working in the egg and the flour alternately until you have a soft smooth dough. Add the salt and leave it to rest for 30 minutes. Bring a pan of salted water to the boil and drop in teaspoons of the dough – the quantity should yield about 12–15 small dumplings. Bring back to the boil and turn down the heat immediately. Poach the dumplings for 12–15 minutes, until the dumplings are well-risen and firm. Drain, toss with butter and keep them warm while you finish the venison.

Remove the venison pan lid and turn up the heat to reduce the sauce a little. Stir in the soured cream just before you serve it, accompanied by the dumplings and perhaps a dish of wild mushrooms stewed in butter.

POT-ROAST SADDLE OF HARE WITH CHESTNUTS
Hasenbraten mit Kastanien (Austria)

Hares used to be considered royal game – suitable for the noblest table – and are at their best at this time of year. The age of the animal can be detected from its size, and from the yellowness of the teeth. A young hare will have small white teeth and claws well hidden by fur. The older hare will have longer claws and slightly greying wavy fur. Undressed, it can weigh as much as 12lb/6kg, but it will lose at least a third of that in the skinning and paunching. A large brown lowland hare will feed 8–10 people, a smaller 'blue' mountain hare 6–8.

Quantity: Serves 6–8.

Time: Start a few hours ahead. 2 hours intermittent attention.

Equipment: A larding needle, a small saucepan and a lidded casserole.

1 saddle of hare (include the back legs if the hare is small)
2oz/50g fat bacon or pork
1 large carrot, scraped and sliced
6 peppercorns, crushed
1 small piece root ginger
2 bay leaves
1 teaspoon dried thyme
1 glass water

1lb/500g fresh chestnuts, or 8oz/250g dried chestnuts, soaked for a few hours
1 tablespoon wine vinegar
salt
1 large onion, peeled and sliced
1 garlic clove, peeled and crushed
1 teaspoon dried marjoram
½ pint/300ml red wine
1oz/25g butter

To finish
1/4 pint/150ml soured cream, mixed with 1 teaspoon of flour

Rub the inside of the hare with vinegar, and clean out any blood clots in the ribcage with salt. Use a sharp knife to remove the tough membrane skin from the back and the legs (if you have included them). Cut the bacon or pork fat into thin strips and use them to lard the saddle – hare meat is dry and lean, as befits such an energetic wild creature.

Put the joint in the casserole with the onion, carrot, garlic and aromatics and add the wine and water. Bring it all to the boil, then turn down the heat and simmer gently for 5 minutes. Remove from the heat and leave the hare to marinate for a few hours.

Take the hare out of the marinade (reserve the liquid and all its bits) and pat it dry. Melt the butter and turn the hare in the hot fat till it takes a little colour. Add a couple of spoonfuls of the marinade, bubble up, turn down the heat, lid tightly and roast at 375°F/190°C/Gas 5 for about 45 minutes, pouring in spoonfuls of the marinade as the juices dry out, until all the marinade has been added.

Meanwhile, prick the fresh chestnuts and put them to roast in the oven with the hare. Skin them when they are soft. If using dried chestnuts, simmer them in enough milk to cover them for 30–40 minutes (in the oven with the hare if you like), and drain them. Mash the cooked chestnuts a little, and add them to the juices round the hare for the last 30 minutes of the cooking time.

Remove the lid for the last 10 minutes of cooking to gild the hare and reduce the juices.

Transfer the hare to a warm dish and stir the cream into the pot juices. Bubble the sauce up, and simmer gently for 5 minutes, until it thickens.

Serve the hare with plain boiled brown lentils. Hand the cream and chestnut sauce separately. You have been out on the hill all day – so who's worried about a little cream?

PIG-KILLING: *CIRCA* NOVEMBER 19TH

The annual pig-killing was an occasion of great importance in the rural calendar. The event was not without its poignancy: the household pig was almost a member of the family – an important member, in good standing, who had been cared for and fed on the kitchen scraps ever since he was a small piglet. The ritual customarily took place after the animal had been turned into the fields to glean, or given the run of the chestnut and acorn woods after the autumn gathering. This was the time when he was at his plumpest and most succulent – guaranteeing plenty of lard for the winter.

The Belgians, of all western Europeans, perhaps most love their pork and the *cochonailles* which are a source of national gastronomic pride. Marcel Rémy remembered the pig-killings of his youth in *Les ceux de chez nous* (Brussels, 1925):

> I was so excited before the event, I don't think I took off my stockings to sleep in all the week which preceded it. When the day finally dawned – such happiness. At last. We could hear the pig in the sty squealing for his morning feed; then my uncle pulled open the heavy wooden door of the pig-sty and hid himself behind it. And the pig trotted out into the courtyard snuffling and making his noises. If it had been me, I'd have made a run for it. He stopped and screwed up his little eyes like a farmworker whose nap in the hay has been disturbed, then he wrinkled up his nose and squealed a thousand times louder, until my uncle straddled him and gave him the fatal blow. He made a little pouff, like a puff-ball exploding, and that was all. I don't think he even noticed.

In pre-war rural Hungary, a village household informed its neighbours there was a pig-killing by hanging in the window a beautifully carved fork, a small branch stripped of its bark, with the new twigs on each side cut down to form spikes, on which would be speared pieces of bacon, sausage and crackling as the day progressed. The ritual often took place on November 19th, Hungarian St Elisabeth's Day, when the saint shakes her petticoat and it snows. Or people might wait until Catherine's, Andrew's, or Lucia's Day. Or even between the two Christmases, the birth of Christ and the birth of the New Year.

Károly Viski, in *Hungarian Peasant Customs*, described the event:

> A poor man begins with one sucking pig, to end up with one weighing a ton; but at a well-to-do house, particularly on the Great Plain, especially if there are summer workmen to be catered for, six to eight pigs are killed in one winter. The killing of the pig is counted as a family feast, the children do not go to school on that day. Work begins before the light of dawn. The friends and relations come with lamps, on their shoulders they bring pitch forks, a few of them carry knives. First of all they take a swig of plum or peach brandy. Then a few hot cakes, or boiled sausages if there are any left from last year. By the time it has dawned, the victim has already been brought back from the end of the village, where the actual killing and the singeing of its skin is done with great care and cleanliness.
>
> Meanwhile everyone at home is preparing – the water is being boiled, pepper and paprika pounded, bread-pap thinned, firkins cleaned, fresh dish-cloths prepared. The dissecting and preparing is done with great skill, no trained butcher could do it better. They know every part of the animal, and each part is used for a different purpose. By evening everything is ready: white and other sausages, black pudding, a pudding made of sow's maw; even lard all salted, lies in its place. Dinner too is ready – a gift of gratitude for help proffered by friends and neighbours. The menu is: chicken soup with thin noodles, stuffed cabbage, fresh sow's maw pudding and different kinds of spicy sausages. At wealthy households this is followed by roast capon; the fried sweet is brought in last: doughnuts, cream cheese pudding, flead cakes or other suchlike things, and of course plenty of wine to remedy the defects of so many heavy dishes. Normally there is no lack of toasts – the feast would not be complete without them.

The Belgians get much of their *charcuterie* from the Ardennes. There are still pig-killings in isolated Ardennes villages in the autumn – sometimes of a single animal shared between two or three families and fed off the combined households' scraps. The hams are cured for several days in spiced apple vinegar, rubbed with saltpetre and pickled in a wooden tub in unrefined rock salt imported through Liège or from the Lorraine. After it has taken the salt, the ham is hung up for smoking – a process which can take several months. The wood for smoking the pride of the Ardennes is chosen with passionate care – and usually includes broom. Old houses in the rural areas still have the brick smoke curing areas built in the loft where the chimney came through.

In Britain, Dorothy Hartley recorded her own household's reverent treatment of the pig from the miller at Melton Mowbray in about 1935:

First his sides were laid for bacon, the spareribs therefrom made boney pie, the hams, so skilfully cut, were sugar-cured by a treasured recipe. The head and trimmings and ears made brawn, the fry was a day's dinner; the sausage meat went into its skin; and the porkpie meat, strewed with seasoning, went into its deep panshon. Then the porkpie crust was made. Boiling water and lard were poured into the warm flour in frothing dusty cascades: pummel briskly up and down till the dough is elastic. Then as the pieces were cut off, they were 'raised' round our wooden pie-moulds, with swift admonishing pats and pokes, and little anxious in-drawings of the breath, and a satisfactory little snort that put the cooling paste aside to set.

The lard was rendered down in a big iron pot, just as in the mountains they render down the mutton fat. As the clear transparent oil was ladled from the pot to cool, whitening in the deep jar, the little bits of skin (flead) dried and brown, fried crisp, these scratchings, as they called them, were scratched up from the bottom of the pan, sprinkled with chopped parsley and eaten for breakfast, or made into scratchy pastry, this last a variant of the beaten flead cake of Kent . . . So end all good English pigs according to their breed.

Hens, that other stalwart of the independent farmer's barnyard, like to get together with a loose pig, because he's such a good forager. He digs, they hang around and peck. It all leads to eggs and bacon for breakfast – all round Europe.

Eric Newby, in the early 1980s, visiting a small village in former Yugoslavia, sampled the fruits of the autumn pig-killing:

The prflut was delicious, a rare delicacy. The smoking of this sort of ham is usually carried out in late autumn or in winter and the process of preparing it is only commenced at the time of the full moon. At any other time an inferior product will result. Like many other peasant communities around the Mediterranean, the inhabitants of the Kras are still to a great extent governed by the moon in their everyday life. To prepare this ham it was first kept in salt for a week, then it was put in what looked a bit like an old-fashioned letter press for another week, the pressure being increased daily. It was then hung in a chimney to smoke over a fire of ash wood and after that it was hung for anything from seven months to a year in a dry place, having been previously sprinkled with pepper as a protection against flies, which together with dampness, were its principal enemies. By the time a prflut reached Trieste, a good one was about as expensive as smoked salmon.

PORK MEATBALLS IN BEER
Boulettes à la bière (Belgium)

The *plat spécial* of the pig-killing meal – the highlight of the *kermesse aux boudins* which now marks Belgian high days and holidays – is the head, ears, trotters of the pig, simmered with spices and lambic beer for at least 2 hours, served with a rather more manageable dish of meatballs, and presented on a large platter surrounded by its accompaniments.

Quantity: Serves 4.
Time: Allow 1 hour intermittent attention.
Equipment: A bowl. A heavy shallow saucepan.

1lb/500g minced pork
2oz/50g breadcrumbs, soaked in 4 tablespoons
  milk
salt and pepper
2oz/50g butter
1 stick celery, washed and sliced
1½ pints/900ml light beer (*bière blonde*)
2oz/50g raisins

1 egg
1 teaspoon dried marjoram
½ teaspoon grated nutmeg
3–4 shallots, peeled and chopped
1 tablespoon flour
1 carrot, washed and sliced
1 bay leaf and a sprig of thyme
4oz/100g prunes (with their stones)

To finish
¼ pint/150ml double cream
1 heaped tablespoon parsley

salt and pepper

Work the pork into a firm mass with the egg, breadcrumbs, marjoram and nutmeg, salt and pepper, and one of the shallots sweated briefly in a little of the butter. Form the mixture into a dozen balls and roll them lightly in a little flour.

Melt the rest of the butter in the saucepan and turn the meatballs in the hot froth for a moment or two. Add the remaining shallots, the celery and the carrot. Let them take the heat for a moment. Pour in the beer and let it bubble up. Add the bay leaf and thyme and the dried fruit and bring everything back to the boil. Turn down the heat, lid, and leave to simmer until the meatballs are tender and the prunes soft – 35–40 minutes.

Remove the meatballs and the fruit and keep them warm while you reduce the sauce to about ½ pint/300ml. Stir in the cream and allow it all to bubble up. Taste and add salt and pepper as necessary – not too much, as the flavours are subtly sweet.

Serve the meatballs lightly sauced, and sprinkled with parsley arranged on a platter flanked with plain-boiled Brussels sprouts and nutmeg-spiced mashed potatoes or sliced potatoes sautéed with butter and onion. Hand the extra cream sauce and a sharp apple purée separately. Beer must accompany, of course.

LARDY CAKES
(Britain)

These fleadcakes, and similar ones made with the scratchings left from the rendered lard, were tradition-ally made all over Europe on pig-killing day. In England they developed into delicious currant-and-rais-ing-enriched sweet doughs which remain popular the year round – now particularly a speciality of Wiltshire and the West Country, where the pigs fatten on the cider pulp and the apple-orchard gleanings. They were served for tea on Saturday and Sunday.

Quantity: Makes 1 cake to serve 4–6.
Time: Start a couple of hours ahead.
Equipment: A mixing bowl and sieve. A rolling pin and board. A roasting tin and cooling rack.

1lb/500g flour
1oz/25g fresh yeast (½oz/12g dried)
½ pint/300ml warm water
8oz/250g mixed currants, sultanas and
 crystallized peel

½ teaspoon salt
6oz/175g lard
3 tablespoons granulated sugar mixed with 1oz/25g
 mixed spice

Sieve the flour with the salt. Rub in the yeast (if using dried, follow the instructions on the packet) and 1 tablespoon of the lard. Make a well in the middle and mix in enough warm water to give a soft sticky dough. Knead it well on the floured board until it is no longer sticky.

Form the dough into a neat ball and put it in a warm bowl, covered with a clean cloth. Leave it in a warm place to double in size – about 1 hour should be enough.

Knock down the dough and knead it briefly to distribute the air bubbles. Roll the dough out on the floured board. Dot it with one third of the rest of the lard cut into walnut-sized lumps, about 1½in/4cm apart, and sprinkle 1 tablespoon of spiced granulated sugar and a third of the dried fruit. Fold the dough into three from the ends, and then into three from the sides. Repeat the process twice, each time putting on dabs of lard and sprinkling with sugar and fruit.

After three foldings and lardings, roll the dough out to fit the well-greased roasting tin. Score it with a sharp knife into portions. Put the dough back in its warm place to rise again for another 20–30 min-utes, until it puffs up again.

Bake the lardy cake in a hot oven, 425°F/220°C/Gas 7, for about 30 minutes until deliciously brown – but keep an eye on it in case you have to turn the oven down. Remove it carefully to the rack to cool.

It smells so delicious, it's almost impossible to leave it until it cools. But don't touch it immediately it comes out of the oven – sugar can give a nasty burn.

PAPRIKA SAUSAGES
(Hungary)

Most pig-killing meals included fresh sausages – usually the only time when the peasantry ate them. On market-day, too, little sausages and spiced liver and such small treats, cheaply bought by the pedlars from the local butcher, were grilled on the spot and sold to the housewives, exhausted by their morning's mar-keting on either side of the counter.

Quantity: Serves 6–8.
Time: 30 minutes intermittent attention.
Equipment: A bowl. A funnel if you are using proper casings. A grill or frying pan.

2lb/1kg roughly minced belly pork

1 tablespoon salt

1 teaspoon ground white pepper

grated rind of 1 lemon

1 garlic clove

1 teaspoon paprika

1 teaspoon crushed marjoram

sausage casings (*optional*)

Work all the ingredients together (except the optional casings) into a firm smooth paste. Either stuff the mixture into sausage casings through a funnel (remembering to push the skin up the funnel, instead of trying to squirt the mixture down the tube), or form the meat into patties – easier to handle if you dust them with flour.

Grill the sausages, or fry them in a little lard, until well browned and sizzling.

Serve with thick chunks of bread, mild mustard and grated horseradish.

PIG'S KIDNEYS WITH SHERRY
Riñones al jerez (Spain)

When I lived in Andalucía with my growing family, we kept a household pig – it would have been very ill-seen by the neighbours if we had thrown away the vegetable trimmings from our meals, which also fed two maids, a gardener, and our many visitors. Besides which, we inhabited an acorn-loaded cork-oak forest, and what could be better for fattening the fellow in the autumn? On the appointed day, the pig met his maker, and everyone in the valley came over to help and advise. We made black puddings, *chorizos*, fillet of pork preserved in red lard. We salted the sides for bacon, and sent the hams up to the mountains to be salted and cured in the dry air of the Sierra Morena. Those who were still there at the end of the day were rewarded with the kidneys cooked in the sherry we had been sipping from mid-morning onwards. I had to include the liver, finely sliced, with appropriate increases in the other ingredients, since the party always seemed to double by sundown.

Quantity: Serves 4.
Time: Start 1 hour ahead. 15 minutes.
Equipment: A bowl. A heavy frying pan.

a pair of pig's kidneys, skinned and trimmed
  of the core

1 onion, peeled and chopped

1 teaspoon paprika

1 tablespoon chopped parsley

1 glass water

1 teaspoon vinegar for soaking

2 tablespoons lard or olive oil

1 clove garlic, peeled and crushed

1 tablespoon fresh breadcrumbs

1 glass dry sherry

salt and pepper

Slice the kidneys finely and put them to soak for 1 hour or so in water acidulated with vinegar, to rid them of some of the ammoniac taste. Or, if you are in a hurry, scald the kidney slices with boiling water.

Warm the lard or oil in a pan. Put in the onion and garlic and let them soften for a moment. Add the kidneys and turn them in the hot oil. Stir in the paprika, then the breadcrumbs and parsley. Pour in the sherry and bubble up to evaporate the alcohol. Add the water, stir well and bring back to the boil.

Lid tightly, turn down the heat, and simmer gently for 10 minutes, until the kidneys are tender and the sauce well thickened. Taste and add salt and pepper.

Serve with thick chunks of country bread, and more ice-cold dry sherry.

TRUFFLE HARVEST

Monsieur Bréman, of Mirabel aux Baronnies on the slopes of Mont Ventoux in upper Provence, is the proud owner of a patch of truffle oaks. I had the good fortune to be invited, one cold morning in early December, to accompany him on his weekly scour of the stony ground for *Tuber melanosporum*, the black diamond of the Périgord. M. Bréman's half-hectare of Kermes oaks was planted forty years ago, pushing aside the vines which take their unique bouquet from the mixture of lavender, thyme and truffle oaks which surrounds them, in a favoured patch where oaks had already produced truffles.

The countryside is low and hilly, edging the valley of the Rhône, rich red acres of well-husbanded vines, thyme grown in rows and square hectares planted with truffle oaks – squat little trees with prickle-edged leaves, brittle and brown but still hanging on their branches in December. Nothing like the scallop-leaved giants of our own countryside whose leaves fall off the silver-barked branches in autumn. The presence of the proprietors and their dogs on their truffle patches is betrayed here and there by the tail of a small rusting grey van protruding from the edge of a line of oaks. However full his mattress may be with the proceeds of his profitable trade, even the richest of Provençal farmers buckets about in an old *camionette*.

The process of where and how the truffle grows remains mysterious – the inconstant tuber is essentially a wild crop, as unpredictable as any game bird. France is not the only place where *Tuber melanosporum* flourishes, either. It is found in Spain as far south as Valencia, and in northern Italy too. But the best are harvested, say the natives of the Périgord, between the limits of the 43rd and the 45th parallel.

It is impossible to predict what will be found under the few inches of earth beneath the carpet of prickly leaves which is the black diamond's preferred habitat. One memorable year M. Bréman had 60lb/30 kilos in his single weekly gathering. He – in common with the other farmer-proprietors who find the crop a highly profitable sideline – would be the first to seed his oaks artificially if he had any faith in such tricks:

'They have done a great deal of work on the trufficulture. Each year there's a new excitement about artificial cultivation. You can sow the oaks with the mycelium, but it's not reliable, and in my experience, doesn't seem to make good truffles. The worst-looking trees often produce the best truffles. You can plant a hundred trees and only get ten which produce – one year it'll be one which has the fungus, the next year another. It's a matter of weather too. You need rain in July and August for a good harvest the following winter. Oak is not the only host-tree either – you find them on the roots of hazel, poplar, lime and several others – although in my experience the oak produces the best.'

We fetch Noireau, M. Bréman's all-important assistant, from his confinement in the farmyard, and set out in the cold crisp air, down a little track in between lines of neatly pruned vines. Noireau is a little black dog, eight years old and of no particular breeding: there's black labrador retriever in there somewhere – cockers and setters are highly rated – with a bit of poodle and terrier for good measure. Noireau has bright intelligent eyes and a very pointed noise. He has had no supper or breakfast and is eager for an outing.

The dog is not naturally interested in the black tuber. That is the pig's forte – except that the pig cannot be trained not to gobble up what he grubs. *Tuber melanosporum* is, after all, just another lump of black fungus to a mutt. He has to be trained to pick out that special perfume, richer as the truffle matures. A human can nose out his own truffles, of course – old spinsters with little on their mind are said to be the best – and there are sometimes a few indicators to help: a crack in the soil near a host tree, or a cloud of tiny reddish flies on a warm day. But a truffle-hound will find ten times as many, scenting them out deep down under the hard packed earth.

A good dog can fetch a million *ancien francs* at the truffle-and-hound market at Bagnols-sur-Cèze, so owners generally train their own companions. Each truffler has his own method. M. Bréman starts with a bit of truffled omelette to give the dog the taste for the job. Then he buries a real truffle in a patch of ground, shows it to the trainee, and rewards him when he finds it. After that the reward is a bit of bread, scented by contact with the truffle the dog has just found.

'You must treat a dog well. He needs a lot of love and encouragement. He must be quarantined the night before of course – if there is a bitch on heat nearby, that's bad, as he will lose concentration. One day there was one down there at the farm, and he smelled it for miles.'

M. Bréman uses a bread stick as a reward. 'It's easy to break into lengths. Noireau is clever, though – he measures the bread stick when we begin the hunt. When he knows there is no bread left, he will give up.'

Noireau sets out along the line of oaks: casual but eager, like a dude on a Saturday night. He scrabbles quickly in the earth, wags his tail and wanders away. M. Bréman goes over with his little pick. He hacks for a few moments and sniffs. There's something there, but he doesn't want to overwork the ground. He calls Noireau back – you don't let a dog scrape too long or he hurts his paws and won't work any more. The dog scrapes again to the left of the hole. Ah. Yes indeed – there it is, a fine black truffle – about 50 grams (2oz), but it has a good colour and smell. The truffles gathered at the beginning of the season are not as good as those gathered in the high season – January and February are the best, December is a little early and March a little late.

We quarter the grove – some finds are large and fine, others not quite ripe, a few are well overdue and as pungent as a well-hung steak, one is enormous. M. Bréman scratches the earth-crusted tuber with his fingernail and examines it carefully. 'See that? Too many white veins. Its flavour will be only moderate. You can never tell. Some trufflers will squeeze a bit of extra earth into the contours – like that, so you don't see it.' He demonstrates, squashing the brown paste into the contours, plugging a hole. 'With the price of truffles as it is, every little extra is a small fortune.'

The truffles are prey to a grub which bores into them. It seems a pity to have to share the prize with the greedy little creatures. M. Bréman shrugs. 'It does no harm – you just shake them out. We have a problem with them here – in sandy soil they don't seem to get them. You see the little fly which hovers over the truffle when it is mature enough to push up the ground – that's the little reddish fly which lays its eggs in the truffle.'

The black truffle of France has a robust, meaty scent – a blend of musk and rare fillet steak – which pervades everything with which it comes into contact. Fresh truffles must be eaten within 2–3 days, and their flavour develops with cooking. If you have to keep them, either sterilize them in small strong jars (just sprinkle the truffle with a little salt first) for 2 hours – the classic Provençal housewife's solution to the storage problem – or slice them and put them up submerged in pure first-pressing olive oil, and use the oil as well as the truffle in your favourite recipe.

The Italians specialize in the white truffle – *Tuber borchii*, the Alba or Piedmont truffle – gathered from the end of October until late December. Like the black, it is symbiotic with oaks and lime trees, but is at its best when it takes its nourishment from the poplar. The delicate white truffle has a flavour which has been described as the perfect marriage between garlic and mature parmesan, and should be eaten raw, grated over a good home-made pasta, risotto or cheese *fonduta*. The Italians also harvest the black truffle, but do not rate it nearly as highly as the white – the French, on the other hand, rate *Tuber borchii* low on the gastronomic truffle table, and prefer the white summer truffle, *Tuber aestivum*, harvested in May, June and August, which also flourishes in Britain.

John Evelyn found summer truffles in seventeenth-century Northamptonshire, and Sacheverell Sitwell dreamed of them *circa* 1965 in *Truffle Hunt*:

> I have always wanted to eat an English truffle. There are quantities of truffles under the beech trees in Wiltshire and Buckinghamshire, but nobody bothers to go and find them. They are not black like the *truffes de Périgord*; nor are they white like the Italian *tartuffi bianchi*. They are apparently green in colour. I had a letter from the last of the English truffle hunters, long retired from business, and he enclosed a snapshot of himself and his dog, a kind of poodle of a particular breed, rather a queer-looking quadruped. If English truffles are as good as white truffles eaten at the Antico Pappagallo in Bologna, English epicures are missing something.

SCRAMBLED EGGS WITH TRUFFLES
La brouillade de truffes (France)

The beautiful and wise Marquise de Pompadour, mistress to Louis XV, kept her *bien aimé* in fine amorous fettle with her delicate dishes of truffles – very useful when the royal lover, as happened not infrequent-ly, had a *défaillance*. This is the way the truffle-hunters themselves prepare those of the harvest which are too small to command a good price in the market place.

Quantity: Serves 4.
Time: Start the day before. 10 minutes to cook.
Equipment: A bowl and whisk. A heavy-bottomed saucepan.

10 fresh eggs
1 small glass olive oil

1 small truffle (about 1oz/25g) per egg
salt and pepper

Leave the eggs and the truffles overnight in the same bowl, tightly covered. The next day, brush and rinse the dirt swiftly off the truffles, pat them dry and cut them into fine slices – or matchsticks, if you prefer.

Call everyone to table. This dish waits for no man – not even the King of France.

Put the oil to warm on a low heat with the truffles.

Crack the eggs into the bowl and whisk them lightly together. Season with salt and pepper. When the oil is hot, but not yet smoking, stir in the eggs. Turn them with the oil and truffles until they form very soft juicy curds.

Serve immediately, with bread and good red wine.

TRUFFLES WITH RED WINE
Ragoût de truffes (France)

The enthusiasm with which the opening of the truffle season is greeted by France's gourmets was recorded by Sacheverell Sitwell in *Truffle Hunt*:

> A friend motoring in France arrived at Poitiers during the dinner hour, and going to the dining room was a little startled to find a number of persons seated at a table with their heads enclosed in pillow-cases. Delighted sounds were emerging from those white hoods, and it was nothing more than a conference of gourmets trying out a new dish of truffles. The pillow-cases were to protect their palates from contamination by the outer world.

Quantity: Serves 4.
Time: Start an hour or two ahead.
Equipment: A little brush, a bowl and a small saucepan.

8oz/250g truffles	4 tablespoons olive oil
2–3 anchovies	1 sprig thyme
8 little white onions or neatly trimmed shallots, skinned	2 glasses of a generous red wine
salt and pepper	5 egg yolks – one for each 2oz/50g of truffle

Brush the truffles, quickly rinse off the dirt, and slice them thickly. Put the slices to soak in the olive oil for an hour or two.

Heat the oil and the truffles in a small saucepan, and add the anchovies, thyme, onions and red wine. Lid, and simmer for 30 minutes.

Whisk the egg yolks lightly, and stir them into the sauce off the heat. Heat the mixture gently to thicken the eggs.

Serve as soon as it thickens, with plenty of bread and more of the same red wine. Look for a good vintage of Châteauneuf du Pape – or any fine wine from truffle-country: the truffles add their special perfume to the wines from the areas they colonize.

CHICKEN WITH TRUFFLES AND CHAMPAGNE
Poularde aux truffes (France)

Farmers' wives of the Périgord fatten their own geese, ducks and capons, and someone will often set up a little trestle near the truffle-market to take advantage of gastronomic urges inspired by the irresistible scent of the black diamonds. This is the most famous of all truffle recipes – with quite a reputation to support. Napoleon himself, on learning from one of his young subalterns, a native of Sarlat, that the young man's father had sired nineteen sons, each one exactly nine months after consuming a *poularde aux truffes*, ordered a consignment of fresh truffles brought from the Périgord, and had his cook prepare the famous dish. Nine months later, the future King of Rome was born, and the young subaltern received instant promotion to colonel of his native regiment.

Quantity: Serves 4.
Time: 45 minutes to prepare. About 1 hour to cook.
Equipment: A lidded casserole.

1 very white chicken (2–3lb/1–1.5kg)
4oz/100g black truffles (more if you have them)
4oz/100g butter
1 onion or 2 shallots
8 fl oz/200ml double cream

salt and pepper
¼ pint/150ml chicken stock (made with the neck
    and giblets, peppercorns and pot-herbs)
¼ bottle dry champagne

Wipe the chicken and season it inside and out. Brush the dirt off the truffles and rinse them quickly under cold water to dislodge any grit. Dry and slice very thinly. Lift up the skin of the chicken with a sharp knife and insert slices of truffle, like big dark freckles, all over the bird, just between the skin and the flesh, but taking care not to cut through the skin. Put the chicken neck and giblets, and the feet and head if you have them, into a small pan of fresh water with peppercorns and a bit of carrot, onion and celery, and leave it to simmer.

Melt the butter in the casserole and sauté the chicken on all sides until it has taken a deliciously golden colour. Lid tightly, turn the heat right down, and cook for 40 minutes, until the chicken is nearly done. You can do this in a medium oven, 350°F/180°C/ Gas 4, if you prefer. Add the onions and let them fry for a minute or two.

Pour the champagne round the bird, bring to the boil, cover, and leave to simmer until the chicken is tender. Remove it from the casserole, joint it neatly, and keep it warm while you finish the sauce.

Pour the well-reduced stock into the buttery hot juices in the casserole, scrape in all the sticky bits, and then stir in the cream. Bubble it all up, let it reduce and thicken for a minute or two.

Pour some of the sauce over the jointed chicken, and serve the rest in a sauceboat. You can strain it or not as you please.

A deliciously earthy purée of celeriac and potatoes would keep appropriate company with the truffled *poularde* – just enough to soak up the juices.

WHITE TRUFFLES WITH PASTA
Tagliatelle al tartuffo bianco (Italy)

Naturally a truffle whose scent is of garlic and parmesan is at its best on home-made all-egg pasta – or perhaps a perfect risotto made with love and care and Arborio rice.

Quantity: Serves 4–6.
Time: About 1 hour.
Equipment: A large mixing bowl. A rolling pin and board. A roomy saucepan. A draining spoon or colander. A little grater.

The pasta
14oz/425g flour
4 eggs

1 teaspoon salt

To finish

1 white truffle (about 4oz/100g)

1–2 cloves garlic, skinned and crushed

2–3 anchovy fillets (*optional*)

1 small glass olive oil

salt and pepper

grated parmesan

First make the pasta. Sieve the flour into a bowl with the salt. Make a well in the middle, and crack in the eggs one by one. Mingle the eggs together with your fingers curved into a hook, drawing flour from the edges as you do so, till a dough-ball forms. When it is soft and smooth and pliable, shake a little flour on to the board and roll out the dough. Leave it to rest for 10 minutes. When the dough has rested, roll it loosely, like a small yellow carpet, and then slice it across into thin strips.

Pile the rolls of cut pasta loosely on the table, then pick up each roll and toss it in the air until the surface has dried a little and there is no longer any danger of the threads sticking together.

Brush the truffle and rinse it quickly to get rid of the dirt. Warm the olive oil with the garlic, salt and pepper, and the anchovies, well crushed down.

Poach the pasta in plenty of water – 2–3 minutes is enough. Drain it quickly and not too thoroughly, and toss with the warmed olive oil. Stir in a sprinkling of parmesan.

Grate on the truffle just as you serve the pasta, so that the sumptuous aroma can be fully appreciated.

SUMMER TRUFFLES BAKED WITH POTATOES AND CREAM
(Britain)

This is my favourite way with all edible fungi. The rich earthy flavour of wild mushrooms is wonderful with the tender sweet flesh of the potato. I'm sure the seventeenth-century gourmet and diarist John Evelyn, who described the English truffle in his vegetable cookbook, *Acetaria*, would have agreed – had the New World potato achieved its modern status – that there could be no companions more perfectly compatible.

Quantity: Serves 4 as a main dish.
Time: 15 minutes. 1 hour to cook.
Equipment: An earthenware casserole. A small saucepan.

8oz/250g truffles or wild mushrooms (more if
   you have them)

1 clove garlic, skinned and sliced finely (wild
   garlic leaves would be even better)

1 pint/600ml single cream

2oz/50g butter

3lb/1.5kg floury potatoes, peeled and sliced as thin
   as a penny

salt and pepper

Brush the truffles or mushrooms, rinse them briefly and slice them thickly – never soak fungi in water, a brief shower is all they need. Melt the butter and turn the fungi in it for a moment or two.

Layer the potatoes and the fungi in the casserole – starting and finishing with potatoes, and sprinkling with garlic, salt and plenty of freshly milled pepper as you go.

Bring the cream to the boil and pour it into the casserole – it should nearly submerge the potatoes. Lid tightly, or cover with foil.

Bake in a medium oven, 350°F/180°C/Gas 4, for 50–60 minutes, until the potatoes are quite tender.

Bring the casserole still well-lidded to the table – the scent released when you open it is at least a quarter of the pleasure. Serve with a salad of winter leaves – whatever you can find.

PROVENÇAL OLIVE HARVEST – *LES OLIVADES*: NOVEMBER TO JANUARY

The olive harvest has been the winter work of the Mediterranean peasantry for going on 5,000 years – probably ever since the first hunter-gathering cook discovered that the bitter little wild fruits yielded a sweet golden juice with remarkable properties. In rural communities methods of processing have changed little over the millennia. The olives have to be picked patiently by hand – there is to date no mechanical substitute for human labour. The skilled harvester pulls the fruit off its short stalk only with the lie of the twig, so that the branches are not harmed. Such care in the picking requires equal selectivity in the choice of miller – and the oil-millers of Mirabelle aux Baronnies, in France's premier olive-growing district of Nyons, in upper Provence, are among the best in the business.

Paul and Alain Farnoux, father and son – like grandfather Farnoux and his grandfather before them – still mill the olives from the ancient trees much as their ancestors did in Roman times, when the silvery giants were first planted. The olive harvest is in full swing from November to January. When I visited the Farnoux mill in 1988 for my annual supplies of the thick emerald-green first pressing virgin olive oil for whose peppery smoothness there is no substitute, Alain Farnoux was gradually taking over the daily running of the business from his father.

'It's hard in the season – we might work all night because people pick during the day and bring in the fruit when the sun goes down – about 5.30 or 6.00. We pick from our own trees, and we press for other people as well. There is a special price for pressing only – many people like to have their own oil for their year's supply. When anyone has too much for their own use, we take it and sell it for them.'

The medieval equipment – including the wooden shaft hewed out of a whole tree-trunk – is still in position at the back. The great cool stone mill-room, half carved out of the living rock, is equipped with its own natural water spring. Water is essential in the process, as it is needed to wash the oil – although donkey or man-power might have been used to turn the mill-wheel. The modern press, too, is a matter for pride. There have been no presses made in France since 1956 – the year of the big freeze, when many of Provence's olive trees died. Now all the presses are imported from Italy or Spain.

Outside the mill a ladder has been propped against the thick unmortared stone wall. It is narrower at the top than at the bottom, so that it can easily be manoeuvred through the canopy of the tree and rested against the less robust branches of the crown. It is a very long ladder. 'Ah, but we have longer ladders,' Paul says. 'Don't forget that you are seeing mostly the post-1956 olive trees – and they are only just achieving their true height. Wait for another twenty years, and you will see some well-grown trees.'

The first job is to sort the fruit. Small olives go for the oil, and the big ones are for pickling. During the season there is a small wholesale market at Mirabelle every Friday morning at about 8.30, when the buyers come in to negotiate with the growers for their pickling olives – the best and fattest of the crop.

Then the milling olives are spread over the mill-stones in the heavy steel vat. The great twin wheels of Italian granite from the mines at Florence are linked together by an axle. Nothing goes in but the ripe fruit.

Alain grins as the mill-wheels grind. 'The modern factory way is to bruise the fruit with four big stone hammers, and then it is done in no time.' When the olives are well crushed into a thick paste, Alain scoops it on to 2-foot diameter discs – they used to be made of esparto grass or hemp, and are now made of plastic fibre.

Alain threads the discs through their central hole on to a pole. The pole is on a trolley – all ready for trundling under the press. By the time the pile has reached 6 feet/2 metres in height, the sheer weight of the stack has begun to produce a steady trickle of fresh golden juice. It runs down the sides like maple syrup off pistachio ice cream.

Leftover paste, 'le grignan', is sent off to be made into soap (olive oil soap is lovely – soft and smooth and good for the skin). Some of it is kept back to be used for fuel. The Farnoux family heat their whole house from a boiler in the mill which is fuelled by grignan. Or the grignan can be sold to the oil-process-ing factories, where it is heated and washed and processed to be sold as olive oil – although, having been treated, it is no longer virgin.

'The industrial process does not use a press like this,' Alain explains. 'It employs a hot water method – up to 60°C is permitted for virgin olive oil – to separate the oil from the water. With this method there is no heat at all, and no loss of vitamins or acidity, and our acidity is usually around 0.3 per cent. The shorter the time from olive to press, the lower the acidity.'

Paul thrusts a lipped bottle under the cloudy green-gold stream emerging from the primitive gravity press and holds it up to the light. 'Pure fruit juice,' he smiles happily. 'The butter of Provence.'

The juice is pumped up to a cask. Oil being lighter than water, the oil rises to the surface. A pipe lead-ing from the top of the barrel skims off the oil and funnels it into the bottles. The water is piped away from the bottom: it is of no further use. The corks are rammed home and that's it: time to celebrate with the first oil of the season, poured, oil-miller style, straight on to a thick wedge of bread toasted over the grignan fire.

OIL-MILLER'S TOASTS
Roustido du moulin (France)

Frédéric Mistral, the poet of Provence, described in *Memori e raconte* the dance of the Olivettes – an ancient ritual which accompanied the harvesting of the olives in the Alpilles – supposedly to amuse the pickers and encourage them in their exhausting, icy task. It features the noisy warlike behaviour familiar in all such ceremonies, designed to scare away malevolent spirits, but given an added poignancy, as in lower Provence it also serves to record the difficulties the villagers had in gaining access to their harvest during the Moorish occupation.

> A party of sixteen young men, dressed in Roman costume, headed by various officers – a king, a prince, a general – and preceded by a harlequin clown and a herald, march in double file to the beat of military drums. They perform various figures and tattoos – the figure of eight, the chain, and several others – while the herald twirls his baton, and the clown apes the herald's movements to the amusement of the spectators. The Olivettes come to a halt in the town square and stage a mock-battle by clashing their swords together in a rising crescendo. The king and the prince duel. Their subjects cheer them on and the whole rout is completed with a cavalcade of the participants, riding their swords like hobby-horses, in a circle round the harlequin.

This is the traditional supper offered to their pickers on the completion of the harvest by the millers of Provence. The tradition is rapidly vanishing – although it is still usual to *esquicher les anchois* after the harvesting. The flavours and the habit live on, in spirit at least, in the *anchoiade* of recent restaurant invention.

Quantity: Serves as many as the bread will satisfy.
Time: 10 minutes.
Equipment: A grill, or a toasting fork and the glowing embers of the fire.

a large loaf of rough country bread, sliced thickly
garlic cloves (1 per slice)
anchovy fillets (about 2 per slice – if they are from
  the barrel, soak them in milk for an hour or two
  and de-whisker them first – but only if you do
  not like your pleasures rustic)

a flacon of first-pressing virgin olive oil (about 2
  tablespoons per slice)

Set out all the ingredients and admire them. Each person should construct their own *roustido* – how else to decide on the right proportions for your taste?

Baptize the bread with thick green fresh olive oil. Spread a crushed garlic clove and two fillets of anchovy on each slice. You will need no salt, as the fish are quite salty enough. Vary the quantities as you please.

Grill or toast the bread under or at the highest heat, until it roasts and sizzles. Enjoy it immediately – at its best with plenty of the wine of the country, for which it provides a fine internal cushion.

FUNERAL FEASTS

In Saxon Britain, the funeral feast was the heir-ale or Norse *Arval* – at the end of which the heir was announced. The spirit of the dead man was welcomed at the feast, and had to be offered a share, although the ghost could eat only ghostly nourishment – leaving the real food to be enjoyed by the mourners. After the advent of Christianity, the ghost's share of the food was given to the poor of the parish so that they might offer prayers for the departed.

In western Europe we are no longer so robust in our view of the final rites, and firmly separate the dead from the living – with the reading of the will timed to put a dignified distance between the subject of the funeral and his heirs. Even in Ireland the traditional keening of the professional mourners is no longer heard, although sorrows are still liberally drowned in that blessed distillation which the Irish claim as their own. Ham and cold meats are the funeral feast of Ireland – with *crabeens* – pig's trotters, plain boiled – to line the stomach for the libation of poteen which is still a cottage industry, however illegal, all over the Emerald Isle.

The taste for funeral cold cuts is shared by the English – who prefer their funerals, as with all their celebrations, to have a generous seasoning of pomp and circumstance, a predilection nicely observed by that chronicler of the petty bourgeoisie, H.G. Wells, describing the obsequies attendant on the orphaning of his fictional tragi-comic hero, Mr Polly:

All the preparations for the funeral ran easily and happily under Mrs Johnson's skilful hands. On the eve of the sad occasion she produced a reserve of black sateen, the kitchen steps and a box of tin tacks, and decorated the house with festoons and bows of black in the best possible taste. She anticipated the long contemplated purchase of a table-cloth for the front room, and substituted a violet-purple cover for the now very worn and faded raptures and roses in plushette that had previously done duty there. Everything that loving consideration could do to impart a dignified solemnity to her little house was done.

Later, at the funeral tea:

There were two cold boiled chickens, which Johnson carved with great care and justice, and a nice piece of ham, some brawn, and a steak and kidney pie, a large bowl of salad and several sorts of pickles, and afterwards some cold apple tart, jam roll, and a good piece of Stilton cheese, lots of bottled beer, some lemonade for the ladies, and some milk for Master Punt; a very bright and satisfying meal.

In Mediterranean lands, the trappings of death were never so disposable. The black garments of mourning for the women, the crêpe bands on the arms for the men, are worn not for an afternoon but for years on end. When I lived in Andalucía in southern Spain fifteen years ago, the mourning period was five years for a parent, and a year for any other relation. Still today, in primitive rural areas, any woman over the age of thirty-five may expect to wear black for one reason or another until the end of her days.

Patrick Leigh Fermor, in pre-war rural Greece, found the isolated communities greeting death with naked hand and undraped emotion – much as our ancestors did:

All over the Greek world – indeed, wherever the religion of Byzantium holds sway – village funerals are accompanied by outward signs of lamentation that come as a great surprise to those who have only witnessed the prim obsequies of north-western Europe. The mourning is the work of the women. It begins as a like-wake, a wailing and keening round the body by candle flame, and when the coffin is carried out into the daylight with the corpse rocking from side to side on the carrying shoulders, the mourning lifts to a crescendo that only fitfully subsides during the funeral service in church, to rise once more on the way to the cemetery in the wild cries of the kinswomen. The physical fact of death has no palliations or disguises. The sealed coffin of western Europe and the cosmetics and mummifications of North America are undreamed of. Every Greek child has heard and heard again the agony of the death-rattle and seen the shrunken grey chaps, the fallen jaw and the closed eyelids of their elders. The coffin is left open until the last minute and only lowered into the grave when everyone has kissed the dead cheeks good-bye.

Károly Viski had a merrier time of it in pre-Communist Hungary:

When the mourners come back from the graveyard, the funeral feast begins. At first all the poor who have assembled for the occasion are given food. During the funeral feast there is more gaiety than at the vigil, where sometimes a few jokes break through. And in some parts it gradually changes into a joyous feast, as though the funeral had been exchanged for a wedding. Because of this strange kind of wedding feast in many parts even the very old women are buried in their wedding dress, and old men in the clothes which they were given by their fiancées many years previously. This last wedding is especially the due share of an unmarried lad or girl. They are the bridegrooms or brides of Heaven. So they have a right to a wedding celebration. At this kind of wedding feast, people dance, sing and enjoy themselves as though it were the real thing.

Most of us find it increasingly difficult to deal with death – the unavoidable consequence of birth. Perhaps this is because the sterilized environment which we now inhabit – a consequence of solutions to the problems posed by large populations – has insulated us from appreciating funerals and their accompanying festivities as a celebration of life as well as its natural conclusion.

The necessary formalities of bereavement were – and are – more comfortably accommodated by those who have direct contact with birth and death – whether of animals or humans – and who do not consider it anything but a natural event, whatever their religious beliefs.

MEMORIAL PORRIDGE
Koliva (Greece)

All three Saturdays of Carnival are sacred to the memory of the dead. This is the dish which is made as an offering to them – the last surviving relic of a repertoire of ancient funeral foods, mostly grain porridges garnished with significant ingredients, prepared by the people of pre-Christian Europe. If the porridge is to be served for an actual funeral, a dish of it is taken to church to be blessed, and then it is handed out, wrapped in little paper bags decorated with a cross and the deceased's initials, to those who attend the funeral.

Quantity: Serves 12 small helpings.
Time: Start a few hours ahead. About 1 hour intermittent attention.
Equipment: A saucepan. A jelly mould.

8oz/250g whole wheat grains	1½ pints/900ml water
1 teaspoon salt	2 tablespoons sugar
4 tablespoons home-made toasted breadcrumbs	2oz/50g sultanas
the seeds of a pomegranate	1 tablespoon toasted almonds or sesame seeds

To finish

icing sugar	sugared almonds
silver sugar balls	flat-leaved parsley

Pick over the wheat. Bring the water to the boil with the salt. Drop in the wheat, stir it round, bring it back to the boil and simmer it gently for about 40 minutes, until the wheat is soft and the water has all been absorbed. Stir in the rest of the ingredients and tip the mixture into the jelly mould.

Tip it out when it has set, and sprinkle it with icing sugar. Decorate with sugared almonds and silver balls, with a few parsley leaves to add immortality.

A word of warning: the porridge must be eaten the same day or the wheat may ferment.

BREADCRUMBED HAM
(Britain and Ireland)

Ham is a perfectly appropriate centrepiece for a northern funeral meal. Solid, dignified and quietly cheering, it combines the virtues of the most welcome of funeral guests. Furthermore, it needs no attention while cooking, and can be left to be ready for carving when the party gets home. It would not be honey-baked for such a meal – that is left for more frivolous celebrations. The parsley-stuffed christening chine on p.310 is also quite proper for the occasion – I saw it served for a funeral tea in Nottinghamshire in 1989.

Quantity: Serves 20.
Time: Start the day before. 10 minutes.
Equipment: A very large lidded stew-pot. Old coats and blankets.

1 whole brined ham on the bone
  (12–18 lb/6–9kg in weight)
1 pint/600ml beer or cider water

2lb/1kg vegetable trimmings – carrots, onions,
  leeks, turnips, celery, apples

To finish
about 6oz/175g home-made toasted breadcrumbs

Put the joint in the stew-pot, tuck the vegetables down the sides, cover with the beer or cider and enough cold water to submerge everything, and slowly bring to the boil. Boil for 20 minutes if the ham weighs 12lb/6kg, adding 5 minutes on for each 1lb/500g. Remove the whole pan, ham, liquor and all, from the fire and snuggle it under a heavy covering of old coats and blankets. Leave it for about 12 hours. Drain it. The ham will be perfectly cooked.

Remove the skin and press the toasted breadcrumbs all over the white fat. Serve with salads, pickles and potatoes baked or boiled in their jackets.

KNUCKLE OF VEAL WITH WINTER VEGETABLES
Jarret de veau aux légumes d'hiver (Belgium)

The Belgian view of the funeral feast is as robust as its native cooking:

> All our ceremonies, whether christenings or funerals, end around a table, and nobody is shocked by the laughter which emerges at the end of a funeral meal. The reason we regale ourselves over a tomb is to prove that, in the end, life triumphs over death, and this is accepted by even the most pious among us.

Veal was always reserved for festive occasions, both in Belgium and across the border in Germany, where roast veal knuckle is one of the delights of the *Kermesse*. A request for *osso buco* should produce more or less the right cut – a jarret is from the shank, and is cut more on the cross.

Quantity: Serves 6.
Time: Allow 30 minutes to prepare. 1 hour to cook.
Equipment: A large lidded stewpot.

6 veal-shin steaks cut right through the bone – *osso buco*
2 tablespoons lard
4 large carrots, scrubbed and chunked
2 onions, skinned and sliced
2 medium parsnips, peeled and chunked
2 pints/1.2 litres Pils or lager
sprig of thyme

salt and pepper
1 tablespoon flour
1 tablespoon butter
4 leeks, washed and chunked
2 medium turnips, peeled and quartered
2–3 sticks celery, washed and chunked
1–2 bay leaves

Wipe the veal steaks and dust them with seasoned flour. Melt the lard and butter in the casserole and turn the meat in the hot fat until it takes a little colour. Push the meat to one side and add the vegetables. Let them cook for a moment, and then pour the beer – it should come two-thirds of the way up the meat and vegetables. Allow it all to bubble up and boil until the alcohol has evaporated. Add the herbs, and season with salt and pepper. Turn the heat down, lid and leave to simmer for 1 hour, until the meat is perfectly tender.

Serve piled up on a big dish with plain-boiled potatoes seasoned with a pinch of caraway seeds, and steamed whole quartered cabbage hearts. Hand a jug of the cooking juices separately.

POSTSCRIPT

The circle completes itself. Fast precedes feast. Grey-beard winter, dozing by the fire, wakes to the light tread of spring. Death yields place to new life. Once again it is time to prepare for Christmas, the great festival of renewal.

BIBLIOGRAPHY

(Chief sources consulted or quoted in the text)

d'Agnel, Arnaud and Dor, Leopold. Noël en Provence. Marseilles, 1982.

Ashby, Thomas, Some Italian Scenes and Festivals. Methuen, London, 1929.

Ayrton, Elisabeth. The Cookery of England. André Deutsch, London, 1974.

Baerlein, Henry. Baltic Paradise. Muller, 1943.

Ballou, Maturin M. Due North — Glimpses of Scandinavia and Russia. Boston, 1887.

Beauviala, Anne-Christine and Vielfaure, Nicole. Fêtes, coutumes et gâteaux. Paris, 1984.

Beeton, Isabella. Household Management. Ward Lock, London (1912 edition).

Berenguer, Luis. El Mundo de Juan Lobon. Madrid, 1967.

Blythe, Ronald. Akenfield. Allen Lane, London, 1969.

Bolitho, Hector. The Glorious Oyster. Knopf, USA, 1929.

Bontempelli, Guy. La Truffe. Aix-en-Provence, 1988.

Boswell on the Grand Tour: Germany and Switzerland 1764. Heinemann, London, 1953.

Brockenden, William. Journals of Excursions in the Alps. London 1833.

Butler, Frank Hedges. Through Lapland with Skis and Reindeer. Fisher Unwin, London, 1917.

Butlin, F.M. Among the Danes. Methuen, London, 1909.

Camporesi, Piero. Bread of Dreams. Polity Press, 1989.

Casas, Penelope. The Foods and Wines of Spain. Knopf, USA, 1982.

Chamoux, Simone. Les Olives dans la Cuisine. Lys, France, 1985.

Clair, Colin. Of Herbs and Spices. Abelard Schuman, London, 1961.

Clark, Rev. John A. Glimpses of the Old World. London, 1840.

Clébert, Jean-Paul. Les Fêtes en Provence. Avignon, 1982.

Cooper, James Fenimore. Excursions in Switzerland. London, 1836.

Dallas, E.S. Kettner's Book of the Table. Centaur Press, London, 1877.

David, Elizabeth. French Provincial Cooking. Michael Joseph, London, 1960.

Davidson, Alan. North Atlantic Seafood. Viking, London, 1979.

Davidson, Alan. Mediterranean Seafood. Allen Lane, London, 1972.

Deane, Tony and Shaw, Tony, The Folklore of Cornwall. Batsford, London, 1975.

Dixon, William Hepworth. The Switzers. London, 1872.

Douglas, Norman. Old Calabria. Secker Warburg, London, 1915.

Eyre, Mary. A Lady's Walks in the South of France. London, 1865.

Fermor, Patrick Leigh. Mani. John Murray, London, 1958.

Fiennes, Celia. Through England on a side saddle in the time of William and Mary. Ed. Mrs Griffiths, London, 1888.

Fisher, M.F.K. The Cooking of Provincial France. Time-Life Books, London, 1969.

Fitzgibbon, Theodora. A Taste of Ireland. Dent, London, 1968.

Forbes, John. A Physician's Holiday, or A Month in Switzerland. John Murray, London, 1849.

Fraser, Mrs Hugh. A. Diplomatist's Wife in Many Lands. Hutchinson, London, 1912.

Frazer, Sir James George. The Golden Bough. Macmillan, 1929 ed. Abridged by the author.

Fytrakis, Eva. Traditional Greek Cooking (trans. Diana Reid). Athens, 1981.

Gallop, Rodney. A Book of the Basques. CUP, Cambridge, 1930.

Gallop, Rodney. Portugal, A Book of Folk-ways. CUP, Cambridge, 1936.

van Gennep, Arnold. Manuel de Folklore Français Contemporain. Paris, 1937–49.

Goldring, Douglas. Journeys in the Sun. Macdonald, London, 1946.

Gomme, George L. Ethnology in Folklore. London, 1892.

Grigson, Jane. Charcuterie and French Pork Cookery. Michael Joseph, London, 1967.

Hamilton, Andrew. Sixteen Months in the Danish Isles. London, 1852.

Hare, Augustus. The Story of My Life. London, 1896–1900.

Hartley, Dorothy. The Countryman's England. Scribner/Batsford, 1935.

Hartley, Dorothy. Food in England. Macdonald, London, 1934.

Henningsen, Henning. Dystløb [Danish water battles]. Copenhagen, 1949.

Henningsen, Henning. Bådeoptog [Danish Boat Processions]. Copenhagen, 1953.

Hobhouse, Henry. Seeds of Change. Sidgwick & Jackson, London, 1985.

Hole, Christina. English Traditional Customs. Batsford, London, 1975.

Hole, Christina. English Folklore Customs. Batsford, London, 1940.

Illyes, Gyula. The People of the Puszta. Budapest, 1967.

Johnston, Isobel Christian. The Cook and Housewife's Manual of Mrs Margaret Dods. 1826.

Lang, George. The Cuisine of Hungary. Athenaeum, London, 1971.

Lawson, John Cuthbert. Modern Greek Folklore and Ancient Greek Religion. CUP, Cambridge, 1910.

Leib, Ollie. Bayerische Leibspeisen. Munich, 1979.

Levai, Vera. Culinary Delights. Budapest, 1983.

Liman, Ingemar. Traditional Festivities in Sweden. Stockholm, 1983.

Llanover, Lady. The First Principle of Good Cookery. London, 1867.

Long, George. The Folklore Calendar. London, 1930.

Luard, Nicholas. Andalucía. Century, London, 1984.

Mabey, Richard. Food for Free. Collins, London, 1972.

McGee, Harold. On Food and Cooking. Scribner, USA, 1985.

McNeill, F. Marian. The Scots Kitchen. Blackie, Edinburgh, 1929.

McNeill, F. Marian. The Silver Bough, MacLellan, Glasgow, 1957.

Maple, Eric. Old Wives' Tales. Robert Hale, London, 1981.

Marryat, Horace. A Residence in Jutland, the Danish Isles and Copenhagen. John Murray, London, 1860.

Médécin, Jacques. Cuisine Niçoise (trans. Peter Graham). Penguin, London, 1983.

Miles, Beryl. Candles in Denmark. John Murray, London, 1958.

Morton, H.V. In Search of Ireland. Methuen, London, 1930.

Max Müller, Mrs Georgina. Letters from Constantinople. Longmans, London, 1897.

Newall, Venetia. An Egg at Easter. Routledge & Kegan Paul, London, 1971.

Newby, Eric. On the Shores of the Mediterranean. Harvill, 1984.

Notes and Queries, Choice notes from N & Q. London, 1859.

Olsson, Brita. Baka Matbröd. Sweden, 1984.

O'Neill, Timothy. Life and Tradition in Rural Ireland. Dent, London, 1977.

Pagnol, Koscher & Mattern. Les Recettes de la Table Provençale. Strasburg, 1982.

Palmer, Geoffrey, and Loyd, Noel. A Year of Festivals. Warne, London, 1972.

Pohren, Donn. Adventures in Taste: The Wines and Folk Food of Spain. Seville, 1972.

de Pomiane, Edouard. Le Code de la Bonne Chére. Paris, 1930.

Pritchett, V.S. Foreign Faces. Chatto, London, 1964.

Reboule, J.-B. La Cuisinière Provençale, Marseilles, 1985.

Reynolds-Ball, Eustace A. Unknown Italy: Piedmont and the Piedmontese. London, 1925.

Riddervold, Astri and Ropeid, Andreas. Popular Diet (Ethnologia Scandinavica), 1984.

Root, Waverly. The Food of France. Cassell, London, 1958.

Shand, P. Morton. A Book of Food. Cape, London, 1928.

Sitwell, Sacheverell. Sacred and Profane Love. Faber, London, 1940.

Sitwell, Sacheverell. Primitive Scenes and Festivals. Faber, London, 1942.

Sitwell, Sacheverell. Splendours and Miseries. Faber, London, 1943.

Sitwell, Sacheverell. *Truffle Hunt*. Robert Hale, London, 1953.

Sitwell, Sacheverell. *Denmark*. Batsford, London, 1956.

Spicer, Dorothy. *The Book of Festivals*. New York, 1937.

Stowe, Mrs Harriet Beecher. *Sunny Memories of Foreign Lands*. London, 1854.

Stromastad, Asse. *Eat the Norway*. Oslo, 1984.

Stubbes, Phillip. *The Anatomie of Abuses*. Repro. 1585.

Thonger, Richard. *A Calendar of German Customs*. Wolff, 1966.

Tower, Charles. *The Moselle*. Constable, London, 1913.

Ullus, Luc. *Coutumes Culinaires au Pays de Liège*. Brussels, 1981.

Vidoudez, Michele and Grangier, Jacqueline. *A la Mode Chez Nous*. Lausanne, 1976.

Viski, Károly. *Hungarian Peasant Customs*. Budapest, 1932.

Whittick, Arnold. *Symbols, Signs and Their Meanings*. London, 1960.

Wilson, C. Anne. *Food and Drink in Britain*. Constable, London, 1973.

de Windt, Harry. *Through Savage Europe*. Fisher Unwin, 1907.

Wolff, Henry W. *Rambles in the Black Forest*. Longmans, London, 1890.

Wright, Arthur R. *British Calendar Customs*. London, 1936.

and Cheese Sunday, 99-100
Lent in, 109, 116, 119
Easter, 139, 142-148
and Feast of Assumption, 243-245
honey in, 249, 250
wine harvest, 270
funerals, 308-309
Green George (Green Man), 166
Green Thursday, 131-132
Grégoire, Gaston, 174
Gregory the Great, Pope, 109
Groaning victuals, 81
Grouse (*Lagopus scoticus*), 240-242
Grout, John, 276-277, 283
Guadalquivir delta (Spain), 179, 185-187
Gulvâl (Cornwall), 249
Hallowe'en (All Hallows Eve), 284-288
Hamilton, Andrew 170,277
   Sixteen Months in the Danish Isles, 168,278
Hannover (Germany), 125
Hanseatic League, 21, 41, 105, 110
Hartley, Dorothy,
   The Countryman's England, Food in England, 47,
      171, 243, 248, 295
Harvest-homes and festivals, 272, 275-283
Hawker, Rev. R.S., 276, 278
Heaton, Eliza Putnam, 217
Henningsen, Henning, 91
Henry VIII, King, 285
Herefordshire, 66, 73, 81
Hesketh, Christian, Lady (*née* McEwen), 284
Hogmanay, 10, 44, 67-70
Hole, Christina,
   English Folklore, 81
Holland (Netherlands)
   and St Nicholas, 14-16, 17
   Carnival, 91
   herring consumption, 111-113
   Easter, 126
Holy, 43
Holy Thursday (Red Thursday), 149-150
Honey harvest (St Bartholomew's Day), 248-
   250
Hood, Robin, 178

Household Words (journal), 143
Hungary
   and St Lucia, 19
   Christmas Eve, 33
   Friend's Basket, 83
   Christenning feast, 84
   and St Valentine's Day, 89
   Carnival, 92
   Lent, 114
   Easter eggs, 125-126, 137
   Good Friday, 134
   Easter food, 135, 137
   May Day, 167-168
   Whitsun, 179
   St John's Day, 198
   weddings, 209,221-225
   wine harvest, 268, 270
   harvest festivals, 278
   pig-killing, 294
   funerals, 308
Illyes, Gyula, 156, 167, 179, 209, 221-222
Innocent III, Pope, 10
Ireland, 110, 113, 125, 240, 284, 286, 307,
   310
Irminsul (stone column), 165
Isle of Man, 134, 197
Istanbul
   spice trade, 254-256
   and bonito fishing, 257
Italy
   Advent in, 11
   Christmas, 53
   Carnival, 91-92
   Lent, 117
   Easter eggs in, 125-126
   Easter food, 138, 139
   wine harvest, 270
   truffle harvest, 299, 301
Jabugo (Spain), 259-260
Jack-in-the-Green (or Bush), 166
Jack-o'-Lent, 127
James II, King, 127
Jenkin, Hamilton, 81
Jerez (Spain), 185, 186, 192, 268

crayfish festival, 239
mead in, 249
Switzerland, 14, 159, 162
Tarascon (France), 179-180, 181
Tennyson, Alfred, Lord, 168
Thanksgiving, 272, 278
Theodosimus, Pope, 10
Therea (Greek island), 143
Thérèse of Schleswig-
Hildburghausen (wife of
Ludwig of Bavaria), 273
Thonger, Richard, 31
Thor (Norse god), 7, 42
Three Kings (Wise Men), 15, 72, 73, 174
Thuringia, 125
Timothy, Bishop, 8, 90
Tinos, Cyclades (Greek island), 243
Tom Bawcock's Eve, 44
Tomte (Scandinavian Christmas gnome), 10, 22
Torskens Dag (Day of the Cod), Lofoten, 104-105
Toulouse (France), 98
Trajan, Roman Emperor, 8
Transfiguration, Feast of the, 243
Transhumance, 158, 160, 284
Transvestism, 9
Transylvania, 116, 278
Tromsö (Norway), 183
Truffle harvest, 299-305
Turkey, 82, 254-255
(see also Istanbul; Ottoman Turks_
Turkeys, 9, 43
Twelfth Night, 72-73
Tyrol, 9, 181, 268
Urban IV, Pope, 173
Vaison-la-Romaine (France), 11, 53, 55, 59, 198
Valborg, Feast of, see Walpurgis Night 164
Valentine, St, 88
Vapunaato, see Walpurgis Night
Venice, 254, 256
Versailles (France), 226-227
Viana do Castella (Portugal), 244
Victoria, Queen, 32
Vienna, 125, 290

Villedieu, Paulette, 198, 211
Vincent, St, 77
Virgin of the Dew (Rocío),
Andalucía, 185-186
Viski, Károly, 9-10, 19, 52, 80, 92, 179, 198,
209, 221, 223, 268, 278, 294, 308
Volksfest, 272
Vosges (France), 14
Walpurgis Night, 164-173
Weddings, 206-225
Wells, H.G., 307
Wendron (Cornwall), 282
Wesley, Charles, 282
Weyhill sheep market, 234
Whangs-o'-luck, 81
White, Florence, 51, 84, 129-130
Whitstable (Kent), 252
Whitsun, 177-193
Wild Man of the Woods, 166
William I of Wurttemberg, 272
Wilson, Anne, 132
Wiltshire, 297-268
Wine, 267-268
Winter solstice, 7, 9
Witches, 94, 164, 284
Wolff, Henry, 110
Rambles in the Black Forest, 210
Yarmouth (Norfolk), 112
York
miracle plays, 177
Yorkshire, 51, 288
Yugoslavia, 33, 295
Yule, 7-8
log, 52-54

INDEX OF RECIPES